African Underclass

EASTERN AFRICAN STUDIES

Revealing Prophets
Edited by DAVID M. ANDERSON
& DOUGLAS H. JOHNSON

*East African Expressions of
Christianity*
Edited by THOMAS SPEAR
& ISARIA KIMAMBO

The Poor Are Not Us
Edited by DAVID M. ANDERSON
& VIGDIS BROCH-DUE

Potent Brews
JUSTIN WILLIS

Swahili Origins
JAMES DE VERE ALLEN

Being Maasai
Edited by THOMAS SPEAR
& RICHARD WALLER

Jua Kali Kenya
KENNETH KING

Control & Crisis in Colonial Kenya
BRUCE BERMAN

Unhappy Valley
Books One & Two
BRUCE BERMAN
& JOHN LONSDALE

Mau Mau from Below
GREET KERSHAW

The Mau Mau War in Perspective
FRANK FUREDI

*Squatters & the Roots of
Mau Mau 1905–63
African Womanhood
in Colonial Kenya**
TABITHA KANOGO

*Economic & Social Origins
of Mau Mau 1945–53*
DAVID W. THROUP

Multi-Party Politics in Kenya
DAVID W. THROUP
& CHARLES HORNSBY

Empire State-Building
JOANNA LEWIS

*Decolonization & Independence
in Kenya 1940–93*
Edited by B.A. OGOT
& WILLIAM R. OCHIENG'

Eroding the Commons
DAVID ANDERSON

Penetration & Protest in Tanzania
ISARIA N. KIMAMBO

Custodians of the Land
Edited by GREGORY
MADDOX, JAMES L. GIBLIN
& ISARIA N. KIMAMBO

*Education in the Development
of Tanzania 1919 – 1990*
LENE BUCHERT

The Second Economy in Tanzania
T.L. MALIYAMKONO
& M.S.D. BAGACHWA

*Ecology Control & Economic
Development in East African History*
HELGE KJEKSHUS

Siaya
DAVID WILLIAM COHEN
& E.S. ATIENO ODHIAMBO

*Uganda Now
Changing Uganda
Developing Uganda
From Chaos to Order
Religion & Politics in East Africa*
Edited by HOLGER BERNT
HANSEN & MICHAEL
TWADDLE

*Kakungulu & the Creation
of Uganda 1868 – 1928*
MICHAEL TWADDLE

Controlling Anger
SUZETTE HEALD

Kampala Women Getting By
SANDRA WALLMAN

Political Power in Pre-Colonial Buganda
RICHARD REID

Alice Lakwena & the Holy Spirits
HEIKE BEHREND

Slaves, Spices & Ivory in Zanzibar
ABDUL SHERIFF

Zanzibar Under Colonial Rule
Edited by ABDUL SHERIFF &
ED FERGUSON

*The History & Conservation of
Zanzibar Stone Town*
Edited by ABDUL SHERIFF

Pastimes & Politics
LAURA FAIR

*Ethnicity & Conflict
in the Horn of Africa*
Edited by KATSUYOSHI
FUKUI & JOHN MARKAKIS

*Conflict, Age & Power
in North East Africa*
Edited by EISEI KURIMOTO
& SIMON SIMONSE

*Property Rights & Political
Development in Ethiopia & Eritrea*
SANDRA FULLERTON
JOIREMAN

Revolution & Religion in Ethiopia
ØYVIND M. EIDE

Brothers at War
TEKESTE NEGASH &
KJETIL TRONVOLL

From Guerillas to Government
DAVID POOL

*A History of Modern Ethiopia
1855–1991* (2nd ed.)
BAHRU ZEWDE

Pioneers of Change in Ethiopia
BAHRU ZEWDE

Remapping Ethiopia
Edited by WENDY JAMES,
DONALD L. DONHAM, EISEI
KURIMOTO & ALESSANDRO
TRIULZI

*Southern Marches
of Imperial Ethiopia*
Edited by DONALD L.
DONHAM & WENDY JAMES

A Modern History of the Somali
(4th ed.)
I.M. LEWIS

*Dhows & the Colonial Economy
in Zanzibar 1860–1970*
ERIK GILBERT

*In Search of a Nation**
Edited by GREGORY H.
MADDOX & JAMES L. GIBLIN

*A History of the Excluded**
JAMES L. GIBLIN

*Islands of Intensive Agriculture in
Eastern Africa*
Edited by MATS WIDGREN &
JOHN E.G. SUTTON

Leaf of Allah
EZEKIEL GEBISSA

Mau Mau & Nationhood
Edited by E.S. ATIENO
ODHIAMBO & JOHN LONSDALE

African Underclass
ANDREW BURTON

*Black Poachers, White Hunters**
EDWARD I. STEINHART

*Crisis & Decline in Bunyoro**
SHANE DOYLE

* forthcoming

African Underclass
Urbanisation, Crime & Colonial Order in Dar es Salaam

ANDREW BURTON
Assistant Director
British Institute in Eastern Africa

The British Institute in Eastern Africa
in association with

James Currey
OXFORD

Mkuki na Nyota
DAR ES SALAAM

Ohio University Press
ATHENS

The British Institute in Eastern Africa
10 Carlton House Terrace
London SW2Y 5AH
& P.O. Box 30710, 00100 GPO, Nairobi

in association with

James Currey Ltd
73 Botley Road
Oxford
OX2 0BS

Mkuki na Nyota
P.O. Box 4246
Dar es Salaam

Ohio University Press
The Ridges, Building 19
Athens
Ohio 45701

Copyright acknowledgments:
The author and publisher acknowledge permission to use material from '*Jamii ya wahalifu*. The growth of crime in a colonial African urban centre: Dar es Salaam, Tanzania, 1919–1961', *Crime, History and Societies*, 2004, no. 2, with permission of Librairie Droz S.A.

British Library Cataloguing in Publication Data
Burton, Andrew
African underclass : urbanisation, crime & colonial order in Dar es Salaam. - (Eastern African studies)
1. Urbanization - Social aspects - Tanzania - Dar es Salaam
2. Urbanization - Tanzania - Dar es Salaam - History - 20th century 3. Crime - Tanzania - Dar es Salaam - History - 20th century 4. Dar es Salaam (Tanzania) - Social conditions - 20th century 5. Dar es Salaam (Tanzania) - Politics and government - 20th century 6. Great Britain - Colonies - Africa - Administration - History - 20th century
I.Title
307.7'6'09678232

ISBN   0-85255-976-3   (James Currey Cloth)
       0-85255-975-5   (James Currey Paper)

Library of Congress Cataloging-in-Publication Data is available on request from the Library of Congress

ISBN   0-8214-1635-9   (Ohio University Press Cloth)
       0-8214-1636-7   (Ohio University Press Paper)

Typeset in 9/11pt Baskerville
by the British Institute in Eastern Africa
Printed and bound in Malaysia

[I]n Africa nothing is quite as it should be to the European mind. The European mind requires logic and order and civilisation, and so it tries to bring these to Africa. Historically this is desirable, but for the individual European often exhausting, like trying to prod a dinosaur along a narrow path with a small stick.

J.C. Cairns (former District Officer, Dar es Salaam),
Bush and Boma (London, 1959), p. 117

Straightness is one of the things the Europeans have brought here. We Africans must learn it, like arithmetic.

Abdullah (Cairns' servant), *ibid.*, p. 20

Dedication

To Margaret Dutton

Contents

Contents

PART II

PART III

List of Maps, Figures & Tables

Maps

Figures

Tables

Acknowledgements

This book has been a labour of love. Living in Dar es Salaam to conduct the main body of my doctoral research in 1996-7, I was smitten. From dinner at Uhindini's cosmopolitan New Zahir restaurant brushing shoulders with Gulf Arabs, culturally insensitive tourists, alongside the whole gamut of coastal and upcountry Tanzanians, while the *muezzin*'s call to prayer wafted down Mosque Street; to Remmy Ongala in full flow on the dangers of unprotected sex on a ramshackle stage in the heart of Mikoroshoni; to the evening rides home down Kilwa Rodi with *Ndani ya Bongo* pounding out of humming *daladala* speakers and naked flames flickering in the inky darkness on either side, barely illuminating roadside stalls: this and much more inspired an enduring affection for and curiosity about what must be Africa's most affable metropolis. That such a large city can remain such a relatively benign place is a tribute to its inhabitants past and present. It may seem overly sentimental singling out what is a demographic settlement, however, because Dar es Salaam was and remains to me such a vibrantly human place, and because the many experiences and interactions I have encountered there over the past seven years lie at the heart of this book, it is the city itself with all its diverse inhabitants, institutions, corners and crevices I want to acknowledge first.

Much as I would have liked it to, the text that follows sheds little light on the manner in which Dar es Salaam developed a harmony and social integration rare in African cities. Instead a darker part of the city's past is uncovered. My research, alongside that of other scholars working on Dar es Salaam, indicates there is more to the sleepy 'Haven of Peace' than meets the eye. The enduring intolerance of colonial and post-colonial officials, and an emerging bourgeoisie, towards the urban poor forms one stark reminder of the ongoing conflicts that have unfolded in the city over the past century. Similarly, the great poverty of the majority of urban residents as catalogued in the following pages during the colonial period, and their daily struggle to earn a living and to evade repressive state action, continues to characterise the contemporary experience of a large proportion of the city's population.

Nevertheless, the good humour in which these struggles are generally conducted provides one clue as to why the overriding impression of Dar es Salaam is of a well-integrated and easy-going town, even if this is only half the story. Alongside the city's emergence over the past decade or so as a prime example of the changing face of urban Africa, this relative harmoniousness also helps account for the wave of Bongophilia currently sweeping Western academe, of which this book is but one example.

Much of my thinking on Dar es Salaam's past was informed by countless interactions with anonymous Darmites, both fleeting ones on *daladalas* or at roadside stalls and rather lengthier ones, usually conducted in palm-fringed bars. To all those involved in passing encounters with this *mshenzi* making ill-informed and/or ill-advised enquiries I extend my humble thanks. To my drinking buddies at the now demolished bar off Kurasini Road in particular – cheers. At the *Jeshi la Wokovu*, where in 1996/7 *banda* C6 became an unanticipated home from home for this God-less researcher, Bonifacia Haule and Bernard Chacha in particular provided hospitality and good humour. I would like to thank Gabriel Mwakalinga for his selfless efforts in attempting to set up interviews in Kisutu and Temeke; Justina Tumaini for exposing herself to the great embarassment of asking my half-baked questions in interviews at locations throughout Dar es Salaam; and Luna Mkayula for introducing me to Mabrouk Swedi Mabrouk and Abubakar Saidi Mgomba. These latter two Magomeni residents were among the many Dar es Salaam *Wazee* who graciously deigned to humour the enquiries of this researcher: I am most grateful for the time and effort they all thereby wasted. At the University of Dar es Salaam in November 1997 a rather green researcher was given a warm welcome and orientation by Tanzania's history *Mzee*, the venerable Professor Isaria Kimambo. Also up on 'the hill', J.M. Lusagga Kironde, another enthusiastic student of Dar es Salaam, provided invaluable advice, hospitality and much-appreciated copies of his thesis and subsequent publications. More recently, on my trips down from Nairobi, Yusufu Lawi's warm welcome and practical support meant that his office in the history department was invariably one of my first ports of call. Meanwhile, my stint in Dar es Salaam happily coincided with Peter Bofin's work in the town for the Irish NGO Concern. His enthusiasm for all things Bongo was then, and has continued to be, positively infectious. Thanks to this shared affection for Dar es Salaam, alongside a penchant for a Serengeti or two, our physical and conversational explorations also played an important part in my understanding of the town.

Also in Dar es Salaam, I have been fortunate enough to establish valued friendships with other researchers working on and in the city. Although I first met Jim and Blandina Giblin by chance on a beach on Lake Nyasa, they have become indelibly associated with Bongoland: their Segerea home providing a haven of good food, warm hospitality and valued insights into Tanzanian life, past and present. Jim has also – both formally through comments on parts of this manuscript at various stages in its existence, as well as informally through long conversations in Segerea and elsewhere – influenced how this book eventually turned out. Again, although I first met Mike Jennings as a rookie Ph.D. candidate at SOAS in 1995, our friendship blossomed after we both found ourselves in Dar es Salaam the following November. Sharing the daily trials, tribulations *and* delights of research in Tanzania with Mike was highly valued, as were the nightly deconstructions of the day's events at Kurasini's great Tumbaku Club, which served to refine and clarify my thinking on Tanzania and much else besides.

I have had the good fortune to work on the history of Dar es Salaam when it is receiving an unprecedented amount of interest from numerous other scholars who have not only offered invaluable information and advice, but also provided good company in Dar es Salaam and further afield. On first hearing from Jim Brennan in 1996 that he too was working on the history of Dar es Salaam during the British colonial period (and after), my first reaction was concern. This was before I realised that another ten researchers would fail to get to the bottom of Dar es Salaam's colonial history, and that in any case having such a thoughtful and rigorous fellow scholar working alongside me was a substantial boon. By the time I met Andy Ivaska in Uhindini in December 2000 any concerns about academic overcrowding had therefore been superseded by a positive enthusiasm for fellow historians pursuing elusive truths about Dar es Salaam's past – an enthusiasm that has proved fully justified in this case by the work that Andy has produced since and by his good companionship in Bongo and elsewhere over the last few years. I regret to say that I was unable to consult his thesis before this book had to be submitted (though I was fortunate enough to consult works in progress), and that it is therefore no doubt all the poorer for it. Ned Bertz is another fellow historian whose work is regrettably appearing too late for this book to have benefited from his insights therein. Nevertheless, I have enjoyed Ned's company in Dar es Salaam, and have greatly profited from his comments on my work. By contrast, Eileen Moyer's Ph.D. thesis arrived just in time for me to read and incorporate references to it. Eileen declared delight and surprise when first coming across my historical research on Dar es Salaam, which complemented her own work on youth in the contemporary city so well. Having now read her thesis, I can express my own delight. I urge anyone who reads this book to search out Eileen's work, which explores many of the same issues I raise in this study of the colonial period in present-day Dar es Salaam; and by so doing, I am pleased to say, demonstrates that this is not simply a piece of arcane historicism. I am also very grateful to fellow Bongo scholars Franck Raimbault and Alex Perullo, who kindly furnished me with valuable information arising from their own research on the German period and the contemporary music scene respectively; and to David Henry Anthony for sending me an electronic copy of his 1983 thesis on Dar es Salaam.

This book began life as a Ph.D. thesis at the School of Oriental and African Studies, and it has most certainly been enhanced by a number of relationships I established there. First and foremost, I have benefited from the friendship, good counsel and support of my former supervisor David Anderson in

Acknowledgements

innumerable ways. Much water has passed under the bridge since, as a nervous mature student long out of higher education, I tentatively knocked on his study door to be interviewed for the MA in African Area Studies. Fortunately, I had neither long hair nor was I a hippy, which sealed my participation on the course and the rest is, erm... history. Dave's empathy, intelligence and limitless energy and enthusiasm have proved an inspiration for myself and countless other graduate students to whom he has acted as supervisor. Also at SOAS, Professor Andrew Roberts' comments on early versions of my work on Dar es Salaam were much appreciated. Richard Reid provided the ideal drinking partner after African History Seminars, and, being in the later stages of writing up his thesis, valuable orientation for a fledgling graduate student in the world of doctoral research. Finally, I would like to thank participants at the SOAS African History Seminar whose comments on presentations I frequently found very useful.

Over the years I have also been lucky enough to receive insightful commentary from a variety of scholars who have agreed to read my work. John Iliffe must, at one point or another, have given inspiration to most historians working in and on sub-Saharan Africa. I was fortunate enough to have Professor Iliffe as an examiner for my Ph.D. and his comments in that role, and in a subsequent letter, helped me to re-evaluate parts of the thesis as well as to adopt a framework more suitable for a published monograph. More recently, Justin Willis and Laurent Fourchard selflessly pored through drafts of the manuscript, offering much useful advice that I have incorporated wherever possible. Meanwhile, Richard Waller's generosity in providing detailed and insightful feedback was responsible for my re-evaluating several key areas, as a result of which the book has, I think, been significantly strengthened.

At an earlier stage in the project, whilst I was still accumulating data, a number of people were also very generous with their time. Nick Westcott deserves special thanks from all those interested in the history of Dar es Salaam for microfilming a copy of E.C. Baker's 1931 social survey in the early 1980s. By the time I arrived in Dar es Salaam in 1996 all surviving copies of this important document (including at least one in the national archive and another at the national library) had gone missing. I would also like to thank Nick for giving me copies of his notes to interviews with A.H. Pike, and from various TNA files that were unavailable in 1996/7. Another individual who has earnt the gratitude of students of the town is J.A.K. Leslie, whose extraordinary *Survey of Dar es Salaam* has provided an essential source ever since its formal publication in 1963. I would also like to thank John Leslie and his wife for their hospitality on the two occasions I went to their Berkhamsted home to conduct interviews. Randall Sadleir was another former Darmite who showed this researcher unstinting Irish hospitality. Finally, I am most grateful to all those former residents of Dar es Salaam who went out of their way to respond to my letters in *The Overseas Pensioner* and *Tanzanian Affairs*, and to my subsequent questionnaire.

Acknowledgements

The research and writing up of this book was facilitated by financial support from a number of institutions including SOAS, the University of London Central Research Fund and the Royal Historical Society, to all of whom I extend my thanks. I also received a minor grant in 1998 from the British Institute in Eastern Africa. I feel privileged to have subsequently worked for the Institute as its Assistant Director since September 2000. This role has not only afforded me the opportunity to meet countless scholars of the region, interactions with whom have considerably enhanced my own understanding of East Africa, but it has also provided me with the ideal environment in which to work on *Wahuni* (the original Swahili title of this book and the name by which I'll always know it) and other projects. All the staff at the Institute have in some way or another facilitated my research, and it is perhaps invidious to single out individuals. I would nevertheless like to express special thanks to Philip Owiti, who is responsible for many of the maps and scanned images, and Paul Lane who has been such a good and understanding colleague. I would also like to thank all the graduate students attached to the Institute who carried out research for this project; notably Gerard McCann, Jane Humphris, Helen Liddington, Sarah Walters, Anna Smith and Jo Parish.

Thanks must also go to those people responsible for supplying illustrations herein that provide welcome respite for the reader's eye. These include Joan Thompson for sending me photos from her husband's collection arising from his work in the Dar es Salaam police; the staff of Tanzania Information Services, who kindly organised the reproduction of photos from their collection, and granted permission for their use; Kate O'Hearn at Hodder Headline for her efforts in obtaining permission to reproduce text and an illustration from J.C. Cairns' *Bush and Boma*; Mauras Malikita for allowing me to use his *tingatinga* depiction of a roundup of *machinga*; Mahmood A. Karimjee for the copy of a postcard of a Dar es Salaam rickshaw; and Daniel Branch for doggedly obtaining a digital copy of the 1934 aerial photo of Dar es Salaam from Rhodes House.

Finally, and most importantly, Paulette and Alexandra provide the home from which I go to work – one much appreciated for all the humour and love contained therein. It is they who have suffered the periodic absences partly resulting from work on this book. While it probably doesn't fully compensate for the consequent neglect of my role as husband/father, I hope the end result at least goes some way to justifying these absences. It would have been dedicated to the two of them, but they have already had one book dedicated to them, and in any case there is another woman in my life to whom I owe even more: my mother. Bringing up baby in this case was, given the circumstances, no mean feat, particularly when baby grew up into something of an *mhuni* himself. I received a better education and more patience and love than I probably ever deserved. Dedicating this book to Margaret Dutton barely begins the repayment.

Abbreviations & Glossary

AA	*African Affairs*
AA	African Association
ADO	Assistant District Officer
Ag	Acting
AO	Administrative Officer
APO	Assistant Political Officer
AR	Annual Report
Askari	Soldier/Policeman/Guard
Baraza	Meeting
Boma	District Administration Headquarters
CS	Chief Secretary
CP	Commissioner of Police
DAR	District Annual Report (Dar es Salaam, unless otherwise stated)
DC	District Commissioner
DO	District Officer
Dsm	Dar es Salaam
DMS	Director of Medical Services
DT	*Dar es Salaam Times*
Duka	Shop
EARC	East African Royal Commission, 1953–55
ECB	Economic Control Board
EP	Eastern Province
GN	Government Notice (as published in the official Gazette)
Idd	Islamic holiday
IJAH	*International Journal of African Historical Studies*
ILO	International Labour Organisation
JAH	*Journal of African History*
JMAS	*Journal of Modern African Studies*
JSAS	*Journal of Southern African Studies*
Jumbe	African Officials in the urban Native Administration
KNA	Kenya National Archive
Kwetu	African Newspaper (1930s–1950s)
LC	Labour Commissioner
Legco	Legislative Council
Liwali	African head of the urban Native Administration
LO	Labour Officer
MAAO	Municipal African Affairs Officer
MC	Municipal Council
Mhindi	Indian
MLG	Member for Local Government

MLO	Member for Law and Order
MOH	Medical Officer of Health
MS	Municipal Secretary
Mshenzi	(pl. *Washenzi*) Coastal term for an 'uncivilised' person
MSS	Member for Social Services
Mzee	Elder ✦
Mzungu	European
Ngoma	Dance (meeting)
OiC	Officer in Charge
PAR	Provincial Annual Report (Eastern Province, unless otherwise stated)
PC	Provincial Commissioner
PRO	Public Records Office
PWD	Public Works Department
QPR	Quarterly Police Report
RH	Rhodes House
RM	Resident Magistrate
Shamba	Plot of land
SN	*Sunday News*
SOAS	School of Oriental and African Studies
SP	Superintendent of Police
SSCol	Secretary of State for the Colonies
TA	Township Authority
TAA	Tanganyika African Association
Tangazo	Official notice
TANU	Tanganyika African National Union
TAWCA	Tanganyika African Welfare and Commercial Association
TC	Town Clerk
TCSS	Tanganyika Council of Social Services
TH	*Tanganyika Herald*
Tingatinga	Style of painting originating in 1960s Dar es Salaam
TNA	Tanzania National Archive, Dar es Salaam
TNR	*Tanganyika* (later *Tanzania*) *Notes and Records*
TO	*Tanganyika Opinion*
TS	*Tanganyika Standard*
TT	*Tanganyika Times*
UDsm	University of Dar es Salaam
Uhuni	Delinquency
Uhuru	Independence
UMCA	Universities Mission to Central Africa
Wakili	Senior officials in urban Native Administration
Wahuni	'Delinquents'/'Hooligans'
WN	*Weekly News*
ZNA	Zanzibar National Archive

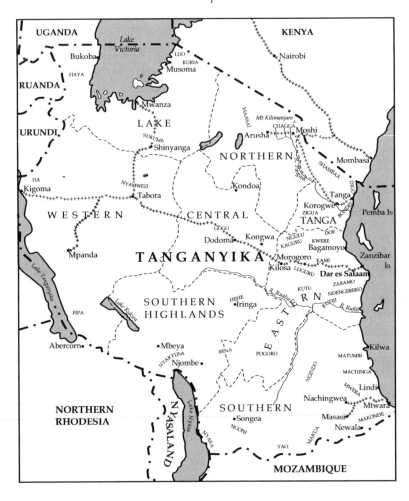

Map 1 *Tanganyika Territory, with administrative centres and selected ethnic groups*

Introduction

Wahuni!
The Making of a Colonial Underclass

This is a book about crime. More specifically, the crime of being in the wrong place at the wrong time. As an African in colonial Dar es Salaam, without a pass issued by the District Office or evidence of having lived in the town for a substantial period (by 1958, four out of the past five years), your very presence was technically an offence. If you were unemployed or informally employed that was doubly offensive. Moreover, regardless of your work status, your mobility was circumscribed by municipal by-laws that forbade your presence in parts of the town at night and required you to carry a light at all times everywhere else between nightfall and sunrise. By the 1950s, if not earlier, apprehension for any combination of the above offences commonly resulted in the removal of individual Africans from Dar es Salaam, and up to 2,000 persons were forcibly repatriated to their rural homes annually. The British colonial administration had presided over – indeed, through its obsession with a particular kind of order and its legislative fecundity, actually produced – a substantial increase in criminality. And while it was also responsible for creating a context in which growing numbers of Africans were attracted to urban areas and to Dar es Salaam in particular, if you were lacking the prerequisites of urban citizenship, as defined by the British regime, simply being there was a crime.

This intolerance towards the African presence in Dar es Salaam is linked to the book's other main theme: urbanisation. Under British rule, Dar es Salaam underwent a transformation from a small, neglected colonial town to a city of almost 200,000. The administrative, socio-political and, from the point of view of many European, Indian *and* African observers, the moral consequences of this phenomenon were profound. In the hyperbolic words of Tanganyika's Minister for Social Services, writing in 1951, '[t]he 15th century [wa]s being changed into the 20th century in a matter of months'.[1] Ever-growing numbers of Africans coming from societies identified as having no traditions of urbanism made their way to Dar es Salaam and

[1] Minute, 25 September 1951, TNA/18950/Vol. III.

1

other lesser urban centres, and here were exposed to all the temptations and vices of modernity. African societies (or more accurately, social relations) were, according to European and African testimony, endangered by 'tribesmen's' exposure to urban life. Meanwhile, within the towns European and Indian settler populations, and respectable African urban residents, suffered from what was perceived as the fallout of this contact: in the shape of the insubordination of African youth, growing crime rates, and the unsightly and insanitary presence of beggars, hawkers and the like. More prosaic, though ultimately more serious, concerns centred on the provision of employment, housing, health and social services, and urban infrastructure. Rapid population growth significantly complicated urban governance, most particularly when, as a result of the low wage levels prevailing in the town or the restricted availability of formal employment, rural migrants arriving in Dar es Salaam were not significantly adding to municipal income.

The pressures faced by colonial officials in Dar es Salaam were, of course, by no means unique to the city or to the period. The process of urbanisation was perhaps the single most noteworthy trend of twentieth-century world history.[2] In 1900 only one country, Britain, could be described as 'urbanised'. By the end of the century those countries that had larger rural than urban populations had become the exception instead of the rule, and shortly thereafter it was envisaged a majority of the human race would reside in towns.[3] Nowhere has this urban revolution been more profound than in the Third World. Here, societies that were overwhelmingly rural in character at the beginning of the century had by its end become increasingly urban.[4] Towns and cities in Africa, Asia and Latin America grew at rates that far exceeded those experienced by the industrialised world. In the 1940s and 1950s, the urban population in these three regions grew at rates approaching 5 percent.[5] In sub-Saharan Africa, between 1960 and 1980 the average growth rate of primary urban centres was as high as 7 percent.[6] By contrast, in European countries at the point of their fastest urban population growth (mostly in the late nineteenth century) the average gain per year was around 2 percent.[7] Moreover, the context in which this phenomenon has occurred

[2] A technical definition of urbanisation is the proportion of people living in urban settlements (usually of 10,000 or more). Thus an urbanised society is one in which more than half the population lives in a town. It has other, less precise meanings, however, that include the social, cultural and economic processes associated with the shift from a rural to an urban society.

[3] Habitat, *Global Report on Human Settlements* (Oxford, 1987 & 1996), pp. 23 and 12.

[4] Just 18% of Africans lived in towns in 1960. *Ibid.*, p. 52.

[5] By the 1990s the average population increase in Third World cities was estimated at 175,000 persons per day. Habitat, *Global Report on Human Settlements* (Nairobi, 2001), p. 3.

[6] An average of 7.09% is arrived at from the figures given for Ouagadougou, Douala, Nairobi, Tananarive, Bamako, Dar es Salaam, Kampala, Kinshasa and Harare, in Charles M. Becker and Andrew R. Morrison, 'The growth of African cities: Theory and estimates' (Table 6.1), in Archie Mafeje and Samir Radwan (eds), *Economic and Demographic Change in Africa* (Cambridge, 1995).

[7] Kingsley Davis, in 'The Urbanization of the Human Population', *Scientific American*, 1965, (reprinted in R.T. LeGates and F. Stout (eds), *The City Reader* (London, 1996)), p. 8, cites urban growth rates in the 1940s and 1950s of 4.7% for a sample of seven African countries, 4.7% for 15 Asian countries, and 4.3% for 12 Latin American countries. Peak growth rate in nine European countries was just 2.1%. See also Alan Gilbert and Josef Gugler, *Cities, Poverty and Development: Urbanization in the Third World* (Oxford, 1992), pp. 7–12.

does not recapitulate the experience of the West. Urbanisation in Africa, Asia and Latin America is happening in circumstances of 'far higher absolute population growth, at much lower income levels, with much less institutional and financial capacity'.[8] The rapid growth of Third World cities has meant that their economic development has frequently failed to keep pace with their demographic expansion, resulting in widespread unemployment and inadequate infrastructure and services. Large populations of urban poor have emerged living and working on the margins of the modern city.[9]

Anxious to promote controlled urban development, Third World politicians and administrators have been dismissive of the initiatives of the urban poor to provide themselves with an income and a home. Difficult to supervise, the shanty communities are perceived by ruling classes as contaminating the urban environment, or as threats to urban order. A frequent response to their presence has been to remove them from the cities and/or to attempt to prevent rural–urban migration in the first place.[10] These initiatives rarely (if ever) achieved the desired effect. However, despite their manifest historical inadequacies, officials continue to favour such policies as a response to rapid urban growth. In 1998, a law was passed by the Cuban government giving Havana administrators the power to forcibly repatriate migrants to their homes in the provinces.[11] In China, influx control is currently occurring on a monumental scale. A New York human rights organisation estimates that several million Chinese are locked up each year as a result of the Government's 'custody and repatriation' policies.[12] '[M]igrants picked up by the authorities', observes *The Economist*, 'represent a bigger affront to the concept of human rights than do the persecuted dissidents so publicised in the West'. If urbanisation was one of the twentieth century's most noteworthy historical trends, a frequent response to rapid urban growth was for governments to attempt to limit it through highly coercive measures.

Like the populations of other Third World cities, Dar es Salaam's inhabitants have experienced Government campaigns aimed at controlling urban growth and residence. Although in the more recent past large-scale coercive action against the urban poor seems mercifully to have actually

---

[8] Habitat, *Global Report* (2001), p. 3.

[9] For Africa, see John Iliffe, *The African Poor: A history* (Cambridge, 1987), chapters 10 and 13.

[10] Armstrong, for instance, mentions (among others) campaigns in the Philippines in 1963; in Indonesia in 1976; in Kampuchea in the late 1970s; and in Nigeria in 1984. Hardoy and Satterthwaite cite instances in Senegal in 1977 and in Indonesia and the Philippines in 1970 and 1982 respectively. Allen Armstrong, 'Urban control campaigns in the Third World: The case of Tanzania', Geography Dept, University of Glasgow, Occ. Papers no. 19 (1987), p. 5; Jorge Hardoy & David Satterthwaite, *Squatter Citizen: Life in the urban Third World* (London, 1989), p. 51; for neighbouring Kenya, see Lynn M. Thomas, *Politics of the Womb: Women, reproduction and the state in Kenya* (Berkeley/Los Angeles, 2003), p. 157; and for Northern Rhodesia, J. Van Velsen, 'Urban squatters: Problem or solution', in David Parkin (ed.), *Town and Country in Central and Eastern Africa* (London, 1975), pp. 294-307.

[11] *The Economist*, 23 October 1999, p. 94.

[12] In October 1999, for example, 'to ensure a spick-and-span capital' for the Communist Party's fiftieth-anniversary celebrations, Beijing authorities expelled 300,000 migrants from the city. *The Economist*, 16 October 1999, pp. 99–102; see also, 21 December 2002, p. 79.

declined in frequency,[13] in the first two decades after independence Dar es Salaam underwent a series of concerted — if ineffectual — urban purges aimed at removing unemployed, underemployed and informally employed persons from the city.[14] In the course of these campaigns those lacking waged work were demonised by official propaganda. They were *kupe* (parasites); *wazurulaji* (loiterers); *wavivu* (idlers); and *maadui wa siasa ya ujamaa na kujitegemea* ('enemies of the policy of socialism and self-reliance').[15] The politics of post-independence Tanzania resulted in the adoption of a distinctive slant to justify the state's attempts at urban 'cleansing'. It was those accused of being 'unproductive' who were perennially the targets of such campaigns. However, the origins of the campaigns are to be found in an earlier period. It was in the colonial era that both the phenomenon of rapid urbanisation emerged and coercive measures aimed at controlling the urban population were first employed. The marginalisation of that section of the urban population existing outside the formal economy also occurred at this time. It is the period of British colonial rule that provided the formative influence on post-colonial attitudes towards the urban poor.

While post-independence politicians employed a wide range of Swahili terms in their propaganda against the urban *residuum*, the principal source of colonial officials' anxieties can be reduced to just one category in Swahili: the *wahuni*.[16] The term *wahuni* had by the 1950s, if not before, come to refer to all the unemployed, underemployed, and nefariously employed Africans who, from the colonial point of view, cluttered the streets of Dar es Salaam. More specifically they were the target of repatriation campaigns conducted under the Removal of Undesirable Natives (later 'Undesirable Persons') Ordinance. *Wahuni* derives from the Swahili verb *huni*, which, according to Johnson's *Standard Swahili–English Dictionary* (an excellent source for colonial

---

13   In part, as a result of shifts in thinking about the state's social and economic role. Since the late 1980s the Tanzanian government — in marked contrast to the earlier post-colonial period — has pursued an often distinctly *laissez-faire* path. Indeed, Ali Hassan Mwinyi — who replaced Julius Nyerere as the country's second president in 1983, and was particularly associated with the liberalisation policies of the late 1980s and early 1990s — acquired the nickname '*ruksa*' (Swahili for permission), thanks to his willingness to leave things to the market (however venally this may at times have operated). For a good account of policy towards the informal economy in 1980s Dar es Salaam, see Aili Marie Tripp, *Changing the Rules: The politics of liberalization and the urban informal economy in Tanzania* (Berkeley, 1997).

14   See Andrew Burton, 'The Haven of Peace purged: Tackling the undesirable and unproductive poor in Dar es Salaam, *c.*1954–1984', in Andrew Burton and Michael Jennings, *The Emperor's New Clothes? Continuity and change in late-colonial and early post-colonial East Africa* (forthcoming).

15   Joe Lugalla, *Crisis, Urbanization, and Urban Poverty in Tanzania* (Lanham, 1995), p. 164. For an intriguing analysis of those identified as the 'enemies of national development' in Tanzanian nationalist discourse, see James Brennan, 'Sucking with straws: Exploitation and citizenship in Tanzanian nationalist thought and rhetoric, 1958–1976', in Burton and Jennings, *Emperor*.

16   Interestingly use of *mhuni/wahuni* was banned in early post-colonial Zanzibar, because — in line with its socialist philosophy — 'all people should be equal, and both words made light of irresponsible youth' (*Ngurumo*, 19 June 1965, cited in *ibid.*). However, it remained in use on the mainland, and its centrality to the contemporary city is reflected in one term for Dar es Salaam's street slang, the *lugha ya wahuni* [literally, 'language of the *wahuni*'].

usage), means to wander about for no good purpose, disobey or to be a vagabond. This made the *wahuni* 'profligates', 'wastrels', 'gadabouts', 'lawless persons' or 'outcasts'. In a contemporary dictionary, the singular form, *mhuni*, is — tellingly — first defined as an 'unmarried person', and then as an 'idler', 'vagrant' or (again) 'outcast'.[17] A generational definition identifying *wahuni* as young bachelors certainly had resonance in colonial Dar es Salaam, particularly among more senior Africans.[18] However, the term has important behavioural associations, and for both the colonial period and the present *wahuni*'s closest modern English equivalent is 'hooligans'.[19]

It is unclear when the term was first applied to sections of the urban population, although the adoption by a dance group of the title *Ngoma ya Kihuni* ('the hooligan's dance society')[20] in Sadaani in 1911 indicates its early usage along the *Mrima* (the northern Tanganyikan coast). This society was formed by 'low class, up-country immigrants to coastal towns'.[21] Their use of *kihuni* may well have been a defiant response to prevalent negative stereotypes.[22] By the 1930s *wahuni* had passed into common usage as a pejorative term in Dar es Salaam. According to a 1939 editorial in *Kwetu*, which provided a forum for Tanganyika's aspirant educated African elite, 'the well-known *Wahuni*' were to be encountered 'loafing in the bazaars and hotels, walking out late at night, and sleeping in obscure nooks'.[23] Sometime thereafter the term was adopted with increasing frequency by colonial officials to describe the growing number of young male Africans in the town without formal employment.[24] It was a conveniently inclusive

[17] Taasisi ya Uchunguzi wa Kiswahili, University of Dsm, *Kamusi ya Kiswahili–Kiingereza* (Dsm, 2001).

[18] The description 'young' here is highly relative. One oral informant, Mabrouk Swedi Mabrouk, aged the *wahuni* at anything from 16 to around 40 (basically, as long as they were fit enough to run or jump walls to evade capture!). Officials probably had a more restrictive conception of who might be termed *wahuni* (see e.g. fn. 24 below)

[19] For historical treatments of related phenomena in other parts of the world, see Stephen Humphries, *Hooligans or Rebels? An oral history of working-class childhood and youth, 1889–1939* (Oxford, 1981); Geoffrey Pearson, *Hooligan: A history of respectable fears* (London, 1983); Joan Neuberger, *Hooliganism: Crime, culture, and power in St. Petersburg, 1900–1914* (Berkeley/Los Angeles/London, 1993).

[20] The *ki-* prefix in Swahili is a diminutive.

[21] John Iliffe, *A Modern History of Tanganyika* (Cambridge, 1979), p. 238.

[22] By 1935 a Dar es Salaam successor to the *Ngoma ya Kihuni* had come to the attention of the *Tanganyika Standard* in the form of 'The Loafer Band'. *TS*, 16 March 1935. In the neighbouring Congo, in the 1950s, a band featuring the future African superstar, Franco, derived its name (*Watam*) from the local equivalent to *wahuni* (*watama*). Graeme Ewens, *Congo Colossus: The life and legacy of Franco & OK Jazz* (North Walsham, 1994), p. 58.

[23] *Kwetu*, 21 February 1939. Quoted in David Henry Anthony, 'Culture and society in a town in transition: A people's history of Dar es Salaam, 1865–1939', unpub. Ph.D. thesis, University of Wisconsin (1983), pp. 159–60. See also the letter on *wahuni* from M.F. Kassam in *Kwetu*, 13 January 1942.

[24] The first official reference I have come across, in the 1941 annual report of neighbouring Temeke District (p. 2), defines 'Muhuni [sic] as a 'young bachelor between the ages of eighteen and twenty five who has no fixed place of abode and obeys noone'. Wahuni, according to the report (p. 4), 'spend their time in more or less dishonourable employment in the township of Dar es Salaam and elude every effort at capture'.

term[25] that encapsulated, and simultaneously marginalised, a troublesome section of the urban population, about whose movements and actions colonial officials had little knowledge.[26]

Wahuni's increasing usage from the 1940s was associated with an unease, arising from what has come to be known as 'over-urbanisation', that preyed on the minds of colonial officials and other inhabitants of Dar es Salaam. The failure of the state to provide adequate infrastructure and amenities, and of the urban economy to provide sufficient formal employment, or satisfactory wages for those in employment, fed into other anxieties over the social processes accompanying African urbanisation. Concern about the proper conduct of urban immigrants, informed by both Western and African notions of morality and discipline, were at the heart of debates over urban growth conducted in both official correspondence and reports, and the European, Indian and African press. Occupation of urban space was made conditional upon conformity to certain forms of behaviour: notably industriousness (usually linked to formal employment), respectability and deference to (colonial and African) authority. However, in a town stratified (and often segregated) along class, race, ethnic and religious lines, such notions were contested. Patterns of work and leisure emerged that contradicted European, Indian and (respectable) African ideals, which from their point of view contributed only to the disorderliness and the depravity of the urban environment. More seriously still, in a social context characterised by marked economic inequality, even property rights were not always accorded the respect they were supposed to command.

Urban space, order and authority in colonial Dar es Salaam

Perceptions of space have been central to analyses of urban policy in colonial Africa.[27] Towns and cities have been portrayed as spaces within and from which order was imposed and — paradoxically — an arena in which the forces of disorder threatened to undermine the wider society. Evidence of the physical impact of European rule is particularly abundant in the urban areas, where the colonial imprint has been most visible and enduring.[28] This is true of both their functional role within wider territorial or international

[25] C.C. Harris, who more than any other official was responsible for intensified action against this section of the population, translated *wahuni*, in his autobiographical account of his colonial service, *Donkey's Gratitude* (Edinburgh, 1992), variously as 'bachelors' (p. 297), 'young town stiffs' (p. 304), 'wandering vagabonds' (p. 341) and 'layabouts' (p. 351).

[26] In colonial Mombasa, the 'Swahili' occupied a similar discursive space in colonial rhetoric. According to Justin Willis, 'the association of the word "Swahili" with a lazy and criminal population that defied regulation came to dominate European attitudes'. 'Swahili youth' were described by one official as 'a generation of drunken wasters'. *Mombasa, the Swahili, and the Making of the Mijikenda* (Oxford, 1993), pp. 110–11.

[27] See especially Frederick Cooper, 'Urban space, industrial time, and wage labour in Africa', in *Struggle for the City* (Beverley Hills, 1983), pp. 23–38 *et passim*.

[28] David M. Anderson and Richard Rathbone, 'Urban Africa: Histories in the making', introduction to *Africa's Urban Past* (Oxford/Portsmouth, NH, 2000), p. 9.

networks,[29] and in the character of the towns themselves.[30] In their very locations, towns could have a 'symbolic value, forming a spatial inscription of colonial power'.[31] Moreover, they performed important political and administrative functions, providing a base from which colonial rule could — however imperfectly — be imposed over wide regions.[32] The attempt to assert colonial order was nowhere more ambitious than in the urban centres, where legislative and planning interventions often involved ruthless and far-reaching attempts to organise space. Africans were subject to a wide array of urban laws and by-laws aimed at controlling their movements and behaviour. Although these frequently out-stretched the capacity of the colonial state to enforce them, the African in towns was subject to more direct supervision by colonial agents of enforcement than in the countryside.[33]

A great paradox of the colonial town, however, was that while it was where the regalian state was most in evidence, it was also a space of refuge where Africans could evade state exactions as well as escape rural patriarchal authority that colonialism had done much to buttress.[34] Although the administrative presence was more in evidence in the towns, large, heterogeneous and shifting urban populations offered a degree of anonymity

[29] Underdevelopment theorists in particular emphasised the enduring role that Third World cities have played in the extraction of wealth. For a critique, see Cooper, 'Urban space', pp. 13–15. For a discussion of the spatial location of Jinja, Uganda, see Andrew Byerley, 'Manufacturing Jinja. Rounds of space production and place making in an African industrial town' (Ph.D. thesis, University of Stockholm, forthcoming).

[30] Anthony D. King, *Colonial Urban Development: Culture, social power and environment* (London, 1976); Anja Kervanto Nevanlinna, *Interpreting Nairobi: The cultural study of built forms* (Helsinki, 1997); Seltene Seyoum, 'Land alienation and the urban growth of Bahir Dar', in Anderson and Rathbone, *Africa's Urban Past*, pp. 235–45; William Cunningham Bissell, 'Conservation and the colonial past: Urban planning, space and power in Zanzibar', in *ibid.*, pp. 246–61; Andrew Burton, 'Urbanisation in Eastern Africa: An historical overview, *c*.1750–2000', introduction to *The Urban Experience in Eastern Africa, c.1750–2000* (Nairobi, 2002), p. 23.

[31] Burton, 'Urbanisation', p. 16. For the example of Arusha *boma*, see Thomas Spear, '"A town of strangers" or "A model East African town"? Arusha and the Arusha', p. 113; and for the administrative 'Plateau' of Brazzaville, Florence Bernault, 'The political shaping of a sacred locality in Brazzaville, 1959–97', p. 289, both in Anderson and Rathbone, *Africa's Urban Past*.

[32] For a discussion of the role small administrative centres played in the imposition of colonial order in Samburu District, a part of Kenya Colony far from the main centres of power, see Peter Waweru, 'Frontier Urbanisation: The rise and development of towns in Samburu District, Kenya, 1909–1940', in Burton, *Urban Experience*, pp. 85–97.

[33] See e.g. John McCracken, 'Coercion and control in Nyasaland: Aspects of the history of a colonial police force', *JAH* 27 (1986), pp. 127–47; David Killingray, 'The maintenance of law and order in British colonial Africa', *AA* 85 (1986), pp. 411–37; David M. Anderson, 'Policing the settler state: Colonial hegemony in Kenya, 1900–1952', in Dagmar Engels and Shula Marks, *Contesting Colonial Hegemony* (London, 1994); David M. Anderson and David Killingray, 'Consent, coercion and control: Policing the empire, 1830–1940', introduction to *Policing the Empire: Government, authority and control, 1830–1940* (Manchester, 1991). For policing in Dar es Salaam, see Andrew Burton, 'Brothers by Day: Colonial policing in Dar es Salaam under British rule', *Urban History* 30:1 (2003), pp. 63–91; and for the district administration, Andrew Burton, 'Adjutants, agents, intermediaries: The Native Administration in Dar es Salaam township, 1919–1961', in Burton, *Urban Experience*, pp. 98–118.

[34] Pre-colonial towns could also act as places of refuge. See e.g. Steven Feierman, *Peasant Intellectuals: Anthropology and history in Tanzania* (Madison, 1990), p. 112 *et passim*.

that was more or less impossible in a village. So, for example, tax collection was much more effective in the countryside than in the urban areas,[35] and towns often formed a 'haven' for the 'professional [labour] contract breaker'.[36] The urban world was also a youthful one that offered freedom from elders' control and opportunities for advancement to young Africans.[37] Similarly, the manner in which women used urban areas to escape rural patriarchy, and often to prosper, has been well documented.[38] Experience of urban life among young men and women not only undermined 'traditional' authority but also led to their contamination by an unrespectable modernity. In recollecting his colonial service, a Kenyan police officer complained that:

> Old men came to my station looking for lost sons. They were puzzled and bewildered. The young wanted to smoke, drink and drive motor cars. Their daughters painted their lips, smoked cigarettes and grew cheeky. They lived with other men and drank methylated spirits. They said 'Go home you old fool. Go and look after your goats'.[39]

In the urban areas the over-reach of the colonial state was particularly evident. Initial, unsuccessful, efforts to limit the exposure of Africans to urban life gave way to attempts to mediate the process of modernisation that was understood as being part and parcel of African urbanisation. However, contact with 'modernity' in the towns resulted in not only the advancement of 'progressive' goals associated with late-colonial (and post-colonial) developmentalism, but also the fashioning of new identities and behaviour (among young men and women in particular) that complicated and/or undermined state initiatives.[40] In the case of Dar es

---

[35] Willis, *Mombasa*, pp. 106, 198; Andrew Burton, 'Dealing with the defaulter: Native taxation and colonial authority in Tanganyika, 1920s–50s' (in preparation).

[36] Justin Willis, 'Thieves, drunkards and vagrants: Defining crime in colonial Mombasa, 1902–32', in Anderson and Killingray, *Policing the Empire*, p. 223.

[37] See e.g. Willis, *Mombasa*, p. 93 *et passim*; Joanna Lewis, *Empire State-Building: War and welfare in Kenya, 1925–52* (Oxford/Nairobi/Athens, OH, 2000), p. 135; and for Dar es Salaam, Andrew Burton, 'Urchins, loafers and the cult of the cowboy: Urbanisation and delinquency in Dar es Salaam, 1919–1961', *JAH* 42 (2001), pp. 199–216.

[38] The literature is extensive. For East Africa, see e.g. Luise White, *The Comforts of Home: Prostitution in colonial Nairobi* (Chicago, 1990); Claire Robertson, *Trouble Showed the Way: Women, men and trade in the Nairobi area, 1890–1990* (Bloomington, 1997); Bodil Folke Frederiksen, 'African women and their colonisation of Nairobi: Representations and realities', in Burton, *Urban Experience*, pp. 222–34; Thomas, *Politics of the Womb*, p. 68. Inez Sutton, '"Rich enough to pay for what they want": Independent townswomen in colonial East Africa' (f/c – ms in author's possession); Ophelia Mascarenhas and Marjorie Mbilinyi, *Women in Tanzania: An analytical bibliography* (Uppsala, 1983), pp. 36, 121–37; Birgitta Larsson, *Conversion to Greater Freedom: Women, Church and social change in North-Western Tanzania under colonial rule* (Uppsala, 1991), pp. 111–38, 210–13; Janet Bujra, *Serving Class: Masculinity and the feminisation of domestic service in Tanzania* (London, 2000), pp. 90–1.

[39] Sidney T. Kelson, p. 10, RH/Mss.Afr.s.735. Quoted in Lewis, *Empire State-Building*, p. 135.

[40] For state attempts at the mediation of modernity, see Justin Willis, '"Clean spirit": Distilling, modernity, and the Ugandan state, 1950–1986', in Burton and Jennings, *Emperor*; Andrew M. Ivaska, '"Anti-mini militants meet modern misses": Urban style, gender and the politics of 'national culture' in 1960s Dar es Salaam, Tanzania', *Gender and History* (f/c); and Burton, 'Urchins'. For colonial attempts to separate 'modern' and 'traditional' sectors, see Frederick Cooper, *Decolonization and African Society: The labor question in French and British Africa* (Cambridge, 1996), Part III.

Salaam, the manner in which the town became for African women a space of unprecedented autonomy, and sometimes prosperity, *contra* the expectations and desires of both colonial administrators and African men, has been described.[41] The town was also a place where young Africans were able to evade the assertions of both elders and officials: where they adopted patterns of behaviour that subverted both the developmental hegemony of the late-colonial (and postcolonial) state and rural patriarchal authority.[42]

The relative freedom offered African youth by the urban environment and the anxieties induced by the phenomenon are — alongside the administrative response to urbanisation — at the heart of this book. Waning authority over migrant youth was a perennial concern. The 'constant stream of unskilled, young, and usually unmarried' male migrants entering the town posed a threat to elders' authority and to that of the colonial regime.[43] Anxieties over both the collapse of 'customary regulations' on social behaviour and the uncontrolled impact of modernity on guileless 'tribal' immigrants found a focus in the form of the *wahuni*. The timing of the emergence of the term into official rhetoric in the 1940s and 1950s is telling. Prior to WWII it was the 'detribalised native' that was the source of concern; a category whose unspecificity more than anything signalled European antipathy towards the African urban presence and the lack of colonial knowledge of what was actually occurring in the township. With the post-war shift to a local government policy (as opposed to indirect rule) and social engineering initiatives aimed at modernising African society, urban administrators sought to replace tribal links with civic and class-based identities. A restricted urban population was envisaged, engaged in formal employment and living in nuclear families, whose connections with the backward rural areas were to be kept to a minimum.[44] Above all else, it was the burgeoning tide of youthful immigrants making their way to Dar es Salaam that undermined the emerging policy. Physical control of the town was lost as the spiralling African population placed considerable strain on the urban infrastructure, and large unplanned settlements arose to meet migrants' needs. The urban economy — in which officials had hoped better wages would result in the inculcation of Western time and work discipline and improvements in African productivity — was similarly swamped, and a burgeoning informal sector emerged. Moreover,

---

41   Mbilinyi, 'Unforgettable business'; Geiger, *TANU Women*, p. 44; Ivaska, 'Anti-mini militants'; Andrew M. Ivaska, 'Negotiating "culture" in a cosmopolitan capital: Urban style and the Tanzanian state in colonial and pos-colonial Dar es Salaam' (Ph.D. thesis, University of Michigan, 2003).

42   Ivaska, 'Negotiating culture'; Burton, 'Urchins'.

43   Harris, *Donkey's Gratitude*, p. 297. In addition to urbanisation, other processes arising during colonial rule also resulted in heightened inter-generational tension and the perceived delinquency of young Africans. For a study of rural *uhuni*, see Richard Waller, 'Disciplining youth in colonial Maasailand', paper given at the ASA conference, Boston, 30 October–2 November 2003. For an intriguing account of the shifting relationship of alcohol and patriarchal authority in East African society, see Justin Willis, *Potent Brews: A social history of alcohol in East Africa* (Oxford/Athens, OH/Nairobi/Kampala/Dar es Salaam, 2002).

44   E.g. *East African Royal Commission 1953-55 Report* (*EARC Report*) (London, 1955), p. 214. For an extended historical treatment, see the work of Frederick Cooper, especially *Decolonization*.

greater independence of mind among those exposed to the urban milieu resulted in a less deferential population, and the urban police and district administration found the task of social control increasingly demanding.[45]

The most alarming aspect of this failure to impose order was a growing problem of urban crime. In large part, the upsurge in criminality was actually improvised by colonial legislation that often reflected official anxieties over the nexus linking urbanisation, demoralisation and vice. Attempts to assert an alien colonial order could instead promote disorder. An array of laws and by-laws prohibiting diverse pursuits were ignored by many urban residents, who in so doing both contested their legitimacy and added to the crime statistics. For example, the prohibition of certain informal economic activities in a context in which the formal economy was failing to provide sufficient jobs or incomes was viewed by some as the true offence rather than the urban presence of, say, petty traders or mendicants. As the capacity of the colonial state to enforce such legislation grew after WWII, increasing numbers of Africans were apprehended in breach of the law — thereby contributing to the spiralling number of offenders, which in turn gave rise to official concern. More serious still was an upsurge in property crime, alongside — to the dismay of Europeans, Indians and many Africans — the failure to entrench the sanctity of personal possessions among sections of the urban population. Massive disparities in income, combined with the conspicuous affluence of the few, the extraordinarily low level of wages and widespread unemployment and underemployment, served to endorse some illicit redistribution. Such phenomena merely tended to confirm suspicions about both the moral consequences of urbanisation and the ill-preparedness of Africans for town life.

Official policy, then, failed to have the anticipated impact on African urbanisation. Instead, it served to marginalise a large proportion of Africans present in the town, whose rights to urban citizenship were undermined by both colonial legislation and administrative practice. The anti-urban prejudices of officials, settlers and elite Africans at one and the same time helped to define an 'underclass', and to justify action against the undesirable urbanites which this underclass comprised, most prominently the so-called *wahuni*.[46] Both policy and prejudice, as they emerged in colonial Dar es Salaam, were to bequeath a considerable legacy to post-colonial urban governance, as administrative practice — despite its transparent failure to meet its goals both before and after independence — continued to discriminate against significant sections of the urban population.[47]

---

[45] See Burton, 'Urchins' (for insubordinate youth), 'Brothers by Day' (the police) and 'Adjutants' (the urban Native Administration).

[46] The term 'underclass' is used not in Marxian class terms, which would identify that section of society under discussion here as a 'lumpenproletariat'. Rather, it is used to describe a community of urban poor whose emergence in the colonial period coincided with its social and economic marginalisation; and which has continued to suffer marginalisation in post-colonial Tanzania.

[47] See Burton, 'Haven'; Brennan, 'Sucking by straws'; Ivaska, 'Negotiating culture'.

Urban order and colonial knowledge

The failure to impose its own urban order reflected both the ambition and the corresponding shortcomings of the colonial state. Various laws and by-laws were in place that sought to restrict urban residence and control the behaviour of Africans in the town. However, social and economic changes accompanying colonial rule resulted in growing numbers making their way to Dar es Salaam, particularly from the late 1930s. Moreover, within the town the capacity of the administration to supervise and discipline the African population was limited. Urban legislation proved either inadequate or unenforceable with the resources available. From the 1940s, officials adapted to the new reality of increasing urbanisation by accepting a restricted community of Africans in Dar es Salaam, while adopting initiatives aimed at directing the way in which urban African society evolved and simultaneously intensifying efforts to exclude those who were deemed to have no place in the town. While more ambitious and better-resourced, this new urban policy was no more successful than that pursued between the wars. In part, the weakness of the urban regime stemmed from the fact that even with an expanded district administration and police force, alongside greater resources for the construction of urban infrastructure and amenities, the unanticipated pace and scale of African urbanisation simply overwhelmed initiatives aimed at addressing the phenomenon. However, an equally important source of weakness was a fundamental ignorance of urban African society.

Official knowledge of the African community in Dar es Salaam remained limited at best throughout the colonial period. This stemmed in part from disapproval over the African urban presence. Up to the early 1940s the African in town was defined not by what he (or she) was becoming but instead in negative terms, as the 'de-tribalised native'. Little effort was made to investigate urban communities that were both small and viewed as impermanent. Even the growing acceptance of African urbanisation in the 1940s and 1950s was informed more by colonial notions of how African urban society ought to be than how it actually was. The position was further complicated by both the heterogeneity and the mobility of the urban population. As the principal economic and administrative centre in Tanganyika Territory, Dar es Salaam attracted a great diversity of people from surrounding districts in Eastern Province, from further afield in Tanganyika Territory, and from neighbouring colonies in East and Southern Africa. Mobility was high. Movement between the upcountry rural areas and the capital was constant. There were great seasonal fluctuations of population. Moreover, times of economic slump not only forced jobless workers to return to their rural homes but also often resulted in a drift of the unemployed to peri-urban areas to engage in *shamba* cultivation.[48] In addition, within the town itself the African urban population was characterised by its mobility, with frequent shifts of address being common.[49]

[48] E.g. J.A.K. Leslie, *A Survey of Dar es Salaam* (Oxford, 1963), p. 93.
[49] Leslie estimated in 1957 'that a quarter of younger people move house every three to four months'. Leslie, *Survey*, p. 250.

Theoretically, colonial Dar es Salaam should have been an orderly, regimented town in which people's residential and occupational space was well defined and had been internalised by members of its diverse communities. However, at no time did the well-ordered capital envisaged in colonial legislation, in which inhabitants of the town knew their proper place, correspond to reality — although it remained an ideal informing decisions made by colonial and post-colonial administrators alike. Building laws failed to prevent a degree of residential intermingling of African, Indian and European communities.[50] Regulations aimed at restricting rural–urban migration, alongside those aimed at controlling migrants once they had arrived in the town, were equally ineffective. Throughout the British period, in the midst of Dar es Salaam's longer-term inhabitants, the disturbing presence of a 'floating population' loomed large in the official imagination, representing a persistent threat to colonial urban order.

British officials had difficulty in fathoming such a fluid community.[51] Africans in Dar es Salaam were perceived as an aggregate mass about which, one official complained in 1930, '[w]e know less … than we do of remote tribes'.[52] Twenty years later, the situation was much the same: sociologists working for the Government in Dar es Salaam in 1951 were told that '[p]eople make wild guesses about the native population but we don't know their habits.'[53] This lack of knowledge magnified anxieties about the African urban presence. Where to the European mind no apparent order was discernible, a portentous disorder was often assumed.[54] Confronted with a faceless and yet heterogeneous population, colonial officials tended to anticipate the worst and to demand ever-increasing powers to assuage their exaggerated concerns. The demonisation of the *wahuni* formed a prime expression of this.

The lacunae in colonial knowledge are only too apparent in the primary sources that have survived, which invariably are much stronger on the perceived causes of official anxiety than they are on everyday urban life. Even the best-informed and most sympathetic observers had only a partial view of African society. They were especially ignorant of the movements and actions of that section of the population drifting between urban and rural life, and/or intermittently engaging in waged employment, otherwise resorting to petty trade,

---

50   Throughout 'Indian' is used to refer to persons originating from the Indian subcontinent, Muslim and non-Muslim alike. 'Asian' is used to refer to persons of Indian and Arab (and in some cases Chinese) descent.

51   The same was true of colonial Mombasa. See Willis, *Mombasa*, pp. 106, 190. See also Phyllis Martin on the Poto-Poto quarter in Brazzaville, *Leisure and Society in Colonial Brazzaville* (Cambridge, 1995), p. 42.

52   Quoted in the Report by R. and C. Sofer on a possible sociological survey of Dsm, p. 14, TNA/18950 Vol. III.

53   Notes leading up to recommendations that a sociological survey of Dsm should take place (by the Sofers?) in Dsm Ex-Prov. Dist. Book Vol. V.I.

54   Urban society in neighbouring Northern Rhodesia was characterised by A.L. Epstein — a sociologist, no less — as 'inchoate and incoherent, where the haphazard is more conspicuous than the regular, and all is in a state of flux'. 'The network and urban social organization', *Rhodes-Livingstone Institute Journal* 29 (1961), p. 29. Quoted in James Ferguson, *Expectations of Modernity: Myths and meanings of urban life on the Zambian Copperbelt* (Berkeley, 1999), p. 18.

to scavenging or to crime to get by; who by the late-colonial period formed a large proportion (probably a majority) of the urban African population. This lack of knowledge expanded at a rate comparable to the growth of the town.

So the social surveys produced by Baker and Leslie, in 1931 and 1957 respectively, can be viewed as yardsticks of colonial knowledge that provide pictures of similar comprehensiveness and reliability at different stages of the town's development. By 1957, the African population of Dar es Salaam had increased fourfold, its geographical extent by three or four times, and urban economic, social and cultural activities had proliferated at a comparable rate. All of these factors substantially complicated any attempt by even the most enthusiastic and sympathetic colonial officer[55] to get a grasp of the African town. Meanwhile, the administration of Dar es Salaam was mainly in the hands of officials who either hadn't the time or the inclination (or both) to familiarise themselves with African urban society. The African township as viewed from the *Boma* (District Office) differed as much from Leslie's more informed perceptions as these differed from the African experience of Dar es Salaam.

The shortcomings of the official record provide obvious problems for the historian of the town. While windows can be opened up on the lives of the so-called *wahuni* using data gleaned from the various colonial reports and correspondence, these windows are invariably located in the *Boma*. For example, where informal economic activities do come to light, they are generally viewed simply as a problem to be controlled. We get little idea of their location, their extent, who exactly is engaging in them, their profitability or any number of other aspects that may be of interest.[56] Moreover, other surviving records also fail to illuminate those areas neglected in official sources. In European reminiscences, and in the settler, the Indian, and even the African press (which was of course the voice of a literate elite), the *wahuni* occupy a similar space to that which they occupy in Government correspondence or reports. Here too they generally emerge as a faceless mass and a source for concern. In Dar es Salaam, as elsewhere, the poor leave behind only 'sporadic traces'.[57]

In his book on late-nineteenth and early-twentieth century Mombasa, Justin Willis has highlighted the problem of reliance on official sources for the historian, and how this can lead to reconstructions in which urban populations remain 'a disorganised rabble, just as the administrators of the time were wont to perceive them'.[58] A similar criticism could be made of this account of the *wahuni*. In my defence I would make the following observations. This is not a history of the African community of Dar es Salaam, though inevitably aspects of the city's social history do emerge. It is principally a study of urban administration and of 'folk devils and moral panics' in the colonial setting.[59] Nevertheless, I hope that the sympathetic treatment of

---

[55] Which Leslie undoubtedly was.
[56] The reports by Baker and Leslie are the exception, although even these present only a limited snapshot of such activities.
[57] Iliffe, *African Poor*, p. 2.
[58] Willis, *Mombasa*, p. 2.
[59] The expression is from Stanley Cohen, *Folk Devils and Moral Panics: The creation of mods and rockers* (St Albans, 1973), which provides an excellent account of popular anxieties surrounding youth culture in 1960s Britain.

those people labelled *wahuni* will leave the reader with an impression of their human qualities: some idea, at least, of their motivations for entering the city and the activities they engaged in once there. Broad patterns do begin to emerge from the historian's privileged overview of data surviving from the four decades of British colonial rule in Tanganyika: it is possible to gain some impression of what was going on in Dar es Salaam beyond the colonial ken. Also, while the official record may have significant weaknesses, it is extremely strong on how the colonial administration responded to the phenomenon of rapid urban growth. Parts One and Three of the book take advantage of this rich material. Sandwiched between these, in Part Two, is an account of those urban phenomena, rendered criminal by colonial legislation, that were the occasion for such official disquiet, and which led to the emergence of *wahuni* as colonial bogeymen *par excellence.*

Chapter overview

The purpose of the first chapter is to place what follows in a wider context. Attitudes towards urban growth in Tanganyika were influenced by earlier responses to mass urbanisation in Western societies. Equally, urban policy in Tanganyika was a part of, and influenced by, policy elsewhere in Africa. A comprehensive overview of colonial urban policy in Eastern Africa and South Africa (which provided a model for urban administrators throughout the sub-region[60]) provides background for the detailed case study that follows. Chapter 2 gives a snapshot of Dar es Salaam between the wars, in which aspects of the town's demography, administration and social economy are discussed. With limited resources at their disposal, officials were hard-pressed to impose a comprehensive colonial order. Meanwhile, although the town attracted labour from throughout Tanganyika (and further afield), the low level of urban wages led to an impecunious existence for most Africans. The poor living conditions prevalent in the town contributed to official anxieties over the African urban presence, which are discussed in chapter 3. In the inter-war period, officials displayed a fundamental suspicion towards urbanisation, among young Africans in particular. A number of legislative measures were adopted in order to deal with the phenomenon. However, officials were hard-pressed to enforce these laws. The situation deteriorated substantially from around 1938, when an acceleration in rural–urban migration placed increasing strain on the town's administration, infrastructure and economy. Alongside shifts in colonial thought emerging from Whitehall (and from elsewhere in Africa), this led to a reappraisal of urban policy that is discussed in chapters 4 and 5. There was now greater official acceptance of the African urban presence; this coincided with a recognition that more

[60] In particular the 'Durban system' was held up as an example for urban administrators. See e.g., 'Controlling Natives in Townships: Lessons for East Africa from Durban', *East Africa*, 21 November 1929, p. 311.

had to be done to enhance conditions in the town, through the provision of infrastructure, better wages and a more efficient urban administration. However, prior to 1947 little *was* done to effect the new goals emerging from the debate over urban policy. Ironically, one area in which rather more administrative energy was expended was in the attempts to refine and enforce legislation aimed at controlling African urbanisation. While officials envisaged the emergence of a permanent urban African community, urban residence was to be restricted to those who fulfilled certain criteria, notably formal sector employment. Those who failed to meet these criteria were, increasingly, subject to eviction from the town.

Part Two provides a discussion of crime and colonial order. Although Dar es Salaam was actually a relatively peaceful place, crime in the town was inextricably linked to arguments over African urbanisation and to the kind of society that colonial officials endeavoured to create. In chapter 6, the problem of defining and interpreting crime in the colonial situation is addressed. It is observed that in a society governed by laws framed by an alien minority, notions of illegality and illegitimacy often fail to coincide. Urbanisation in Tanganyika led, as elsewhere, to the emergence of a distinctive urban criminality, which forms the subject of the following chapter. The growth of an indigenous 'class' of professional criminals, including the activities of criminal gangs in the late-colonial period, is observed. However, the conclusion is reached that the vast majority of crime in Dar es Salaam was opportunistic and petty in form. This is followed, in chapter 8, by a discussion of an emerging urban informal economy. The legitimacy of colonial legislation prohibiting such activity was contested by Dar es Salaam's African population, with laws and by-laws routinely breached. The illegal trade in alcohol and street trading provide two case studies of such crimes. Other aspects of what in European historiography has been termed 'social' criminality arise in the following chapter. In Tanganyika, various legislation existed on the statute books aimed at restricting African mobility both within and to Dar es Salaam. It had limited success. The emergence in the town of an undifferentiated mass of unemployed and underemployed Africans who to the colonial mind represented a constant threat to urban order is described. It included jobless 'loiterers', rickshaw-pullers, beggars, and perhaps most seriously unruly adolescents. Attempts were made to control all these groups, but with the meagre resources available to the urban administration they had limited effect. Anxieties provoked by the presence of these urban undesirables were confirmed by the periodic breakdown of order that occurred in the town. The second half of chapter 9 provides a detailed overview of those instances of disorder recorded in surviving sources.

Part Three begins with a snapshot of Dar es Salaam after WWII, a time when rapid urban growth resulted in significant changes to the town's physical and demographic make-up. This, alongside a colonial willingness to invest greater resources in urban development, led to the expansion of the town's administrative, social and economic infrastructure. Despite this expansion, however, the pace of demographic growth undermined the administration's ability to control the town; meanwhile, living conditions experienced by the bulk of the urban population remained grim. The following chapter documents the attempt to address this through a new urban policy, whose roots lay in the debates of the 1940s, but which only began to be implemented in the final decade of colonial rule. At the heart of the new policy was the attempt to nurture a stabilised urban African population, enjoying better wages and living conditions. If an enhanced role for Africans in the town was envisaged in this policy, however, at the same time it involved the marginalisation of a growing community of unemployed, underemployed and informally employed Africans. Increasingly, from the 1940s, and more particularly the 1950s, the right of urban residence was technically denied this section of the urban population, which was earmarked for forced removal from the town. Chapter 12 provides a discussion of the debates surrounding legal and administrative measures aimed at controlling movement to and residence in Tanganyikan towns in the late 1940s and 1950s. This is followed by a detailed account of the increasingly coercive application of such legislation. It ends with short biographical sketches of some of the victims of repatriation campaigns, which by the mid-1950s had become a daily feature of African life. Through these a chink of light is shed upon the lives of individual Africans evicted as *wahuni*.

One

'These Great Marts of Human Corruption'

Urbanisation & Urban Policy in Comparative Perspective[1]

The concern provoked among colonial officials by the phenomenon of African urbanisation was by no means unique to Tanganyika. Such anxiety was characteristic of social relations in urban centres in Western societies at least since the industrial revolution began to change the character of their towns and cities from the early nineteenth century. In part these anxieties arose from the loosening of traditional structures of control. The urban arena was one in which old social, economic and political formations were broken down and over time replaced by new ones. Urbanisation led to the atomisation of individuals, and the emergence of distinct and conflicting interest groups. In Victorian Britain, the first modern society one can characterise as urbanised, the concentrations of landless workers that began to congregate in the large industrial cities were viewed with mounting concern by contemporary politicians and observers.[2] The first half of the nineteenth century had witnessed the shift from a predominantly rural to a predominantly urban society and there was great uncertainty among 'respectable' classes over the consequences of this process. These concerns were articulated in terms of the loss of an idyllic agrarian society characterised by the reciprocal links between rulers and the ruled. They found expression in nineteenth-century nostalgia for *Merrie England* and in the poetry of the Romantics. As the crucible of the emerging industrial society, urban centres were characterised as the location of demoralisation and depravity. Stedman-Jones, writing of London's respectable classes in the late nineteenth century, notes that while 'the countryside had symbolised the forces of simplicity, strength, phlegm, loyalty and deference' to these people, 'the growing preponderance of the urban population portended the sway of dangerous and volatile populations'.[3] To nineteenth-century observers the towns were particularly associated with the acquisition of

---

[1] Quote from Friedrich Engels, *The Condition of the Working Class in England*, trans. & ed. W.O. Henderson & W.H. Chaloner (Stanford, CA, 1958), p. 135.

[2] For examples, see Asa Briggs, *Victorian Cities* (Harmondsworth, 1968), pp. 59–87.

[3] Gareth Stedman-Jones, *Outcast London* (Harmondsworth, 1984), p. 150.

vices. Even Freidrich Engels, a sympathetic commentator on the plight of the urban poor, observed that it was in the cities that 'virtue ... is depressed from the obscurity in which it is involved: guilt is matured from the difficulty of its detection: licentiousness is rewarded by the immediate enjoyments which it promises.'[4] For many, such as the MP and liberal reformer, Charles Masterman, who viewed with concern the emergence of 'a new race ... this New Town type' in the East End of London, what was occurring with the shift to the city was a kind of 'demographic degeneration', in which second generation urban citizens were not only physically weak but also morally stunted.[5]

In fact, there was widespread ignorance about the working-class communities emerging in the towns. Middle-class concern over urban growth stemmed from this lack of knowledge. According to Emsley:

> H.A. Frégier coined the term 'les classes dangereuses' in 1840; and while the Parisian poor may, in the event, have been far more dangerous to the bourgeoisie than any of their British counterparts, Frégier's term was rapidly anglicised and taken over by British men of property as much to define their fears as any social group lurking in the city slums.[6]

Briggs observes that to the Victorian middle classes '(t)he "dark city" and the "dark continent" were alike mysterious, and it is remarkable how often the exploration of the unknown city was compared with the exploration of Africa and Asia'.[7] William Booth, the founder of the Salvation Army, for example, asked in 1890:

> As there is a darkest Africa, is there not also a darkest England? Civilisation, which can breed its own barbarians, does it not also breed its own pygmies? May we not find a parallel at our own doors, and discover within a stone's throw of our cathedrals and palaces similar horrors to those which Stanley has found existing in the great Equatorial forest?[8]

He equated the English slum to the African jungle in its 'monotonous darkness, its malaria and its gloom, its dwarfish de-humanised inhabitants, the slavery to which they are subjected, their privations and their misery'.

Towards the end of the nineteenth century these uncharted territories began to be penetrated by Victorian philanthropists, men such as Charles Masterman and Charles Booth (no relation to William Booth), both of whom were particularly concerned by the breakdown of community and associated problems in the overcrowded East End of London. In contrasting the organic type of communities to be found in rural areas with the more individualistic, alienated society of the cities, later social scientists refined

4   Engels, *Condition of the Working Class*, pp.135–6.
5   C.F.G. Masterman, *The Heart of Empire: Discussions of Modern City Life in England* (1901), quoted in Andrew Lees, *Cities Perceived: Urban society in European and American thought, 1820–1940* (Manchester, 1985), p. 155; see also, Pearson, *Hooligan*, pp. 68–73.
6   Clive Emsley, *Crime and Society in England, 1750–1900*, 2nd edn (London, 1996), p. 36.
7   Briggs, *Victorian Cities*, p. 62.
8   General William Booth, *In Darkest England and the Way Out* (1890), quoted in Lees, *Cities*, p.110.

concerns of pioneers such as Booth and Masterman and began to theorise the social and cultural processes that were occurring in modern society. Ferdinand Tonnies' *Gemeinschaft–Gesellschaft* dichotomy, for example, contrasted

> traditional society, generally equated with rural society, [in which] people live in a face to face community where social mobility is low, customs and actions are legitimated in terms of customs and precedent; [with] modern society [which], in contrast, is impersonal and a variety of voluntarily formed associations regulate different aspects of social life.[9]

Durkheim's concept of anomie – a state where 'common values and common meanings are no longer understood or accepted, and new values and meanings have not developed'[10] – is perhaps the best known of these theories of social change and one that was seen to have particular relevance to conditions in the towns and cities of the industrialised world. Durkheim, like many earlier commentators on the process of urbanisation, was 'concerned that the city, together with the spread of "modern civilisation", was destabilising the "equilibrium" of certain individuals and prompting degeneracy and deviance'.[11] In America, Robert Park, one of the pioneers of the Chicago school of urban sociology, reached similar conclusions. 'Everyone is more or less on his own in the city,' he wrote in 1915. 'The consequence is that man, translated to the city, has become a problem to himself and to society in a way and to an extent that he never was before'.[12]

Concerns aroused by the processes of industrialisation and urbanisation in nineteenth-century Britain, and later other Western societies, influenced attitudes towards the similar processes occurring a century later in sub-Saharan Africa, as we shall see in the case of Dar es Salaam. In the colonial rhetoric regarding the effects of urban growth in Tanganyika are traces of the Victorian anxiety towards the transformation of British society. There is the same idealisation of country life and corresponding concern over the detachment of the urban migrant from his rural community. In the colonial context, though, urban administrators viewed the African jungle – or 'bush', at least – as a virtuous environment instead of a metaphor for vice and demoralisation. Similarly, *Merrie England* could be equated with a conception of *Merrie Africa* in which existed integrated rural African societies governed by unchanging customary regulations. Colonial officials expressed the same concern over the breakdown of traditional structures of control, and the licentiousness of the urban environment. They were, like their counterparts in the West, anxious about an emerging urban 'mass'. In the 'detribalised native' we have the colonial counterpart to Masterman's 'New Town type'. Surveys of the African populations of Dar es Salaam and other colonial

---

[9]   Emsley, *Crime*, p. 94.
[10] This definition is from the Encyclopaedia Britannica CD ROM (1997) version.
[11] Emsley, *Crime*, p. 94.
[12] Robert Park, 'The city: Suggestions for the investigation of human behaviour in the urban environment' (1915), quoted in Lees, *Cities Perceived*, p. 301.

towns, which found widespread malnutrition and concluded that large numbers of urban Africans were as a result more or less 'unemployable', uncovered a 'demographic degeneration' similar to that which had been described by Masterman in London's East End. The colonial state, like nineteenth-century industrial capitalism, had created a monster of its own making. The grand project of 'civilising' and — later — modernising African society had as its by-product the exposure to the demoralising currents of urban life of subsistence agriculturalists who were considered even more poorly equipped to withstand them than landless peasants in nineteenth-century England. Among the immigrants to the urban areas it was African youth who were a prime focus for concern. The emergence of *wahuni* in Dar es Salaam, or the 'wharf rats' of Accra or Lagos, were equally unwelcome as the 'street urchins' in the rookeries of London. Moreover, colonial perceptions of the negative consequences of African urbanisation were coloured by a sense of the 'other' — resulting from an ignorance about African life in the towns — that corresponds with the fear of the unknown inhabitants of the Victorian slums. In the Tanganyikan case the ignorance was deeper still because the cultural barrier between the colonial masters and their subjects was much greater than that which separated the Victorian urban poor from their bourgeois contemporaries. This gap in colonial knowledge only began to be bridged when, as had also happened in the West, attention was belatedly directed towards the urban areas as the process of urbanisation became acknowledged as irreversible, late in the colonial era. By this time, some observers were even explicitly connecting what was occurring in Africa to what had earlier occurred in Western societies. P.M. Henry wrote in the *New Commonwealth* in 1954:

> When we cease looking upon Africa as a completely exotic land, we shall recognise the many familiar features of the Industrial Revolution of the nineteenth century. Obviously the situation is complicated by racial differences, but fundamentally it is the same.[13]

Colonial urban policy in East and Southern Africa

Cultural antipathy to the process of urbanisation in Western society reinforced colonial prejudices about African subjects. This was particularly true of East and Southern Africa where, in contrast to West Africa, evidence of pre-colonial traditions of urban settlement was negligible.[14] In fact, the process

---

[13] As witnessed by the staging of a conference on the 'Social impact of industrialization and urban conditions in Africa' in Dakar, organised by UNESCO, the Council for Technical Cooperation in Africa and the French Government. This lead to the UNESCO publication, *Social Implications of Industrialization and Urbanization in Africa South of the Sahara*, London (1956).The quote is from Henry, 'African Townee', p.220.

[14] European prejudices were epitomised by a refusal to believe that the complex urban settlement of Great Zimbabwe was a product of African initiative. See Martin Hall, *Archaeology Africa* (Cape Town/London, 1996), pp. 23–30 *et passim*; Graham Connah, *African Civilizations: Precolonial cities and states in tropical Africa: An archaeological perspective* (Cambridge, 1987), p. 183.

of urbanisation had actually been accelerating in the region in the course of the nineteenth century.[15] However, aside from exceptional groups such as the Swahili, whose long traditions of urban settlement were well documented, the African was treated as a fundamentally rural being by incoming colonialists. His (or her) social identity was inextricably bound up with the ethnic community to which he (or she) belonged. Up to the 1940s, the colonial state drew authority from the rural areas. Through varying systems of indirect rule it was the 'consumer of a power generated within the customary order'.[16] This 'customary order' was perceived to be in danger of unravelling in the cities.[17] Where the demands of the local economy threatened to undermine colonial social and political structures by drawing the 'native' away from his home, the institution of migrant labour sought to preserve tribal structures of identification and social (and political) control. Once in the town, restrictions on African urban residence were in place to dissuade migrants from deciding to remain there. However, despite such attempts to control the process of urbanisation, and in spite of widespread resistance to the phenomenon — among not only officials but Africans also[18] — in the course of colonial rule increasing numbers of Africans made their way to the towns.

Antipathy towards the process of African urbanisation was most marked in the period up to WWII.[19] This is ironic, for although towns were in many cases growing at rapid rates at this time, they were considerably smaller and more easy to control, albeit with limited resources, than after 1945. Nairobi, East Africa's largest urban centre, had an African population of less than 30,000 in 1936. In the same year, the five main urban centres in Southern Rhodesia had a combined African population of just 93,000.[20] While small, the African populations usually far outnumbered urban settler communities.

---

[15] For Eastern Africa, see Burton, 'Urbanisation'.

[16] Karen E. Fields, *Revival and Rebellion in Colonial Central Africa* (Princeton, 1985), p. 31.

[17] Even in colonial West Africa — where traditions of urbanism were more abundant. John Parker, writing about Accra, observes: 'The structuration of town and country in the official mind closely informed the emerging ideology of indirect rule, a policy which never fully came to terms with the existence of an African in the heart of the colonial capital'. 'The cultural politics of death and burial in early colonial Accra', in Anderson and Rathbone, *Africa's Urban Past*, p. 212.

[18] According to John Lonsdale, most Africans in colonial Kenya 'seem to have been more vigorously anti-urban in thought than the British'. 'Town life in colonial Kenya', in Burton, *Urban Experience*, p. 212. For African anti-urbanism in colonial Southern Rhodesia, see Tsuneo Yoshikuni, 'Linking urban history with precolonial/rural history: From the Zimbabwean experience', pp. 158–63, in *ibid.*; for Tanganyika, see Burton, 'Urchins', pp. 202–6, and below, pp. 75–8.

[19] In British Africa this was determined in part by recruitment policy into the Colonial Service. Recruitment was controlled by the Whitehall mandarin, Sir Ralph Furse, who favoured candidates to whom 'modern industrialisation and urbanisation were anathema'. R. Heussler, *Yesterday's Rulers* (London, 1963), p. 104, quoted in Anne Phillips, *The Enigma of Colonialism: British policy in West Africa* (London, 1989), p. 4.

[20] Dar es Salaam's African population at this time was under 25,000 (see Appendix). David M. Anderson, 'Corruption at City Hall: African housing and urban development in colonial Nairobi', p. 140, in Burton, *Urban Experience*; J. Clyde Mitchell, *Cities, Society, and Social Perception: A Central African perspective* (Oxford, 1987), p. 45.

However, the towns were considered fundamentally European. In Southern Rhodesia, observed Gray, '[a]ccording to the theory of segregation they [urban Africans] were not there':

The towns were part of the white man's world. There his interests alone should be considered and his outlook should prevail. The black man's needs and security were to be provided for in the Reserves; there was the centre and focus for his life, and his periods of labour for European employers were merely brief interruptions.[21]

In neighbouring South Africa, the 1922 Stallard Commission decreed that 'the Native' should only be allowed entry to towns when he was willing 'to minister to the needs of the white man, and should depart therefore when he so ceases to minister'.[22] Similar views were held by both officials and settlers throughout the region. Controlling the African urban presence was essential for the peace of mind of non-native communities, who often harboured profound anxiety about contact between the races, the so-called 'black peril', which encapsulated everything from European sexual paranoia to the threat of African crimes of violence or against property.[23] The perceived threat of disease had a substantial impact on policy, notably on urban planning.[24] In towns throughout the region municipal laws enforced strict segregation between racial populations where Europeans occupied the most favourable locations, often elevated above densely populated 'native' areas in which desperate living conditions (partly the product of colonial neglect) contributed to widespread ill-health and disease, thereby fuelling fears of contagion that Europeans in a circular fashion used to legitimise segregation.[25]

Africans themselves needed to be protected from exposure to the urban milieu. Town life was held to have a corrosive effect on their identity and

---

[21] Richard Gray, *The Two Nations* (London, 1960), pp. 110 and 229.

[22] Stallard Commission report, quoted in Deborah Posel, *The Making of Apartheid, 1948–61: Conflict and compromise* (Oxford, 1991), p. 40.

[23] For 'black peril' in turn of the century Johannesburg, see Charles Van Onselen, *New Babylon New Nineveh: Everyday life on the Witwatersrand* (Jeppestown, 2001), pp. 257–68.

[24] See e.g., L.H. Gann, *A History of Southern Rhodesia: Early days to 1934* (New York, 1969), pp. 192–3; Maynard W. Swanson, 'The sanitation syndrome: Bubonic plague and urban native policy in the Cape Colony, 1900–1909', *JAH* 18 (1977), pp. 387–410; Willis, *Mombasa*, p. 151; Paul Maylam, 'Explaining the Apartheid city: 20 years of South African urban historiography', *JSAS* 21:1 (1995), pp. 24–5. See also, Philip Curtin, 'Medical knowledge and urban planning in Tropical Africa', *American Historical Review* 90 (1985), pp. 594–613; and for West Africa, Raymond F. Betts, 'The establishment of the Medina in Dakar, 1914', *Africa* 41 (1971), pp. 143–52; John Cell, 'Anglo-Indian medical theory and the origins of segregation in West Africa', *American Historical Review* 91 (1986), pp. 307–35; Odile Goerg, *Pouvoir Colonial, Municipalités et Espace Urbain: Conakry–Freetown des années 1880–1914* (Paris, 1997); and Laurent Fourchard, *De la Ville Coloniale à la Cour Africaine. Espaces, pouvoirs et sociétés à Ouagadougou et à Bobo-Dioulasso (Haute-Volta) fin 19ème siècle–1960* (Paris, 2001).

[25] Milcah A. Achola, 'Colonial policy and urban health: The case of Nairobi', in Burton, *Urban Experience*, pp. 119–37. Segregation was not only a feature of colonial towns. In mid-nineteenth century Tunis, for example, Julia Clancy-Smith observes that 'the topographical gradient… and the social gradient of its inhabitants' residential space were nearly identical'. 'Gender in the city: Women, migration and contested spaces in Tunis, c.1830–81', in Anderson and Rathbone, *Africa's Urban Past*, p. 196.

behaviour, as well as their health. Megan Vaughan has noted that the deculturation that was considered to accompany the move to the towns was often associated with the increased incidence of disease among Africans — including insanity and sexually transmitted and what are termed 'industrial' diseases. 'Africans got sick', Vaughan writes, 'because they had forgotten who they were, they had ventured across boundaries of difference and chaos had ensued.'[26] The 'detribalised' African was a prime focus of concern: an anomic individual existing in the administrative — and classificatory — interstices of colonial rule. The social process of urbanisation — more or less coterminous with detribalisation[27] — could only bring trouble and was, as far as possible, to be resisted. G. St J. Orde-Browne, a Colonial Office labour adviser, and former Tanganyikan official, in 1935 complained that detribalised Africans were

> without any real standard of behaviour, and obey only such police or company regulations as may be effectively enforced. …Divorced from the old traditions and restraints, they no longer have a mass of public opinion to guide and control their actions.[28]

'A wholly industrialised Wemba', lamented a North Rhodesian District Officer in 1935:

> is, I should think, a very unpleasant person indeed, and it will come when this generation grows up here. …[H]e will find himself down here an individual instead of as in his own country a section of his family group. I think he will be a very difficult man indeed to manage, and his son will be worse.[29]

Accompanying this antipathy towards the social aspects of urbanisation, was a corresponding neglect of infrastructure and services in the African townships.[30] If the African's true home was in the countryside then improving urban conditions was pointless — indeed it might only contribute to the problem by drawing more Africans from their tribal homes. Visiting the colonies in the late 1930s, Lord Hailey observed among 'many members of the colonial services a desire to prevent or postpone urbanisation or the stabilisation of labour, and a reluctance to give to natives who insisted on living in a town the advantages of government expenditure'.[31] '[I]f African

---

[26] Megan Vaughan, *Curing Their Ills: Colonial power and African illness* (Cambridge/Oxford, 1991), p. 202.

[27] Though detribalisation also occurred in rural areas characterised by in-migration and mixed ethnicity, notably those surrounding places of employment such as mines or plantations. M.J.B. Molohan, in his 1957 report on *Detribalization* (Dsm, 1959), p. 11, gives the following definition of the term: '…the effect on Africans that is occasioned by their separation from family, clan and tribal authority as well as from the social codes of behaviour, discipline, custom and perhaps religion which originally guided their thoughts and actions, with the object of making them useful members of the tribe or community to which they belonged'.

[28] Major G. St J. Orde-Browne, *The African Labourer* (Oxford, 1933), pp. 103–4.

[29] Quoted in Gray, *Two Nations*, p. 111.

[30] See e.g. for Nairobi, Achola, 'Colonial policy'; for Ndola, A.L. Epstein, *Urbanization and Kinship: The domestic domain on the Copperbelt of Zambia, 1950–1956* (London, 1981), p. 23.

[31] Lord Hailey, *Native Administration and Political Development in British Tropical Africa* (London 1940–2), p. 38. See also, *EARC Report*, p. 201.

workers were really just primitive "target workers", they did not require a "real town" and cheap barracks and rude huts would suffice", observed R.G.B. Moore, a missionary on the Copperbelt in the years 1933–43.[32]

While this anti-urbanism was most evident in the settler colonies like Kenya and the Rhodesias — and of course in South Africa — it was nevertheless present in some shape or form in colonies throughout the region. It was best exemplified by legislation designed to control residence in, and movement within and to, the urban centres. Restrictions on African urban residence, for example, were common. In Southern Rhodesia, on arrival in a town Africans had to obtain a pass to seek work from the Town Pass Officer.[33] After work and accommodation had been obtained, the municipality issued a 'certificate of service' that was usually valid for a period of three to six months. In Northern Rhodesia, the Townships Ordinance required 'every native staying more than 36 hours in a Township to possess either a resident's or a visitor's permit'.[34] In the Kenyan capital, Nairobi, an African could only legally enter the town with a letter from the DC's office in their home area explaining that they were seeking employment. Once in the town visitors to Nairobi were required to obtain a temporary residence permit from the City African Affairs Officer.[35]

Such restrictions were not confined to British colonies. In the Belgian Congo, according to Valdo Pons, up to 1931 although

> few positive measures had [been] taken to influence the development of African settlements around the main 'European towns'… The tendency had been to discourage Africans from permanent settlement away from the tribal areas.[36]

Nevertheless, by the mid 1920s the urban 'loafer problem' had become 'so serious that the Labour Commission of 1925 expressed very strong views and recommended drastic remedies'.[37] 'Positive measures' were eventually introduced in 1932. In that year, under the *Décret sur les Centres-Extra-coutumiers*, a number of African townships (*Centres-Extra-coutumiers* [CECs]) were declared, which, although technically semi-autonomous, remained 'closely supervised' by European officials. To enter a township an African required the approval of the CEC administration. With this approval a man searching for employment was admitted to the town *à titre temporaire* for one month, after

---

32 *These African Copper Miners: A study of the industrial revolution in Northern Rhodesia* (London, 1948) [published posthumously], p. 60. Quoted in Ferguson, *Expectations*, p. 34.

33 See Native Registration and Pass Laws, n.d. (1945), TNA/28685 (hereafter 'Native Registration'); and 'Ndola report', pp. 63–6, for controls on urban migration and residence in East and Central Africa. For Southern Rhodesia, see also Teresa A. Barnes, *'We Women Worked So Hard': Gender, urbanization and social reproduction in Harare, Zimbabwe, 1930–56* (Portsmouth, NH/Oxford/Harare/Cape Town, 1999), pp. 11–12.

34 *Ibid.*

35 *Ibid.* and personal communication from David Anderson.

36 Valdo Pons, *Stanleyville: An urban African community under Belgian administration* (Oxford, 1969), p. 35.

37 Report by Maj. G. St J. Orde-Browne on 'Labour conditions in Tanganyika Territory' (Dsm, 1926) [hereafter: Orde-Browne, 'Labour'], para. 115, copy in PRO/CO/691/83.

24

which he would be repatriated to his home if he had not found a job. Those in waged work remained in the town *à titre précaire* — permitted to reside in the town, but remaining subjects of their rural *chefferies* and 'liable to expulsion in the event of prolonged unemployment'.[38] Only those born in the CECs or who had resided there for more than ten years were granted the 'formal status of permanent residents'.

Alongside this legislation aimed at restricting urban residence were a variety of measures designed to limit movement within and to urban areas. Within the towns, African mobility was strictly controlled. 'Natives' lived in segregated areas (often referred to as 'locations') and by-laws curbed their movements in both these areas and — more strictly — in other 'non-native' parts of town. The Southern Rhodesian Urban Locations Ordinance of 1905 decreed that '[n]o native... may reside within [a] municipal or other prescribed area... save and except within the area of the location established'.[39] By-laws governing African residence in the Kenyan capital laid down similar restrictions. Meanwhile, in both Nairobi and Salisbury various regulations limited freedom of movement. The Nairobi Municipality by-laws of 1944 stipulated that all Africans outside of the 'native locations' between 10pm and 5am required a pass signed by the Town Clerk, police officer or an African's employer. A pass issued by an employer was valid for just 24 hours and had to state specifically 'the place or places in which such native may be'.[40] Even movement within the 'locations' was technically restricted. Between 10pm and 5am no African could 'without valid excuse' (proof of which was upon him/her) be abroad 'in any vehicle or unoccupied building or wandering or loitering in any highway, yard or other place in the native locations'. A similar by-law held in Blantyre, in Nyasaland, where police patrols 'were instructed to prevent Africans "sitting or loitering on the Township roads" and... regularly arrested men and women for being out in the open after dark'.[41] In Lusaka, Northern Rhodesia, no fewer than six kinds of passes governed African movement around the town.[42] Such by-laws were in place in urban areas throughout the region.[43]

So too was legislation aimed at controlling movement *to* the town. South African 'pass laws' were of course the most notorious (and longest lasting). The Native Urban Areas Act of 1923 and Native Laws Amendments Act of 1937 (and with the introduction of *apartheid* the Group Areas Act of 1950) provided comprehensive controls over rural–urban migration among black

---

[38] Pons, *Stanleyville*, p. 36.

[39] Gann, *Southern Rhodesia*, p. 193.

[40] GN no. 366 of 1944.

[41] McCracken, 'Coercion and control', p. 133.

[42] Norman C. Rothman, 'African urban development in the colonial period: A study of Lusaka, 1905–1964', Ph.D. thesis, Northwestern University (1972), pp. 325 & 330, cited in Iliffe, *African Poor*, p. 190.

[43] For the Rhodesias see 'Native Registration'; for the particularly coercive regime in Lourenço Marques, see Jeanne Marie Penvenne, *African Workers and Colonial Racism: Mozambican strategies and struggles in Lourenço Marques, 1822–1962* (Portsmouth,NH/Johannesburg/London, 1995), chapter 7; for the Witwatersrand, Van Onselen, *New Babylon*, p. 246.

South Africans.[44] While the South African situation was, for a number of reasons, exceptional,[45] pass laws were in force throughout Eastern and Southern Africa and were responsible for a high proportion of criminal prosecutions. Africans in Southern Rhodesia were required to carry an identification certificate in the rural areas, and if moving to a town to seek work or for other purposes had to obtain an additional — temporary — pass under the Native Passes Act of 1914. In 1942, some 22,000 out of a total 63,000 convictions in the territory were against pass law offences. Similar requirements were in force in Northern Rhodesia under the Native Registration Ordinance of 1929, and although the pass laws were not so strictly enforced there, in 1942 they constituted an even higher proportion of criminal convictions.[46] African mobility was also restricted by legislation in 'the tidy-minded Belgian Congo',[47] with those wishing to go to the towns being required to first obtain a *passeport de mutation* from their rural *chefferie*.[48]

Pass laws were as much a method of controlling labour as they were a means of restricting African mobility. Nowhere was this more clear than in Kenya where they took the form of what was called the *kipande* system — enforced under the Registration of Natives Ordinance (1915) — which required every male over 15 years to carry a finger-printed certificate of identity that contained detailed information about his employment record.[49] In 1939 almost five thousand convictions were obtained under the ordinance — over 10 percent of the territorial total of criminal convictions and the third highest category. The pass system played an equally important part in overall labour policy in Portuguese East Africa: in the capital Lourenco Marques, in the late 1920s, around 20 percent of the African population was sanctioned for registration violations annually.[50] Other colonial legislation criminalised destitution. The Belgian Congo's first vagrancy law was passed as early as 1896.[51] In British colonies similar legislation was also in force. In

[44] Between 1916 and 1981 over seventeen million offenders were prosecuted for contravening pass law regulations. Hermann Giliomee and Lawrence Schlemmer, *Up Against the Fences: Poverty, passes and privilege in South Africa* (Cape Town, 1985), p. 1; see also Laurine Platzky and Cherryl Walker, *The Surplus People: Forced removals in South Africa* (Johannesburg, 1985); Doug Hindson, *Pass Controls and the Urban African Proletariat in South Africa* (Johannesburg, 1987); Posel, *Apartheid*.

[45] Including the size and well-established presence of a non-native community; the resources available to the South African state to enforce such legislation; and the high levels of industrialisation (and urbanisation).

[46] 'Native Registration' puts it at an unlikely 6,977 out of a total 9,944 convictions. See also, Ferguson, *Expectations*, pp. 53–4; Elena L. Berger, *Labour, Race, and Colonial Rule: The Copperbelt from 1924 to independence* (Oxford, 1974), p. 18.

[47] Iliffe, *African Poor*, p. 190.

[48] Pons, *Stanleyville*, p. 36.

[49] See David M. Anderson, 'Master and servant in colonial Kenya', *JAH* 41 (2000), pp. 459–85; Anthony Clayton and Donald Savage, *Government and Labour in Kenya, 1919–1939* (London, 1974), pp. 131–4; Sharon Stichter, *Migrant Labour in Kenya: Capitalism and African response* (London, 1982), p. 46; Roger van Zwanenberg, *Colonial Capitalism and Labour in Kenya, 1919–1939* (Nairobi/Kampala/Dsm, 1975), pp. 183–9. For early-colonial Mombasa, see Justin Willis, 'Thieves'; and Willis, *Mombasa*, pp. 164–6; 198–9.

[50] Anderson, 'Policing', p. 195; Penvenne, *African Workers*, p. 107 *et passim*.

[51] Iliffe, *African Poor*, p. 190.

East Africa, for example, the Vagrancy Ordinances of Uganda and Kenya empowered officials to imprison and/or repatriate persons 'found wandering without any visible means of subsistence'.[52]

African urbanisation and late-colonial policy in East and Central Africa

While legislation controlling African mobility often remained in place throughout the colonial period, official attitudes towards the more general process of African urbanisation began to shift from the 1930s. A growing awareness of the permanence of African communities emerged.[53] This occurred first in the Belgian Congo. The *Décret sur les Centres-Extra-coutumiers* of 1931 resulted from 'a complete review of urban policy by the central government'.[54] Up to then the tendency had been to 'assume that the urban labour force consisted overwhelmingly of migrant labourers who would return to their villages after periods of earning'.[55] However, the decree formed

> an integral part of a wider set of measures... to make better use of the colony's limited resources of man-power, and to stabilise and develop the labour force. In sharp contrast to the first thirty years of colonial administration, labour migration was now to be opposed, the perpetuation of 'tribalism' in towns was to be discouraged, and the development of urban communities was to be actively promoted.[56]

This was not a simple acceptance of African urbanisation *per se*, but an attempt by the Belgian administration to guide and control it. As we have seen, entry to and residence in the towns remained strictly supervised. This was considered

---

[52] 'Ndola Report', p. 67. It is important to note that the enforcement of legislation restricting African movement was dependent upon the ability of colonial administrations to apply it. It is likely — as we shall see in the case of Tanganyika — that much of the legislation discussed in this section was enforced intermittently at best, and was more representative of colonial ideals than of reality. Apparently, it was in the settler colonies of Southern Rhodesia and Kenya, and of course in South Africa, where the most concerted attempts were made to enforce these laws. Though even here the state overextended itself. In Kenya, for example, both Willis ('Thieves') and White (*Comforts*, p. 97) note the unenforcable nature of much urban legislation. Ferguson makes the same point for Northern Rhodesia, *Expectations*, pp. 53–4.

[53] Cooper, writing on British and French Africa, characterises the decade 1935–45 as a 'break point', during which 'the idea of "tribal" Africa was losing its usefulness, and officials were casting about for conceptual tools to regain their sense of control'. *Decolonization*, p. 18. Lewis, meanwhile, sees WWII as a 'watershed in the history of twentieth-century government practice' when 'colonial officials had begun to sign up to a more positive view of African capabilities and to a more professionally responsive type of colonial government'. *Empire State-Building*, p. 16.

[54] Pons, *Stanleyville*, p. 35.

[55] *Ibid.*, p. 35.

[56] *Ibid.*, p. 35.

27

essential if health and security were to be maintained, if the labour force was to be stabilized and the growth of slums prevented; it was also seen as an 'educative measure' to promote a sense of order and responsibility, and as part of a more general policy supposedly designed to lead Africans towards *évolution* and a 'civilized' way of life.[57]

The new policy soon led to an unusually high degree of permanence among urban African populations in the Belgian Congo, compared to other colonies in the region.[58]

A shift in British policy occurred somewhat later. The consequences of African urbanisation were first faced by British officials on the Northern Rhodesian Copperbelt. Here, by 1940 'there were clear signs of a tendency of unskilled workers to "stabilise" themselves regardless of European policies.'[59] The situation had come to a head in 1935, when a major strike occurred, unsettling officials in Rhodesia and London. In the wake of the strike, Governor Young singled out detribalisation and industrialisation as 'the most important problems that confront not only Northern Rhodesia but other parts of Africa'.[60] Nevertheless, a commission formed to investigate the causes of the unrest and make recommendations for future policy — after identifying a choice 'between the establishment of native authority, together with the frequent repatriation of natives to their villages; or... the acceptance of definite detribalisation... of the mining population under European control' — opted to 'reaffirm the authority of the chiefs and reinvigorate... the system of migrancy'.[61] However, shifts at both local and imperial levels meant this exclusionary response to the problem of African

---

[57] *Ibid.*, p. 37.

[58] In 1950 as many as 23% of Léopoldville's African population had been born in the city; a survey conducted in Stanleyville two years later found that almost half of those surveyed had spent over 16 years living in urban areas (including Stanleyville). Over 20% had spent 26 years or more in towns. J.S. LaFontaine, *City Politics: A study of Léopoldville, 1962–63* (Cambridge, 1970), p. 30; Pons, *Stanleyville*, p. 50. Contrast this with the position in Nairobi as late as 1968–70, where a survey found that just 3% of people living in the city had been born there. R.M.A. van Zwanenberg with Anne King, *An Economic History of Kenya and Uganda, 1800–1970* (London, 1975), p. 269.

[59] Andrew Roberts, *A History of Zambia* (London, 1976), p. 189; see also Godfrey Wilson, *An Essay on the Economics of Detribalization in Northern Rhodesia* (Livingstone, 1941). Roberts observes a difference in the types of mines to be found in Katanga Province of the Belgian Congo (the principal area of industrial employment in the colony) that helps account for the earlier shift in Belgian urban policy. Mines in Katanga were mostly open-cast in which it was possible to use large-scale machinery. 'As a result,' observes Roberts, 'the Katanga company, Union Minière, developed a strong interest in forming a relatively skilled and stable African labour force.' The underground mines of Northern Rhodesia offered much less scope for mechanisation. Though, in contrast to Government policy, mining companies there — competing for labour with industries to the south — from early on encouraged the presence of women and children in the mining camps. George Chauncey, Jr, 'The locus of reproduction: Women's labour in the Zambian Copperbelt, 1927–1953', *JSAS* 7 (1981), pp. 135–64.

[60] Quoted in Cooper, *Decolonization*, p. 59.

[61] The first quote is from *Report of Commission Appointed to Enquire into the Disturbance in the Copperbelt, Northern Rhodesia* (Lusaka, 1935), quoted in Cooper, *Decolonization*, p. 59. The second is by Cooper.

urbanisation could no longer be sustained indefinitely, in Northern Rhodesia and elsewhere in the region. The British Secretary of State, J.H. Thomas, in response to developments on the Copperbelt, had observed that it was 'necessary to accept a degree of detribalisation'.[62] Three years later, in his survey of colonial Africa, Lord Hailey wrote of African urban populations that while '(t)he growth of this class is viewed with some apprehension', colonial administrations foresaw 'the expansion of a class which will eventually become in the full sense detached from tribal life'. Hailey recommended that a new policy should be adopted 'directed to building up an organic social life of a type of which Africa itself offers little experience'.[63] Indeed, after WWII colonial administrations did become increasingly concerned about the social welfare of urban African populations. In part this was a response to the perceived loss of moral and material support suffered by the town-dwelling African, detached as he was from his kith and kin in his tribal home. However, it was also a result of political, economic and social strains in the urban environment that were becoming apparent to British officials throughout the region at this time, which their Belgian counterparts had attempted to avoid through the establishment of the CECs.

The 1940s saw an acceleration in rates of rural–urban migration, which led to rapidly growing urban populations throughout British East and Central Africa.[64] In Salisbury, Bulawayo, Umtali, Gwelo and Que Que — the five main centres of Southern Rhodesia — for example, the number of African men in employment more than doubled between 1936 and 1946, from 43,305 to 94,929.[65] Ian Phimister attributes the rapid increase in African urbanisation in Southern Rhodesia at this time to a combination of factors: job opportunities in newly established secondary industries, African population growth resulting from increased fertility, and the proletarianisation of increasing numbers of landless (or land poor) peasants.[66] Similar factors were at work in Kenya, where urban growth rates were equally impressive. In Mombasa, the colony's main port and second city, the African population grew by around 50 percent in the years 1939–45, from 40,000 to 63,000.[67] The African community in Nairobi was expanding even faster: from 28,000 in 1936 to over 65,000 a decade later.[68] Administrations had great difficulties developing urban infrastructures to keep pace with this rapid demographic growth. Nowhere was this more apparent than in the shortage of housing. By 1947, in Nairobi, the Kenyan administration estimated that 82,000

---

[62] Thomas to Young, 24 December 1935, PRO/CO/795/76/45083. Quoted in Frederick Cooper, *On the African Waterfront* (New Haven, 1987), p. 255.

[63] Lord Hailey, *An African Survey* (London, 1938), p. 544.

[64] The same appears to have been true of the Belgian Congo. Between 1940 and 1950, Léopoldville's African population grew from 46,884 to 190,912. LaFontaine, *City Politics*, p. 28.

[65] Mitchell, *Cities, Society, and Social Perception*, p. 45.

[66] Ian Phimister, *An Economic and Social History of Zimbabwe: Capital accumulation and class struggle* (London, 1988), p. 259.

[67] Cooper, *Waterfront*, p. 57.

[68] Anderson, 'Corruption', p. 140.

Africans were living in housing designed to accommodate only 54,000. Between 1946 and 1957 accommodation designed for 30,000 occupants was constructed: however, over the same period the African population grew by 52,000.[69] Investigating the living conditions of Africans in Southern Rhodesian towns, the Howman Committee in 1944 found overcrowding everywhere, with the result that 'Africans squeeze into what rooms they can find, seek out all kinds of shelters about the towns and "married" couples share rooms with bachelors.'[70] In Bulawayo's industrial areas 'some 4,000 male employees in addition to an unknown number of women and children' lived in 'conditions of indescribable squalor'.[71] Similarly, in Harare, the African township of Salisbury, overcrowding was endemic. As a result, south of Salisbury's Mukuvisi River 'black slums sprang up all over, constructed of the simplest and cheapest materials: poles and dagga, grass and tins, tied and nailed together to form some form of shelter.'[72] Thanks to accommodation shortage, similar shanty settlements were beginning to emerge in other towns in the region from the 1940s.[73]

The malnutrition and poor health endemic among African urban communities was another problem that began to receive increasing attention. In 1939, the Committee on Nutrition in the Colonial Empire found evidence of widespread malnourishment throughout the empire, prompting more detailed investigations in various colonies.[74] In Southern Rhodesia, the 1944 Howman Committee observed that malnutrition was 'seriously prevalent everywhere in the urban areas'.[75] Poor sanitation in urban African locations meant that hookworm and other intestinal diseases were common. Meanwhile, malnutrition, tuberculosis and pneumonia all increased in frequency in the 1940s.[76] Conditions were not helped by the low wages received by most Africans: surveys conducted between 1942 and 1944 found that as many as 90 percent of Africans were paid less than the minimum required to raise a family.[77] On the Copperbelt in the early 1940s, while the average wage was found to be enough to meet basic needs, large numbers of men were earning considerably less.[78] In Kenya, where in 1939 the minimum wage to meet the cost of living in Nairobi was calculated to be Shs. 20/75,

[69]   Van Zwanenberg, *Economic History*, p. 270.
[70]   Southern Rhodesia, *Report of the Committee to Investigate the Economic, Social and Health Conditions of Africans Employed in Urban Areas* (Howman Report), January 1944. Quoted in Gray, *Two Nations*, p. 252.
[71]   Quoted in Phimister, *Zimbabwe*, p. 260.
[72]   L. Vambe, *From Rhodesia to Zimbabwe* (London, 1976). Quoted in Phimister, *Zimbabwe*, p. 260.
[73]   For Nairobi, see Andrew Hake, *African Metropolis: Nairobi's self-help city* (Brighton, 1977); Terry Hirst and Davinder Lamba, *The Struggle for Nairobi* (Nairobi, 1994). For Dar es Salaam, see below, p. 218.
[74]   *Report of the Committee on Nutrition in the Colonial Empire* (HMSO, 1939), p. 151.
[75]   Gray, *Two Nations*, p. 223.
[76]   Phimister, *Zimbabwe*, p. 260.
[77]   *Ibid.*, p. 262.
[78]   See A. Lynn Saffery, *A report on some aspects of African living conditions on the Copperbelt of N. Rhodesia* (Lusaka, 1943); and R.J.B. Moore, 'Native wages and standard of living in Northern Rhodesia', *African Studies* 1 (1942).

the Davies Report found that, out of a workforce of 36,000, nearly 16,000 were earning under this amount. From the mid 1940s, the increasing incidence of diseases associated with extreme overcrowding, malnutrition and poor sanitary facilities — notably tuberculosis and venereal disease — aroused 'official concern bordering on panic' in the Kenyan capital.[79]

The low rates of pay prevalent in colonial economies were a product of the predominance of migrant labour. Most Africans working in the towns were on short-term contracts and travelled there alone. This absolved employers of the responsibility of providing a family wage. Migrant workers' continued links with the rural areas subsidised the cost of their labour. Indeed, the notion that wages were merely pocket money for African workers was a widely held belief. 'Their [Africans'] pocket is a different one from ours,' a Provincial Commissioner told an enquiry into the 1935 Copperbelt strike,

> and the money they put into it still remains for almost the whole population of this territory an unnecessary luxury... If I am deprived of my salary I starve, but the native in similar circumstances can go home and live as happily as ever.[80]

As Gray has pointed out, this point of view was riddled with error. An African's links with the rural areas were 'in many cases... financially a mixed blessing' with the expectations of rural kin often outweighing the benefits these might bring.[81] Nevertheless, attitudes such as these allowed the payment of often spectacularly inadequate wages to urban African workers to go mostly unremarked until WWII.

From the early 1940s, however, reports on conditions in urban African communities in East and Central Africa were increasingly concluding that supposedly 'cheap' migrant labour was not in actual fact cheap at all, as it was linked to inefficiency. In Southern Rhodesia, for example, both Percy Ibbotson, in his *Report on a Survey of Urban African Conditions in Southern Rhodesia*,[82] and the Howman Committee both advocated a minimum wage. It was considered that this would

> give protection against the casual, inefficient rural visitor; lead to more efficient use of labour by certain employers; prevent exploitation; link up with a 'compulsory education' recommendation by preventing the employment of juveniles; and finally would 'provide a floor above which wages would be encouraged to rise' by various measures designed to increase efficiency.[83]

A later Kenyan report, written by Labour Commissioner Carpenter, concluded that under conditions in which migrant labour predominated it was 'clearly illogical to expect that the African worker... [would] be capable of that concentrated and sustained physical effort which we like to associate with the

---

[79]   Achola, 'Colonial policy', pp. 123–4.
[80]   Quoted in Gray, *Two Nations*, pp. 116–17.
[81]   For (later) examples of the often dubious 'advantages' of rural links, see LaFontaine, *City Politics*, p. 112; and Ferguson, *Expectations, passim.*
[82]   Bulawayo (1943).
[83]   Gray, *Two Nations*, pp. 213–14

western conception of manual work'. In order to inculcate Western attitudes to work it was considered necessary 'to first remove the African from the enervating and retarding influences of his economic and cultural background'.[84] In addition, the migrant labour system was found to be inefficient on account of its high labour turnover and the associated need to continuously recruit and train new workers. A better trained, more reliable workforce was increasingly what was required by post-war urban employers. The labour shortage that was a marked feature in much of East and Central Africa up to the Depression at least, was from the 1940s giving way in towns throughout the region to an overabundance of workers as a result of spiralling urban growth rates. Consequently, the need to check the potential cost (or to ensure the availability) of a scarce commodity (African labour) was no longer the priority: in the post-war period the productivity of African employees instead acquired primacy. Administrative concerns associated with a system of migrant labour — notably the threat posed by a growing mass of poorly housed, poorly fed Africans congregating in the urban areas, over whom traditional, rural sources of authority exercised a diminishing influence[85] — would also be addressed by a policy of stabilisation. The Howman Committee report stressed

> the grave need to provide the fullest possible community facilities, housing and educational machinery that would make possible the growth of a natural family, community and social urban life. [Evidence demonstrated] that given such facilities... the African does respond and there is no reason whatever why in time an urban culture with its own standards, civic consciousness, leadership and spontaneous controls should not emerge.[86]

In contrast to the position of neglect prior to WWII, urban policy scaled the imperial agenda after the war. By 1954, '[t]he urbanisation of the native population in Africa' was, according to one observer, 'now recognised as the paramount social development'.[87] The *Report of the East African Royal Commission*, published the following year, observed it was

> essential to break down the barriers which prevent Africans from full participation in the life of towns. The African must come to regard the towns as places which fully provide him with an outlet for his courage, ability and initiative.[88]

By this time a consensus was emerging, in both London and the colonies, over the adoption of labour stabilisation as the central plank of this new urban policy.[89] At a regional conference held in Ndola in 1958, measures

---

[84] Kenya Colony, *Report of the Committee on African Wages* (Nairobi, 1954), pp. 11 & 32.

[85] This threat was demonstrated in a wave of strikes that occurred in towns throughout sub-Saharan Africa during and after the war. For Anglophone and Francopohone Africa, see Cooper, *Decolonization*; for Kenya, *idem*, *Waterfront*; for Uganda, Gardner Thompson, 'Colonialism in crisis: The Uganda disturbances of 1945', *AA* 91 (1992), pp. 605–24; and for Tanganyika, Iliffe, 'Dockworkers' and below, pp. 187–92.

[86] Quoted in Percy Ibbotson, 'Urbanization in Southern Rhodesia', *Africa* XVI:2 (1946), p. 75.

[87] Henry, 'African Townee', p. 220.

[88] *EARC Report*, p. 250.

[89] The issue of urban development, and its social and cultural ramifications, was the subject of the Colonial Office Summer Conference on African Administration, held at King's College, Cambridge, 23 August–4 September 1954. See PRO/CO/879/160.

aimed at encouraging greater permanence and productivity of African labour were endorsed by officials from Uganda, Kenya, Tanganyika, Zanzibar and the Central African Federation. According to the conference report, stabilisation was 'an essential condition of the advance of the African... [one] which should be carefully encouraged and we believe it is a movement which in any case will gradually take place'.[90] Indeed, the move towards better remunerated and more skilled African labour was already occurring. Average African wages on the Copperbelt, for example, increased between 1949 and 1955 by 116 percent, at a time when prices rose by just 28 percent; and between 1954 and 1962 the number of employees contracted. In Kenya, in the decade after 1955 'production rose substantially, African wages doubled, prices rose only slightly, but employment actually fell off.'[91]

Complementing this policy of labour stabilisation were a series of measures aimed at shaping the social and cultural transformations accompanying African urbanisation. British officials in post-war East and Central Africa sought to inculcate civic responsibility among emerging urban African populations. Thanks partly to the disparate tribal backgrounds of African urbanites, town populations were perceived to lack a sense of community. Although fears of detribalisation were receding, the urban environment was still viewed as holding few positive influences, and many negative ones, for the African innocent newly detached from his rural home. Through a significant expansion in spending on infrastructure and amenities servicing the 'locations' after WWII (though never enough to meet the demands or the needs of spiralling urban populations), urban social welfare and community development activities, and increased African participation in municipal government, officials sought to mould a respectable and responsible African urban class.[92] An early example of such thinking was expressed by a Nairobi public health official in 1941, who called for 'the acceptance of the fact that the urban type of native exists' and for 'his education in the rights and duties of citizenship'. '[T]he development of the urban African', he continued, must 'include... all the usual amenities required in a modern town'.[93] In Uganda, on newly constructed housing estates in late-colonial Jinja, officials attempted to engineer 'a regulated community life... to mitigate social anomie'.[94] This was achieved partly through the organisation of African social and leisure activities.[95] The construction and nature of urban housing in itself formed an important part of the economic and cultural objectives of stabilisation. According to Uganda's Secretary for Social Services, the

[90] 'Ndola report', pp. 6–7.
[91] Cooper, *Decolonization*, p.346 (for Uganda, see p.459); Hugh MacMillan, 'The historiography of transition on the Zambian Copperbelt – Another view', *JSAS*, 19:4, p.700; Cooper, *Waterfront*, p.180; Stichter, *Migrant Labour*, pp.133–9.
[92] For Dar es Salaam, see Burton, 'Townsmen'.
[93] Quoted in Lewis, *Empire State-Building*, p. 138.
[94] Andrew Byerley, 'The production of space: Uganda/Jinja Town/Babu Quarters', paper given at 'The urban experience in Eastern Africa, 18th century to the 1980s' workshop, Nairobi, July 2001, p. 19.
[95] Byerley mentions imported sports and competitions for the best-kept homes and gardens on the housing estates.

underlying aim of the territory's housing policy in the 1950s was

> to build up a stabilised labour force of all the classes in the main urban centres... In order to do this it is necessary not only to provide homes for African workers but also to provide a satisfactory community life in circumstances which have not previously existed in Uganda and which will fulfil the needs of the different classes and adequately replace the rural social organisation which the stabilised urban populations have abandoned.[96]

'As far as possible', observed the Labour Commissioner in neighbouring Kenya, urban housing schemes were to 'embody the concept of the "neighbourhood unit".'[97] On the Copperbelt, African workers were encouraged to put down 'respectable roots... principally by means of house-ownership and the development of organized town communities'.[98] By the 1950s, towns had become 'laboratories of modernity'[99] in which the African townsman (and woman) was to be socially engineered.[100]

Urban policy in South Africa

The evolution of colonial policy in which an emerging African urban class was envisaged as playing a growing part in township affairs stood in marked contrast to the course of events in South Africa.[101] As the most economically developed territory in the region, the problems associated with African urbanisation that British and Belgian officials were increasingly aware of from the 1930s on, were in even greater evidence here. They also emerged significantly

---

[96] Quoted in Byerley, p. 17.   [97] Carpenter report, quoted in *EARC Report*, p. 213.

[98] R.L. Prain, 'The stabilization of labour in the Rhodesian Copper Belt', *AA* 55 (1956), pp. 307–8.

[99] Administrative laboratories from the point of view of colonial officials conducting social engineering; academic laboratories to social scientists — most famously those working from the Rhodes-Livingstone Institute in Northern Rhodesia — observing the impact of urbanisation on African society. The phrase is from A.L. Stoler, *Race and the Education of Desire: Foucault's history of sexuality and the colonial order of things* (Durha, NC, 1995).

[100] See e.g., Cooper, *Decolonization*, chapter 8; Timothy Scarnecchia, 'Residential segregation and the politics of gender, Salisbury, Rhodesia, 1940–56', Ph.D. thesis, University of Michigan (1993); Lewis, *Empire State-Building*, pp. 134–42; Bodil Frederiksen, 'Making popular culture from above: Leisure in Nairobi, 1940–60', in Liz Gunner (ed.), *Collected Seminar Papers* (London, Institute of Commonwealth Studies, 1992); Frederiksen, 'African women'; Byerley, 'Manufacturing Jinja'.

[101] The partial exception is Southern Rhodesia where — in a 'struggle between the owners of capital and the white working class' — a policy of African stabilisation was resisted by white skilled workers. See Carole Rakodi, *Harare: Inheriting a colonial settler city: Change or continuity?* (Chichester, 1998), p. 25. According to Timothy Scarnecchia, 'a more stable work force' was sought 'by encouraging married workers to settle [in the towns] with a nuclear family', and the apparent success of this policy is indicated by a substantial decline in the ratio of African men to women in Salisbury. ('Poor women and nationalist politics: Alliances and fissures in the formation of a nationalist political movement in Salisbury, Rhodesia, 1950–56', *JAH*, 37 (1996), pp. 287 & 295). However, Cooper (*Decolonization*, p. 140) observes that although Southern Rhodesia did 'indeed try to move hesitatingly toward a policy of urban stabilization, '[it] would pull back in the name of segregation and low wages — both demanded by white settlers — and the issues raised by th[e Howman] report would still be unresolved when colonial Rhodesia became independent Zimbabwe in 1979'.

earlier than in the European colonies to the north. Rapid urbanisation was occurring from the late nineteenth century. Cape Town's population numbered as many as 51,000 in 1891. It was soon superseded by Johannesburg, which in 1896 — only ten years after its foundation — contained a population of 100,000. The country's total urban population rose from 1.2 million in 1904 to 3.2 million in 1936.[102] Rapid urban growth led to conditions familiar to colonial officials in 1930s and 1940s East and Central Africa. Urban slums emerged before WWI in which 'malnutrition was widespread… sanitation was usually non-existent; the water supply was often an irrigation furrow; and many Africans had to house themselves in shanties built from packing-cases, flattened tins and sacking.'[103] 'Natives throng to Cape Town', complained the *Cape Times* in 1922, 'and make their homes in the slums, where it is a quite common experience to find fifty or sixty of them herded in small four-roomed houses at night surrounded on all sides by the demoralising attractions of illicit liquor dens and brothels.'[104] The Native Urban Areas Act of 1923 (and subsequent legislation in 1937) was designed to address the 'native urban problem' through the implementation of segregation and a system of pass laws. However, the scale of the problem dwarfed that present in other African colonies and the enforcement of such controls proved beyond the capacity of South African administrators. 'A revolutionary change is taking place among the Native peoples… through the movement from the country to the towns,' observed Field-Marshal Smuts in 1942. 'Segregation tried to stop it. It has, however, not stopped it in the least. The process has been accelerated. You might as well try to sweep the ocean back with a broom.'[105]

The 1940s was a time of decision for South African politicians and administrators, just as it was for their colonial counterparts to the north. According to one observer, Professor Hoernlé, industrialisation required 'African workers as permanent residents… in urban areas':

> If this is incompatible with 'segregation', then our choice is between segregation without industrialization, or industrialization without segregation. …The present system prevents most workers from becoming fully efficient; it wastes a large proportion of the productive capacity of our population; and condemns the workers, separated for long periods from their families, to unnatural and demoralizing conditions of life. The only salvation is to integrate African workers and their families, as completely and thoroughly as possible, into our economic system….[106]

However, this vision of future urban policy was hotly contested. These divisions were reflected in the contrasting policies recommended by two commissions of enquiry that were set up prior to the 1948 election — the Fagan and Sauer Commissions. While both agreed on the need to control

---

[102] John Iliffe, *Africans: The history of a continent* (Cambridge, 1995), p. 275.
[103] A.P. Walshe, 'Southern Africa', p. 552, in Andrew Roberts (ed.), *Cambridge History of Africa, Volume 7: 1905–1940* (Cambridge, 1986), pp. 544–601.
[104] Quoted in Iliffe, *African Poor*, p. 115.
[105] Quoted in Ibbotson, 'Urbanization', p. 75.
[106] Quoted in *ibid*, p. 76.

African urbanisation through a stringent national pass system, the two reports articulated different positions on the place of the African in towns. Like Smuts and Hoernlé, the Fagan Report viewed African urbanisation as inevitable and recommended the promotion of this trend 'within the framework of urban residential segregation'.[107] The Sauer Report, on the other hand, called for the reversal of the trend toward African urbanisation. Although, contrary to conventional wisdom, in the wake of the National Party's victory in the election concerted efforts were made to stabilise the existing African urban population (while strenuously resisting its expansion), it was the Sauer approach that was broadly adopted.[108] The moral panic over detribalisation, which was at this time receding elsewhere in Africa, continued to inform official policy in South Africa. Verwoerd, the first Minister of Native Affairs in the National Party government, declared that 'the position in the urban areas has become intolerable', and warned of

> the 'social danger' of 'detribalisation'... When the Native Affairs Department translated these injunctions into elements of practical apartheid, the attempt was to freeze the process of detribalisation: classified as temporary urban residents, migrant workers were, in the language of an explanation given in Parliament, 'periodically returned to their homes to renew their tribal connections'![109]

In contrast to the British and Belgian colonial administrations, the National Party government continued to identify and to administer Africans as rural beings, attempting to check urbanisation through a rigid system of segregation and pass controls.[110]

Influx control in late-colonial East and Central Africa

While the *apartheid* state and European colonies to the north diverged over African *urbanism* from 1948, in their approach to African *urbanisation* there

---

107 Mahmood Mamdani, *Citizen and Subject: Contemporary Africa and the legacy of late colonialism* (Princeton/ Kampala/Cape Town/London, 1996), p. 99. See also, I.T. Evans, 'The political economy of a State Apparatus: The Department of Native Affairs in the transition from segregation to Apartheid in S. Africa', Ph.D. thesis, University of Wisconsin (1986), pp. 59–61.

108 For stabilisation initiatives in the late 1940s, see Philip Bonner, 'African urbanisation on the Rand between the 1930s and 1960s: Its social character and political consequences' *JSAS* 21 (1995): 1, pp. 121–2.

109 Mamdani, *Citizen*, pp. 99–100, (the original quotes are taken from Posel, *Apartheid*, pp. 61, 81–2).

110 In fact, the South African government did eventually adopt policies similar to those enacted to the north, though not until the 1960s. According to Glaser (*Bo-Tsotsi*, p. 129), it was then that 'the Vorster government accepted the presence of a permanently urban African population' and 'sought to sharpen the distinction between urban insiders and outsiders. While Section 10 rights (to permanent urban residential status) were entrenched and even extended in certain categories, those who did not qualify for urban status were hounded with greater intensity'. Even the high degree of coercion employed by the South African state to prevent urbanisation — both before and after the 1960s — resulted in failure. By 1980 Johannesburg's African township, Soweto, which was designed for a population of 600,000, housed some 1.6 million people (Iliffe, *Africans*, p. 282). The pass laws were proving unenforceable and in the mid 1980s major influx control regulations were rescinded. William Beinart, *Twentieth Century South Africa* (Oxford, 2001), p. 256.

were marked similarities between policies pursued in South Africa and elsewhere in the region. Like their South African counterparts, colonial officials continued to view the urban areas as places where rights of residence were to be restricted, though from the 1940s urban citizenship was no longer racially defined in the colonies.[111] To enforce these restrictions various legislative and administrative measures were adopted which, like the pass laws in the Republic, were aimed at checking the rural–urban flow.[112] The growing tolerance of the African urban presence that occurred throughout East and Central Africa from the 1930s was from the outset acknowledged as being limited. Hailey emphasised the need to check what he termed 'uneconomic urbanisation'. 'The future of African towns', he wrote in 1942,

> and particularly of the native locations of East and Central Africa, will depend largely upon the extent to which the administration adopts a policy of excluding from permanent residence in them those who do not fulfil a useful function in urban life.[113]

'The provision of decent living conditions and the development of forms of urban government with active African participation', Hailey observed, 'will be difficult unless residence in urban areas is controlled by a system of permits.' Similarly, while the Southern Rhodesian Howman Committee advocated stabilisation, it was deemed essential that this be accompanied by measures aimed at the 'deliberate control of urban life'.[114]

Indeed, throughout East and Central Africa tolerance of (restricted) African urbanisation was accompanied by policies of 'deliberate control'. In the new urban regime adopted in the Belgian Congo in the 1930s, access to the towns was to be strictly regulated with '[w]omen, children, and elderly men unable to work… normally refused admission'.[115] Married women who entered the towns with their husbands were only allowed to stay as long as the marriage lasted. Although the long-term goal of the establishment of CECs had been 'to promote urban communities led and administered by Africans', the CEC regime, according to Pons, 'remained a system of close supervision in which the colonial authority retained full control'.[116] Visiting Haut Katanga province in 1954, a Tanganyikan official observed that 'every attempt (was) made to strictly control the entry of Africans into Elisabethville… to try and ensure… that only the requisite number of workers in relation to the work available [was] permitted to enter the city.'[117] When,

---

[111] Willis observes a similar shift from 'racial discrimination' to 'social or cultural discrimination' with regard to East African colonial policy on access to alcohol. *Potent Brews*, p. 176.

[112] However, these new laws tended to operate after Africans had migrated to the towns rather than attempting to restrict African urban migration from the rural areas, as was the case in South Africa.

[113] Hailey, *Native Administration*, p. 39.

[114] Howman Report, quoted in Cooper, *Decolonization*, p. 140. See also Scarnecchia, 'Residential segregation'.

[115] Pons, *Stanleyville*, p. 37.

[116] *Ibid.*, p. 36.

[117] C.C. Harris, Report on a visit to the Belgian Congo to examine African housing, September 1954, TNA/225/DC01/3/3.

in the late 1950s, unemployment began to emerge as a serious problem in the African areas of the territorial capital, Léopoldville, the 'stringent controls that had always been applied' to restrict urban immigration were intensified, and resort was made to a policy of police checks and repatriations to the rural areas.[118]

In the British colonies, as urban growth rates picked up and official attitudes towards African urbanisation shifted from the 1940s, diverse legislation was enacted aimed at regulating the new urban African communities. In Buganda in 1940 a special Vagrancy Bill formed an early example of such legislation. It was designed to 'provide simple machinery by which unemployed and destitute natives' — who 'in recent times… ha[d] been collecting at various big centres, particularly Mengo, Mpigi and Masaka… giv[ing] considerable trouble to the authorities' — could be returned 'to their homes'.[119] In Kenya, the 'Limitation of Labour' regulations, passed under the wartime Emergency Powers (Defence) Acts in 1944, made provision for 'compelling any native who has resided in a township without employment for more than 48 hours either to be directed to take up approved employment or to be repatriated to his reserve'.[120] Between May and December 1944, 2,968 Africans were apprehended under the regulations in Nairobi alone, half of whom were repatriated.[121] After the war, what was intended to be more permanent legislation was passed in the shape of the 1946 Removal of Undesirable Natives Ordinance, which enabled officials to remove from towns (among other categories) any unemployed Africans. After concerns were raised about its racially discriminatory nature the Voluntarily Unemployed Persons (Provision of Employment) Ordinance was passed in its place in 1949. This required any unemployed person in the town to report to his (the legislation was directed at men[122]) local labour exchange and to show proof that he was 'genuinely seeking work'. It provided powers for labour officers to force 'voluntarily unemployed' persons into work or to send them to 'labour reception centres'.[123] However, it was the ordinance's administrative functions that were most valued by officials and, according to a 1950 report, 'repatriation was found to be the most satisfactory way of dealing with the majority' of persons apprehended under the ordinance.[124] In a confidential despatch to the British delegation at the United Nations in January 1950, the Secretary of State for the Colonies admitted that 'the real object of

---

[118] LaFontaine, *City Politics*, pp. 12 & 14; Ewens, *Congo Colossus*, p.85.

[119] Memo by Attorney General of Uganda, 4 January 1941, PRO/CO/859/79/8.

[120] 'Native Registration'.

[121] Cooper, *Waterfront*, p. 76.

[122] Though a call was made in October for the ordinance to be applied to adult females. Deputy CS to CP, Nairobi, 11 October 1950, KNA/ABK/14/25.

[123] For the military-style regime in these centres, see instructions for running Labour Reception centres, Memo to PCs, DCs and LOs, KNA/DC/KSM/1/23/101.

[124] The police were reported to have 'made considerable use of the provisions of the ordinance'. Report by DC, Nairobi, June–September 1950, 14 October 1950, KNA/ABK/14/25.

this legislation is to cope with the serious drift of males to urban centres such as Nairobi and Mombasa'.[125] In Southern Rhodesia, the Native (Urban Areas) Accommodation and Registration Act formed the principal plank of a revised urban policy from the late 1940s. The supply of housing restricted the number of Africans present in the urban areas, access to which was supposed to be strictly confined to those holding 'certificates of service' (work passes).[126] Women were denied the right to live in urban locations, and those who 'tried to make their way in a difficult world... were the subject of intense police harassment'.[127] According to Scarnecchia, the act 'criminalized many residents of the urban areas involved in non-formal employment', and Salisbury Municipality attempted to 'coerce compliance through its powers to raid and evict any man or woman who failed to produce the proper work papers'. To the north, on the Copperbelt — one of 'British Africa's prime laboratories for stabilization'[128] — similar controls over African urban residence were also in force in the 1950s. Here, nobody was allowed to remain in a location without the permission of the Location Superintendent, and getting such permission 'depended chiefly on being able to show that one was "usefully occupied"'.[129] As in Southern Rhodesia an attempt was made to control residence through urban housing, though owing to an inadequate supply many of those in employment ended up staying with kin or friends (as much as one-third of the population in Ndola). They were required to obtain a special permit 'if they were not to run the risk of arrest'. An African correspondent to *The Northern News*, complaining of the housing problem, noted that among these houseless citizens were some who had 'two to five sheets of paper covered by over 200 date stamps, denoting how many times they have called at the housing offices'.[130] Comparing the situation in Dar es Salaam favourably to that in Central Africa, Leslie observed that in Northern Rhodesian towns there was 'a constant battle of wits between the authority and "illegal occupants" who are always drifting in, overfilling the accommodation which did not have them in mind'. 'Checking and getting rid of these people', he

---

[125] SSCol to UK Delegation, UN, New York, 26 January 1950, PRO/WO/276/133. A petition to the UN had been sent by the East African Trade Union Congress complaining about the ordinance. The *East African Standard* (20 August 1949) reports an attempt by Eliud Mathu, an African member of the Legco, to prevent the passage of the Bill. After its enactment Mathu complained 'it had been "steamrollered" through by immigrant races and that his people would interpret it as making them "something like slaves"'. It appears that resentment towards this legislation was partly behind the general strike of 1950. See David Hyde, 'The Nairobi General Strike (1950): From protest to insurgency', in Burton, *Urban Experience*, pp. 235–53.

[126] Scarnecchia, 'Poor women', p. 286.

[127] Cooper, *Decolonization*, p. 335, citing Scarnecchia, 'Residential segregation'.

[128] Though here too official policy met with fierce resistance from a white working class. Cooper, *Decolonization*, pp. 336–48.

[129] Epstein, *Urbanization*, p. 26.

[130] 22 October 1955, quoted in *ibid*.

reported, 'is a process which gives rise to endless friction.'[131]

Despite the diverse measures adopted throughout Eastern and Southern Africa aimed at curbing rural–urban movement, what Hailey had termed 'uneconomic urbanisation' continued to occur. In urban policy, as in so many other areas of colonial administration, the pretensions of the colonial state outstripped its capacity for enforcement.[132] In Stanleyville, according to Pons, despite the small size of the three townships making up the CEC, 'the detailed rules and regulations… were soon found difficult to apply'. Annual reports repeatedly referred to 'the enormous difficulties in keeping the population register up to date and, particularly, in enforcing the regulations governing the entry of newcomers'.[133] In Léopoldville, between 1945 and 1955, the African population mushroomed from 96,116 to 290,377; and, although a limit was placed on immigration from 1955, and inducements offered for urban residents to return to the countryside, it grew by a further 100,000 between 1955 and 1960. By the late 1950s serious urban joblessness had emerged in the city, the percentage of unemployed men rising from just 4.41 in 1955 to 18.9 in 1958.[134] Moreover, a delinquent sub-culture had purportedly arisen of 'la jeunesse bandit' or the *watama*, who 'smoked cannabis, imposed "curfews", fought with weapons over territories and girls, raped women, and preyed especially on the squatter settlements' and were 'symptomatic of a disintegration of society'.[135]

Spiralling urbanisation rates throughout British colonies in East and Central Africa were placing similar strains on urban administrations there. In Nairobi, for example, officials had more or less relinquished control of the town's African locations in the late 1940s.[136] The general strike of 1950, and subsequently the outbreak of Mau Mau, offered the administration the opportunity to reassert itself.[137] However, it was not long before the initiative was once again lost. Despite the clearance of most Kikuyu, Embu and Meru (who at the time formed a majority of the urban population) from the city in

---

[131] Leslie, *Survey*, p. 153. The practice of expelling unemployed Africans from the towns was, of course, by no means restricted to British and Belgian colonies. Iliffe observes that in the French colonies 'officials, with an ingrained fear of urban riot, made a "banal and daily" but ineffective practice of deporting the *population flottante*, which meant almost any unemployed immigrant'. Iliffe, *African Poor*, p. 190. For the example of Brazzaville, see Florence Bernault, *Démocraties ambiguës en Afrique centrale. Congo-Brazzaville, Gabon, 1940–1965* (Paris, 1996).

[132] Though it should be emphasised that the 'weakness' of colonial administrations did not prevent them employing significant levels of coercion in their attempts to put a brake on African urbanisation.

[133] Pons, *Stanleyville*, p. 37.

[134] LaFontaine, *City Politics*, pp. 28–31.

[135] Quotes from Iliffe, *African Poor*, p. 189, and *ibid.*, p. 167. See also Paul Raymaekers, 'Pre-delinquency and juvenile delinquency in Léopoldville', *International African Labour Institute Bulletin* 10 (1963), pp. 329–57; J.S. LaFontaine, 'Two types of youth group in Kinshasa (Léopoldville)', in P. Mayer, *Socialization: The approach from social anthropology* (London, 1970), pp. 191–213; Ewens, *Congo Colossus*, p. 58; and Gary Stewart, *Rumba on the River: A history of the popular music of the two Congos* (London/New York, 2000), p. 78.

[136] See David Throup's chapter on 'Outcast Nairobi', *The Social and Economic Origins of Mau Mau* (London, 1987).

[137] Hyde, 'Nairobi General Strike'.

Operation Anvil in early 1954,[138] official restrictions on the freedom of movement in force during the Mau Mau emergency barely restricted the rate of rural–urban migration to manageable levels — the African urban population growing from 64,397 in 1948 to 115,000 a decade later.[139] After the emergency was lifted in January 1960, the Kenyan capital experienced a massive wave of immigration — around 50,000 entering Nairobi Extra-Provincial District in that year.[140] The burgeoning population placed an ever-greater strain on the city's infrastructure and amenities.[141] While illegal squatters in the city were in the early 1950s numbered in the hundreds, by 1962 an estimated 15,000 lived in the Kariobangi slum alone, and Nairobi was experiencing a veritable explosion of shanty construction.[142] At the same time, urban unemployment had reached unprecedented levels.[143] By the late-colonial period, towns and cities throughout the region were undergoing similar phemonema. Faced with an urban crisis in the early 1940s, colonial administrations had turned to stabilisation policy as a central means of addressing the problems they faced in the towns. By the late 1950s, as stabilisation measures were adopted throughout the region, its failure as a comprehensive urban policy became ever more apparent. Facing a second urban crisis on a substantially greater scale than that of the early 1940s, colonial administrators bequeathed the ever more insurmountable problems of urban governance to their African successors.[144]

Tanganyika was unusual compared to most of those territories in East and Southern Africa discussed above. Not only did it have a significantly smaller European population, but it was governed under a League of Nations mandate (and later as a UN Trust Territory) which bound the British administration to promote 'the material and moral well-being and the social progress of [the] inhabitants'.[145] At the same time, the resources available to Tanganyikan officials to assert control over the African population were also more negligible than those utilised by their counterparts in colonies

---

[138] Twenty-eight thousand were sent to camps and to the rural areas. Those who remained were subject to 'an elaborate pass system and a nightly curfew'. Van Zwanenberg, *Economic History*, p. 271.

[139] C.J. Martin, 'Sample population census of Nairobi, 1958', copy in KNA library.

[140] Andrew Burton, 'Emergence of an African underclass: Nairobi, 1954–71', MA dissertation, SOAS (1993), p. 13.

[141] See Anderson, 'Corruption'; Achola, pp. 134–36; and especially, Hake, *African Metropolis*.

[142] Burton, 'Underclass', p. 17; see Hake, *African Metropolis*, for a full account. In Northern Rhodesia, a 1957 study on Lusaka estimated that 45% of the total African population lived in 'unauthorised settlements'. Helmuth Heisler, *Urbanisation and the Government of Migration: The inter-relation of urban and rural life in Zambia* (New York, 1974), p. 117.

[143] A.G. Dalgeish, in his *Survey of Unemployment*, Nairobi (1960), identified the problem as being the flip side of stabilisation. The higher wages paid to urban workers were leading to more economical use of labour by employers, and at the same time high wages were attracting ever greater numbers of rural–urban migrants. See Cooper, *Waterfront*, pp. 180–1. For the case of Tanganyika, see Andrew Burton, 'Raw youth, school-leavers and the emergence of structural unemployment in late colonial urban Tanganyika', (in prep.).

[144] See Cooper, *Decolonization*, Part IV.

[145] Quoted in Iliffe, *Modern History*, p. 247.

such as Kenya, Northern Rhodesia or the Belgian Congo.[146] Meanwhile, the relatively underdeveloped state of the Tanganyikan economy meant that the demand for labour stabilisation in the late-colonial period was less pressing than in neighbouring colonies with more substantial industrial sectors.

Nevertheless, urban policy in the territory followed the same broad patterns as those outlined above — from an initial distaste for and reluctance to acknowledge African urbanisation, to late-colonial policies of stabilisation and social engineering, accompanied by attempts at influx control. The following chapters examine the manner in which local events in Dar es Salaam and wider shifts in colonial thinking combined to form the familiar, and yet distinctive, administrative policy that was pursued in the Tanganyikan capital.

[146] For comparisons with Kenya and Uganda see Appendix III, C, in D.A. Low and Alison Smith (eds), *History of East Africa* (Oxford, 1976).

Part I

African Urbanisation
& Colonial Policy

c.1916–46

The population is… increasing in breadth and strength.
It is an aggregate of masses, our conception of which clothe themselves
in terms which express something portentous and fearful.

William Cooke Taylor, quoted in Briggs, *Victorian Cities*, p. 61

Two

Dar es Salaam Between the Wars

Historical background

Situated on a fine natural harbour, Dar es Salaam was selected by Seyyid Majid, Sultan of Zanzibar, in 1862 as a base to consolidate his hold on the East African coast and the caravan trade with the interior.[1] Prior to Seyyid's arrival, the area was the location of a chain of small coastal villages — including Mzizima, Msasani and Kunduchi — inhabited by a number of 'Swahili clans' collectively known as the Shomvi, and by dispersed settlements inland occupied by Zaramo. A number of stone buildings were constructed under Majid's orders, and by the late 1860s a small community that included Indian and Arab traders had emerged that was administered by an *Akida* appointed by the Sultan.[2] After the death of Majid in 1870, the settlement was neglected by his successor, Seyyid Barghash. Nevertheless, fuelled by an expanding trade in agricultural products with the predominantly Zaramo hinterland, Dar es Salaam continued to grow. By the mid 1880s the population numbered several thousand, including indigenous Shomvi, numerous Zaramo, Arab officials, soldiers and traders, and Indian merchants.

After a period of local resistance in the late 1880s Dar es Salaam was subordinated to German colonial rule, becoming in 1891 the capital of

[1]   This section is based on Admiralty War Staff, Intelligence Division, *A Handbook of German East Africa* (London, 1916); Baker, 'Memorandum', pp. 1–7; Clement Gillman, 'Dar es Salaam, 1860 to 1940: A story of growth and change', *TNR* 20 (1945); Sir John Gray, 'Dar es Salaam under the Sultans of Zanzibar', *TNR* 33 (1952); and John Sutton, 'Dar es Salaam: A sketch of a hundred years', *TNR* 71 (1970). I am most grateful to Franck Raimbault for sending me his comments, information from which has been incorporated into the text. For Dar es Salaam under the Germans, see Franck's forthcoming (University of Paris) P.h.D thesis; and 'Les élites Arabes et Indiennes face à la colonisation. Le cas de Dar-es-Salaam à l'époque de la domination Allemande (1890–1914)', *Hypothèses* (2001). See also, Jürgen Becher, *Dar es Salaam, Tanga und Tabora: Stadtentwicklung in Tansani unter deutscher Kolonialherrschaft* (Stuttgart, 1997).

[2]   According to the Holy Ghost Father Hoerner (who visited in 1867), it consisted of 900 inhabitants.

Deutsch Ost-Afrika. In subsequent years the kernel of the modern town was developed. A port was constructed on the western side of the creek on which the town is situated, and official and European residential buildings were erected to the north, alongside a botanical gardens. Administrative and commercial buildings were established along Kaiserstrasse, an esplanade running along the harbour. The heart of the town centred on the principal business street, Unter den Akazien, the top end of which was known by the Hindi name *Barra Rasta* (literally 'big road'), Arab Street and India Street.[3] Here an Indian commercial and residential area emerged — the bazaar — which has constituted an important business centre ever since. To the north and west of the bazaar, lay the African residential area, to which immigrants came from both near and far attracted by the opportunities arising from commercial, administrative and small-scale industrial activity that was supplanting the pre-colonial plantation economy. Although the Germans in 1891 defined residential zones for Europeans, Asians and Africans, these were not strictly enforced. However, after 1912, when the administration began purchasing nearby *shambas* for African settlement, more effective segregation was envisaged.[4] Urban development was consolidated by the construction of a railway into the interior (begun in 1905), which by 1914 connected the town to Kigoma on Lake Tanganyika, and all points between. The population grew rapidly after 1891 — particularly the African and Asian communities (see Appendix). By 1913 the town had a population of around 22,500, including 19,000 Africans (up from 3000 to 4,000 in 1887) and 2,500 Asians (of whom there were only a handful present in 1887).[5]

The Germans maintained a firm grip on the town. According to a later British observer, '[r]ules and regulations were promulgated' alongside a 'legal code which was not in any way representative of local opinion'.[6] A *Liwali* was installed through whom the urban African population was administered; he was assisted by a network of *Majumbe* (headmen) each responsible for a section of the township. While the Germans displayed greater tolerance towards African urbanisation than was characteristic of early British officials — at least in part because of their need for African labour — supervision of the African community was effected through these indigenous agents, and through the *Knüppel askari* and *Geheimpolizisten*. German discipline of miscreants was severe, with the use of the *kiboko* hide-whip being heavy and frequent. 'It was important', Franck Raimbault observes, 'that German

---

[3]   Kaiserstrasse, Unter den Akazien and Arab Street are today called Sokoine Drive, Samora Avenue and Nkrumah Street respectively. I am indebted to Gitanjali Surendran for the translation of *Barra Rasta*.

[4]   An African suburb on a grid pattern, west of the centre, at what became Kariakoo, was planned by the Germans but not completed.

[5]   It should be stressed that population figures from surveys and censuses conducted prior to WWII are unreliable, and all discussion of such statistics in this book should be treated as indicators. Population data and sources are contained in the Appendix.

[6]   Baker, 'Memorandum', p. 6.

Map 2.1 *Dar es Salaam in 1905*
Source: Gillman, *'Dar es Salaam'*

Fig. 2.1. *Aerial photo of Dar es Salaam, 1934*
Source: RH/Mss.Afr.s. 392. (© Bodleian Library, University of Oxford)

domination manifested itself by displays of violence on a daily basis'.[7] In the British period, European, Indian and African commentators frequently remarked upon the harshness of German rule, in some cases expressing nostalgia for the strict orderliness that was held to have prevailed prior to WWI.[8]

Dar es Salaam under British rule

Dar es Salaam was first occupied by the British in 1916, and for the remainder of the war acted principally as a military base in the campaign against von Lettow-Vorbeck's retreating German forces. When, in October 1918, a British civil administration eventually took over,[9] it was faced with a difficult situation in the territorial capital arising out of both the impact of WWI and adverse climatic conditions that had resulted in a shortage in foodstuffs accompanied by a significant hike in the cost of living.[10] A slowdown in economic activity and shrinking job market were also contributing to what DC Brett observed, in 1921, was 'an unfavourable comparison between the prosperous times enjoyed under the late German administration and the hardships experienced by the native since the war'.[11] Rising prices and the shortage of employment were no doubt connected to an increase in urban crime in the wake of military occupation, as was British unfamiliarity with the town and the low precedence set upon urban administration during the course of the war.

With the installation of a civil administration the imposition of urban order became a high priority. Township Rules were introduced for Dar es Salaam under the Regulations for Peace and Good Order in 1920 (and updated in 1923).[12] Areas covered by the rules included sanitation requirements, building and trading licences, the establishment of markets, public order offences such as 'loitering', prostitution and gambling, as well as residence rights for Africans and regulations restricting African mobility in the town. A later addition to the rules legislated for the separation of Dar es Salaam into three zones.[13] Zone I, in which only 'residential buildings of a European type' were allowed to be

---

[7] Personal communication, 17 May 2003.
[8] See e.g. *TH*, 11 June 1932; *TS*, 28 June 1952; and Report on the Question of Imprisonment in Tanganyika Territory in PRO/CO/691/126/1. See also, F.S. Joelson, *The Tanganyika Territory* (New York, 1921), pp. 201–5; Anthony, 'Culture', chapter 2; and Juhani Koponen, *Development for Exploitation: German colonial policies in mainland Tanzania, 1884–1914* (Helsinki, 1994), pp. 359–66 *et passim*.
[9] While Dar es Salaam was handed over to the 'civil authorities' on 1 October 1918 (Sayers, *Handbook*, p. 93), civil administration in Tanganyika as a whole was not introduced until 21st January 1919 (Gillman, 'Dar es Salaam', p. 16). The League of Nations mandate did not formally come into effect until July 1922. Kenneth Ingham, 'Tangayika: The Mandate and Cameron', in Harlow *et al.* (1965), p. 545.
[10] See D.F. Bryceson, 'A century of food supply in Dar es Salaam', in J.I. Guyer, *Feeding African Cities* (Manchester, 1987), pp. 162–3.
[11] Dsm DAR, 1921, p. 7.
[12] GN no. 6 of 1920.
[13] GN no. 160 of 1924.

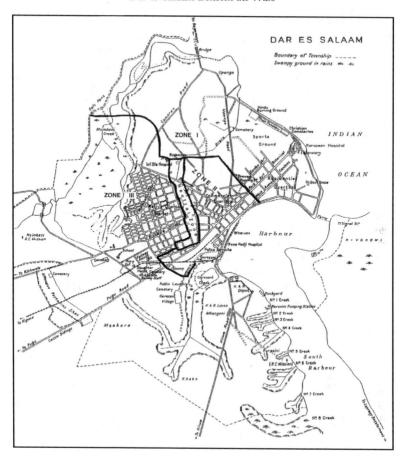

Map 2.2 *The zoning of inter-war Dar es Salaam, 1925, showing Zones I–III and the 'Neutral Zone'*
Source: TNA/12589/Vol. 1

built, was bordered by Versailles Street to the south-west, the Msimbazi Creek to the north, and the Indian Ocean to the east. It encompassed the main government offices, the botanical gardens and a predominantly European residential area of bungalows set in spacious surroundings. By the 1930s, when Zone I was extended northwards, upmarket suburbs were emerging along the coast to the north of the centre at Sea View and Oyster Bay.[14] Zone II, the congested commercial area in which 'residential and trading buildings [in permanent materials] only' could be erected, provided both home and bazaar to the majority of the growing Indian population. It ran from Versailles Street in the north-east to the so-called 'Neutral Zone' or 'Open Space', known today as Mnazi Mmoja, in the west. This space — 100 yards wide and almost a mile in length — was designed as a buffer to protect the European and, to a lesser extent, the Indian communities from the insanitary conditions perceived to be prevalent in the African township (see Map 2.2).[15] The township was located in Zone III, which encompassed all those areas to the west of the open space and Zone II up to the town boundary. Here 'native houses' could be constructed in impermanent materials. The main centre of population in Zone III was Kariakoo (so named because it was the location of a depot for British army porters — the Carrier Corps — during WWI), a planned African residential area, consisting predominantly of six-roomed 'Swahili' houses constructed initially from mangrove poles and mud walls, and *makuti* thatched roofs, which grew up around a market originally built by the Germans in 1914.[16] It also included the urban villages of Gerezani and Keko (or Kheko), close to the southern town limits. Ilala, a planned extension to Kariakoo — in which Africans evicted from Gerezani, the Open Space and other areas in the late 1920s were offered plots[17] — was by the early 1930s expanding apace. In 1931 Zone III contained 2,035 houses 'of native construction' (of which 40 had corrugated iron roofs); there were a further 380 such houses in Zones I and II.[18] On the peri-urban perimeter were numerous villages containing both large Zaramo (Mtoni, Yombo, Msasani, Magogoni, Buguruni), and upcountry populations (Yombo, Mtoni), many of whose inhabitants had links to the town either through the sale of agricultural produce or through employment (see Map 2.3).

The unstated ideal of colonial administrators was for racial segregation between Dar es Salaam's three zones.[19] One official in 1920 remarked upon

---

[14] Baker, 'Memo', p. 9.

[15] Establishment of the open space was facilitated by the occurrence of a fire in 1921, which destroyed many African houses in the area, although it was some time before the space was fully cleared. A similar 'cordon sanitaire' was originally planned between Zones I and II. However, the value of existing property in the area prevented it being cleared. See Kironde, 'Land use', pp. 169–73; Brennan, 'Nation', chapter 1.

[16] For inter-war African housing see Baker, 'Memo', pp. 14–28.

[17] See TNA/12589/I and *ibid.*, p. 11.

[18] *Ibid.*, p. 15.

[19] The three zones came to be identified with the main 'races' in their coloquial names: Uzunguni (literally, 'place of the European'); Uhindini ('place of the Indian'); and Uswahilini ('place of the Swahili'), though the latter refers to a form of African urban culture rather than the people.

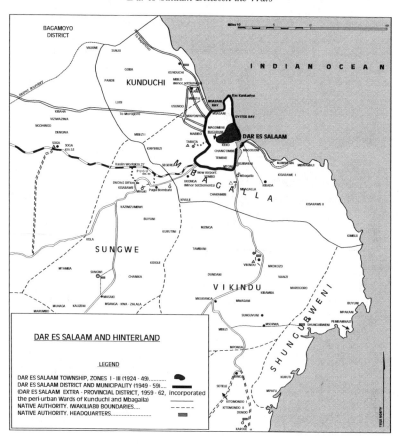

Map 2.3 *Dar es Salaam and hinterland*
Source: Based on insert from M.J.B. Molohan, *Detribalization* (Dsm, 1959)

51

the 'universal agreement as to the wisdom and necessity of segregation', although he recognised 'we cannot adopt the principle of segregation as such, for that would lead us into a position where we should be in conflict with the terms of... the [League of Nations] Mandate'. Nevertheless, he concluded, 'proper segregation' could be ensured by means of building and township regulations, the policy subsequently adopted in 1924.[20] As Kironde has observed, a 'sanitation syndrome' was evident in early British urban policy, with medical officers playing a prominent role in planning.[21] The establishment of the Open Space was only the most obvious example of this. In 1929, in Gerezani — a village of 106 huts located close to the European railway quarters — conditions were said to be 'almost ideal for the production of an outbreak of malaria amongst Europeans', and the village (where some occupants had been living since the early 1900s) was subsequently demolished.[22] Similarly, when Zone I was extended to cover areas north of the centre in the early 1930s, 'the methods of life' of Africans resident in Upanga were deemed 'a constant menace to the health of the non-native community' and their eviction deemed essential.[23] Nevertheless, although strict segregation remained the ideal of officials, members of the three main racial groupings could still be found residing in each zone. Zone I contained African residences in the sparsely populated northern area, as well as wealthier Indians occupying 'European-style' accommodation. European traders were to be found in the commercial area, to the north of which was also the African settlement of Kisutu, dating back to the early German period.[24] Meanwhile, some Europeans working for the railways had their quarters in Zone III, and Kariakoo was the location of a growing number of Indian commercial and residential premises in the inter-war period.[25] The most 'stunning contradiction' to racial zoning was to be found in the location of the city's central market — which was moved from Zone II to central Kariakoo in 1923. The relocation resulted in a substantial influx of Indian traders into Zone III.[26]

[20]   Min., 22 January 1920, TNA/3152.
[21]   Kironde, 'Land use', p. 156; for 'sanitation syndrome' in colonial planning see above, p. 22.
[22]   Snr HO to CS, 13 February 1929, TNA/12589/I; for the demolition of Gerezani, see Kironde, 'Land use', pp. 177–80.
[23]   PC to CS (paraphrasing MS Helps), 16 December 1935, TNA/12589/II; for African residence in Upanga, see Kironde, 'Land use', pp. 181–6. Europeans were equally concerned about Indian modes of living — the Indian community being condemned as 'one of the greatest offenders against all forms of sanitation'. Minute quoted in Brennan, 'Nation', p. 27.
[24]   Baker, 'Memorandum', pp. 9–10.
[25]   According to Baker, over 8% of the houses in Zone III were occupied by 'non-natives'. 'Memorandum', p. 16; see also, Brennan, 'Nation', chapter 1.
[26]   See Brennan, 'Nation', pp. 46–7, for the relocation of the market, and *passim* for a discussion of the political ramifications of zoning and its failure. The porousness of the town's zones stemmed in part from the difficult choices that had to be made in the context of 'the notorious frugality of British rule'. As Brennan (p. 21) observes, 'often those policies costing the least or extracting the most won out'.

The urban population

Dar es Salaam's population in the 1920s was already highly cosmopolitan. Among the 600 Europeans, German, Greek, Swiss, French, Belgian, Portuguese, Italian and other nationals were present in groups of thirty or more, as well as larger numbers of British officials and traders.[27] The 4,000-strong Indian community was also heterogeneous, comprising of Christian Goans, Sinhalese, Sikhs, Hindus and the majority Muslims, who were subdivided into Ismaili and Ithnasheri Khoja, Bohora Shia, Sunni and Ahmaddiya sects. Other 'Asiatics' present in the town were Chinese and Arabs. Arab identity was as opaque in Dar es Salaam as it was elsewhere on the East African littoral. The term embraced Arabised coastal Africans, migrants from the Hadhramaut and elsewhere on the Arabian peninsula and their descendants, as well as local people of mixed race descent. The ambiguous position of 'Arabs' in coastal society was reflected in colonial indecision over whether or not they should be classed as 'native' or 'non-native'.[28] There was also a small Chinese community in Dar es Salaam, the residue of an unsuccessful attempt by the German colonial administration to import labour from the Orient in the late nineteenth century.[29]

The 20,000-strong African community was characterised by the greatest ethnic diversity. The 1931 census identified members of 167 different 'tribes' residing in the town.[30] Zaramo predominated, making up approximately a third of the African population (6,642 out of 22,732). Other groups numbering over a thousand were the Rufiji (2,022), Yao (1,268) and Manyema (1,221).[31] Movement between the town and the rural areas was common among all ethnic groups, and frequently singled out by officials as one of the main complicating factors of urban administration.[32] A number of causes

---

[27] 1929 DAR, p. 20.

[28] For example, in respect to landholding, Arabs were classed as natives under the 1923 Law of Property and Conveyancing Ordinance, while 'anyone with Arab blood' were non-natives according to the *Land Ordinance* of the same year. H.H. McCleery, 'Extent and conditions under which Natives are occupying land in the outskirts of Dar es Salaam' (1939), p. 16, RH/Mss/Afr.s.870. For a discussion of non-native landholding and its repercussions see Brennan, 'Nation', chapter 1.

[29] References to the Chinese community are few and far between, though they are briefly mentioned in both Baker's and Leslie's surveys. Iliffe, *Modern History*, p. 152, and Thaddeus Sunseri, *Vilimani: Labour migration and rural change in early colonial Tanzania* (Portsmouth, NH/ Oxford/Cape Town, 2002), p. 55, mention the attempt to import labour.

[30] DO Fryer to PC, EP, 10 July 1931, Native census results, TNA/61/167.

[31] Tribal categorisations are used here to give some impression of the geographical origins of the urban population. African ethnicity in Dar es Salaam was in fact probably relatively permeable and/or multivalent, notably in the case of the autochthonous Zaramo and Shomvi. For a useful discussion of ethnicity and identity in Dar es Salaam, see Brennan ('Nation', pp. 93–118).

[32] The shifting urban population was a long-standing problem for officials. In discussing German attempts to control malaria in 1901, Clyde observes: 'the greatest problem that confronted Ollwig [a medical officer in the German administration] was the transient nature of the population ... People were continually coming and going'. D.F. Clyde, *History of the Medical Services of Tanganyika* (Dsm, 1962), p. 25.

Table 2.1 *Principal ethnic groups as identified in the 1931 census*

	Male	Female	Male child	Female child	Total
Zaramo	3,313	1,973	857	499	6,642
Rufiji	1,351	359	203	109	2,022
Yao	795	369	64	40	1,268
Manyema	445	654	61	61	1,221
Nyasa	577	305	45	34	961
Kami	690	136	71	44	941
Nyamwezi	540	234	45	27	846
Ngindo	498	234	48	29	809
Ndengereko	304	201	99	38	642
Nyagatwa	328	160	47	24	559
Ngoni	332	128	42	38	540
Mwera	384	83	20	19	506
Makonde	356	88	33	15	492
Kutu	209	42	26	18	295
Hehe	172	87	19	8	286
Makua	175	48	11	3	237
Nyakyusa	164	34	14	5	217
Matumbi	143	49	14	10	216
Ganda	135	54	13	11	213
Wanubi	76	79	22	20	197
Pogoro	147	33	8	4	192
Shomvi	52	49	8	12	121
Total	**13,323**	**6,206**	**1,988**	**1,217**	**22,732**

All those groups numbering over 190 are included plus the Shomvi.
Source: DO Fryer to PC, EP, 10 July 1931

lay behind this mobility. It was often interpreted by administrators as evasive behaviour on the part of the African: attempting to escape the control of village chiefs and elders (and husbands in the case of women) and the tax demands of the colonial state. However, it was more commonly associated with the agricultural cycle in the town's hinterland: the urban population growing significantly outside the main planting/harvesting months of June to August and October to December.[33] In addition, large numbers of labourers made their way to the town from upcountry in search of employment and/or on their way to and from Zanzibar for the clove picking season, or to plantations in Eastern and Tanga Provinces. According to G.A.

[33] Report on a possible sociological survey of Dsm by R & C Sofer, 21st April 1951, TNA/ 18950/Vol III. Beidelman observes the main clearing/planting months in Uzaramo as August-September (harvested in January) and October-December. T.O. Beidelman, *The Matrilineal Peoples of Eastern Tanzania*, London (1967), p. 16.

Debenham, a Labour Officer in the late 1920s, workseekers arrived 'by almost every train'. Lacking accommodation on arrival they slept 'as best they can in odd corners'. 'The streets of the town at night', he observed, 'are full of these people.'[34]

Mobility was particularly prominent among the Zaramo, whose heartland lay in the areas surrounding Dar es Salaam, though the town no doubt contained urbanised Zaramo too. The home areas of the Rufiji were also located close to the town, in the southern parts of Dar es Salaam district and neighbouring Rufiji district; they likewise displayed a high degree of mobility. Yao originated from south-western Tanganyika and further afield in Portuguese East Africa and Nyasaland. Although their areas of origin were quite distant, they too appear to have retained strong links with their rural homes. Manyema, on the other hand, were highly urbanised. They were composed mostly of former-slaves (and their descendants), principally from areas to either side of Lake Tanganyika, who had settled in and around the town (and in other Tangayikan towns[35]) after their emancipation. In the words of a later survey, they were 'the citizens of Dar es Salaam *par excellence*',[36] and were well established in the lucrative property sector and in petty commerce. The community of Sudanese and Shangaan ex-*askaris*, who had settled in the town in the late nineteenth and early twentieth century after completing their service in the German army, were a smaller grouping who, having largely cut ties with their homes like the Manyema, were unusually committed to permanent urban residence. The Shomvi were another noteworthy group, closely linked to the Zaramo,[37] inhabiting coastal villages — notably Msasani — existing prior to the founding of Dar es Salaam that continued to prosper as semi-detached suburbs of the town into the colonial period and beyond.[38] Nyamwezi also maintained a high profile in the area.[39] Estimates enumerating their presence vary wildly.[40] However, as porters on the coastal caravans they were among the earliest regular upcountry visitors to Dar es Salaam, and lived in substantial numbers in both the town itself and in surrounding villages.[41]

[34]   Debenham to LG, 27 April [1927?], TNA/61/76.
[35]   See e.g. Sheryl McCurdy, 'Transforming associations: Fertility, therapy, and the Manyema Diaspora in urban Kigoma, Tanzania, *c*.1850–1993', Ph.D. thesis, Columbia University (2000).
[36]   Leslie, *Survey*, p. 149. Quoted in Iliffe, *Modern History*.
[37]   Brennan observes 'the fluidity of Shomvi and Zaramo identity, underscored by regular intermarriage, indicates that neither ethnonym corresponds to the sociological category of "tribe".' See also, Leslie, *Survey*, p. 20.
[38]   Baker, 'Memorandum', p. 1.
[39]   Though who exactly the term referred to is by no means straightforward, the label often incorporating the related Sukuma and possibly members of other groups from western Tanganyika involved in the coastal trade with the interior.
[40]   In 1894, the Nyamwezi were found to constitute around 7% of Dar es Salaam's population (Iliffe, *Modern History*, p. 161). In 1905, a Malaria research team put the proportion at an implausible 27% (actually more than the Zaramo — 26%). (Sigvard von Sicard, *The Lutheran Church on the Coast of Tanzania, 1887–1914*, Uppsala, 1970), p. 171). In the 1931 census they made up less than 4% of the population — a suspiciously small proportion, this time.
[41]   See Leslie (*Survey*, pp. 43–4), who states a preponderance lived in the rural areas either side of the town boundary, which perhaps accounts for the discrepancies in the estimated size of the Nyamwezi community.

Although the population was predominantly male, substantial numbers of women were present in Dar es Salaam from early on. Censuses carried out in 1928, 1931 and 1940 numbered African women in the town at 9,139, 7,417 and 16,550 respectively (compared to 12,791, 15,299 and 18,200 men). The female:male sex ratio — according to this data, around 71:100 in 1928, 49:100 in 1931, and 91:100 in 1940 — was, compared to other towns in the region, high.[42] According to the 1931 census most women were dependants of husbands (4,470) or kept as mistresses (461); 160 were designated prostitutes. However, the distinction between these three categories was not necessarily so clear cut,[43] nor did their classification as dependants tell the whole story. Women in Dar es Salaam were, in fact, engaged in a range of economic activities. Baker found there were 'six or so' brothels in the town 'frequented by native and non-native', though he observed these were not typical of African life; he considered the African man tended 'rather to concubinage than to promiscuity in his relations with women'. Local Manyema women, according to Baker ('if one can trust native opinion'), often divorced their first husband and — with their parents' permission — became concubines, with 'a greater hold over their lovers than they would over their husbands'.[44] More commonly, women engaged in petty trade, selling charcoal and firewood, along with cooked foodstuffs such as *vitumbua* (rice cakes), fried fish and *togwa* (a non-alcoholic millet drink), from the verandahs of their houses. They also engaged in mat making.[45] In his 1950s survey, Leslie noted that some women had over time accumulated sufficient resources from their petty trading activity to build properties, from which they derived a comfortable income.[46] The most lucrative trade dominated by women in the inter-war period was the brewing and sale of alcohol. From 1926 the consumption of alcohol was officially only allowed at the Kariakoo *pombe* market.[47] The trade was monopolised by twelve women — many of them old — who each employed six staff who helped brew and sell the (millet) beer. Profits were handsome, Baker estimating them at around Shs.150/- per month (even after having paid Shs.100/- for a licence). When East African Breweries temporarily took over responsibility for the brewing of all 'native beer' in the township in the mid 1930s, the Provincial Commissioner observed that the women brewers had 'had a marvellous time for many years. They have made a lot of money'. Some owned as many as four houses which were rented out 'very profitably'.[48]

---

[42] For example, in 1930s Nairobi the rate was anything from 25:100 to 12:100 (White, *Comforts*, pp. 57–8); in Salisbury in 1950 it was as low as 6:100 (Scarnecchia, 'Poor women', p. 295).

[43] Luise White (*Comforts*) has documented how in neighbouring Kenya the distinctions between those women offering sex and those offering companionship or domestic housekeeping skills to townsmen was by no means clear. In his survey of Broken Hill, Northern Rhodesia, Wilson makes the same point. *Detribalization Pt. II*, p. 64.

[44] Baker, 'Memorandum', pp. 83–4.

[45] *Ibid.*, pp. 25, 38.

[46] Leslie, *Survey*, pp. 117 & 168. According to Brennan ('Nation', p. 108), it was Manyema women again who were the principal female rentiers.

[47] *Ibid.*, pp. 32–5; see also, Mbilinyi, 'Unforgettable'.

[48] Legco debate on the Native Liquor Ordinance Amendment Bill, Nov. 1934, TNA/18893. Though officials may have exaggerated such profits. Willis, see *Potent Brews*, pp.100–1.

The urban population was also characterised by its relative youthfulness. According to Baker the number of elderly men was 'strikingly low'.[49] Young Africans, by contrast, appeared keen to sample urban life. Frequently, the move to Dar es Salaam occurred around the time young men became eligible for tax; it was motivated either by the need to find waged employment or by the desire to evade payment.[50] '[T]his class is always increasing', observed Baker, 'and is recruited from the youths of Lindi, Bagamoyo, Kilosa, Morogoro and Tabora who, finding that economic crops have little value, make their way to the capital in the hope of getting work.' 'The number of detribalised youths' was 'disquieting': some had 'come to the capital from upcountry in the capacity of personal servants and ha[d] been left stranded, others ha[d] travelled down on their own initiative whilst yet others ha[d] been orphaned and left to fend for themselves'.[51] Although children were not so common, the number of young boys without parents in the town was, by the 1930s, also a source of growing concern. Many were employed as domestics or by shopkeepers, or were paid to work as itinerant coffee and cake sellers; others engaged in petty crime.[52]

The social composition of the African population

According to European observation the African urban community was characterised by a lack of coherence. Baker reported

> singularly little consensus of opinion in the native quarter. Members of a household show a lack of interest in their neighbours which is curiously un-African… They are extraordinary individualistic in outlook and take little or no interest in township affairs.[53]

He ascribed the apparent absence of communality in part to 'the fact that there are so few old men in the town that the young ones have no focus round which to gather'. By the late 1930s this purported incoherence was characterised as a lack of 'civic consciousness', which administrative innovations in the 1940s and 1950s were designed to counteract.[54] However, assumptions about a relative

---

[49] Baker, 'Memorandum', p. 80.

[50] E.g. Dsm DARs, 1930, p. 8; 1937, p. 3. In her thesis on contemporary Dar es Salaam, Eileen Moyer identifies, alongside corresponding economic motives, additional, more sinister, reasons for rural–urban migration among African youth: notably to escape physical violence — in the shape of both over-zealous parental correction and sexual abuse by parents or other family members — 'routinely suffered in their childhood homes'. ('In the shadow of the Sheraton: Imagining locality in global spaces in Dar es Salaam, Tanzania', Ph.D. thesis, University of Amsterdam (2003), p. 154). Although I have come across no references to these factors in the colonial period, colonial knowledge about such intimate issues was scarce to non-existent and it seems likely that similar phenomena at this time would also have provided a motivation for the move to town.

[51] Baker, 'Memorandum', pp. 88, 94.

[52] See Burton, 'Urchins'.

[53] Baker, 'Memorandum', p. 69.

[54] See Burton, 'Townsmen'.

absence of African civil society are belied by surviving data recording an apparent abundance of communal, recreational and even embryonic political institutions in the inter-war period. Anthony describes a kind of café society, in the shape of the *mikahawani* and *hoteli*[55] : football, dancing and various ethnic or multi-ethnic associations performed similar integrative functions, encompassing, to varying degrees, all sections of the heterogeneous urban population.[56] However, many of these institutions simultaneously reflected tensions that were intrinsic to the social make-up of the town. So, while *beni ngoma* dance societies were characterised by 'their proud modernity and multi-tribalism', at the same time the competing *marini* and *arinoti* groups came to represent respectively the 'elite' (whether traditional or educated) as opposed to lower status townsmen and women.[57] Similarly, the football teams Young Africans and Sunderland expressed division between locals and newcomers to the town.[58] The fissures in urban society, notably those separating elders and youth, the affluent and indigent, and the (formally) educated and the uneducated, informed prejudices shown towards that section of the population demonised as *wahuni*.

An emerging 'elite' who enjoyed affluence and/or authority came to the fore in inter-war Dar es Salaam. This elite had clear ideas about urban — and wider African — society, which they tried to impose upon fellow residents.[59] Age, education and/or relative wealth gave members of the elite the confidence to condemn the behaviour of their less respectable brethren; they also served to promote anxiety about those townsmen who shared none of these privileges and were disdainful of their supposed betters.[60] Thanks

---

[55]   Anthony translates these as coffee and tea houses, though *hoteli* has come to be more broadly understood as a restaurant.

[56]   Anthony, 'Culture', chapter 4; see also Tadasu Tsuruta, 'Popular music, sports, and politics in Dar es Salaam during the British colonial period', originally published in Japanese in the *Journal of Asian and African Studies* 55 (1998), pp. 93–118 (however, all references are to a substantially revised English version in the author's possession). Burton, 'Townsmen'.

[57]   Iliffe, *Modern History*, p. 391; Terence Ranger, *Dance and Society in Eastern Africa: The beni 'ngoma'* (London, 1975), pp. 64–5 (n.b. the quote by Urban Tamba, a Dar es Salaam resident). Oral informants cited by Tsuruta ('Popular music') also recalled the 'Malofa' ('loafer') Band' (see fn. 22, p. 5 above) and 'Mexico' who represented, respectively, 'mostly boatmen (stevedores)' and 'educated people such as clerks'. By the 1930s *beni ngoma* were restricted to the 'riff raff' alone, according to E.C. Baker's report on Tanga; the modernising functions of *beni* for the educated elite were assumed by the African Association. Ranger, *Dance*, pp. 94–6.

[58]   Tadasu Tsuruta describes the two groups as *watu wa pwani* (coastal people) and *watu wa bara* (upcountry people). ('Simba na Yanga: Football and urbanisation in Dar es Salaam, 1920s–1970s', paper given at the conference, 'Dar es Salaam in the 20 century: Urbanisation and social change in an emerging East African metropolis', UDsm, 1 July 2002). Brennan ('Nation', p. 103) describes them as *wenye mji* (owners of the town) and *watu wa kaja* (immigrants). Both are valid: Zaramo/Shomvi could identify themselves in opposition to other 'coastal' peoples as the town's true indigenes, and at other times identify themselves in a wider coastal grouping as against upcountry Africans (sometimes referred to as -*shenzi*, or 'uncivilised'), who might not integrate so easily into the dominant urban Islamic Swahili culture.

[59]   'Being the few who have the benefit of education', Mzee bin Sudi wrote to Kleist Sykes in 1932, 'we are obliged to lead our less fortunate fellows'. Quoted in Iliffe, *Modern History*, p. 410. For the 'self-styled' Zulu spokesmen (*abakhulumeli*) of urban South Africa between the wars, see David B. Coplan, *In Township Tonight! South Africa's Black city music and theatre* (London/NY, 1985), p. 79.

[60]   The pages of *Kwetu* are full of examples of such condemnations and elite *angst*.

to their position in African society, members of the elite enjoyed relatively privileged access to European officials, whose vision of urban society was no doubt influenced by their representations.[61] Educated Africans, for example, were from the late 1930s appointed to Dar es Salaam's film censorship board where they voiced particular concern over the impact of cinematic depictions of crime on their fellow townsmen.[62] Poorer urban residents occasionally attempted to counter such representations. However, they lacked the educated African's articulacy and struggled to get their voices heard. Europeans, complained Saleh bin Fundi, organiser of a domestic servants union in 1940s and 1950s Dar es Salaam, and former leader of the *arinoti*, listened only to

> the well to do Africans who do not care about the poor... those are the people who are fighting for their own interests.... The common town people are those who know the needs of the people because they can starve for two or three days, but you... hold your meetings with the rich people so you cannot find out the difficulties of Tanganyika Territory.[63]

The African elite included self-styled elders from coastal and upcountry groups, who based their authority along the tribal, gerontocratic lines to which inter-war administrators were so receptive.[64] The relative independence of urban youth represented a challenge to their authority, a fact frequently bemoaned to (and by) European officials.[65] It is the educated elite, however, who are most visible in the extant sources. They viewed themselves as the progressive leaders of African society, but in most cases were socially and culturally distant from the bulk of the urban population. Their education set them apart from an overwhelmingly non-literate majority. In the 1931 census, out of a workforce of 13,754, just 2,639 indicated an ability to read or write. It also gave them privileged access to high-status, renumerative employment. In his 1939 report on the town, DO Pike remarked upon substantial inequality in the urban workforce, with the highest-paid African clerks receiving as much as Shs. 200/- per month when 60 percent of urban workers earned under Shs. 15/- monthly, some receiving as little as Shs. 7/-.[66] In addition, there was a degree of residential differentiation, the eastern part of Kariakoo (close to Zone II, where many Africans worked) being occupied by 'better-paid Africans who were educated and politically aware'.[67]

Africans who had received a Western education most commonly originated from districts far from the capital (often from neighbouring territories), and were, in contrast to the Muslim majority, frequently practising Christians

---

[61] Not least in the emergence of the term *wahuni* into official parlance.
[62] James Brennan, 'Democratizing cinema and censorship in Tanzania, 1920–76', paper given at the first conference on 'Comparative Imperial and Post-colonial Historical Studies', Michigan State University, 14 February 1999.
[63] Quoted in Bujra, *Serving Class*, pp. 68–9. For background on Saleh bin Fundi, see Iliffe, *Modern History*, pp. 397–8.
[64] Baker, 'Memorandum', pp. 70–1; Brennan, 'Nation', pp. 104–5.
[65] See below, pp. 75–8.
[66] Pike, 'Report on Native Affairs in Dar es Salaam Township' [hereafter, 'Report'], p. 8, TNA/18950/Vol. II.
[67] Iliffe, *Modern History*, p. 387.

(Baker talks of 'an alien intelligentsia'). For example, Samwil Chiponde, who came to Dar es Salaam after WWI and became a High Court interpreter, was a product of the Universities Mission to Central Africa school at Kiungani, Zanzibar. Cecil Matola, an 'aristocratic Yao teacher' at the Government School, and Benedict Madalito, a Makua clerk in the District Office, were also educated at Kiungani. Other African civil servants, such as Edwin Brenn and Rawson Watts, both clerks in the secretariat, were products of the Church Missionary Society school at Mombasa.[68] The most prominent African in the inter-war period, though, was the anglophile civil servant, Martin Kayamba. The grandson of nineteenth-century Shambaa leader, Kimweri ye Nyumbai, and son of a UMCA-educated father, Kayamba was the product of 'not only the old aristocracy... but also the new elite created by early mission teaching'.[69] The most senior African employee in the colonial administration, he resided in Dar es Salaam between 1932 and 1938. Thanks to his lineage and his education, Kayamba viewed himself 'in clearly aristocratic terms'.[70] 'This was not unusual for his associates in Dar es Salaam', Anthony observes, 'most of whom shared a sense of difference from their non-Christian and less literate fellows.'

The educated elite was not solely composed of Christians. Kleist Sykes, a Railways clerk, for example, was a modernising Muslim member of the elite, who anxiously sought 'the education and enlightenment of the Swahili brethren [sic]'.[71] Nevertheless, Sykes also came from an atypical background to most Dar es Salaam residents. He was born to a Shangaan father and Nyaturu mother in Tanga Province, and became the adopted son of Effendi Plantan, the 'Zulu' leader of Dar es Salaam's former-*askari* community before WWI.[72] Other prominent Muslims were of local origin, such as Ali Saidi, a Zaramo building inspector, and Ramadhani Ali, a Zaramo trader and one-time 'King' of the town's *marini ngoma*. In 1929 Saidi and Ali, alongside fellow Muslims such as Sykes, and educated Christians such as Matola and Watts, founded the Tanganyika African Association. According to Ranger, this superseded the *marini* as an outlet for the ambitions of the urban elite by the early 1930s. However, the association was divided 'between those who favoured a territorial alliance of educated men and those who sought unity between different social strata in the capital', the split appearing to reflect tensions between local Muslims and upcountry Africans.[73]

In the mid 1930s the association was temporarily taken over by a rival organisation, the Tanganyika African Welfare and Commercial Association

---

[68] *Ibid.*, pp. 266, 407; Baker, 'Memorandum', p. 69.

[69] John Iliffe, 'The spokesman: Martin Kayamba', in *idem* (ed.), *Modern Tanzanians* (Nairobi, 1973), p. 68; see also, 'The story of Martin Kayamba', in Margery Perham (ed.), *Ten Africans*, London (1936).

[70] The quote is from Anthony, 'Culture', citing an unpublished 1968 conference paper by Iliffe on the African Association.

[71] *Samachar*, 14 September 1930, quoted in Brennan, 'Nation', p. 144.

[72] Iliffe, *Modern History*, p. 408; Daisy Sykes-Buruku, 'The Townsman: Kleist Sykes', in, Iliffe, *Modern Tanzanians*, pp. 95–114. For further background on the Muslim 'elite', see Mohamed Said, *The Life and Times of Abdulwahid Sykes (1924–1968): The untold story of the Muslim struggle against British colonialism in Tanganyika* (London, 1998).

[73] *Ibid.*; Ranger, *Dance*, pp. 94–5.

Fig. 2.2 *Newspaper photograph of Erica Fiah, Founder (and Editor) of* Kwetu *and the Tanganyika African Welfare and Commercial Association. Source:* Kwetu, 14 January 1939, p. 11

(TAWCA), which represented urban traders and the more radical civil servants. It was the creation of another prominent member of the African elite, Erica Fiah. Fiah had come to Tanganyika from Uganda during WWI, working as a clerk for various government and private organisations in the 1920s, and later becoming a shopkeeper, activist and eventually newspaper proprietor. *Kwetu*, which he owned and ran between 1937 and 1951 (though it appeared only sporadically in later years), formed an even more important outlet for the educated elite than the African Association: providing a platform for literate Africans throughout Tanganyika, but most particularly those residing in the capital, not least Fiah himself who composed its opinionated editorials. Inspired by Marcus Garvey, the self-educated Fiah viewed himself as a natural leader of the town's African population. However, despite his ambition and energy, he was poorly qualified for such a role. According to Westcott, Fiah 'kept himself somewhat aloof from Dar es Salaam's society.... As an educated Ganda he probably felt superior to the Muslims and educated Tanganyikans, and he was certainly never a very popular figure around town'.[74] While more aloof than most, Fiah's relationship with his fellow townsmen was probably representative of other educated Africans.

---

[74] Nicholas Westcott, 'An East African radical: The life of Erica Fiah', *JAH* 22 (1981), p. 87. 'People thought Fiah despised them', observed A.H. Pike (DC, Dsm, 1938–45). Handwritten notes from an interview with Pike, Guildford, 19 March 1979. I am most grateful to Nick Westcott for letting me have copies of these notes.

Controlling the town

Administrative structures to govern Dar es Salaam's heterogeneous population were erected shortly after WWI. A Township Authority was established under the Township Ordinance of 1920. In 1931 its membership consisted of the District Officer, the Senior Health Officer, a member of the Public Works Department, the Municipal Secretary, and two nominated unofficial representatives from both the European and Indian communities. The authority was responsible for the management of the whole town, and tended to be dominated by European and Indian interests at the expense of the African community. Municipal revenue was collected predominantly from European and Indian private and commercial sources. For example, in 1930, non-African land rents amounted to £3,037, municipal house tax to £5,313, and house tax to £7,767; as opposed to African land rents of £1,740, municipal house tax, £1,051, and hut and poll taxes (combined), £3,650.[75] Nevertheless, complaints were frequently made — by both officials and Africans — that the African areas did not receive a fair share of funds invested in their development (in addition to the above, revenue of £2,210 was collected in fees from traders at the Kariakoo market and municipal eating house; and a further £720 from *pombe* market fees).[76] In the late 1920s, social amenities for the African population, according to the Deputy Director of Sanitary Services, were negligible:

> there are no playgrounds worthy of the name, no public garden, no suitable cinemas, no public bath or proper bathing place, no public library, no proper bookstall for the sale of suitable literature; nothing shortly to occupy the Native's leisure time except the occasional football match on Upanga Sports Ground, cards, beer sold under very sordid conditions, and women.[77]

Even basic infrastructure was sorely lacking. The growing African suburb of Ilala — which by 1930 had a population of 1,600 — had in 1932 just one standpipe, one public toilet, and no refuse collection service, street lighting or police patrol.[78] A committee appointed in the early 1930s to make recommendations for the administrative reorganisation of Dar es Salaam had as one of its terms of reference the need 'to ensure that… [the African areas] receive adequate attention and a reasonable return for the municipal taxation paid by them'.[79] However, the reorganisation that ensued in 1934, leaving the Municipal Secretary, E.H. Helps, responsible both for the municipal administration and for African affairs in the town, only served to

[75] Baker, 'Memorandum', pp. 63–5.
[76] The revenue figures are from *ibid.*, pp. 31 and 34. For resentment towards the amount spent on African amenities, see Kironde, 'Land use', p. 203; and for 'growing resentment in the minds of some Africans', PC, EP to CS, 21 September 1939, TNA/20795/IV.
[77] Letter to CS, 18 May 1927, TNA/61/76.
[78] 1930 DAR, p. 9; Kironde, 'Land use', p. 204; for the lack of policing, see Andrew Burton, 'Brothers'; and for the resultant crime problem in Ilala, Burton, 'Wahuni', p. 94.
[79] Report of Dsm Township Adminstration Reorganisation Committee, July 1932, TNA/20795/1.

compound the neglect of the African areas, according to a later report that found 'an air of stagnation which must be rectified if all communities in the township are to progress side by side'.[80]

Alongside the Township Authority, a district administration was established whose primary responsibility was African affairs in the township.[81] The principal European official was the District Officer (later, District Commissioner). Meanwhile, the *Liwali*, an Arab, was the most senior non-European, acting as an arbitrator in most civil matters but performing no direct supervisory role. In 1921, the German administrative system of unpaid headmen was overhauled and five paid officials were installed — still called *Majumbe* — who were supervised by an *Akida*. However, establishing the authority of African intermediaries in the township was problematic, and the Native Administration was to undergo a number of changes in the inter-war period. Complications arose from the heterogeneity and sophistication of the urban population. Colonial administrators failed to identify individuals who had sufficient legitimacy among urban African communities, and at the same time were willing — and able — to carry out unpopular measures demanded of them by the District Office. Revising his 1931 social survey in 1940, Baker bemoaned the lack of assistance in the maintenance of law and order provided by town headmen, who did 'little but collect tax'.[82] The apparent laxity of the urban administration is striking — particularly so given the apparent ambitions to control African behaviour as represented by the Township Regulations.[83] These shortcomings were in part responsible for the marked antipathy that colonial officials showed towards African urbanisation. 'More supervision and control over the native population', according to one early DO, was 'very desirable'.[84]

Complementary structures aimed at administering the law among Dar es Salaam's African population also played an important part in the attempted assertion of colonial order. In the initial dispensation of judicial powers after WWI Dar es Salaam's (European) Resident Magistrate, who dealt with all criminal and civil matters involving Europeans and Asians in the town, was given jurisdiction over the more serious criminal cases in which Africans were involved (including all offences against property). It was thought advisable, however, that an indigeneous (though 'Arab') authority should be responsible for presiding over more petty offences committed by urban Africans, along with all civil disputes in which both parties were African. Accordingly, in May 1921, the *Liwali* was empowered to hold a Native Subordinate Court, with limited jurisdiction, located at the District Office (from the early 1930s, in a new court house in Kariakoo). His court played a useful role in the promotion

---

[80] 'Memo on the Administration of Dsm Township in relation to Dsm District' by DO Huggins (Huggins, Memo), 22 March 1937, pp. 4–5, TNA/61/207/1.

[81] Apart from the brief hiatus between 1934 and 1938 when Helps assumed responsibility for African affairs. For the urban administration, see Burton, 'Adjutants'.

[82] Amendments by Baker to 'Memorandum', 10 January 1940, TNA/18950/Vol. II.

[83] This is evidenced by comparing tax collection — one of the district administration's principal responsibilities — in rural and urban areas. See Burton, 'Defaulter'.

[84] 1924 DAR, p. 9.

of urban order. 'The result of the parental correction administered by the *Liwali*', commented the annual report with some satisfaction, 'has been beneficial and has had a distinct tendency to reducing the number of cases of assault and rowdiness.'[85] On its own, however, it was not considered sufficient to meet the needs of the urban African population. Much of the *Liwali*'s time was taken up with civil matters, such as marriage and divorce, and in administering Islamic law.[86] So in 1927, when new Native Courts had been proclaimed throughout the rural parts of the district in which the *Wenyemzi* (sing. *Mwenyemzi*) headmen acted as judges, the chance was taken to introduce an additional Native Court alongside that of the *Liwali*, presided over by the *Mwenyemzi* of Dar es Salaam and attended by at least three of the town *Majumbe*. Although initially successful, the *Mwenyemzi*'s court was scrapped in 1930, after which the *Liwali*'s remained the sole urban Native Court up to 1942, when two *Wakili*'s courts were introduced.[87] However, the bulk of criminal prosecutions — against Africans, Asians and Europeans alike — continued to occur in the town's Resident Magistrate's Court.

The Tanganyika Police formed the third branch of the state at the heart of the imposition and maintenance of urban order. Indeed, of all three, it was perhaps the most essential. While the colonial regime, in its administrative and judicial initiatives in Dar es Salaam, attempted to establish structures of governance that retained the broad acceptance of the African population, its success in this endeavour was in the end greatly facilitated by the background presence of an organised police force. Their legitimacy was always to some degree reliant upon the coercive potential of the colonial state, which in Dar es Salaam the police represented. In the aftermath of WWI a local police force was formed, officered by Europeans and Indians and with a large intake of former African soldiers as constables. A network of beats and patrols was elaborated that formed an important source of crime prevention. However, the police presence in the African parts of Dar es Salaam was negligible. Resources for the policing of the town were in short supply, as were those for its general administration and development. While police activity in the town resulted in the arrest of many offenders responsible for a variety of criminal acts, major and minor, it is likely that many more offences against the penal code and the municipal by-laws — the effectiveness of which depended upon the active presence of agents of enforcement — went undetected.[88] Those offenders who were apprehended were incarcerated in the town prison, prominently located close to the harbour on Main Avenue. Remand prisoners being escorted 'along the seafront manacled and ragged' to the Magistrate's Court on Azania Front formed a very public reminder of the potential consequences of transgressing colonial laws.[89]

[85]   1921 DAR, p. 5.
[86]   1923 DAR, p. 5.
[87]   Three *Wakili*, appointed in 1942, acted as intermediaries between the *Majumbe* and the *Liwali*/District Office. See Burton, 'Adjutants', for a more detailed discussion.
[88]   For the Dar es Salaam police, see Burton, 'Brothers'.
[89]   DO Davey to PC, EP, 26 August 1937, TNA/61/118/Vol. 1.

Labour in inter-war Dar es Salaam

As Tanganyika's main commercial centre, opportunities for African employment in Dar es Salaam were varied. In addition to the port and Government departments (including public works and the railways) — who were the main employers — the town contained a variety of private companies.[90] In 1930, approximately 14,000 Africans were employed in the town.[91] Around 3,000 were engaged as domestic servants by Indians and Europeans.[92] For the 2,500 casual labourers in the town, building work was an important source of employment — as it was for more skilled employees such as masons, carpenters, and painters — though it fluctuated according to the strength of the economy.[93] The Public Works Department was the largest Government employer, hiring a daily average of about 2,000. Approximately 2,000 labourers worked on sisal estates in the areas surrounding the town.[94] Most plantation workers came from further afield, as locals preferred other, better-remunerated, forms of employment. Indeed, the difficulty of obtaining labour for the plantations in the district was a perennial complaint of officials throughout the colonial period, even at times of high urban unemployment.[95] By contrast, dock work was favoured by Dar es Salaam residents. In 1931, 1,893 men were employed as labourers, boatmen and winchmen in the port. In the same year, the census identified 454 African clerks residing in Dar es Salaam, 428 *askaris* and 394 messengers (see Table 2.2).

Alongside the diverse opportunities for African employment were numerous forms of self-employment.[96] At least 600 Africans were engaged in petty trade in 1931, many of whom sold foodstuffs at the Kariakoo market. Baker found the rate of profit could be high — in respect of dried cassava, an average of 200 percent. However, the capital involved was so small (from 20 to 40 shillings) that the trader rarely made 'more than is sufficient to pay for food and clothing on a moderate scale'. Hawkers carried a variety of goods for sale from street to street: coffee, milk, *vitumbua* (rice cakes), fish (cooked and fresh), vegetables and charcoal.[97] They operated in all parts of town. Goods were taken from house to house in Zone I, where European consumers purchased items at lower prices than prevailed

---

90 A number of large import-export firms were based there, such as Smith Mackenzie and Co., the African Mercantile Company, Lehman's, Karimjee Jivanjee and Co. and Esmailjee Jivanjee and Co. Also present in the town by the late 1920s were five oil mills, five flour mills, five printing presses, four soda factories, four garages, three ginneries, two brick factories, a tannery and a salt factory close to Oyster Bay. G.F. Sayers, *Handbook of Tanganyika* (London, 1930), Appendix X; 1929 DAR.

91 These and subsequent employment figures are from the 1930 DAR, p. 24; and DO Fryer to PC, EP, 19 August 1931 reporting the results of that year's census, TNA/61/167.

92 In the 1950s, Leslie also found that Indians also employed 'quite a few relations' as servants. Interview, Berkhamstead, 7 August 1998.

93 Dsm TA mins, 18 July 1927; Dsm DAR, 1930, p. 24.

94 On the Ruvu, Alavi, Hussen, Mbagala, Msasani, Mbezi and Chikongo estates.

95 E.g. DARs, 1924, p. 17; 1922, p. 8. The same was true of sisal estates surrounding colonial Mombasa. Willis, *Mombasa*, p. 199.

96 Except where otherwise indicated, this paragraph is based on Table 2.2; and Baker, 'Memorandum', pp. 31-41.

97 There were also Indian hawkers selling sweetmeats and cheap china; and Arabs selling cheap clothing.

Table 2.2 *Occupational data from the 1931 census*

Nature of Employment	Number	Number unemployed	Literate
Clerks	454	67	454
Cooks	566	106	182
Domestic servants	2,873	260	1,009
Messengers	394	34	0
Carpenters	397	93	198
Masons	366	58	111
Painters	170	7	37
Smiths	291	35	85
Tailors	233	- 30	• 86
Electricians	47	0	6
Sailors	8	0	2
Agriculturalists	271	0	11
Traders	583	50	203
Casual labourers	2,425	0	682
Overseers	111	0	42
Rickshaw boys	146	0	32
Motor car drivers	225	64	82
Hospital dressers	71	0	33
Forest guards	2	0	2
Survey chainsmen	11	1	4
Dispensers	15	0	15
Dhow builders	2	0	1
Telegraph linesmen	34	0	6
Sanitary inspectors	20	0	20
Teachers (Koranic and school)	54	0	54
Askaris	428	0	258
Sweepers	27	0	4
Boatmen	242	40	55
Dhobis	204	40	37
Railway firemen	34	0	3
Dock labourers	1,642	450	315
Water carriers	318	0	100
Barbers	5	0	4
Fishermen	250	0	25
Winchmen	9	0	0
Night watchmen	97	0	9
Detectives	8	0	5
Bootmakers	14	0	3
Bridge builders	1	0	1
Brick makers	4	0	0
Butchers	20	0	2
No occupation	530	530	80
Soap makers	11	0	1
Builders	47	0	9
Machine men	8	0	5
Mixed occupation	35	0	11
Beggars	9	0	0
Nurses	42	0	0
Totals	**13,754**	**1,865**	**2,639**

Source: DO Fryer to PC, EP, 19 August 1931, TNA/61/167

in official markets. Pedlars of foodstuffs were to be found 'squatting along Azania Front'. They were also active in Zone II, along Main Avenue and Acacia Avenue, and in Uhindini. In Zone III, in 1932, the Medical Officer complained of the increasing number of Africans trading without a licence from their houses, estimating that at least 20 percent of 'Native houses' in the town were selling charcoal and firewood. 'After 4pm', he observed, 'Swahili Street and Msimbazi Street are covered with hawkers sitting on both sides of the streets.'[98] The poor state of the infrastructure in the African township, provided opportunities for the 318 people operating as water carriers. Carpenters produced furniture of varying quality for the urban market.[99] Meanwhile, 146 Africans worked as rickshaw 'boys', though these were being 'rapidly superceded' by taxis — in the census, 225 people gave motor car driver as their profession, though the bulk of these would have been waged employees.[100] As many as 204 African *dhobis* or laundrymen worked at the Municipal Washing Shed at Gerezani Creek — paying Shs. 12/- per month for a stand. Meanwhile, 291 smiths practised their trade in the town: tinsmiths made a living mending broken domestic utensils and through the manufacture of small tin lamps that were sold to Indian retailers at a modest profit; blacksmiths and goldsmiths were also present.[101] In addition, 271 urban residents identified themselves as agriculturalists and 250 as fishermen. Most of the cultivators living in the town farmed on private coconut plantations on the outskirts of Dar es Salaam. Use of land was allowed in return for maintaining the plantation, or in cases where fertile valley land was occupied the farmer often shared the produce with the landowner.[102] Unauthorised squatter agriculture also appears to have occurred. In 1937 as many as 133 people were found to be cultivating on Busse's *shamba*, a former German plantation near Temeke leased to an Indian businessman, without the authorisation of the lessee.[103]

For most Africans in the town, life was by no means easy.[104] A Labour Department investigation into conditions in Dar es Salaam in 1928 revealed a position that was 'distinctly disquieting'. 'The whole problem of municipal control and development and the management of urban labour', concluded that year's labour report, 'is one that presents perhaps more difficulties than any other in the country.'[105] It found 'conditions of living for the native population... far from satisfactory'. Those receiving wages at the end of the month would use a third to a half of their salary paying off debts. By the twentieth of the following month

---

[98] *TS*, 25 August 1932; extract from Monthly Sanitation Report, April 1934, TNA/450/249.

[99] According to Baker, the least proficient would have starved 'were it not for the poorer African who cannot afford to buy a well-made table but who wishes to adopt a mode of life modelled on that of the European'.

[100] Rickshaw operators and, no doubt, taxi drivers, were in fact not technically self-employed, as the vehicles they operated were owned by Indians, to whom the bulk of the profit probably went. Similarly, many hawkers sold goods as agents of Indian traders (and continue to do so in contemporary Dar es Salaam).

[101] 1919–20 DAR, TNA/1733:1, p. 69.

[102] Baker, 'Memorandum', pp. 48–9.

[103] See TNA/61/101/A/Vol. 1 and Brennan, 'Nation', pp. 62–4.

[104] Except where indicated, the following paragraphs are based on Baker, 'Memorandum', pp. 53–61; 86–90.

[105] Labour AR, 1928, pp. 18–19.

funds were exhausted, and debts were incurred once again. Many went without food for the last two or three days before receiving their salary. Pawnshops played an important part in the monthly budget — the number of shops increasing from eight in 1928 to 14 twelve years later.[106] The need to pawn arose from low wages and a high cost of living. From the early 1930s the situation was exacerbated by depression. By late 1931 40 percent of those Africans normally in work were jobless. Between January and April the number of Africans employed by the Public Works Department was reduced from 3,243 to 1,260.[107] The slump persisted through the early 1930s. In 1932, Fryer's successor, T.P.S. Dawkins, observed much unemployment in town — 'both Native and non-Native'. African employment had continued to contract and many of the jobless were eking 'a precarious existence on casual employment and the assistance of more fortunate friends'.[108] Building in the early 1930s was 'at a standstill'. It was not until 1936 that the town finally began to emerge from the downturn and a new construction boom was under way in the bazaar.[109] For those fortunate enough to have retained employment through the depression, workloads increased and wage rates declined. Government labourers, who in early 1931 received 77 cents per day, by the end of the year got just 60. Dockworkers, who were considerably better paid, also suffered a cut in wages, from Shs. 2/- to Shs. 1/50 per day.[110]

For the unskilled majority, urban life was a struggle. At prevailing rates, a casual labourer employed by a government department and fortunate enough to get six day's work per week, received just Shs. 20/- per month in 1930 and Shs. 15/60 twelve months later. Those working for private firms received between Shs. 20/80 and Shs. 22/10 monthly if they were working a six-day week in 1930. These amounted to starvation wages barely adequate to cover a single man's essentials. One of the 'cheapest budgets' Baker said he had seen was that of an unmarried man, who, before he had put aside anything for clothes (for which a monthly amount of Shs. 1/25 was required), had already spent Shs. 23/06. Baker calculated that even on the equivalent of prison rations a monthly outlay of Shs. 31/57 would be required to feed, house and clothe a man and his partner.[111] Given the severe inadequacy of wages received by African labour it is little wonder that officials harboured deep anxieties over the consequences of African

---

[106] An alternative form of pawning involved the deposit of a box of clothes with an Indian trader, who would keep the box as surety and offer the depositor credit when he required it. PC Brett to CS, 5 May 1928, TNA/61/286/1, cited in Brennan, 'Nation'; Baker's 'Memorandum' amendments, 10 January 1940, TNA/18950/Vol. II.

[107] DC Fryer expressed surprise that he had not received more complaints about this situation, taking the lack of unrest as an indication of the 'growing numbers of a labour class as opposed to agriculturalists' who 'accepted without demur the reduced wage and are only too pleased to obtain work'. Dsm DAR, 1931, p. 2.

[108] Dsm DAR, 1932, pp.1, 15.

[109] DMS to CS, 12 August 1936, TNA/23629.

[110] Although dockworkers may have received higher daily rates, demand for their labour fluctuated and the majority worked only intermittently. There was a core of 'permanent' workers on monthly or fortnightly contracts. See Iliffe, 'Dockworkers', p. 122.

[111] And these budgets were worked out at a time (1931) when prices had actually decreased over the last couple of years. How people survived remains unclear, though peri-urban farming and petty commerce appear to have played their part. See Brennan, 'Nation', pp. 63–4.

urbanisation. However, at this stage the solution did not lie in an increase in African wages, which, according to the Labour Commissioner, would only result in inflation and 'the flow of deluded victims towards the maw of the town harpy'.[112] Many officials were keen to erect controls over the movement of Africans within the territory. However, although frequently recommended, no thoroughgoing system of controlling African mobility was organised. Meanwhile, the circumstances of poorly paid workers in Dar es Salaam were neglected until the outbreak of WWII, when official attention was once again drawn to their plight.

Official insouciance towards the desperately poor living conditions suffered by most African urban residents was made possible in part by the character of the town at this stage in its development. Dar es Salaam in the inter-war period was a small urban centre, whose African population between 1919 and the late 1930s grew only negligibly. What is more, strong rural links among the urban population meant Africans working in the town were responsive to changing economic conditions and often returned to the countryside when employment was scarce.[113] In different circumstances, the low wages and high cost of living would have pressurised the colonial Government into action. As it was, a prominent characteristic of the inter-war administration of Dar es Salaam was simply neglect.[114] This partly arose from an official policy that saw the African as a rural being and that invariably located efforts to administer Africans in the countryside — the most notable expression of which was of course indirect rule.[115] It was also a consequence of the scant resources available to officials. Dar es Salaam was the capital of East Africa's 'Cinderella' territory, and compared to neighbouring Kenya, and to a lesser extent Uganda, the Tanganyika Government was poorly endowed.[116] As a result, the main agents of colonial control in the town were underfunded, and while a raft of legislation existed that was aimed at regulating the African urban population, its application was patchy. However, as we shall see in the following chapter, this neglect was not indicative of official complacency. While the small size of the town between the wars meant that social change accompanying urban growth posed little threat to the colonial administration, anxieties were frequently expressed over African urbanisation.

[112] Orde-Browne to CS, 14 March 1928, TNA/61/295/45, quoted in Brennan, 'Nation', p. 45.
[113] The most obvious examples being during and after WWI, when there was a marked deterioration in living conditions in the town (between 1914 and 1921 the urban population slumped by, according to one estimate, as much as 17,000 — see Brennan, 'Nation', pp. 22–3); and during the early 1930s (in 1931 there were 15,299 African men in the town; by 1937 this had fallen to 11,550).
[114] In line with the *laissez-faire* policies evident in much of colonial Africa in the inter-war period.
[115] For indirect rule in Tanganyika, see Iliffe, *Modern History*, pp. 318–80; Ralph Austen, 'The official mind of indirect rule', in P. Gifford and W.R. Louis (eds), *Britain and Germany in Africa: Imperial rivalry and colonial rule* (New Haven, 1967). For an insightful analysis of indirect rule in colonial Africa, see Fields, *Revival and rebellion*. And for a more recent discussion of the long-term implications of this form of government in Africa, see Mamdani, *Citizen*.
[116] In 1938 — although the population of Tanganyika was a third larger than that of Kenya, and over a half larger than Uganda's, and, in addition, was physically bigger than the two other East African colonies combined — government expenditure stood at just £2,224,000, compared to £3,649,000 for Kenya, and £2,020,000 for Uganda. Appendix III, Tables 1 and 13, Low and Smith, *East Africa*.

Three

The 'Town Native'
& Colonial Order

1919–38

The native of Dar es Salaam is innately a liar, intriguer and petty conspirator. It is difficult to find honesty of character in any direction.[1]

So, in the first annual report by a British official for the district of Dar es Salaam, written in 1920, APO West bluntly stated what he considered to be the shortcomings of the urban African population. While they may not have chosen to express it in such forthright terms, West's successors would have had some sympathy with his point of view. From the outset, African contact with the urban environment was held to result in demoralisation. In 1926, the Governor of Tanganyika, Donald Cameron, expressed a commonplace of colonial wisdom when he observed that 'the native in a town, even when employed, is exposed to many temptations and is liable to take to evil ways.'[2]

Freedom from the customary constraints of his or her rural home all too often, in the view of colonial officials, combined with the density of the urban population and the dynamism and unfamiliarity of urban life to have a disastrous impact on the native character. 'It is difficult to imagine a speedier means of debauching a whole population', wrote Orde-Browne, then Labour Commissioner, in 1927.[3]

Urban centres were the location of many evils. It was 'fatally easy for a native who finds it difficult to earn what he considers a satisfactory wage, to turn to the profits that he can readily secure from such sources as gambling, liquor and prostitution'. Even at leisure the African in Dar es Salaam was exposed to unsalutary influences. 'The amusements and relaxation provided for the African,' observed the 1924 district report, were all 'unedifying in the extreme': 'Education, mission efforts, and closer supervision and control may, it is hoped, work an improvement; but the present effect of town life on the average African is indubitably most demoralising.'[4] Meanwhile, the

[1] Dsm DAR, 1919–20, p. 3.
[2] Governor Cameron's despatch accompanying Orde-Browne, 'Labour,' in PRO/CO691/83.
[3] Labour AR, 1927, p. 51.
[4] 1924 DAR, pp. 4, 6, 10.

corrupting influence of life in Dar es Salaam was not confined to inhabitants of the town alone. Migrant workers with experience of life away from their 'tribal' homes were frequently considered a disruptive presence on their return.[5]

Africans who existed on the fringes of the urban economy and/or whose transience posed a challenge to colonial order were a particular source of official anxiety. The casual labourer intermittently engaged in employment; the newly arrived immigrant exploiting the hospitality of a town-dwelling relative; the Zaramo from the neighbouring countryside; the contract worker at the end of his contract: all were not only prey to the temptations of town life but were also beyond the supervision of the district administration. Most disturbingly they were exposed to the corrupting influence of that class of 'native' described as 'detribalised'. It was the 'detribalised native' whom officials considered to be their principal foe in their struggle to assert control; who, according to the 1926 Police report, was 'the real culprit against peace and good order'.[6] As increasing numbers of Africans had experience of town life the expansion of this group became a prime concern. Orde-Browne warned of 'the large and growing class of detribalised natives who have fallen away from African social organisation without having qualified themselves to take a place in a Europeanised community'.[7] Longland, Commissioner for Eastern Province in the late 1930s, concurred. '[S]ocial conditions in Zone III,' he informed the Chief Secretary in 1939, 'are creating a new type of African... greatly inferior to his forebears.'[8]

The large numbers of juvenile and young adult Africans attracted by the opportunities and excitements the territorial capital provided were a source of particular anxiety. Part of the problem arose from the inadequate education system within the town, consisting before WWII of just the government and the Mohamedan Schools, which although 'full to capacity' catered for only half the juvenile population.[9] Ill-discipline among urban youth was often bemoaned by officials. 'Children of school age develop an undue amount of independence,' observed Orde-Browne in 1924, 'and it is most difficult to induce the parents to deal adequately with them.'[10] The high proportion of young Africans who left their rural families to come to Dar es Salaam constituted a more serious problem. DO Fryer noticed the presence of 'many young natives between sixteen and twenty' drifting into the town, attracted as much by the novelty of urban life as freedom from familial or customary discipline. According to Fryer, they were being forced 'into contact with

[5] E.g. Kisarawe DAR, 1936, p. 1.
[6] See also, Orde-Browne, 'Labour', para. 165. Similarly, in colonial Mombasa, officials bewailed the role of 'Swahili' (read detribalised) youth as 'loafing through the days, contaminating every tribe in the country through personal example before those of its members temporarily residing in Mombasa'. 1925 Mombasa DAR. Quoted in Willis, *Mombasa*, p. 155.
[7] Orde-Browne, 'Labour', para. 114.
[8] Longland to CS, 21 September 1939, TNA/20795/Vol. II.
[9] Pike, 'Report', p. 12.
[10] 1924 DAR, p. 10.

conditions from which they suffer both physically and morally, their whole lives... often [being] affected'.[11] Baker observed that sporadic demand for their labour had a demoralising effect on African youth:

> Some of these young vagrants do a certain amount of work but they are usually only employed intermittently. A number of them are always to be seen hanging round the markets and coffee shops waiting for any job which may turn up. At night they wander the streets until a late hour and those of them who have no place in which to spend the night sleep in the open or lie on the verandahs of the houses after the owners have retired for the night. They are all of them unwilling to leave the town....[12]

The proper place for such underemployed youth, as far as officials were concerned, was back on the *shamba*. However, growing numbers of young Africans showed a marked disinclination towards agricultural work, which in part motivated the move to the town and was further strengthened as a result of time spent there.[13] A 1938 report on labour recorded dismay at the high proportion of youths who 'should properly be finding wives for themselves and cultivating land on their own behalf or working as wage-earners', but who instead tended 'to drift away from their homes to the townships, where they become loafers, without any anchorage, liabilities to the Territory rather than the assets they should be'.[14] 'In the vicinity of the more developed areas of the Territory tribal discipline has broken down in so far as these youths are concerned', the report concluded, 'and chiefs and elders found the situation beyond them'.

While young and adult males were the focus of official concern, by contrast, scant consideration was paid to African women in Dar es Salaam. Considering its apparent size, the absence of any significant consideration in the existing sources, before the 1950s, of this not insubstantial section of the urban population is remarkable. The peripheral position occupied by women in the colonial economy meant their condition only rarely scaled the urban official's agenda; an agenda that was invariably headed by the prime consideration of the control of African male labour. Indeed, the few times when administrators *were* required to address the situation of women in the town would tend to be in relation to their role in servicing this labour — as prostitutes or brewers of traditional beer, for example.[15] In such cases the main issue would not be the economic status, the wellbeing, or even simply the presence of the women concerned, but their influence on African townsmen. So, while Baker, in 1930, may have deplored the large numbers of young girls born in the township

---

[11] 1931 DAR, p. 19.

[12] 'Under-employment', observed Baker, was 'demoralising since it accustoms the casual labourer to a life half spent in idling, usually in undesirable company in the bazaar'. Baker, 'Memorandum', pp. 70, 88, 94.

[13] *Ibid.*, p. 48; G.W. Hatchell, 'Education and training of Africans,' 8 September 1945, TNA/ 450/404.

[14] 'Report of the Committee on Supply and Welfare of Native Labour in Tanganyika Territory', 1938, p. 10.

[15] See Mbilinyi, 'Unforgettable'.

joining 'the constantly growing class of unhealthy native prostitutes' among whom there was growing incidence of venereal disease, he was 'more particularly interested, however, in saving the growing young men of the District from contact with such conditions'.[16] The demoralisation of African women was regrettable; it was the impact of urbanisation on African men, though, that was the principal source of concern.[17]

African attitudes towards urbanisation[18]

Many Africans shared the European view of the urban arena as an environment in which profligacy and demoralisation abounded. In a society that remained overwhelmingly agricultural, anti-urbanism was a widely held sentiment. Among educated Africans, it was reinforced by Western antipathy towards the process of urbanisation. Such attitudes are immediately apparent in the pages of *Kwetu*. As Anthony has observed, '[a]lmost all the letters which dealt with Dar es Salaam in a typical issue of *Kwetu* viewed the city in negative terms.'[19] The town was the location for drunkenness, for foul language and disreputable behaviour, and for hooliganism and crime.[20] Eryeza Tabula, writing to *Kwetu* in 1942, portrayed the Tanganyikan capital as an unruly place in which the sensitivities of the respectable citizen were under seige:

> In the town of Dar es Salaam there are many locals who go unpunished; they are swearing at each other casually in the streets.... Many people urinate freely all over... drunks are tottering about the streets, at dawn the noise of drunkards never decreases, those sleeping are disturbed by the shouting. Moreover, time after time women are assaulted at random in the streets by *Wahuni*, but in other towns ... I haven't seen such things. Has Dar es Salaam no laws?[21]

'Town life', Robert Lukyaa had succinctly observed three years earlier, 'is deadly'.[22] A large part of the problem was seen to be the high levels of unemployment or underemployment. Repeated calls were made by 'respectable' Africans to clear the town of those without work. 'On more than one occasion,' observed Baker in 1941, 'I have been asked in *baraza* to clear ... ne'er-do-wells from Dar es Salaam lock, stock and barrel.'[23]

---

[16] Unedited 1930 PAR, in TNA/19415. This and other passages were deemed too controversial and omitted from the final report.

[17] Geiger argued that in Tanganyika 'colonial administrators experienced particular difficulties in conceptualising and therefore actually "seeing" urban African women, except when events or circumstances involving them demanded attention'. *TANU Women*, pp. 20, 22.

[18] This section is based on Burton, 'Urchins'.

[19] Anthony, 'Culture', p. 187.

[20] *Kwetu*, 8 February 1939, 13 (cited in Anthony); Francis Athman to *Kwetu*, 22 February 1940; M.F. Kassam to *Kwetu*, 13 January 1942.

[21] *Kwetu* (supplement), 8 March 1942 (original in Swahili).

[22] *Kwetu*, 3 May 1939, p. 4.

[23] Baker to CS, 12 March 1941, TNA/61/688/5.

Invariably, the prescribed fate of such 'undesirables' was to be sent to the rural areas to cultivate. This was the desired solution of H.E. Reuben, writing to *Kwetu* in 1940, who observed that 'it is out of the question for people to sit in towns doing nothing, eating the livelihood of those who have work. It is evident that people of this kind bring famine into the world.'[24]

African elders were especially concerned by the manner in which an evolving urban society undermined the deference they customarily expected as their due.[25] Officials frequently remarked upon the phenomenon. Baker noted in 1931 that parental control — 'the essence of tribal life' — had been weakened and 'in the case of many urban natives had disappeared altogether'.[26] There was in the town 'a section of the native population which is devoid of any sense of responsibility whatever ... composed of unmarried youths between the ages of fifteen and twenty-five years'.[27] More senior African residents of Dar es Salaam had lobbied Baker for a council of elders, 'to deal with matters affecting the African population and work for the creation of a consensus of public opinion by which people and especially young men might be controlled'.[28] By this time, even in the rural areas surrounding the town, Native Authorities exercised diminishing control over youth. 'There is no doubt', wrote the District Commissioner in 1936,

> that the situation of the Territory's capital within the district does act as a disturbing influence on the tribal life and organisation of the Wazaramo, particularly in the case of those Native Authorities bordering the township, and it is not uncommon to hear native elders complain of a lack of obedience among their sons who have become acquainted with the diversions and detribalised life of the township.[29]

According to Baker, the diminishing respect paid to African elders was partly a function of their conservative instincts and unresponsiveness to 'modern' influences. The youthful employee, for instance, who previously would have served an apprenticeship in his village, could become 'proficient in an occupation which his father did not understand and was unable to practice ... [and] too often tended to despise the older generation as old fashioned and unintelligent'.[30] In Dar es Salaam itself, Baker remarked, 'the younger generation considers that it is more competent to deal with present day affairs than [the elders] are and openly scoff them as inefficient and out of date'.[31] This contempt was in part associated with a Western education. L.O.I. Mbawala, a correspondent to *Kwetu* in 1942, observed: 'There is a

---

24 H.E. Reuben to *Kwetu*, 3 January 1940, in TNA/23574/Vol. II.
25 For example, the 1939 *Kwetu* editorial complaining of young trouble-makers '[n]o longer subject to the influence of their parents'. (Quoted in Anthony, 'Culture', pp. 159–60.)
26 Baker, 'Memorandum', p. 6.
27 *Ibid.*, p. 70.
28 *Ibid.*, p. 71.
29 1936 DAR, p. 1. See also the comments by G.W. Hatchell on Tanga, 8 September 1945, TNA/450/404.
30 Baker, 'Memorandum', p. 6.
31 *Ibid.*, p. 69.

rumour in this country that schoolboys are despising not only their elders but also uneducated Africans.... Our school boys are fleeing from our fathers' bomas and try to avoid any racial customs.'[32] Education and the allure of urban life were together responsible for the growing disinclination to engage in agricultural work. Baker observed 'a generation ha[d] arisen which, through lack of practise or distaste, is under the impression that it is physically unable to till the soil and considers that such an occupation is only fit for old men who have not advanced with the times.'[33]

Compared to the drudgery of rural life, Dar es Salaam represented the chance for material advance. The spectacle and excitements offered by the town also proved a powerful magnet to curious young Africans. The leisure activities available to urban residents were without parallel in the territory: cinemas showed Western, Indian, and later home-produced films to African audiences; competitive football was well established by the early 1940s; and gambling was a popular pastime among African youth. The multitude of bars and clubs (both legal and illegal) and the regular *ngoma* provided opportunity for revelry. Here the latest trends in music and dance could be enjoyed, and the latest fashions flaunted. While these aspects of urban society attracted African youth, their elders saw such distractions as responsible for and symptomatic of a degeneration in behaviour. 'Dances performed by the young men,' according to Baker, 'are in no way countenanced by the elders who thoroughly disapprove of them.' Meanwhile, Rufiji elders in the town bemoaned the influence of films on impressionable youngsters and asked that a cinema catering for an African audience be closed.[34]

All of this threatened an emerging African urban bourgeoisie. In 1931, Baker observed the presence of hooligans whose 'amusement after dark [wa]s to annoy the respectable members of the community by acts of discourtesy, assaults or petty thefts'.[35] 'Respectable' Africans also frequently bemoaned gambling in the town. In 1936, Erica Fiah complained of schoolboy gamblers.[36] Six years later, the gaming activities of *wahuni* were singled out by M.F. Kassam in the pages of *Kwetu*.[37] This was the least of their sins, however. In the course of an *ngoma* celebrating *Idd* at Mnazi Mmoja, Kassam complained that *wahuni* had assaulted women, thrown stones at the police, and stolen from 'ordinary citizens'. 'What about the elders who were empowered by the District Commissioner,' he asked, highlighting the toothlessness of African officials, 'do they not observe these disorderly events in the town?'[38] The revelry associated with *ngoma* was a frequent cause for complaint among, in Fiah's words, the 'peace loving Africans of Dar es Salaam who are taxpayers'.[39] And with dancing went drunkenness. Baker observed

---

[32] *Kwetu*, 18 September 1942, p. 3.
[33] Baker, 'Memorandum', p. 48.
[34] *Ibid.*, pp. 74; 98.
[35] *Ibid.*, p. 70.
[36] TAWCA (E. Fiah) to PC, EP, 31 March 1936, TNA/22444.
[37] *Kwetu*, 13 January 1942.
[38] Original in Swahili.
[39] The unrest associated with *ngomas* in the town led to an announcement in March 1942 proscribing them at any place other than Mnazi Mmoja. *Kwetu*, 21 August 1939, p. 12; *Tangazo* (Announcement), 5 March 1942, TNA/540/27/11.

a 'disturbing feature' of township life was the tendency of youths under 18 to patronise the *tembo* (palm wine) clubs. 'These boys', complained L.O.I. Mbawala, 'can be found chiefly in the Dancing Halls, the "Pombe" [traditional beer] clubs etc.'[40]

Undesirables and colonial urban order, 1919–41

Dar es Salaam was used by many Africans living or working in the surrounding districts of Eastern Province not only to escape parental or elders' control, but also as a refuge from husbands, private employers, the Native Authorities as well as the colonial state itself. Of the various fugitives to be found in the town, the commonest were those avoiding payment of tax.[41] Non-payment of taxes first came to the fore as an issue of concern in the late 1920s. At their conference in 1929, Senior Administrative Officers drew attention to the interconnected problems of African migrancy, mobility and evasion in Dar es Salaam. They bemoaned the great difficulties in collecting tax from 'the floating population of labourers, stevedores, motor drivers etc., who are immigrants from upcountry or from neighbouring territories'. Causing particular concern were those young jobless defaulters who drifted in from outlying districts in Eastern Province. '[F]requently', DC Fryer complained the following year, 'there have appeared before the Tax Officer fifty or a hundred natives, eighty percent of them youngsters, all without work, from Rufiji, Kilwa, Bagamoyo and Morogoro Districts, and they are all loafing round town waiting for the time when they can safely return home without being worried for tax.'[42] No solution was found to counter the apparent rootlessness of a large proportion of Dar es Salaam's population. In 1941, an amendment to the Native Tax Ordinance was passed conferring powers of arrest on tax collectors. According to the explanatory memorandum that accompanied the amendment:

> The persons whom this provision is intended to effect are those who have no settled area of residence and who are frequently unknown to local authorities. It is considered necessary that collectors should have this power to enable the tax to be collected from this class of natives who would otherwise escape with impunity.[43]

Given their difficulty in controlling this floating population, alongside the widespread antipathy towards the process of African urbanisation, officials were anxious to seek means of checking rural–urban migration. Lacking both the financial resources and sufficient knowledge of urban African society

---

[40] Baker to CS. 16 July 1941, TNA/12356/Vol. II; *Kwetu*, 18 September 1942, p. 3.
[41] It must be stressed, though, that the commonest form of migrant would have been those who came to the town in order to earn money to meet their tax requirements. For more on taxation, see Burton, 'Defaulter'.
[42] 1930 DAR, p. 8.
[43] Explanatory Memo., PRO/CO/691/181/42003.

to influence the social and cultural transformations accompanying urban growth, the principal form of control employed was over African mobility. In the inter-war period, action against Dar es Salaam's population was actually, by later standards, relatively modest.[44] However, concern over the movement of Africans into the town received a frequent airing and a range of laws were passed to this end in the 1920s. Without the capacity to enforce them, this legislation was more representative of colonial ideals than of administrative reality. Nevertheless, its existence no doubt also performed certain symbolic functions that served to dissipate European and Indian settler anxieties.[45]

One of the British administration's first actions after consolidating their hold on Dar es Salaam was a forceful assertion of spatial organisation. In the 1919–20 annual report, the unwelcome presence in the town of a residue of demobilised *askaris* and military porters was noted. The official response to the situation was instructive of how colonial officials envisaged the future of their newly conquered capital and its relationship with the remainder of the territory. During the last half of 1919 'not less than about four thousand with no right or no employment were forced out of town either to their own districts or to the country to cultivate.'[46] At the very inception of British rule certain criteria for urban residence were alluded to. Those with 'right' to remain in Dar es Salaam and those in employment were unaffected. Conversely those without 'right' (i.e. those without work who originated from outside the capital) were removed to their home districts, or to the rural parts of Dar es Salaam district itself. With the presence of such large numbers of 'alien' natives, and serious concern over the high levels of crime towards the end of and following WWI, British officials were determined to demonstrate their effective control over the urban arena.

Having removed the town's 'surplus' population, legislation aimed at controlling Dar es Salaam's African inhabitants was published in the form of the first Township Regulations. Alongside by-laws prohibiting hawking of goods and public entertainments, *ngoma* or ceremonies of mourning without permission, were others aimed at controlling African movement to the town. Section 8 stipulated that Africans were not allowed to stay longer than six days in Dar es Salaam without written permission from the DO.[47] Section 12 endowed district officials with powers to remove unwanted individuals from the town; to 'repatriate to his home or District of origin… any native whom [the DO] may consider an undesirable inhabitant or sojourner'. Neither the dramatic action taken against the former military employees in the second half of 1919, nor these regulations, exercised sufficient influence

---

[44] This was more probably a result of the limited resources available to urban officials than any disinclination on their part to tackle the surplus African population.

[45] For Namibia, see Robert J. Gordon, 'Vagrancy, law and "shadow knowledge": Internal pacification, 1915–39', in Patricia Hayes *et al.*, *Namibia Under South African Rule* (London, 1998). I would like to thank Richard Waller, who has observed the law having this symbolic function in colonial Kenya, for emphasizing this point.

[46] DAR, 1919–20.

[47] It was not strictly enforced — either through the incapacity or neglect of officials.

over the mobility of the African population. Less than two years later the District Officer, F.W. Brett, complained that

> Although thousands of military employees were repatriated or turned out of town after their demobilisation, there were apparently not satisfactory means to prevent a large number, representative of many tribes, returning to the town life to which they had become accustomed and which they prefer... A number of these people are unable to obtain *suitable* employment and others have no desire to work.[48]

The problem faced by the administration in ridding the town of undesirables was first and foremost a financial one. No vagrancy act was in force in the Territory, and while section 12 of the Township Regulations provided for orders of repatriation to be served against Africans, the cost was debited from the District Travelling votes. This, according to Brett, was beyond the means of the local administration, rendering 'such a course [i.e. repatriation] impracticable in Dar es Salaam, except in a case of extreme emergency'.

In response to such criticisms, the government introduced further legislation aimed at preventing the growth of a class of 'undesirables' emerging in the urban centres. The Destitute Persons Ordinance, enacted in early 1923, empowered police officers to arrest without warrant any person who was 'apparently destitute'. A 'destitute' was legally defined as 'any person without employment and unable to show he has visible and sufficient means of subsistence'. Magistrates could order those convicted under the ordinance to find work, to be detained for a month while work was found for them, or repatriate them to their area of origin (presumed to be in the rural areas). If offenders failed to comply with the order to return 'home', or, having complied with the order, left their district of origin without permission, they were liable to a six-month term of imprisonment or a ten pound fine, after which they would once again be required to return home. Later the same year, sections 8 and 12 of the old Township Regulations — aimed at controlling immigration to the town and removing undesirables from it — were revised and enshrined as Township Rules Section 146(1) and 146(2).

The new legislation failed to quell official concern over unrestrained African mobility. This was in part a product of its neglect. In 1924, the Commissioner of Police complained of the lack of application of either the ordinance or Township Rule 146, observing that district officials could make 'far more extensive use' of the latter in particular 'for ridding the larger townships of the horde of unemployed natives from the outside districts, who eke out a precarious existence by living on other people'.[49] The reason for this inactivity does not appear to have been a disinclination to tackle those deemed undesirable; rather it was the machinery in place to effect their repatriation, which, according to the minutes of a Senior Administrative Officers conference in 1925, was 'cumbersome and required simplification'.[50]

---

[48] 1921 DAR, p. 8 (emphasis added).
[49] 1924 Police AR, p. 58.
[50] Despatches 1925, PRO/CO/691/78.

These shortcomings were also noted by Orde-Browne in his 1926 report on labour, in which he complained that 'the present lack of control or supervision of the travelling native [wa]s leading to a serious increase in the number of vagabonds in and around all the urban centres'. Detribalised natives were in need of closer control, and he considered that 'whatever reluctance may be felt at interference with the native in his village, there can be little objection to measures of supervision over those people who leave their own surroundings in order to live under non-native conditions'. The answer was more systematic use of the existing legislation.[51] 'If the police can get a conviction and arrange with the AO concerned for the repatriation of the offender,' a central government official concurred, 'we shall shake the vagrants up'.[52]

While the decision was made to apply existing legislation with greater rigour, to many officials it was clear this was not adequate to deal with the situation. 'There are very few magistrates', Sayers, a secretariat official, observed of the Destitute Persons Ordinance, 'who would convict a native under the Order as it stands, for the reason that no native, unless he is a complete stranger, is "unable to show that he has visible means of subsistence". If he wishes to stay in town he "borrows" from those of his tribe.'[53] A further problem with the legislation was financial responsibility for the repatriation of unwanted Africans. Although officials were agreed on both the potential damage that exposure to the urban areas may have on the 'unsophisticated' African, and about the need to forestall this process through the removal of Africans who had no place in the town, there was widespread reluctance to assume financial responsibility for repatriation. Sayers used the example of his former servant, a Kenyan Kamba, to illustrate the problem. After having dismissed him for drunkenness, he had written to the District Office in Ukambani and to the Dar es Salaam police to propose 'going halves' on the cost of his repatriation. They both declined and by the time he wrote the minute 'the boy', according to Sayers, had become 'so thoroughly detribalised that he has no intention of returning to his home'. Prosecuting him as a destitute was not possible because he could 'always raise sufficient friends from his own tribesmen here to escape Police action'.[54] In Sayers' opinion, what was required 'in order to rid the town of workless natives is some enactment (a repatriation of Natives Order?) which will empower the police to apply for the repatriation of a native who has no work and has been so many weeks without it, and has no house... shamba, or other interest in the town'.

With the object perhaps of meeting such criticisms, in 1930 a new penal code further criminalised those without formal employment. Sections 166 and 167 of the revised code singled out 'idle and disorderly persons' and 'rogues and vagabonds'. The former included 'common prostitutes'; those gambling in a public place; beggars; and those likely to cause a breach of the peace. On

---

[51] Orde-Browne, 'Labour', para. 113; Labour AR, 1927, p. 8; extract from letter by Orde-Browne, 13 January 1927, TNA/3775/Vol. II.
[52] Min., 28 February 1927, TNA/3775/Vol. II.
[53] Min., 10 February 1927, TNA/3775/Vol. II. Such 'parasites' were a prominent target of Orde-Browne's ire.
[54] *Ibid.*

conviction, offenders were liable to one month's imprisonment or a fine not exceeding Shs. 40/-, or both. Persons convicted as 'idle and disorderly' for a second time became liable to prosecution as 'rogues and vagabonds'. So too were 'every suspected person or reputed thief who has no visible means of subsistence and cannot give a good account of himself'. It was a strikingly vague definition, particularly given its legal origin. The section also criminalised:

> any person found wandering in or upon or near any premises or in any road or highway or any place adjacent thereto or in any public place at such time and under such circumstances as to lead to the conclusion that such person is there for an illegal or disorderly purpose.

Upon conviction an offender was liable for a first offence to three months' imprisonment, and to one year for every subsequent offence. While this new legislation perhaps made the conviction of 'undesirables' more straightforward, it in no way facilitated their removal, and throughout the colonial period prosecution of individuals under these sections of the penal code was rare.

Officials responsible for the administration of Dar es Salaam and other urban centres entered the 1930s with the machinery to tackle the perceived menace of rural–urban migration substantially unchanged; it was limited mainly to use of the Destitute Persons Ordinance and Township Rule 136(2) (in the new penal code section 146 became 136). With the onset of the depression in the early 1930s, the efficacy of this legislation was severely tested, as it was used to deal with the growing problem of urban unemployment. In 1931, the number of repatriations under Township Rule 136(2) was 'considerably in excess of normal years'.[55] A July census had discovered 1,876 Africans without work in the town, of whom 530 were 'alien natives who had never been employed at any time'.[56] The following month the Provincial Commissioner (and former DO), F.W. Brett, stated his intention to 'clear the town of certain natives who are known to be unemployed and of undesirable character, but who may not come within the definition of a "destitute person"'.[57] These included all 530 of the unoccupied 'alien natives'. As ever, there were financial problems associated with their removal. The treasurer recommended that Brett be authorised to incur the not inconsiderable expenditure arising from repatriation against the existing votes. It was anticipated that this may not be sufficient, however, and that he would have to apply for a further allocation of funds. Maintaining an orderly town was an expensive business. 'Repatriation', Brett informed the Chief Secretary the following year, 'is not as simple as it may seem.'[58] Indeed, as a secretariat official observed in a 1933 minute, while the Destitute Persons Ordinance and Rule 136(2) made adequate legal provision for the repatriation of undesirables 'the question of financial provision' was another matter. Such considerations had 'often deterred DOs' from enforcing these laws.[59] Although urban administrators, painfully conscious of the perceived threat to colonial

---

55 Dsm DAR, 1931, p. 20.
56 Min., 22 August 1931, TNA/21616/Vol. 1.
57 PC Brett to Treasurer, Dsm, 11 August 1931, TNA/21616/Vol. 1.
58 PC to CS, 14 May 1932, TNA/18950/Vol. 1.
59 Min. by W.D.E.A., 14 June 1933, TNA/21616/Vol. 1.

order posed by a growing jobless class, were keen to remove this section of the population, their arguments do not appear to have always prevailed among fiscally sensitive officials at the cash-strapped secretariat.[60] As the Depression eased in the mid 1930s, and job opportunities once again began to increase, the numbers of urban undesirables began to diminish to the manageable levels of the previous decade. The low rates of migration experienced by the territorial capital at this time, coupled with a recovering urban economy, relieved administrative pressures arising from the high unemployment levels prevalent at the height of the Depression. This respite was brief, however. The experience of the Depression was simply a foretaste of what was to come. As African urbanisation accelerated from the late 1930s, and unemployment re-emerged, officials made increasing use of the legislation targeting the urban *residuum* that had, up till then, been largely neglected.

In the inter-war period, enacted legislation was representative more of official *angst* than any substantive pressures complicating the administration of the town. Situated at the cutting edge of transformations accompanying colonial rule, Dar es Salaam formed a focus of great concern among officials, settlers and Africans. The urban arena seemed to crystallise anxieties arising from social, cultural and economic change. These included shifts in gender and generational relations. Such anxieties could inform colonial representations in surprising ways. Andrew Ivaska notes how in the Bantu Educational Kinema Experiment film, *Gumu*, made in the mid 1930s, scriptwriters 'managed to gender th[e] moral geography... [of Tanganyika] in a way that ran counter to demographic and political economic realities':

> [D]espite the fact that small-scale agricultural labor was overwhelmingly performed by women, and that large towns were disproportionately male, the film portrayed the town as a feminine trap of decadence and consumption from which the male hero flees to a hardy, healthy and prosperous future working the land.[61]

A corresponding dichotomy identified the town as a youthful space where deference to elders and betters was once again under threat; and rural areas as the repository of gerontocratic harmony and order.[62] In the inter-war period, it was the (mostly young and urban) 'detribalised native' above all who was identified as the prime colonial bogeyman. An individual both too exposed to, and yet insufficiently influenced by, the new order, occupying a dark space in both the colonial mind and the African township. While the British attempted to effect a reorganisation of African society in Tanganyika, the urban centres were arenas in which, as far as they were concerned, old orders unravelled and no adequate alternative orders arose to take their place.

---

[60] See, for example, the denial of a request for funds to repatriate 93 jobless Africans from Tanga, Tanganyika's second town. *Ibid.*

[61] Andrew Ivaska, 'Imagining Dar es Salaam: Culture, morality and urban space in representations of a capital city,' paper given at the conference 'Dar es Salaam in the 20 century: Urbanisation and social change in an emerging East African metropolis', UDsm, 1 July 2002.

[62] See e.g. Baker, 'Memorandum', pp. 69–70, 80–1; Burton, 'Urchins'.

Four

'The Problem of the Urban African'

Accelerating Urbanization & the Colonial Response 1938–47

From the late 1930s a shift in attitude took place among Tanganyikan officials towards the African urban population, one that corresponded with changes occurring in British colonies throughout East and Central Africa. While concern over the demoralising effects of town life was still expressed, many officials recognised that a permanent African community in Dar es Salaam, which in the future was likely to grow substantially, was an established fact. Increasingly, the 'problem of the urban African'[1] was couched in socio-economic instead of moral terms. At the same time, it was recognised that new initiatives were required in order to achieve the proper development of the emerging urban African community. A number of factors led to this reappraisal of policy. From the late 1930s there was a surge in the growth rate of Dar es Salaam's African population. Second, the prospect of a fully urbanised African community, whose links with their rural homes had been severed, was no longer perceived to be such a cause for alarm (as long as it was guided down proper channels). This was partly a reflection of the new African policy emerging from Whitehall, in which indirect rule by chiefs was to give way to representative local government involving educated Africans.[2] The focus shifted from the preservation of traditional loyalties to the creation of a new, purportedly more democratic, set of values, which if anything stood more chance of being inculcated by urban than by rural Africans. Finally, there was growing official awareness of the poor living and working conditions suffered by the majority of Africans in the town. Although changing attitudes towards urbanisation were apparent in official correspondence and reports from the early 1940s, however, it was not until 1947 — when the urban and territorial economies were at last rebounding — that the shift in the colonial mindset actually began to be expressed in concrete form as implemented policies.

---

[1] As phrased by A.H. Pike, 'Development of the African Areas of Dar es Salaam Township', 12 July 1944 [hereafter, 'Development'], TNA/61/643/3.

[2] See R.D. Pearce, *Turning Point in Africa* (London, 1982), for a useful discussion.

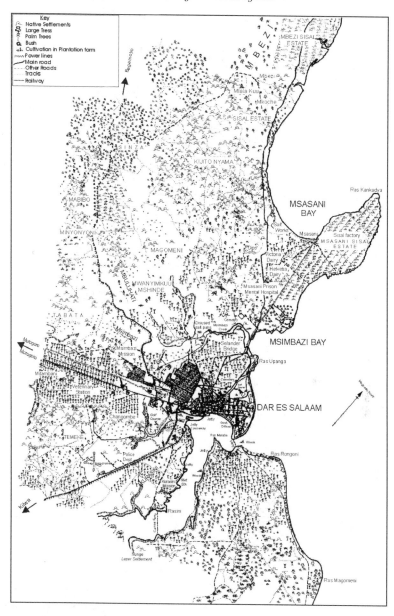

Map 4.1 *Dar es Salaam and environs, 1944*
Source: Based on Dar es Salaam coastal strip map at the Public Records Office

Rapid urban growth

While the first two decades of British rule had seen the comparatively modest growth of the African community in Dar es Salaam from approximately 20,000 to 33,000, the final decades of colonial rule saw a significant expansion of the capital's African population. Over a little more than twenty years it expanded almost four times over. The heightened rates of urban growth first became apparent shortly before WWII. In the early to mid 1930s the capital's African population had actually contracted slightly. By the end of the decade, however, migration from the rural areas into the town was occurring on a previously unprecedented scale, and was set to increase still further with the onset of war. In the six years up to 1944 Dar es Salaam's African population increased by more than 50 per cent, from 26,000 to approximately 40,000, and District Officer Pike anticipated (correctly) that there was 'every prospect that this increase will continue in an ever growing stream after the war'.[3] By 1950 the urban population had expanded to around 60,000.

This influx occurred at a time when living conditions in the town were actually deteriorating. However, Africans continued to enter the town undeterred. Such movement seems hard to account for. Why should people move from rural areas, where both food and accommodation were apparently more easily accessible, to the town, where inflation was resulting in the increasing impoverishment of both wage-earners and the unwaged alike? The relative freedom of town life was probably part of the attraction, as was, no doubt, the glamour of the capital: its modernity, variety and the fast pace of life there. It is unlikely, however, that these aspects played as large a role in immigration to the towns as contemporary officials ascribed to them.[4] As Sabot observes, '[f]or some rural residents the traditional family structure prevailing in the rural areas may be oppressive, while for others it may be a source of support which is left only with reluctance.'[5] Modern economists, in discussing the great post-war drift to African cities, have tended to stress the economic rationality of such internal migration.[6] While unemployment was a common feature of urban life, the opportunities available in the towns nevertheless outweighed those available in the underdeveloped rural areas. Even if waged employment was not secured on arrival in the town, either the risk of benefiting in the long term from formal sector employment made the move worthwhile or informal sector activities provided a subsistence at least equivalent to that enjoyed by many in the countryside.[7]

3   Pike, 'Development'.

4   E.g. Governor's Deputy to SSCol, 12 February 1945, TNA/28685, in which he observes that it is 'the excitements of town life and the attractions of living in a crowd that make the chief appeal… to the gregarious African'.

5   R.H. Sabot, *Economic development and urban migration: Tanzania 1900–1971* (London, 1978), p. 16.

6   See *ibid.*; or, for the Kenyan case, J. Harris and M. Todaro, 'Urban unemployment in East Africa: An economic analysis of policy alternatives', *East African Economic Review* 4 (1968), pp. 17–36; and for sub-Saharan Africa, Josef Gugler, 'On the theory of rural–urban migration: The case of Subsaharan Africa', *Migration* (1969), pp. 134–55.

7   Anthony O'Connor cautions against applying too rigid a distinction between 'pull' and 'push' factors behind rural–urban migration: it is the 'differential, or perceived differential', between the town and countryside that matters. *The African City* (London, 1983), p. 74

In the case of Dar es Salaam, its rapid growth in the 1940s can be accounted for by a mixture of poor conditions in the rural areas along with the opportunities present in the urban environment to get by through informal economic activity, *as well as* the possibility of obtaining waged employment, albeit at reduced rates.

According to Westcott, towns in 1940s Tanganyika offered 'an escape from rural oppression for both men and women' evading efforts by Native Authorities to increase crop production, alongside labour conscription on the sisal estates. Many women and young Africans coming to Dar es Salaam were no doubt motivated by the desire to escape the control of husbands and elders. Moreover, food and commodities, while still scarce, were more widely available in the town.[8] In Dar es Salaam's immediate hinterland conditions in the early 1940s were poor indeed. In 1941, out of 1,700 recruits considered for the army in rural Uzaramo, just 267 were considered fit enough for military service — and of these 163 had to be treated before being accepted. The remainder suffered from a variety of diseases, including hookworm, bilharzia, yaws, hernias and pulmonary disease.[9] The fact that wages in Uzaramo were 25 percent lower than in the township (where opportunities for employment were more plentiful) also encouraged migration.[10] Former DO, A.H. Pike, recalled the early 1940s influx occurred as people were aware of the money-making opportunities arising from wartime conditions, with ships passing through the port on a regular basis and an RAF presence in the town.[11] The increased mobility of the African population of Tanganyika at this time was an additional factor. A huge increase in railway passengers occurred during and after the war, the numbers rising from 470,000 in 1939 to nearly 2,000,000 ten years later. Bus services also became increasingly common.[12] Rufiji migrants, for example, who before WWII faced a two to three day march on foot, from the 1940s had access to motor transport plying the new road to Utete.[13] In Tanganyika, as elsewhere in the region, '[t]he upsurge in rural–urban migration around 1940 might also be viewed as evidence of the deepening penetration of the cash nexus in African societies, and the corresponding need for growing numbers to find waged employment'.[14]

While the move to the town might have made sense to the incoming African, to colonial officials the extent of rural–urban migration was both

[8] Westcott, 'Impact', p. 285; Nicholas Westcott, 'The impact of the Second World War on Tanganyika, 1939–49', p. 147, in David Killingray and Richard Rathbone (eds), *Africa and the Second World War* (New York, 1986).

[9] 1941 Temeke DAR, TNA/61/3/XVI/I/17, cited in Brennan, 'Nation', p. 236.

[10] Engineer, DPW to DC Uzaramo, 25 September 1944, TNA/540/27/21/13, cited in *ibid.*

[11] Notes on interview with A.H. Pike by Nicholas Westcott, 3 November 1978.

[12] Westcott, 'Impact', p. 285. A diverse range of other, more personal, factors no doubt encouraged migration, but these have left little or no trace in the documentary record. In Tanzania, as elsewhere in East Africa, *historical* analysis of rural–urban migration remains neglected and the phenomenon poorly understood. For rare case studies from Kenya and Ethiopia, see Willis, *Mombasa*; and Shimelis Bonsa, 'A history of Kistane migration to 1974', in Burton, *Urban Experience*, pp. 172–86.

[13] Matthew Lockwood, *Fertility and Household Labour in Tanzania: Demography, economy and society in Rufiji District, c.1870–1986* (Oxford, 1998), p. 76.

[14] Burton, 'Urbanisation', p. 21.

incomprehensible and deeply inconvenient. Accelerated immigration put the town's administrators under pressure by placing increasing strain on an already inadequate urban infrastructure; by adding to a growing class of the unemployed, and, as a consequence, by forcing down wages; and by adding to concerns about public order. To officials who already envisaged an African's natural place as being in the countryside, growing rural–urban movement, at a time when urban living conditions were so poor, simply provided further evidence of 'native' irrationality.

Colonial urban policy

Despite exasperation at spiralling migration rates, there was at this time a growing awareness of the permanence of African urban communities and a new sense of urgency to devise a policy to cope with this phenomenon. Prompted by Lord Hailey, Tanganyikan administrators came to realise that 'the urban centres have an importance which has not been fully appreciated by African Administrations'.[15] According to the 1944 report of the Township Development Sub-committee '(t)he whole question of African development in urban communities merit[ed] the closest investigation on the part of Government.' Members of the committee could 'find no record that any considered Government policy in regard of urban Africans has either been propounded or implemented and we recommend that this defect be remedied at a very early date'.[16]

At a time when indirect rule was being abandoned, officials became more sanguine about the dangers of urbanisation in general, and of 'detribalisation' in particular. By the end of the decade attitudes had moved on so far on this score that in 1948 it was pointed out that '(i)n the long run it will probably be accepted that tribalism has a retarding effect on the progress of the African community… and hence the long-term effect of detribalisation cannot be regarded as detrimental'.[17] It was essential, however, that a new set of values emerged to take the place of customary rights and responsibilities. At the end of the war the problems of the towns *and* their inhabitants were seen as being at least in part attributable to administrative neglect between the wars. In Dar es Salaam this neglect was evident not only in the lack of physical 'development' in Zone III but also in the failure to foster among town-dwelling Africans a respectable urban identity to replace their former 'tribal' ones. According to DO Pike,

> (t)he one feature that is predominant in all past schemes in dealing with the urban African is that they have failed and instead of people with some degree of civic consciousness, everywhere one finds the African urban populations steeped in poverty, crime and filth with all the selfishness of town 'stiffs'.[18]

[15]   *African Survey*, quoted in Pike, 'Development'.
[16]   Report of the Township Development Sub-committee, 29 August 1944, TNA/61/643/3.
[17]   Memo on the Effects of Detribalisation dated 2 April 1948, TNA/37520.
[18]   Pike, 'Development'.

What post-war officials should be aiming for was 'to make the urban African a better citizen with a civic conscience'. This would be achieved by devoting more resources to the African community and its area of residence, and in encouraging greater African participation in township affairs. It was hoped an enhanced role for urban elders and educated Africans would reinvigorate an administrative set-up that not only proved 'insufficient outlet for the intelligentsia in the management of affairs' but 'also insufficient discipline for the less sophisticated elements in the population'.[19] A key target of revised policy was the young Africans who were making their way to the urban areas in growing numbers. '[C]haracter training in the schools and supervision after the boys have left school', observed one official immediately after the war, 'have been inadequate in the past and... we have been inclined to overlook the fact that training in the African home is inadequate to meet modern conditions.' To counter the 'ill discipline' of township youth he recommended 'some modification in our present system of training which will place more emphasis on turning the young African into a good citizen with a sense of responsibility and a sense of duty towards himself and towards his neighbour'.[20]

The reappraisal in urban policy was in part influenced by anxieties over the return of demobilised soldiers, among whom, it was anticipated, many would be impatient of life in their rural districts of origin, opting instead to remain in Dar es Salaam. There was going to be, according to a secretariat minute, 'a much larger proportion than hitherto of sophisticated and travelled natives who have seen the world and are likely to be restless and discontented with their conditions, and contemptuous of tribal discipline'.[21] 'Demobilised Africans', predicted Pike, 'will flock to the towns as the only places where can be found the money, the food, the pleasures and not least the comradeship to which army life has accustomed them.'[22] According to Pike, a high proportion of conscripts were 'town roughs'. 'These men', he observed,

> will have learnt discipline and how to work; they will also have gained experience of life. If we can place them in work, they may settle down; if they fail to find work, they will revert to being 'town roughs' — with such additional experience in 'roughness' as will make them a serious problem.[23]

As early as 1942 Baker reported concern on the part of the Governor that measures be put in place to deal with ex-soldiers settling in Dar es Salaam as they otherwise would 'be liable to lead a profitless existence in the town if left to their own devices'.[24]

[19] 1945 PAR, p. 31. See Burton, 'Townsmen'.
[20] G.W. Hatchell, Education and training of Africans, 8 September 1945, TNA/450/404.
[21] Min. by W.E.J. to CS, 7 May 1943, TNA/61/702/3.
[22] DO Pike to the Secretary of the Township Development Sub-committee, 11 September 1944, TNA/61/643/3.
[23] DO Pike to PC, EP, 24 August 1944, TNA/61/686/16.
[24] PC Baker to CS, 16 July 1942, TNA/61/443/1.

Conditions in Dar es Salaam Township

While both accelerated urban growth and wider shifts in colonial thinking had an impact on policy, conditions in the town itself were at the core of new debates over urban policy. Infrastructure in the African township was hopelessly inadequate. This was a direct result of lack of investment. The racially skewed distribution of resources attracted criticism from both Africans and more sympathetic officials. Pike observed in his 1939 report that 'the African on the whole thinks that he gets very little [in return for the revenue collected from Africans] and to substantiate his view it must be admitted there is very little to show for it.'[25]

District officials attributed the neglect suffered by African residential areas to the Township Authority. The relationship between the Provincial Administration and municipal officials was a tense one throughout the colonial period. The differing backgrounds and responsibilities of the two sets of officials led to very different perceptions of how best to administer the town. This was compounded by their position as representatives of distinct communities whose interests often did not coincide. So, while the DC — who was answerable to a Department of Native Affairs that was responsible for the indigeneous population of the Territory — was anxious to promote the welfare of the town's African inhabitants and to encourage orderliness and good behaviour among this community, the Municipal Secretary — answerable to a town council that included no African representative until 1941[26] — tended to be swayed by the demands of the wealthier and more influential, if less populous, European and Indian communities. In addition, the professional background of municipal officials often proved an obstacle to understanding the needs and wants of an urban African community. The town's first Municipal Secretary, E.H. Helps, came from a career in local government in South Africa, where the presence of a large, and relatively affluent, white community, played a determining role in setting the urban agenda. During his tenure, from 1930 to the mid 1940s, Helps' lack of insight into conditions in the African quarter was frequently bemoaned by both district and central government officials.[27] Later municipal officials who had a largely *English* background, were, according to E.G. Rowe, Provincial Commissioner for Eastern Province in the mid 1950s, 'used to a very different environment indeed and had little opportunity to see things through the eyes of Africans or of people who were engaged in African administration professionally'.[28] This tension between district and municipal

[25] Pike, 'Report', p. 28.
[26] In October 1940 the Township Authority consisted of: Helps; DO Pike; the Medical Officer, the Assistant Engineer and the Senior Surveyor; Dr Malik, an Asian community leader; and Messrs Robertson, Patel and Gooch, managers (respectively) of the African Mercantile Co., Mathuradas Kalidas Co. and the Electric Light Co. Min. by Whitlam-Smith, 4 October 1940, TNA/20795/Vol. IV.
[27] E.g. mins by Whitlam Smith dated 13 October 1939, TNA/20795/Vol. IV. However, the lack of attention paid to the African township did not start with Helps' stewardship; it was neglected throughout the inter-war period, for which the District Office also held responsibility.
[28] 'Interview with E.G. Rowe on service in Tanganyika 1928–58', p. 39, RH/Mss.Afr.s 1698; see also Harris (*Donkey's Gratitude*, p. 285), who observes the Municipal Council's 'expatriate officers tended to put African housing problems firmly on the back burner'.

government was at its peak in the late 1930s and early 1940s when, partly thanks to the shortcomings of municipal government in the inter-war period, the re-evaluation of urban policy was taking place. By 1939 the situation in the African township was perceived by both provincial and central government administrators to be very serious indeed. Whitlam Smith, a secretariat official, observed in 1940 that members of the Township Authority 'clearly consider that there is little wrong with the administration in the native areas, and that the latter have been receiving a fair share of their attention and funds'. However, this was

an opinion which those who walk about the town and compare the trim condition of the botanical gardens and the well-to-do residential quarter with the ill-lit, unkempt and uncared for condition of the back streets (which of course are the great majority) of the native part of town will not share.[29]

Although Africans constituted approximately three-quarters of the urban population, and in a normal year contributed £9,000 in direct revenue to Government, just £4,331 out of a total District Office expenditure of £18,245 was spent in Zone III in 1939.[30] The breakdown for the maintenance of roads was £500 out of a total of £2,540; it was £600 out of £2,495 for electricity supplied for street lighting; a measly £140 out of £2,500 for the maintenance and running of water supply stations; and £130 out of £1,095 for general sanitation. Moreover, the full cost of the maintenance of the 'Open Space' — established to serve as a sanitary buffer between the African township and the European and Indian quarters — came out of the Zone III budget, and the only other heading under which the total expenditure was charged to the African areas was the payment of Tax Clerks. Roads in the African township were unsurfaced — just 4.5 miles of road were made up, the remaining 23.3 miles being generally impassable; and poorly lit — there were just 24 street lights on the 27.8 miles of road.[31] Rates of water usage among Africans indicate the negligible provision of piped water in Zone III in contrast to that provided to other communities. Between 1933 and 1938 Africans consumed 0.68 to 0.88 gallons per day per capita, Indians between 7.5 and 14.5, and Europeans 31 to 43 gallons per day.[32] One official commented:

The problem of Dar es Salaam township can be stated simply. It has been governed for years by gentlemen the interests of the majority of whom have been confined exclusively to the non-native commercial and residential areas, with the result that the native areas have been sadly neglected.[33]

This neglect was particularly evident in the poor quality and limited supply of urban housing. Construction of housing had been left almost entirely up

[29] Min., 4 October 1940, TNA/20795/Vol. IV.
[30] 'Proposals for the re-organisation of Dsm Township and District' (Baker, 'Proposals'), Appendix II, 3 July 1940, TNA/20795.
[31] List by Pike, 21 April 1940, TNA/61/207/Vol. III.
[32] ARs of the Public Works Dept. Cited in Kironde, 'Land use', p. 200.
[33] Min., 20 December 1940, TNA/26602; for the racially skewed administration of public services in Nairobi, see the chapters by Achola and Anderson, in Burton, *Urban Experience*.

to Africans themselves between the wars, and even with the accommodation crisis that emerged in the course of WWII it was not until 1947 that Government began to ameliorate the situation by initiating building projects.[34] By the early 1940s, the high demand for, and the limited supply of, housing was leading to ever higher rents, which, along with the poor wages paid to workers, resulted in a growing problem of homelessness. It was, according to Molohan, 'a common sight for natives to be seen sleeping out at night in public places and buildings or on verandahs of private houses simply because they are unable to pay for a night's lodging'.[35] Even for those with accommodation the position was deteriorating. While the population increased between 1939 and 1943 by about a third, the number of African houses in the town actually shrank from 3,155 to 3,123.[36] The approximate density of population rose by 50 percent from 10 to 15 persons per house, and 'slum conditions' were accentuated.[37] Four years later more than two-thirds of the houses in the African township contravened the overcrowding rules.[38] Indians moving into those areas of Zone III closest to Uhindini further exacerbated the housing shortage. At the end of the decade the Provincial Commissioner reported, 'areas which before the war were considered African are now almost entirely Asian'.[39] By the late 1940s unauthorised shanties had arisen; notably at Makaburi, where in 1948 2,500 people were living in basic huts on the outskirts of town.[40]

Lack of development in the African township complicated urban governance, leading to disillusionment among the African 'elite', and to conditions that had the potential to promote unrest among the poor. Longland, in 1939, stated he was 'conscious of a growing resentment in the minds of some Africans... concerning the administration of the native quarter of the town'. 'It is openly said', he reported, 'that Zone III receives little attention and the rest of the Township much in the way of public works and amenities', and this was a result of the fact 'that native representation on the Township Authority is insufficient so that the lack of amenities are not brought to notice'.[41] Africans were at this time beginning to demand a greater role in

---

34   The need for government to intervene was recognised as early as 1942, but no progress was made in various schemes before 1946. Helps, January 1942, TNA/33024; Township Development Sub-Committee Mins in TNA/33024 and TNA/61/643/3; Jackson to SSCol, 27 Nov 1943, TNA/31751. See also Brennan, 'Nation', p. 189; and for a discussion of shifting attitudes towards African urban housing in the 1940s, Kironde, 'Land use', pp. 248–52.

35   Report on Unemployment and Wage Rates in Dsm by DO Molohan, 27 September 1941, TNA/61/443/1 [Molohan, 'Unemployment'], p. 4.

36   Baker's amendments to his 1931 'Memorandum', 10 January 1940, TNA/18950/Vol. II; Memo by DC Pike to DO Molohan, 22 July 1943, TNA/24387.

37   *TS*, 7 August 1943.

38   Iliffe, *Modern History*, p. 372.

39   PAR for 1950, p. 41. See Brennan, 'Nation', pp. 54–7 and 188–96, for a discussion of Indian incursions into Zone III and the repercussions.

40   DC Bone to MS, 24 July 1946, TNA/540/27/1; Development Organisation AR for 1950, p. 17; Sofers' report on a possible survey of Dsm, 1951, TNA/18950/Vol. III; Mascarenhas, 'Urban development', p. 105. According to the Sofers, 'the need for manpower' was at this time 'more important than the adequacy of the conditions under which they were accommodated'.

41   PC, EP to CS, 21 September 1939, TNA/20795/Vol. IV; see also, Baker, 'Proposals'.

township affairs. In a letter to *Kwetu* in 1940, Francis Athman requested that local African officials be given increased powers 'to order and to fix the town'. 'Dar es Salaam', he complained, 'is the dirtiest of all the towns in Tanganyika.'[42] Others expressed their desire for African representation on the Township Authority.[43] This was granted, with a single representative (alongside the Liwali) being appointed from 1941, but it did little to diminish African discontent. By the war's end the District Commissioner reported that 'murmurings from Kariakoo and Ilala are becoming increasingly audible on such subjects as the housing shortage, bad roads, inadequate street lighting, insufficient police protection, [and] unsatisfactory medical facilities.'[44] Pike concurred with this analysis. In his memo on the development of Dar es Salaam the previous year he had described Zone III as 'the Cinderella of the township'. 'The two elder sisters, the European and Asian sections, get everything possible', he complained, 'while the African section gets only the minimum to keep it going.' 'In twenty five years', Pike observed, 'we have nothing to show and cannot have any pride in our past record.' 'The local Africans are becoming increasingly vocal and increasingly antagonistic to the apathy with which they feel Government treats their problems.'[45]

Urban wages, inflation and official intervention

The low rates of pay received by the bulk of the urban African population were an even more important contributory factor to the harsh living conditions prevalent in the township. In 1939, Pike calculated that a majority of employees were paid 'sub-marginal' wages. Conditions actually deteriorated over the next few years. While the cost of living rose steeply in the early 1940s, wages remained at the same low level, becoming, in the words of one Labour Officer, 'more sub-marginal than ever'.[46] Unskilled wage rates in Dar es Salaam had actually fallen since the Depression, and prices had risen. In 1938, there were cases of labourers being paid as little as Shs. 8/- for thirty ten-hour days, when in Dar es Salaam Shs. 10/- was considered the barest minimum.[47] As the effects of the war began to impact upon the colonial economy, inflation further exacerbated the position. A 1942 enquiry found that '87 per cent of Government employees in Dar es Salaam are in receipt of a wage on which they cannot possibly subsist without getting into debt and remaining in debt.'[48] While wages were (just) sufficient for a bachelor, expenditure exceeded incomes by at least Shs. 7/97 each month for a married man without children, and Shs. 14/85 for a man with a family (only 317 out

---

[42] *Kwetu*, 22 February 1940, p. 6. Original in Swahili.
[43] Baker, 'Proposals'.
[44] Uzaramo DAR, 1945, p. 12, TNA/61/504/1.
[45] Development Memo, 1944.
[46] Pike, 'Report', p. 9; Molohan, 'Unemployment', p. 4.
[47] Iliffe, *Modern History*, p. 353; Ag. DO to PC, EP, 31 October 1938, TNA/25912.
[48] 'Report of enquiry into wages and cost of living of low grade African government employees in Dar es Salaam' ('Report... into wages'), September 1942, p. 7, TNA/30598.

of the 2,901 surveyed were found not to be married, or living with a woman). 'It is certain', observed the author of the report,

> that any supplementary sources of income which the employee may have are inconsiderable and generally insufficient to bridge the gap between income and expenditure. At the end of the month the employee has to pawn his clothes and the vicious circle of interest on pawnbroker's tickets commences again.

Sixty percent of government employees were found to be in debt to the extent of a month's salary or more. Private sector employees were, on the whole, even worse off, earning on average less than half that received by government workers — Shs. 12/50–Shs. 15/- per month compared to the Shs. 29/50–Shs. 33/50 earned by an unskilled government employee. '[B]ecause of a lack of proper food', the report concluded, 'a considerable portion of the population of Dar es Salaam are becoming unemployable.' The inadequate diet was felt to be contributing to the high mortality rate prevalent in the town.[49] The poor health of the urban population was dramatically uncovered in 1939, when just ten percent of men volunteering for the army were found to be healthy enough for service.[50] African discontent at the situation was expressed in the columns of *Kwetu*. 'Our chief lamentation today is Pay', a correspondent observed in 1942, 'every corner, official and unofficial, skilled and unskilled, office and field, house and kitchen, grumble for better pay.'[51] The tendency of wage rates, however, was to continue to lag behind inflation.[52]

As we have seen, the low pay received by Africans between the wars had long resulted in poor living conditions prevailing in the township. No attempt had been made to improve the situation. When poor wages and the high urban cost of living once more attracted official attention in the late 1930s, however, circumstances this time demanded an official response. Accelerating urbanisation and the incremental acknowledgment of long-term African urban residence in part necessitated this. In the wake of strikes by Dar es Salaam and Tanga dockworkers in 1939, there was also a growing awareness of the potential for unrest posed by a large impoverished urban population — concerns that were heightened in the wartime context. A living wage, as Pike observed in July 1940, was not merely an economic necessity but also politically expedient.[53] The administration responded by implementing a series of initiatives designed to ameliorate the lot of the urban African. After protracted exchanges over the cost and advisability of increasing government

49   *Ibid.*, and min. by the AG, 17 November 1942, TNA/30598.
50   Director of Manpower to CS, 11 December 1939, TNA/27427, cited in Brennan, 'Nation', p. 171. This trend continued throughout the war, with the overwhelming majority of men from Dar es Salaam checked for military service or plantation work (for which health requirements were lower) deemed not fit to perform either.
51   *Kwetu*, 6 December 1942, cited in Iliffe, 'Dockworkers', p. 128.
52   It was not until after the general strike of 1947 that this trend was reversed, when the 40–50% wage rise received by the dockworkers produced increases of a third or more in other sectors. Iliffe, *Modern History*, p. 404.
53   Min. dated 8 July 1940, TNA/28594. I am most grateful to Nicholas Westcott for giving me copies of his notes to this file.

pay,[54] the daily rate of unskilled employees of government departments in Dar es Salaam and Tanga was raised from sixty to eighty cents per day in October 1940.[55]

Increasing government wage rates remained only a partial solution, however. It was entirely at the discretion of private employers to decide whether they should follow suit. According to the 1942 cost of living enquiry, only a few did so, the small employer being only 'too glad to take advantage of the glut of labour offering and so to avoid any necessity for adding to his wage bill'.[56] Moreover, wartime shortages were resulting in higher prices.[57] In 1941, Government intervened by establishing the Economic Control Board, motivated by the official desire to curb inflation.[58] In the rural areas this was necessary in order to stop producers profiting from rising crop prices and thereby being disincentivised to intensify shamba cultivation or to seek waged employment. By contrast, in the towns officials were keen to prevent unrest among urban communities that might accompany further increases in the price of basic necessities. However, the controls failed to prevent profiteering by wholesalers and prices remained high. In 1942, while the official price of a bag of rice was Shs. 31/-, a bag could in fact only be realistically obtained for Shs. 40/-. Between 1939 and 1942 the cost of living increased by 22.5 percent.[59] The minimum wage paid to Government employees was increased in late 1942 to Sh.1/- per day, but it was not long before the increase was once again eaten up by inflation.[60]

Prevented from increasing wages further by fiscal constraints, opposition from private employers, and the fear of stoking inflationary pressures, Government instead sought to protect African urban labour through direct intervention. Alongside the increase in daily rates, African employees receiving under Shs. 60/- were from 1942 entitled to receive cooked meals at a canteen run by the Railways Administration.[61] Later the same year, the lowest-paid Government employees — those earning Shs. 40/- per month or Shs. 1/50 per day or less (who constituted 87 percent of the Government labour force) — were issued with food rations.[62] According to one official, the provision of

---

[54] See correspondence/minutes in TNA/28594.

[55] CS to all Heads of Departments, PC, EP and PC, Tanga, 20 September 1940, TNA/28594.

[56] 'Report... into wages'.

[57] In 1942, 1943 and 1946 the rains failed resulting in food scarcity. Meanwhile, import restrictions throughout the war years and after led to serious shortages of consumer items. See Westcott, 'Impact'.

[58] After WWII, one official described it as 'a state duty to prevent the cost of living rising'. Quoted in *ibid.*, p. 175.

[59] Molohan, 'Unemployment'; Westcott, 'Impact', p. 170; 'Report... into wages'. The largest increase was in the price of clothes (125%); prices of locally produced items had also gone up — e.g. food (by 11%), and firewood (33%). See also, Summary of the proceedings of the Lighterage Dispute Tribunal (Wilson Tribunal), September 1943, p. 13, PRO/CO/691/183/42191.

[60] LO, Morogoro to LC, Moshi, 17 July 1943, TNA/61/14/22/1.

[61] CS to LC, 22 May 1942, TNA/540 16/15.

[62] Receiving, by 1943, 1 lb of meat, 24 oz of maizemeal, 4 oz beans and 1.5 oz groundnuts daily. Extract from CS to the Secretary of the Dsm Chamber of Commerce, quoted in PC Baker to various officials in Dsm, 24 May 1942, TNA/540/16/15; and LO, Morogoro to LC, Moshi, 17 July 1943, TNA/61/14/22/1.

rations, in conjunction with the increase in the daily rate, was 'reflected in a better type of labourer, big, strong, and fit, and fairly well clothed'.[63] However, these advances were checked in 1943 by a drought that threatened to undermine food supply and once again push up prices.[64] As a result, as part of a wider, regional system designed to regulate the distribution of food throughout East Africa, rationing was introduced for all *bona fide* residents of Dar es Salaam and Tanganyika's other main towns and plantations.[65] This was designed to restrict overconsumption,[66] as well as to ensure that food was obtainable by African urban residents at official prices. To the dismay of officials, the introduction of guaranteed rations, at a time when territorially food supply was scarce, initially 'acted like a magnet in attracting natives to the town who wished to be ensured a regular means of procuring foodstuffs'.[67] Nevertheless, they soon became the focus of much African discontent.[68] As with the earlier price controls rationing was not wholly effective, and a black market soon emerged, which often resulted in Africans being forced to buy food (or clothing) entitlements at escalated prices.[69] Inflation continued through the late war years and beyond. By 1945 prices had officially risen a further 14 percent; in 1947 they were over 20 percent higher than they had been in 1943.[70] Black market prices were considerably higher still. A cost of living allowance was introduced for all workers that was supposed to keep pace with inflation.[71] However, Africans were dissatisfied with the awards, both because they were calculated on the basis of official prices when many goods were only available on the black market, and because — in contrast to the allowances awarded to Europeans and Indians, which were worked out on the basis of 'middle class' incomes — the African award was based on the earnings of the lowest-paid manual worker.[72]

With such conditions prevailing in the township, it is perhaps unsurprising that the labour unrest officials feared eventually occurred in August 1943, when dockers struck for higher pay.[73] Immediate grievances were motivated by the fact that as private employees they did not receive either the cost of

63 LO, Morogoro to LC, Moshi, 17 July 1943, TNA/61/14/22/1.
64 Bryceson, 'Food supply', p. 169.
65 *Ibid.*
66 By Indians and Europeans as well as Africans, though rationing was racially differentiated. See Bryceson, Table 9. This differentiation had important repercussions for the development of racial consciousness among Africans. See Iliffe, *Modern History*, p. 375; and, in particular, Brennan, 'Nation', pp. 173–80.
67 Quarterly Labour report by DO Dsm (for quarter ending 30 September 1943), TNA/61/14/30.
68 E.g. letter from Sembuyagy, *TS*, 11 May 1946. See also, Iliffe, *Modern History*, p. 375; Westcott, 'Impact', pp. 178 and 226; Bryceson, 'Food supply', p. 170; and Brennan, 'Nation', chapter 3.
69 See e.g. *TS*, 9 April 1949, p. 16; for a more detailed discussion of food supply and the black market in post-war Dar es Salaam and its impact on racialised thought, see Brennan, 'Nation', pp. 181–8; see also, Westcott, chapter 5.
70 Iliffe, 'Dockworkers', p. 131. Percentages calculated from Table 18.
71 See e.g. *TS*, 11 September 1943, p. 10; and 10 June 1944, p. 7.
72 Wilson Tribunal, p. 14; *TS*, 10 June 1944, p. 11.
73 See Iliffe, 'Dockworkers', pp. 128–31 for an account of the strike. An earlier strike in 1939, in which dockers demanded the restoration of pre-depression wages, was poorly supported.

living bonus or the rations obtained by lower-paid government employees the previous year (an award known to the dockers as 'bakshishi ya King George'). However, underlying the dispute was the rapidly eroding value of dockers' wages at a time of 'rocketing' prices. Although they received more than was necessary for 'the maintenance of a minimum standard of living' according to the 1943 Cost of Living Committee report, the tribunal set up to investigate the dispute found that:

> Living is, after all, a matter of standards and the labourer's pre-war wage, such as he was still receiving in July 1943, would not allow him anything approaching the same standards of food, clothing and other necessities as in pre-war days.[74]

Concerned about port blockages at a time of war, Government intervened, intimidating the dockers to return to work by making the strike illegal through the declaration of the port as an essential service under the emergency defence regulations and subsequently arresting strikers.[75] In the wake of the tribunal modest increases were achieved by permanent workers, and to a lesser extent casuals, at the port. However, with inflation continuing to undermine the real value of incomes it was only a matter of time before further unrest occurred. When the dockers eventually did take action once again, in September 1947, their dispute soon escalated into a general strike affecting much of the Territory. Dar es Salaam was paralysed for over a week, as the long-brewing grievances of urban Africans were vented (see chapter 9). The strike was, as John Iliffe puts it, 'the climax to the colonial crisis' and served notice that more was required to treat the problem of urban labour than a combination of inadequate salary increments and inefficient rationing and price controls.[76]

The problem of urban youth

While the poor conditions suffered by the bulk of the urban African population worried urban officials, the position of African youth was a source of particular disquiet. Abiding concern over the demoralisation of African youth was now accompanied by anxieties over their socio-economic position. By the late 1930s increasing numbers of young Africans were making their way to the town in search of employment. The provincial report for 1941 complained that:

> Children wander into Dar es Salaam, often without their parents knowledge and obtain employment as houseboys or nurses at a starving wage. Twenty out of thirty children who had left or were irregularly attending a Government school at Vikindu sixteen miles from Dar es Salaam were found to be in the

---

[74] Wilson Tribunal, p. 15.
[75] See Iliffe, 'Dockworkers'; and Issa G. Shivji, *Law, State and the Working Class in Tanzania* (London, 1986), p. 170.
[76] Iliffe, *Modern History*, p. 402.

employment of non-natives in Dar es Salaam at wages of Shs. 3/- to 7/- a month. — Further, youths who dislike rural activities come to town and, if they are lucky, obtain employment at but a slightly increased rate of pay. Many, however, are unemployed or only semi-employed and all, youths and children alike, gain a preference for town life with its accompanying vices.[77]

Two years later, Pike estimated there were as many as 2,000 children roaming the streets of the capital, a large proportion of whom were without work.[78] Widespread unemployment among young Africans was seen as having corrosive moral effects.[79]

The youthful hordes entering Dar es Salaam also had a depressive impact on African wages in the town. According to Baker '[t]he salary paid by the large section of the non-native town-dwellers is based on the smallest wage which the youngest and least efficient child labour will accept.'[80] While the Employment of Women and Young Persons Ordinance of 1940 was introduced to restrict the use of child labour, there remained in the town many children employed as domestic servants (domestic service was exempted) and large numbers of youths just above the legal age of employment. In addition, many employers simply broke the law, continuing to use under-age employees who more readily accepted poor working conditions and low rates of pay.[81] Both Baker and Pike favoured the extension of the Women and Young Persons Ordinance to domestic service, which it was felt would have a salutary influence on 'the social condition of the urban African'.[82] Baker also advocated the introduction of an urban minimum wage, which would mean 'no one would employ child labour on account of the expense.' It took another fifteen years and the changed context of the mid 1950s for an urban minimum wage to be implemented. On the other hand, all forms of employment of children under 12, including domestic service, were prohibited in a 1943 amendment.[83] In addition to providing protection for a section of the community vulnerable to exploitation, it was hoped this would also

---

[77] 1941 PAR, p. 10.

[78] Relayed in Baker's suggestions for PC's Conference Agenda to CS, 20 July 1943, TNA/61/702/3.

[79] As were the livelihoods of many of those fortunate enough to find work. For example, a 1942 Labour report complained of children engaged as touts for brothels. Quarterly Report of LO, EP, September 1942, TNA/61/14/22/1. See also, Pike, 'Report', p. 9.

[80] Baker's suggestions for PC's Conference. The presence of child workers had a similarly deflationary impact upon servants' wages on the Witwatersrand in the early 1900s. Van Onselen, *New Babylon*, p. 227.

[81] Labour Commissioner Hickson-Mahony, estimated that there were over one thousand children employed by Indians (at Shs. 2/- per month or over). Min., 11 March 1943, TNA/28685.

[82] Baker to CS, 3 September 1941, TNA/30134.

[83] No. 4 of 1943. No child under 12 could now be employed except in the company of his/her parents or legal guardian or 'on light work, of an agricultural character, which has been approved by a Labour Officer or an Administrative Officer'. Hickson-Mahony had initially opposed this restriction, feeling that children living with their parents in Dar es Salaam should be allowed to work in order to contribute to the family budget (as well as to keep them off the streets). Min., 11 March 1943, TNA/28685.

facilitate the removal of unaccompanied juveniles found in Dar es Salaam. Within three years, though, further restrictions on employment were demanded; for the legal definition of the age of a child to be raised (from 14 to 16) and the total prohibition of employment of all children 'in domestic service away from their homes' not just those under 12 years of age.[84]

For those children with parents living in or close to the town, it was proposed they be catered for by the extension of the school system and making education compulsory. Educational needs in Uzaramo District (which now included Dar es Salaam) had up to the early 1940s been poorly served. Just four Government or Mission schools, alongside numerous, but tiny, Koranic schools, were struggling to cope with the requirements of a population that by then had grown to almost 190,000 people. It was decided in 1942 that 'a ring of schools near the township boundary' should be erected 'in order to deter children from entering the township by affording them educational facilities near their homes'.[85] In the town itself, compulsory education would have a civilising influence on the urban miscreant. Schooling, it was hoped, would 'instil into children those virtues of character so lacking among the youth of Dar es Salaam today; obedience, discipline, self control, cleanliness and a respect for the property of another'.[86] As with other grand schemes of the early 1940s, however, there were never enough resources devoted to education in Dar es Salaam to establish compulsory school attendance. In 1952, 75 percent of children in the town continued to receive 'no schooling at all'.[87]

The plan to extend education among Dar es Salaam youth, and its failure to be implemented, was symptomatic of many of the administrative innovations mooted by officials in the early 1940s. This was a time when, under pressure from accelerating urbanisation, worsening urban conditions and reformist Whitehall mandarins, a variety of policy options were raised, which anticipated the shape that a mature colonial strategy towards African urbanisation was to take in the 1950s. Most officials acknowledged that the conditions experienced by Africans in Dar es Salaam were simply unacceptable. Something had to be done, not only to alleviate their position but also to effect a more orderly organisation of labour. Social, political *and* economic imperatives made it essential that the 'vicious circle of low wages and sub-human living conditions on the one hand and laziness and unwillingness to work on the other' was broken.[88] Employers, minuted Baker in 1940, 'must get value for money' while the 'labourer and his family' should

---

84   Mins of the PC's Conference, June 1946, Item 24.
85   1942 PAR 1942, p. 24.
86   Pike, 'Report'.
87   1952 Social Development AR, p. 5.
88   Suggestion for PC's conference agenda, AO Mafia to PC, 27 May 1943, TNA/61/702/3. Although this comment was made by an officer presiding over a rural district he pointed out that '(t)his state of affairs is particularly bad in and around townships' — it is likely he had Dar es Salaam uppermost in mind.

'become healthy and contented members of society'.[89] However, it was not until after the 1947 strike that progress towards a true 'living wage' at last began.[90] In the case of urban housing, the position was much the same. While the Township Authority floated a variety of schemes in the early 1940s, action was once again not eventually taken until 1947. Moreover, although officials had identified the need to foster urban citizenship among Africans in Dar es Salaam, few initiatives aimed at cultivating a 'civic consciousness' were implemented prior to 1947, when administrative reforms were eventually introduced aimed at encouraging African participation in municipal governance. Somewhat earlier progress was made by the Social Welfare Office, but once again social development activity only really proliferated in the late 1940s and 1950s.[91]

The principal constraint that lay behind this lack of action was undoubtedly a shortage of resources. According to Ehrlich, at the end of the war Tanganyika was in poor economic shape, 'singularly ill-equipped to initiate and guide development'.[92] Nevertheless, although the policy debate in the early 1940s may be characterised as largely rhetorical it did at least provide a foundation upon which a post-war strategy towards African urbanisation was based. Officials such as Baker and Pike foresaw the need to nurture a class of respectable urban Africans, whose conditions of living and employment were to be closely monitored. Through increased participation in the municipal administration, nurturing reciprocal links between individuals from Dar es Salaam's varied ethnic groups and classes, and the cultivation of edifying leisure habits, it was hoped they would develop into model urban citizens. However, there was a more negative flip-side to this vision of incremental urban improvement. It failed to account for the flow of rural–urban migrants who from the late 1930s placed the town's economy and infrastructure under ever greater strain. For the new strategy to work, a growing class of urban unemployed and underemployed had to be eliminated. While this was a time when the African urban presence was at last acknowledged in Tanganyika, it was only the right type of African whose presence in Dar es Salaam was to be officially tolerated.

[89] Min., 12 July 1940, TNA/28594.
[90] In 1942, the Attorney General noted a 'fallacy ... in Government's approach to the consideration of the 'minimum wage' is that it sets its goal at a wage which will assure the recipient a bare standard of living rather than a decent standard of living.' Min., 17 November 1942, TNA/30598.
[91] See Burton, 'Townsmen'.
[92] Cyril Ehrlich, 'The poor country: The Tanganyika economy from 1945 to independence', in Low and Smith, *History*, p. 298.

Five

Unemployment, Migration & Urban Order
1938–45

At the same time as deteriorating urban living conditions attracted official concern, an emerging problem of unemployment further served to focus officials' minds. In 1938 it was estimated that some 1,500 men in Dar es Salaam were either 'not employed or employed for such periods that they only work one day in three'.[1] This labour surplus was held responsible for wages having reached the 'sub-marginal' limit at which they stood at the outbreak of the war. As officials addressed the problem of urban wages, it was recognised that any increase in rates of pay would only serve to encourage rural–urban migration and hence add to the problem. If Government rates were increased, observed the Director of Public Works in June 1940 (actually anticipating results of a later policy of labour stabilisation), the administration 'would establish a privileged "money" class of Government employees and increase unemployment'.[2] Consequently, from early on in the debate over pay and conditions, the need to both arrest African mobility and to restrict urban residency were identified as essential concomitants to any rise in wages.[3] As with other interventionist policies recommended by officials in the early 1940s, however, the wartime administration was hard pressed to take action in this regard. While the need to act against urban 'undesirables' – a term that increasingly included those without formal employment – was identified at this time, it was not until the late 1940s and the 1950s (especially) that concerted attempts were made to remove such persons from the town. Nevertheless, the debate conducted on this issue, along with the legislation resulting from it, were central to later attempts at regulating the African population.

The urban unemployment problem

By the end of the 1930s African unemployment had emerged in Dar es Salaam on an even greater scale than during the Depression. In 1939, Pike

[1]   Ag DO to PC, EP, 31 October 1938, TNA/25912.
[2]   Min., 12 June 1940, TNA/28594.
[3]   E.g. mins by Baker, 12 July 1940; and by Pennington, 13 July 1940, TNA/28594.

estimated that a quarter of the able-bodied men available for employment in the town were, at any one time, unemployed. Rural–urban migration simply exacerbated the problem. 'A constant, uncontrolled influx of immigrant Africans from the hinterland', observed Pike, made 'the lot of these unemployed unenviable.' Having no means to buy food, most of them were suffering from malnutrition and were 'not only unemployed but unemployable'.[4] A report two years later, by M.J.B. Molohan, an assistant DO and Dar es Salaam's Labour Officer, confirmed the gravity of the situation. Although 'no accurate figure of the number of unemployed [wa]s ascertainable because of the unchecked ebb and flow of natives into and out of the town', Molohan reported that urban unemployment existed 'to an alarming extent'. 'In Dar es Salaam', he warned, 'we may be regarded as sitting on top of a volcano which may erupt at any moment. With the return of demobilised natives after the war the eruption may be all the more imminent.'[5]

Molohan broke down the ranks of the unemployed into three sub-sets:

(a) able bodied natives out of employment, whose numbers may have decreased as a result of conscription and enlistment;

(b) able bodied natives who eke out a bare existence by accepting casual employment as water boys, porters etc; they have little inclination for regular employment. Their number would not be so great were it not for the fact that the Indian has always been ready to exploit this cheap supply of labour;

(c) natives who are already, or are becoming, unemployable because they simply have not the physique to undertake regular employment.[6]

All three categories were regarded with suspicion by district officials. In addition to the threat they posed to urban order, the presence of such large numbers of unemployed and underemployed persons was having a deflationary effect on the wages of those in employment, hence exacerbating poor living standards. Officials in Dar es Salaam were only too aware that similar conditions in Tanga had contributed to a serious outbreak of strike-related disorder there in 1939. 'Professional or genuine' unemployment was common in Tanga, and a subsequent report recommended that, while 'it was unfortunately, inevitable that a certain number of casual labourers should exist in every town… no effort should be spared to keep their number as low as possible'.[7] Baker, in Dar es Salaam, concurred. 'It is vital', he wrote to the Chief Secretary in 1941,

> that unemployment and ill-doing must be checked so far as is possible in urban areas and, with this end in view, it is imperative that those who can

[4]   Pike, 'Report', p. 9.
[5]   Molohan, 'Unemployment', pp. 1-2, & 7.
[6]   *Ibid.*
[7]   In the wake of the strike 55 Africans were repatriated from Tanga. Tanga PAR, 1939, p. 94; 'Report of the Commission appointed to enquire into the disturbances which occurred in the port of Tanga during the month of August, 1939', para. 13, PRO/CO/691/179/42191/13.

find no work ... must be repatriated for their own good as well as that of the community.[8]

He recommended that greater supervision of African movement to the town should be effected through the enforcement of legislation aimed at restricting urban residence – notably Township Rules 136(1) and (2).

Population control measures in Dar es Salaam, 1938–40

In the late 1930s, however, urban administrators still felt that fiscal constraints, along with insufficient manpower, undermined official capacity for action in this respect. Rule 136(1) remained pretty much a dead letter. Provincial Commissioner Longland considered it 'an impossible rule to carry out, at least in Dar es Salaam, because natives come and go without anybody being any the wiser'.[9] The following year, his successor, Baker, declared he would be happy to enforce the rule but he had too few staff to do so.[10] Similarly, DO Pike complained – this time with rule 136(2) in mind – that although '[l]egislation existed to enforce the repatriation of natives who were not in employment... the agents for its enforcement were lacking'.[11]

In an attempt to check the unsupervised movement of Africans into and out of the town (as well as to enhance control over the urban population) a short-lived system of identification was introduced in 1938. Each ward was given a letter and the streets within it a number. Africans registered in a house on a particular street would then receive a number that would identify them.[12] During the remainder of 1938 a concerted attempt was made to record in Native Tax Registers the town's African inhabitants using the new system. However, after completion the official responsible for conducting the registration complained about the persistent shortcomings of the town headmen. Longland shortly afterwards augmented the town's Native Administration, informing the six headmen of Dar es Salaam that each *mtaa* (ward) should be organised along the following lines:

> Every street should have a ... *mnyapara*[13] or policeman ... [who would] keep an eye on all activities in his street: – He would report the arrival of strangers to the *Mkubwa* [headman] of his *Mtaa*... In short he would be the 'eye' of the *Mkubwa* of a street in the *Mtaa*.[14]

However, effective methods of facilitating the social control of the urban population remained stubbornly hard to implement. Neither the system of

---

[8] PC Baker to CS, 12 March 1941, TNA/61/688/5.
[9] PC Longland to DO, 17 January 1939, TNA/61/443.
[10] Baker to CS, 21 May 1940; PC Tanga (to CS, 27 May 1940) was of the same opinion, TNA/28685.
[11] Record of first meeting of Native Welfare Cttee, 19 September 1940, TNA/61/708.
[12] See DO, Dsm to PC, EP, 20 June 1938, TNA/61/207/Vol. 1.
[13] Use of *mnyapara* is revealing of official attitides towards urban residents, it being the term used for overseers on plantations. I owe this insight to Jim Giblin.
[14] PC, EP to DO Pike, 31 January 1939, TNA/61/443.

registration nor the introduction of *wanyapara* as the 'eyes' of the Native Administration appeared to outlive their proponents' term of office in Dar es Salaam.[15] A truly effective means of monitoring the shifting urban populace remained a pipe dream of officials throughout the colonial period.

When Baker became Provincial Commissioner, in 1940, the old problems persisted. Movement into Dar es Salaam had accelerated with the onset of war, while the legal machinery for dealing with the surplus population remained inadequate. Baker judged the problem to be more than simply insufficient material or human resources. He argued that in order for such legislation to be effective it was necessary to establish its legitimacy among the town's resident African population. Rule 136 would,

> if it could be enforced, be of value in controlling this [jobless] class of African. Such a rule, however, cannot be effective without the goodwill of the resident population: unless it has its wholehearted support only a few of the less cunning of the immigrants will be arrested by police constable [sic] and its enforcement may become a source of irritation to the respectable members of society owing to their being continually asked to produce their permits.[16]

The McRoberts ruling

There is some irony in the timing of this call to seek the assent of Dar es Salaam's African residents. Just one year later Rule 136(2), the legislation most frequently used to remove undesirables, was declared *ultra vires* (beyond legal authority) by a Dar es Salaam magistrate, in part because of a lack of consent for it among the general population. In a case of repatriation against one Ramazani bin Mbendo, a 'rogue and vagabond' who had originally been expelled from the town in 1932, Justice McRoberts, while acknowledging that the prisoner was 'the kind of person who is best kept out of town', ruled that the regulation invoked for his removal offended 'against every canon of legality which has ever been established whereby such rules are to be judged'. The Township Rules, he complained, 'are not made "by the people and for the people", nor are they subjected to public criticism by a vigorous press or by public bodies before they become law'.

Rule 136(2) was deemed invalid on three counts. The first was for technical legal reasons. To be valid, the by-law had to be within the authority of the ordinance that enabled it to be made. This, McRoberts concluded, 136(2) failed to do. More relevant to our discussion, however, were the second and third counts: the arbitrariness of the offending regulation and its 'unreasonable' character. 'We might observe', McRoberts pronounced,

> that the public, and every member of the public, is entitled to know under what law he lives....

---

[15] There is no surviving record of either in subsequent years.
[16] Memo. by Baker, 10 January 1940, TNA/18950/Vol. II.

In the matter before me any Native in the place [Dar es Salaam] can be thrown out of it at the behest of the Administrative Officer without any reason assigned, or without such a one as any reasonable man might consider to be any real reason at all. The test is, what the particular District Officer considers to be an 'undesirable inhabitant' and this may differ with every officer who exercises these functions. Just as equity was once said to vary with the length of the Chancellor's foot, so might 'undesirability' vary with the length of an Administrative Officer's temper....

Can it be said that any Native coming to this town can be sure that the DC will not think him 'undesirable' and will have him ejected? Where then is the certainty, and what Native could with absolute safety, build a house, or sink capital in this place?

To validate the third count on which he ruled 136(2) *ultra vires*, McRoberts quoted authority to show that by-laws were unreasonable,

if, for instance, they were found to be partial and unequal in their operation as between different classes; if they were manifestly unjust; if they disclosed bad faith; if they involved such gratuitous or oppressive interference with the rights of those subject to them as could find no justification in the minds of reasonable men....

Regulation 136(2), in his opinion, failed on all counts:

That this by-law is partial and unequal in its operation between the different classes of the community cannot be gainsaid. It applies only to Natives, and both Europeans and Indians are exempted from its operation. It is unjust and oppressive, for it renders any African who is not a Native of the place subject to expulsion without process of law, without appeal, and without lawful reason, for it must be remembered that in exercising this power the District Officer acts administratively and not as a Magistrate. It is a gratuitous interference with the rights of the subject who is entitled to travel where he will throughout the country, and to use the public roads for passage wherever they are established.

The right of transit is preserved by Article 7 of the [League of Nations] Mandate to all and sundry, but no Native must show his face in Acacia Avenue if the fiat has gone forth against him for whatever reason, or for no reason at all. It precludes him from living here even though he may have established his home years before and have his relations, his property, his business, and everything which makes life worth living, here, and he may have no other place in which he may live. But all this is nothing. The DC does not like him. He must go.

It is no good telling me that no DC could be so unreasonable. Give a man despotic power, make him accountable to noone for his actions, excuse him from giving reasons for what he does, and it is perfectly astonishing what such a man may do.[17]

---

[17] McRoberts' ruling is reported in *TS*, 14 March 1941, p. 10. Four years later a similar decision was arrived at in Nairobi, when by-laws restricting African mobility were declared *ultra vires*. Throup, *Mau Mau*, p. 192.

The timing of McRoberts' judgment was remarkable.[18] With the inflow of immigrants adding substantially to Dar es Salaam's problems in the early 1940s, there was a firm consensus among European officials and non-officials, including both those who were more liberal in their outlook as well as the 'hard-liners', that there was an urgent need for increasing the powers available to administrators for dealing with the surplus urban population. Concerns expressed about the civil liberties of the African were incomprehensible to most officials, particular those with some responsibility for Dar es Salaam. Rule 136(2) had, as far as they were concerned, been applied only against an unrespectable class of Africans whose removal from the town benefited the entire community.[19] The possibility, raised by McRoberts, that the wide powers conferred by the regulation could be abused by an overzealous official was dismissed.[20] The application of 136(2) in order to repatriate jobless Africans in 1931 (and no doubt on other occasions for which no records survive) was conveniently forgotten, as were the demands by contemporary officials to apply the same regulation against the growing number of unemployed in Dar es Salaam at that time.

Indeed, the *ultra vires* ruling turned out to be an aberration. While McRoberts found some support from the settler press,[21] his counterparts in the Native Administration were aghast. Circumstances in the capital were far too pressing for officials to concern themselves with the moral force of the magistrate's argument. According to Baker it was

> very necessary that the rule should be retained in its entirety and legalized if necessary. On its enforcement depends, to a large extent, the welfare and comfort of the native community of a large town such as Dar es Salaam.[22]

Three weeks after the ruling, the Chairman of the Township Authority bemoaned the consequent return of natives who had been expelled under 136(2).[23] The *Tanganyika Standard* reported that steps were being taken to meet the new situation. Indeed, less than a month after 136(2) was declared *ultra vires* it was replaced by 'Removal of Undesirable Natives' regulations,

---

18 Although the judgment fitted within a pattern of feuding between the judiciary and the administration that was especially pronounced in East Africa from late 1920s into the 1930s. See especially, the Bushe Commission Report and Evidence for the judiciary's suspicion about administrative motives given the conflation of powers resulting from DOs sitting as magistrates. For a useful summary, see H.F. Morris and James S. Read, *Indirect Rule and the Search for Justice – Essays in East African Legal History* (London, 1972). I am grateful to Richard Waller for pointing this out.

19 Proposals for Agenda of PC's 1941 Conference by DC, Dsm, 28 March 1941, TNA/61/702/1.

20 Baker, for example, could not 'but take exception to Mr. McRoberts criticism of members of the Provincial Administration who are I maintain, as a class, very sympathetic towards the African and careful of his just treatment whether as an individual or as a community'. PC Baker to CS, 12 March 1941, TNA/61/688/5.

21 The Judge's strictures, commented an editorial in the *Tanganyika Standard* (2 May 1941, p. 6), were ones 'with which any ordinary member of the public will fully agree'.

22 Baker to CS, 12 March 1941, TNA/61/688/5.

23 *TS*, 11 April 1941.

passed under the Emergency Powers (Defence) Act that endowed the colonial government with special powers for the duration of the war. These replacement regulations reinstated a DC's ability to 'repatriate to his home... any native he may consider an undesirable inhabitant or sojourner in the township'.[24] They differed from rule 136(2) only in as much as they were not a by-law and hence not subject to the tests by which McRoberts found the original legislation wanting. The speed with which a repatriation mechanism was reintroduced indicates its importance. The ability to remove unwanted residents was increasingly central to the colonial administration of the town.

Influx control initiatives

Despite the immediate reintroduction of repatriation legislation, colonial administrators were nevertheless soon complaining once more about the continuing inefficacy of the machinery to deal with the surplus population. What officials desired above all were some measures to control rural–urban movement. Action under the existing legislation, however rigorous, was in itself inadequate, addressing the symptom rather than the cause. What was required, many argued, was a more comprehensive solution addressing African mobility in Tanganyika as a whole.

The introduction of some form of territory-wide identification system aimed at restricting unauthorised movement of Africans had been raised on a number of occasions between the wars. Each time the political will proved insufficiently strong for action to be taken on the proposals. Orde-Browne first raised the issue in his report on labour in 1926.[25] It re-emerged during a 1929 conference, at which a 'Report on the Identification of Travelling Natives' formed the basis for discussion. Capt. F.C. Hallier, a former DO in Dar es Salaam, and acting Commissioner for Eastern Province, suggested 'a committee be appointed to examine the South African *Urban Areas Act*, which he thought contain[ed] much that is useful and suitable for application in this country'.[26] The majority of officials present, however, were rather more cautious. While it was acknowledged that 'the lack of a proper means of identification is having a rapidly demoralising effect on people who are quite honest by nature', it was 'emphasized that pass laws were not in question'.[27] Although the need for some form of identification system was continually voiced by officials between the wars, other concerns, connected with the

---

[24] GN No. 113 of 1941. The regulations were extended to ten other Tanganyikan towns on 12 June, 1941.

[25] He recommended the introduction of a pass system — based on the retention of tax tickets — aimed at 'increasing control of the travelling native'. While no organised pass system was introduced, the *cheti ya kodi* (tax receipt), which Africans were obliged to carry, became from then onwards the principal means used by officials to identify Africans throughout the colonial period. Orde-Browne, 'Labour', paras 118 and 119

[26] Mins. of the Senior AOs Conference, Dar es Salaam, October 1929, p. 100, in E. Africana, UDsm Library.

[27] *Ibid.*, p. 109.

Territory's mandate status, hindered the endorsement of such proposals by senior administrators both in the Tanganyika secretariat and at the Colonial Office.[28]

In 1940 the subject was back on the Provincial Commissioners' conference agenda. The participants blanched at the introduction of anything as severe as a pass system. On the other hand, an experiment was proposed of getting Native Authorities to issue identity cards 'to any native who wished to leave his own district for any purpose whatsoever and desired to provide himself with a form of travel document'.[29] Native Authorities did begin to issue *ruhusa ya njia* (travel permits) in the early 1940s. However, it was soon apparent that such limited action was not enough to satisfy Dar es Salaam officials. The following year, in response to police complaints about 'destitute natives... found sleeping on open verandahs, and in public markets etc.' (and their inability to deal with the phenomenon), the Native Affairs Sub-Committee of the Township Authority observed the necessity to 'endeavour to limit immigration into the Township'.[30] Provincial Commissioner Baker concurred, deeming control could 'best be achieved by the resurrection in legal form of the old Township Rule 136(1)'.[31] Existing legislation was inadequate. 'The only control the authorities have over this mass of unemployed', wrote Molohan in 1941, 'is that supposed to be granted by the... Regulations which replaced Rule 136(2) of the Township Rules.' This was 'for all intents and purposes regarded as a dead letter' as it only operated after an African had entered a town.[32] What was required, according to Molohan, were 'comprehensive regulations (i) to control the entry of natives into the town, and (ii) to repatriate the existing surplus unemployed back to their home districts'. As an appendix to his report Molohan attached draft legislation that envisaged a strictly enforced system in which Africans leaving the rural areas would be required to obtain a road pass to enable them to proceed to a township. While it is clear that many officials sympathised with Molohan, senior officials at the secretariat and the Colonial Office remained reluctant to endorse any form of pass laws. Those administrators with first-hand experience of the situation in Dar es Salaam, on the other hand, were unanimous in the opinion that there was a pressing need to enhance the current legislation. According to Baker, drastic measures were 'urgently necessary in order to reduce the numbers of unemployed and underfed

---

[28] Further evidence of this reticence, and also perhaps of the tension between different levels of the administration, is to be found in the fact that an Identification Ordinance — which required people leaving their province of origin to be in possession of an official letter of identification — although passed into law as No. 13 of 1935, was never actually brought into force. According to Shivji, it was not implemented because of the potential costs and complications, as well as the fact that it would invite 'harsh criticism from abroad' for being racially discriminatory. Shivji, *Law, State & Working Class*, p. 99.

[29] *Ibid.*

[30] Ag MS to CS, 27 August 1941, TNA/30134.

[31] Baker to CS, 3 September 1941, TNA/30134. McRoberts' ruling on 136(2) was held to have invalidated the whole of section 136 of the Township Regulations.

[32] Molohan, 'Unemployment', p. 2.

natives, both adult and juvenile, who infest the township'.[33]

While the townward drift of 'undesirables' continued to cause consternation, the potentially much greater problem of demobilised soldiers began to arouse equal concern. In June, Pike drew Baker's attention to 'a difficult situation that has started in Dar es Salaam and which shews every sign of developing into an acute administrative problem after the war'. He observed 'the disinclination of discharged soldiers, whether disabled or otherwise, to leave the town and to return to the land'. 'Such a state of affairs' would 'make administration of Dar es Salaam Township, already difficult, quite impossible.' Baker told Pike he was 'endeavouring to organise machinery, of which Government will approve, for prohibiting Africans from residing in Dar es Salaam unless they are in possession of a permit to do so'.[34]

Conditions continued to deteriorate. In spite of taxes being reduced the previous year from Shs. 11/- to 9/- in districts surrounding the capital – an intended disincentive to rural–urban movement[35] – the drift actually accelerated during 1943, exacerbated by the introduction of rationing and lack of rain. In December, Pike complained to Baker:

> The increasing number of natives from other districts of the province (especially Rufiji and Morogoro) who are coming to Dar es Salaam in search of employment shows no sign of decreasing ... they should be discouraged.[36]

At the Economic Control Board meeting in January 1944 it was reported that as a result of a poor harvest 'six hundred natives had entered the town from Western Rufiji alone'.[37] 'This drift', observed Baker, 'besides increasing the difficulties of the Administration means the withdrawal of agriculturalists from food production to non-productive, non-essential jobs and the tendency must be stopped.'[38] In a letter to the Chief Secretary, Crawford, the secretary of the ECB, raised his concerns about the big increase in the consumption of 'native foods' in Dar es Salaam that year – consumption having increased from 3,000 bags in June to 7,000 in December.[39] After Africans in the town were required to register for food rations, Dar es Salaam's population was found to have increased by over 10,000 since the outbreak of war.[40] The situation had become so severe that – 'in order to prevent further overcrowding and the concomitant aggravation of existing conditions' – it was decided to restrict the immigration of non-natives into Dar es Salaam and Tanga.[41]

Even to those without first-hand experience of the town, it was clear that something had to be done. Starting in 1943, a vigorous debate was conducted among officials at all levels of the colonial administration, from District

---

33   Baker to CS, 29 September 1941, TNA/30134.
34   Pike to Baker 4 June 1942; Baker to Pike, 9 June 1942, TNA/540/27/13.
35   The rate in the town remained at Shs. 11/-. 1942 PAR, p. 20.
36   Pike to Baker, 14 December 1943, TNA/61/443/1.
37   Mins of meeting of ECB, 4 January 1944, TNA/61/443/1.
38   Baker to Political, Rufiji, Morogoro and Bagamoyo, 21 December 1943.
39   Crawford to CS, 13 January 1944; ECB Mins, 4 January 1944, TNA/28685.
40   1943 PAR, p. 24.
41   Jackson to SSCol, 27 November 1943, TNA/31751.

Officers to Whitehall mandarins, over the best means of controlling accelerated rural–urban migration. Those officials who were most directly affected by this phenomenon pressed for legislation that established more than just the power to expel undesirable occupants from the urban areas. The Labour Commissioner, Hickson-Mahony, for instance, envisaged the need for both the control of immigration to the town and the restriction of juvenile employment, in addition to the repatriation of 'unemployed undesirables'. Baker agreed, but was anxious that there should be as little interference as possible with the freedom of the individual.[42] In effect, any machinery to restrict African movement within the territory amounted to a pass system. There was still resistance to the introduction of such drastic measures. However, with the situation in the towns so serious and, thanks to the return of growing numbers of demobilised soldiers, only likely to get worse, it was pointed out to the Chief Secretary that such a move should now be contemplated.[43] The previous year, Baker had studied the pass regulations in place in Natal under the Urban Areas Act but had considered them 'harsh and unsuited to Dar es Salaam'. Seven months on, he was inclined to look upon the South African system in a more positive light.[44]

Draft legislation was drawn up and discussed at the 1943 Provincial Commissioners' conference. It was endorsed by the conference participants, eventually passing into law in early 1944 as the Townships (Removal of Undesirable Natives) Ordinance (Cap. 104). The bill was 'considered necessary in the interests both of the natives themselves and of orderly life within [the townships]'.[45] It incorporated a number of safeguards designed to 'avoid the appearance of arbitrary or discriminating treatment' including definitions of potential culprits and powers of appeal to Provincial Commissioners and (eventually) the Governor. While the ordinance did provide a stricter definition of who may be deemed an undesirable than previous legislation, it remained broad enough to include a good proportion of the urban African population. Alongside those who had 'no regular means of employment or other reputable means of livelihood', 'natives having no settled home within the township' were subject to repatriation – the 'settled native' being one who was either liable to house tax or who had paid poll tax for the current and previous year.[46] This meant that any labourer engaged in casual employment could be classed as undesirable; as could any African who, arriving in town within the current tax year, had not paid municipal poll tax the previous year. The ordinance was also racially discriminatory in character (it was the 'Removal of Undesirable *Natives*' ordinance).

Despite the wide powers bestowed by the ordinance upon officials to deal with the surplus urban population, the Governor made it clear in a letter to the Secretary of State for the Colonies that yet further legislation was required.

42   Mins 11 and 17 March 1943, TNA/28685.
43   Min. by W.E.J., 7 May 1943, TNA/61/702/3.
44   Baker to CS, 16 July 1942, TNA/28685; 16 March 1943, TNA/61/443/1.
45   'Objects and reasons' accompanying draft bill, PRO/CO/691/185/42431.
46   Sec. 2, T(ROUN) Ordinance, GN No. 6 of 1944.

The bill was 'a first instalment of legislation of a more drastic character which will be required to deal with post-war conditions'.[47] In response to the Governor's letter, J.V. Wild, a Colonial Office official, pointed out that the problem of the drift to the town was not restricted to Tanganyika: both the Governor of Uganda and the British Resident in Zanzibar had expressed similar concerns.[48] He remained sceptical, nevertheless, of any initiatives to restrict African mobility:

> I do not think that legislation to prevent entry into the townships would be justified unless it were complimentary to development plans in the native areas ... It is a little unfortunate that the first hint we should have had of the Governor's plans for dealing with demobilised soldiers should have been this negative, not to say repressive, measure. These men have become accustomed to cinemas, canteens, and the like, and unless such facilities are made available to them elsewhere, I do not think it would be right to deny them where they already exist ... [A]t present life in the native areas is not sufficiently attractive to justify us in forcing all men to remain there.

Such concerns were shared by others at the Colonial Office. 'When the demobilised soldiers return to their mud huts', observed K.W. Blaxter, the Assistant Secretary for Social Services, 'they will hope for something more by way of local activity to keep them interested than they did before they enlisted.'[49]

Officials in Dar es Salaam, under increasing pressure from the persistent drift to the town, were less mindful of rural initiatives as a solution to the problem. In January 1944, the ECB secretary had recommended to Government that:

> some form of restriction should be imposed on the entry of natives to the township of Dar es Salaam and that complementary powers should be given to the Administration to repatriate natives found in the town without the necessary authority. It had now become a matter of the first importance that the native population of Dar es Salaam should be stabilised, or if possible, decreased.[50]

In response to these demands Baker and Whittle drew up draft regulations – prohibiting the entry into (specified) towns of all but residents and those with permanent employment – which were sent to London for approval. At the Colonial Office, information coming in of the deteriorating situation in Tanganyikan towns had caused Wild to reassess the situation. 'Something

[47] Letter from Jackson, 15 November 1943, PRO/CO/691/185/42431. At the 1943 conference, Baker had stated that this legislation was fine as far as it went, but that it only allowed for removal after entry, which was not enough. Further legislation was needed to prevent the original movement to the urban areas.

[48] Kenyan officials were also at this time drafting legislation designed to deal with the problem in Nairobi and Mombasa. See chapter 1.

[49] Mins by J.V.Wild, 6 December 1943; and Blaxter, 11 January 1944, PRO/CO/691/185/42431.

[50] ECB mins, 4 January 1944, TNA/61/443/1.

clearly has to be done about the entry of natives into townships... when the food and housing shortage is acute,' he wrote. 'Making life in the native areas more attractive and building more houses in the towns' were 'measures which at present are unfortunately out of the question on a sufficiently large scale and... more direct action is needed.'[51] It was decided to go along with the proposals from Tanganyika, and the Secretary of State for the Colonies duly communicated his assent to the introduction of the proposed legislation, which was passed as the Defence (Entry of Natives into Townships: Restriction) Regulations.[52] The regulations made it illegal for an 'alien' native to remain in the town for longer than 48 hours without reporting to the Township Authority and obtaining a permit allowing him to do so.

Disagreements over whether permits should be required of all residents in the town or only those who were new arrivals, alongside a lack of staff to implement the legislation, resulted in the complete neglect of the regulations in Dar es Salaam.[53] Instead, within months of their being passed, officials began clamouring once again for further, more permanent legislation to effect a system of registration covering all urban residents.[54] Both the Municipal Secretary, Helps, and Pike, now acting as Deputy Provincial Commissioner, argued that control of entry into Dar es Salaam would be necessary after the war. Governor Jackson agreed.[55] At a subsequent meeting, it was decided that all male Africans – it was considered undesirable to apply it to Europeans or Asians – liable to tax in the town should be issued with a permit. Women and children under 12 were exempted.[56] A draft bill was drawn up 'for the registration of inhabitants and control of entry into the towns'.[57] If the town was not to be 'flooded with unemployed loafers and potential criminals', wrote Jackson, then more effective legislation had to be introduced for 'this serious social evil' to be dealt with.[58] Others were more dubious about the proposals. Chief Secretary Sandford warned against a 'walled city policy', observing that an unfeasibly 'huge apparatus of control' to check daily entry to and occupation in the town would be required to implement such a scheme.[59]

In the end, the proposed legislation fell victim to changes in the

---

[51] 'Something of this sort has been tried in Zanzibar with some success,' Wild observed. 'Idlers in town have been made to cultivate food crops on plots allotted to them in the neighbourhood of the towns, and this action has had a good effect throughout the Protectorate and not merely in the urban areas directly affected'. Min., 26 February 1944, PRO/CO/691/191/42431.

[52] GN No. 80 of 1944.

[53] The ordinance was enforced in Tanga, the other town to which it was supposed to apply, though 'only to a negligible extent'. Mins by Lamb, 22 February 1944; min. dated 22 April 1944; comments by PC, EP in mins of meeting, 5 September 1944; Governor to SSCol, 12 February 1945, TNA/28685.

[54] Mins by Lamb, 12 May 1944, and Jackson, 13 May 1944, TNA/28685.

[55] Mins of meeting, 19 May 1944, TNA/28685.

[56] Mins of meeting, 5 September 1944, TNA/28685.

[57] At f.123a, TNA/28685.

[58] Min., 13 October 1944, TNA/28685.

[59] *Ibid.*

administration, both in London and Dar es Salaam. On hearing of the proposals, Andrew Cohen – the new head of the Africa department at the Colonial Office – wrote to Sandford that they bore too great a resemblance to South African and Rhodesian systems of population control. Meanwhile, at a meeting in Dar es Salaam to discuss the draft bill, William Battershill, who had just replaced Jackson as Governor of Tanganyika, opened proceedings by declaring his 'vast objections' to the proposed legislation both in principle and detail. Four days later Battershill informed Cohen that he would 'hear nothing more about this Bill'.[60] While concern over conditions in Dar es Salaam was widely felt, in the end political considerations ruled out the introduction of legislation aimed at restricting African mobility. Tanganyika's mandate status made any kind of pass system untenable.[61]

Rural initiatives

Repeatedly thwarted in their attempts to legislate against rural–urban migration, district officials were forced to turn their attention to the principal source of their woes: the rural areas of Eastern Province. Starting in the early 1940s, Dar es Salaam District Office requested that *Tangazo* (Notices) discouraging the move to town be announced in villages throughout the province. In June 1942, for example, the DC contacted his counterpart in Kisarawe requesting that:

> notice be sent out again to the effect that 1) <u>No Work</u> is obtainable in the town 2) and any person from the district found in the town without good reason will be severely dealt with. 'Good reason' does not include sporadic work with Indians.[62]

Five days later a similar message was communicated to the DC in Utete,[63] and the following notice was forwarded by the District Office to headmen to announce to their villagers:

> Many people – especially youths – are coming from Rufiji District to Dar es Salaam Township to look for work. Residents themselves cannot get jobs now as they have been outnumbered by '*Wahuni*' who are increasing day by day. Every effort is being made to return these youngsters and I would be most grateful if you would announce to the youths over there that there are no job opportunities and that they should not come to Dar es Salaam if they

---

[60] Cohen to CS, 10 April 1945; Note of meeting, 1 August 1945; Battershill to Cohen, 5 August 1945, TNA/28685.

[61] E.g. Cohen (to Sandford, 10 April 1945) observed that the proposals 'would probably regarded as an extension of the pass law system and would thus arouse considerable political interest both here and elsewhere'. At a later meeting, the Attorney General said he felt the proposed registration and its racially exclusive application might well have been contrary to the Tanganyika Order in Council but had prepared a draft bill because he had been told it was essential. Note of meeting, 1 August 1945, TNA/28685.

[62] Political, Uzaramo, Dsm, to Political, Kisarawe, Pugu, 12 June 1942, TNA/540/27/13.

[63] Political, Uz., Dsm, to Political, Utete, 17 June 1942, TNA/540/27/13.

do not have a confirmed job as anyone without a job will be severely punished.[64] The letter that accompanied the announcement exhorted the headmen to put pressure on the parents of young adults. It was

up to the elders to convince their youths to stay at home.... The childrens' mistakes are the elders mistakes because it is up to the elders to teach their children from childhood to behave properly.[65]

Such propaganda appears to have had limited success. Further initiatives were forthcoming. In response to complaints received from Uzaramo headmen in 1943, who asked for permission to prohibit any person – man, woman or child – from coming to the town without obtaining a written permit from his *Wakili* to do so, Baker recommended that the most appropriate course of action was for Eastern Province Native Authorities to begin issuing *ruhusa ya njia*.[66] Pike lent *his* weight to such measures, arguing that all Africans proceeding to Dar es Salaam should be given a travel permit by their Native Authority.[67] The message was passed on accordingly to the District Commissioners in Rufiji, Morogoro and Bagamoyo, who were asked to relay it to their Native Authorities, while simultaneously adopting '[a]ll other possible means ... to keep these people on the land and to stop the drift to the town'.[68]

Without allocating increased resources to controlling unregulated movement into the towns, however, the ploy of getting Native Authorities to issue travel permits was merely a stop-gap measure, and not a particularly effective one at that. While it may have discouraged the initial movement, once an African had left his home district lack of a permit to travel did not constitute any offence against the territorial laws. When, two years later, at the 1946 Eastern Province District Commissioners' conference, the feasibility of a Native Authority prohibition on entry into towns was discussed, it was 'decided that the machinery required to make such an order effective was impracticable at present'. 'It was agreed' instead, 'that Native Authorities should constantly be advised to discourage by active propaganda the drift of their people to the townships.'[69] A regime that could not afford to implement some form of pass system, either financially, or, in the final analysis, politically, and which simultaneously was hard pressed to effect improvement in conditions of life in the countryside,[70] could in the end only resort to 'active

64 P.L. Nairac for the DC, Utete-Rufiji to *Mwenyemzi/Mtawala wote* [all headmen and chiefs], 2 July 1942, TNA/540/27/13. Original in Swahili. The English text from which this notice was adapted survives in Political, Uzaramo, Dsm to Political, Utete, 17 June 1942.
65 P.L. Nairac for the DC, Utete-Rufiji, 2 July 1942, TNA/540/27/13. Original in Swahili.
66 Baker to CS, 6 October 1943, TNA/61/443/1.
67 DC, Dsm to PC, 14 December 1943, TNA/61/443/1.
68 Baker to Political, Rufiji, Morogoro and Bagamoyo, 21 December 1943, TNA/61/443/1.
69 Mins of DCs' Conference, EP, held week commencing 2 September 1946, TNA/61/502/pt. 1.
70 See Jackson to SSCol, 12 February 1945, TNA/28685.

propaganda' among rural communities to attempt to stem the drift to the towns.

Embattled officials, overwhelmed by a town-ward tide of rural migrants in the early 1940s, desperately sought administrative solutions to spiralling urbanisation and its attendant problems. While they met with some success in getting a variety of draconian legislation passed into law, restricted human and material resources prevented the new laws from being enforced in any kind of systematic manner. To assert effective control over African mobility it was

> necessary to ensure, in actual fact and not merely in theory, that no African could stay long in the town without having either a registration certificate or an entry permit. This entailed an organisation, police or otherwise, which would be continually checking up people's cards, in the streets, in other public places, and, under certain conditions, in their houses.[71]

This apparatus of control was not to emerge until the following decade (pretty much exactly along these lines). Although officials failed to assert the checks on African mobility they felt were essential in the early 1940s, however, after the war the position did not deteriorate to the extent that was feared. Many demobilised soldiers returned to the rural areas. Meanwhile, for those that decided to stay in Dar es Salaam, an improving urban economy from 1946 meant that work was available. Nevertheless, ever-accelerating African urbanisation added to the administrative difficulties of colonial officials. Although joblessness was not the problem it had been earlier in the decade, the presence of a growing class of intermittently employed Africans, many of them young, was an ongoing concern. They were considered the prime culprits in an emerging problem of urban crime that in the post-war period was to play an important part in the debate over controlling African urbanisation.[72] The problem of crime had in fact featured in the inter-war rhetoric on demoralisation, delinquency being the final stage in the descent of the virtuous tribesman after the move to town. However, in the 1940s and 1950s the growth in recorded crime – which took the form of public order offences as much as, if not more than, more unambiguously felonious behaviour – was viewed with mounting anxiety and was identified as a justification for an increasingly coercive response to rural–urban migration.

---

71 Note of a meeting, 5 September 1944, TNA/28685.
72 Although crime in Dar es Salaam was often invoked by administrators as a justification for legislation aimed at checking movement to the town in the early 1940s, tellingly senior police officers considered the T(ROUN) ordinance sufficient to deal with urban criminality. See comments by the Commisioner of Police reported in Note of a meeting, 17 October 1944. At a subsequent meeting on draft legislation to register and control the entry of Africans, the Commissioner stated he 'could not see why people who were not going to do any harm should not be allowed to come into the town and see the lights and crowds if they wished to'. Note of a meeting, 1 August 1945, TNA/28685.

Part II

Crime in Colonial Dar es Salaam

1919–61

Tanganyika is rapidly developing all the Social Problems of civilised countries.

Rev. R.M. Gibbons, Appendix C in Tanganyika Territory,
Report on the Question of Imprisonment in Tanganyika (Dar es Salaam, 1932)

Six

Interpreting Crime
in Colonial Dar es Salaam

In dealing with crime as a historical phenomenon, scholars of Western societies have 'sought to relate crime and the control of crime to specific economic, social, and political contexts', acknowledging 'that crime is something defined by the law, and that the law was changed and shaped by human institutions'.[1] The value of Dar es Salaam as a subject of study is the manner in which the colonial context, law and institutions impacted upon the incidence of crime in African society. While, in comparison to Western (and some other African) societies at the time, crime in Dar es Salaam was negligible, the period under consideration did witness a remarkable increase in recorded criminality. It is argued that European colonial policy was actually responsible for producing much of the crime that occurred. This was in part a product of dramatic social and economic changes accompanying colonial rule — urbanisation being one such development. However, it also arose from the imposition of alien legislation that often commanded little acceptance among the subject African population. In the colonial context,

---

[1] Clive Emsley, 'The history of crime and crime control institutions', in Mike Maguire, Rod Morgan and Robert Reiner (eds), *The Oxford Handbook of Criminology (Third Edition)* (Oxford, 2002), p. 202. The historiography of crime in Africa is largely undeveloped, though see Donald Crummey (ed.), *Banditry, Rebellion and Social Protest in Africa* (London/Portsmouth, NH, 1986); and Iliffe, *African Poor*, pp. 175–6 *et passim*. What has been written has tended to have a rural focus. The exception is South Africa, where a growing historical literature on crime has emerged over the past two decades. See, for example, Charles van Onselen, *New Babylon/New Nineveh: Everyday life on the Witwatersrand, 1886–1914*, 2nd edn (Cape Town, 2001); Philip Bonner, 'The Russians on the Reef, 1947–57: Urbanisation, gang warfare and ethnic mobilisation', in Bonner, Peter Delius and Deborah Posel, *Apartheid's Genesis, 1935–62* (Johannesburg, 1993); Gary Kynoch, 'From the Ninevites to the Hard Living gang: Township gangsters and urban violence in Twentieth-century South Africa', *African Studies* 58 (1999); Clive Glaser, *Bo-Tsotsi: The youth gangs of Soweto, 1935–1976* (Portsmouth, NH/Oxford/Cape Town, 2000). For Tanzania, see C. Louise Sweet, 'Inventing crime: British colonial land policy in Tanganyika', in Colin Sumner, *Crime, Justice and Underdevelopment* (London, 1982), pp. 61–89; Leonard Paulo Shaidi, 'Explaining crime in Tanzania mainland: An historical socio-economic perspective', Ph.D. thesis, University of Dar es Salaam (1985).

racial attitudes that saw the African as singularly ill-disposed to orderly urban life formed the legitimisation for controls that restricted African freedoms in a manner that would have been untenable even against the most marginalised sections of urban populations in Europe or America.[2]

Defining crime

There is no permanent criminal class at war with the peace of the community but rather a series of separate acts by individuals, whose need or conscience is for the moment in conflict with the provisions of the law.[3]

The British administration presided over a substantial increase in crime in Tanganyika. Whether this indicates a breakdown of morality as defined by the coloniser as opposed to a broader degeneration of behaviour in the terms of the majority African population is not clear. Historians of crime in the Western world have distinguished between illegal actions that were universally condemned by the society in which they were committed, and those considered legitimate acts by significant sections of that society. Emsley, for example, in his survey of crime in England between 1750 and 1900, draws attention to the difference between 'real' (or 'anti-social') crime and 'social' crime.[4] In eighteenth- and nineteenth-century England, laws that appear to have protected the interests of a particular class,[5] were not necessarily accepted by those they discriminated against, who in breaking them felt no sense of wrongdoing.[6] The differentiation of crime along these lines has pertinence in a colonial context. In Dar es Salaam, and elsewhere in the European empires, laws — often, but not always, the product of distinctive Western legal and cultural traditions — were framed by outsiders and imposed upon colonised subjects, their legitimacy in some cases resting solely on the threat of force. In urban centres in particular, Africans were subject to local laws designed to impose municipal order along the lines of that prevailing in European towns and cities, communities that were a part of the industrialised and more affluent societies of the West.

[2] Then or now: the African in colonial Dar es Salaam was subjected to a 'zero tolerance' policy the draconian nature of which substantially exceeded the controversial new crime prevention measures recently adopted in certain American and British cities.

[3] 'Some observations on the treatment of the offender against the law' [in Tanganyika] by Alexander Paterson (1939), p. 1, TNA/27062.

[4] Emsley, *Crime*, p. 2. See also John G. Rule, 'Social crime in the rural south in the eighteenth and nineteenth centuries', *Southern History* 1 (1979), pp. 135–53; and George Rudé, *Criminal and Victim: Crime and society in early 19th century England* (Oxford, 1985), p. 78. Rudé specifies a third category of crime, 'survival' crime, which was committed out of dire necessity.

[5] This is not to say that 'the law' was simply an instrument of the ruling class. Rather, the law mediated and reinforced existing class relations, and offered them ideological legitimation. At the same time it had its 'own characteristics, its own independent history and logic of evolution' and was an institution contested on its own terms. See E.P. Thompson, *Whigs and Hunters: The origin of the Black Act* (Harmondsworth, 1990), pp. 258–69.

[6] The classic example of which is that of poaching. See e.g., Douglas Hay, 'Poaching and the game laws on Cannock Chase', in Hay *et al.*, *Albion's Fatal Tree*, chapter 5.

In Dar es Salaam, while the substantial Indian population complicated matters, the resulting legislation still reflected 'non-native' interests. Here, the *Township Regulations* were

> framed so as to suit the needs and idiosyncrasies of British, Belgian, Portuguese and Greek communities, living among the numerous Asiatic population... while the whole is *imposed* upon the original inhabitants [i.e. Africans].[7]

In the attempt to assert urban order customary pursuits were criminalised; as were many subsistence activities adopted by Africans in the often harsh urban environment. For example, strict liquor laws prohibited the customary usage of alcohol, and municipal regulations restricted the number of people engaging in petty trade. Among the African population legal restrictions aimed at such victimless crimes commanded little acceptance. Evasion of onerous regulations, observes Westcott, 'became an accepted part of life and reduced respect for colonial law'.[8] Indeed, even those crimes that one might characterise as illegitimate, such as theft, may not have been universally considered so among sections of the population who were perplexed — and perhaps aggravated — by the unequal distribution of resources in colonial society.[9]

Some officials acknowledged the problem. In 1932, one senior administrator stressed that 'it must be remembered that there is no real moral turpitude or real criminality involved in breach of the hundred and one rules, regulations, bye-laws etc.'[10] Alexander Paterson, who as British Commissioner for Prisons visited East Africa in 1939, concurred. He considered it was 'inevitable that crime and conscience should not coincide, when a Penal Code that is founded on a European ethic is imposed upon an African people, whose ideas of right and wrong are so completely different'.[11] In his 1957 survey of the town, Leslie observed the frustrations arising from certain municipal regulations:

> All the restrictions which seem to be aimed at preventing a man from making a few pence — no hawking without a licence, no begging, no three card-trick stands — are made by these people [Europeans][12]

Leslie detected widespread indifference towards crime in general among Dar es Salaam's African inhabitants. He ascribed this partly to a general neglect

---

[7] 1924 DAR, p. 4 (emphasis added). It required more than just the enactment of legislation, though, to achieve an orderly urban environment. As a 1925 editorial in the *Dar es Salaam Times* (9 May 1925, p. 2), bemoaning the unruly behaviour of rickshaw 'boys', observed: 'our laws cannot protect us from persons who do not respect the conventions and duties that modern civilisation expects from us.'

[8] Westcott, 'Impact', p. 286.

[9] Leslie, *Survey*, p. 106. For African resentment over differentiated incomes between the races, see Frederick Kaijage, 'Alternative history and discourses from below: Social history in urban Tanga', Dept of History seminar paper, University of Dar es Salaam, 30 November 2000, p. 19; Brennan, 'Nation', pp. 197–9.

[10] Sec. min., 22 September 1932, TNA/21041.

[11] 'Report on a visit to the Prisons of Kenya, Uganda, Tanganyika, Zanzibar, Aden and Somaliland', 1939, [Paterson, 'Report'], p. 1, in TNA/27062.

[12] Leslie, *Survey*, p. 106.

of community interest. '[T]he instinct to help the victim [of a crime] and the forces of law and order', he observed, 'is simply not there'.[13] He considered moral sanctions against criminal behaviour were also not particularly strong. 'The pilferer, the thief, the embezzler,' were 'in the eyes of many — including themselves — hardly criminals but are "winning" something which nobody will miss, and to which they are in any case in some way entitled'.[14]

There is evidence that supports Leslie's conclusions. Throughout the colonial period officials bemoaned the lack of co-operation given to the police.[15] Whether this can best be explained by the loss of communal responsibility, however, is another matter. The police's relationship with the general public in Dar es Salaam was characterised by fear and mistrust.[16] Meanwhile, control measures fundamental to indigenous crime prevention — such as restitution or reparations — were neglected in British legal practice and, according to a meeting convened to discuss crop theft in 1941, 'as a result the African population will not give that co-operation to the police that is essential if law and order are to be secured'.[17] The apparent indifference of the African population to the maintenance of order could also more plausibly be attributed to a lack of commitment to colonial order, not order *per se*. Indeed, the instant justice that could be meted out by Africans to criminals caught in the act was evidence of a dramatic *lack* of indifference.[18]

African attitudes towards theft in Dar es Salaam were no doubt influenced by customary notions concerning property. Although individualised property rights existed in 'traditional' African societies, these were often balanced by re-distributive mechanisms and by kinship obligations in particular. Among the Chagga, for example, individuals rich in livestock placed their herds in the care of others, a system that was, according to Dundas, 'of great benefit to the poor'.[19] Similar mechanisms obtained among pastoral communities.[20]

---

[13] *Ibid.*, pp. 106, 242. Leslie ascribed this not so much to the loss of mutual communal responsibilities on the move to the town, but to 'a fundamental Bantu way of thinking', which viewed only the extended family as worthy of protection. Indifference to crime was simply exacerbated in the town where 'so many people live surrounded by persons for whose protection they accept no responsibility'.

[14] *Ibid.*, p. 109.

[15] See for examples, Molohan, *Detribalization*, para. 80. Molohan observes that the town's inhabitants' sense of 'duty and responsibility for aiding the enforcement of the law... is sadly lacking and instead one finds the public assisting malefactors to escape arrest'.

[16] See Burton, 'Brothers by Day'. The same was true of colonial Nairobi, where David Throup observes that, with so many Africans earning a living in contravention of local by-laws (as in Dar es Salaam), 'the police were identified by the European community as the agency responsible for "cleaning up" the city"' and 'in contrast, the African residents... more commonly viewed the police as colonial agents of oppression'. 'Crime, politics and the police', p. 131.

[17] *TS*, 4 July 1941, p. 15.

[18] For the lynching of a robber along the lines of those which have become so familiar throughout post-colonial Africa, see *TS*, 16 November 1957, p. 1.

[19] Charles Dundas, *Kilimanjaro and its People* (London, 1968; first edn, 1924), p. 298.

[20] See eg., David M. Anderson and Vigdis Broch-Due, *The Poor Are Not Us: Poverty and pastoralism in Eastern Africa* (Oxford/Athens/Nairobi/Dsm/Kampala, 2000), chapters by Potkanski and Anderson.

Excessive differentiation through the acquisition of individual wealth in East African societies was often tempered by an onus on the affluent to display largesse or to sponsor communal rituals.[21] Gluckman, writing broadly on property rights in 'African traditional law', observed that 'no one owns a food or chattel absolutely, because his kinsfolk and even outsiders may have claims upon it which he has difficulty in denying.' He cites the example of *kufunda* or 'legal theft' among the Lozi of Zambia, which 'allowed any kinsman or kinswoman of a Lozi to take anything belonging to the latter, without exposing himself or herself to the charge of stealing'. Long after the imposition of British colonial rule the Lozi king eventually decreed *kufunda* to be a criminal offence, although Gluckman stated he had never heard of 'anyone prosecuting a kinsman for it, though I knew of families that suffered severely under the depredations of ne'er-do-wells'.[22] In Dar es Salaam, colonial officials frequently bemoaned the similar 'depredations' visited upon urban residents supporting newly arrived migrant kin.[23] Sanctions against theft certainly existed in local societies,[24] but property rights were heavily mediated by social relations within the small-scale rural communities from which most townsmen and women originated.[25]

It is hard to say how customary practice influenced attitudes towards crime in Dar es Salaam, whose heterogeneous and differentiated population

[21] For coastal Tanzania, see Jonathon Glassman, *Feasts and Riot: Revelry, rebellion and popular consciousness on the Swahili Coast, 1856–1888* (Portsmouth, NH, 1995); for an excellent discussion of differentiation, social obligation and change among the Maka of Eastern Cameroon, see Peter Geschiere, *The Modernity of Witchcraft: Politics and the occult in postcolonial Africa* (Charlottesville/London, 1997).

[22] Max Gluckman, 'Property rights and status in African traditional law', in *idem*, (ed.), *Ideas and Procedures in African Customary Law* (Oxford, 1969), pp. 259–60.

[23] See e.g. the Chief Secretary's introduction of the *Townships (Removal of Undesirable Persons) Amendment Bill*, Legco Mins, 19 February 1958. A Dar es Salaam shopkeeper who came from Mwanza explained to Leslie in 1956 that 'to conduct his shop on business lines he must outdistance his relatives'. *Survey*, p. 137. In post-colonial Dar es Salaam, Hill notes that 'Matengo urban migrants' built '"elbow room" into their urban community because not to do so would have invited replication of the pushes toward redistribution and cultural levelling so necessary in the rural homeland, but seen as inimical to "progress" in the city'. Stephen Hill, '"I am a partial person": the urban experience of rural music', in Brennan, Burton and Lawi (eds), *Dar es Salaam in the Twentieth Century: The history of an emerging East African metropolis*, (in preparation).

[24] Among the Luguru, for example, serious theft was punished by payment in slaves, and persistent offenders had their hands cut off; among the Ngulu a persistent thief was sold into slavery; among the Zaramo, Burton claimed that thieves were beheaded though if this were the case it would likely have been for a particularly serious offence. Beidelman, *Matrilineal Peoples*, pp. 22, 32, 62.

[25] In contemporary Dar es Salaam, Moyer has observed a distinct ambivalence among poor urban youth towards illegally acquired wealth. Money earned through work, a loan or a gift would 'more likely … be used to start a business, or to be re-invested in an established one. "Dishonest" money is certainly appreciated and fully enjoyed, but to build one's future on it would be considered both immoral and stupid. … The young men and women [surveyed] … were certainly concerned with … bettering their positions in Dar es Salaam society but they were also critical of those … who they believed relied on criminal … means to do so'. Moyer, 'Shadow', pp. 42–3.

complicated the emergence of a unified moral community. Nevertheless, the high degree of economic inequality in colonial society (between the races especially) was unprecedented, and such ill-distributed wealth could serve to endorse unilateral redistribution, particularly at times of need.[26] Thus Rajabu bin Alfani, complaining of low rates of pay in a letter to *Kwetu*, observed that '[m]any Africans are enduring without food for four or more days [per month], but for others who are not able to endure it is necessary to turn to crime.'[27] Kondo bin Waziri, caught stealing a bicycle in 1942, endeavoured to justify a criminal career, which up to then had stretched to six convictions for property offences over a twelve-year period. According to the presiding judge's summary, Waziri sought

to excuse his life of crime by putting the blame for it on other people. He is compelled to steal for a livelihood, he says, because the police do not find him work when he is released from prison. This particular theft, he alleges, was forced upon him by the Native authorities who were pressing him to pay his tax. Even when he has sought to make a living by honest toil in the fields the bush pigs have rendered his efforts nugatory by stealing his crops by night.[28]

Frederick Kaijage reports a fundamental ambivalence towards property in colonial Tanga that no doubt mirrored attitudes in the capital. According to one of his informants, theft was widespread and tolerated in the town; dockworkers distinguishing between *wizi halali* ('legitimate theft') and *wizi hasada* ('illegitimate theft') — the former representing 'a justifiable redistribution of resources' that supplemented meagre African wages.[29] In Dar es Salaam, in 1940 *Kwetu* observed that 'theft from Indian shops was common and its end was for the thief to distribute stolen items among his friends.'[30] According to Leslie, the prevalence of thefts by servants also occurred partly as a result of a redistributive impulse:

the servants in the houses, working for a pittance, have to handle meat and fish and butter and drink and do without themselves; their employers have so many sheets and towels and shirts that they have to be counted, yet if one is missing there is the devil to pay: why cannot there be more of a share out?[31]

Corresponding with the general indifference towards crime in Dar es Salaam, Leslie also observed that no real stigma seemed to attach itself to those who

---

26 Ranger, summarising R.G.B. Moore (*These African Miners*), has described the kind of conditions that perhaps served to justify crimes in Copperbelt towns: 'African workers, Moore asserted, experienced "a constant thwarting of their ambitions owing to their low wages". They saw that a few privileged clerks were able to achieve these ambitions… They envied these men. But above all they resented "the limitless resources and wealth" of the Europeans; the careless expenditure of those who demanded such austerity from their African employees.' *Dance and Society*, p. 136.
27 *Kwetu*, 26 March 1942, p. 4 (original in Swahili).
28 *TS*, 28 August 1942, p. 9.
29 Kaijage, 'Alternative history', p. 19.
30 *Kwetu*, 8 March 1942. Cited by Jim Brennan in a draft chapter of 'Nation' (omitted in the final thesis).
31 Leslie, *Survey*, p. 106.

had been convicted of crimes and/or imprisoned.[32]

Most Africans in Dar es Salaam, sharing similar backgrounds and the same impecunious conditions of existence as offenders (the bulk of whom were opportunists and not recidivists), would probably not condemn the petty offences — such as shoplifting or theft from the workplace — which were the commonest form of property crime in the town, nor would they condemn 'social' crimes such as gambling, hawking or begging. However, also present in Dar es Salaam were a minority of Africans who, through education or employment, enjoyed a somewhat better standard of living than the majority of their compatriots. They shared the anxieties about African criminality felt by Europeans and Indians. Although a minority, it was this group who were best placed to articulate their concerns and to lobby the colonial administration for protection. Africans such as those appointed to the Dar es Salaam cinema censorship board, who expressed identical concerns to European and Indian members over the depiction of crime in films shown to African audiences.[33] In a *Kwetu* editorial complaining of an increase in urban crime in 1940, Erica Fiah also advocated similar measures to his European counterparts:

> For Government to be allowing the jobless to stay in the town is very bad indeed ... Now I bring to the attention of Government and the District and Municipal administrations the policy of removing thieves from the town; unemployed persons should be forced out and be made to cultivate; homeowners should compile lists of the names of their tenants in work and send them to the administration.[34]

M.F. Kassam, in a letter to *Kwetu* two years later, complained of *wahuni* collecting together and harassing women, throwing stones at *askaris* and buildings, gambling and stealing. He asked the DC to 'remove this trouble from the town so that it should be cleansed'.[35] Many African complainants ascribed heightened crime rates to the laxity of the British penal regime, again echoing the laments of European and Indian settlers.[36] Fiah, writing to the *Tanganyika Standard* in 1952, considered that: 'We, the Africans cannot be good people unless we are taught by punishment of beating.' To combat laziness and the penchant to steal, he recommended the reintroduction of the lash (*kiboko*), which the German administration had employed so freely.[37]

---

[32] Ibid., p. 239; see also Paterson, 'Report', and Cairns, *Bush*, p. 17. Cairns observed: 'Prison is one of the hazards a man may encounter in life, like drought, famine, a lazy wife, or rats eating his store of maize seed. Nothing especially moral or immoral is involved'.

[33] In 1941, for example, Kleist Sykes endorsed the board's rejection of the Indian film *Flying Rani* on account of scenes depicting robbery and murder. This policy was maintained after independence: in 1966, the chief film censor, Yusuf A. Marsha, explained that (among others) 'films which show extreme forms of crime and can lead people to learn for example the art of thieving' were banned. Brennan, 'Democratizing cinema'.

[34] *Kwetu*, 12 March 1940, p. 1 (original in Swahili).

[35] *Kwetu*, 13 February 1942 (original in Swahili).

[36] For a classic example of which, see 'What the Governor might have said', a 1930 cutting from the *Tanganyika Times*, RH/Mss.Afr.s. 1072.

[37] *TS*, 28 June 1952; see also, M. Mkonimwe to CS, undated (1944/5?), TNA/10849; and the letter from Lawi Kardi, *TS*, 18 June 1957, p. 4.

Criminality was a contested notion among Dar es Salaam's various strata. Colonial definitions of crime were broad, their object being an orderly and strictly regulated urban environment. Attempts to criminalise particular forms of behaviour were frequently resisted by Africans. Petty economic activities may have been proscribed by colonial law, but they also provided incomes and services to the African population. Even certain property crimes appear to have been condoned by many Africans. Theft was described by Engels as 'the most primitive form of protest', and in Dar es Salaam property crime can plausibly be interpreted as having been in part unfocused (and/or unconscious) resistance against colonial economic and political iniquities.[38] Faced with a massively skewed distribution of wealth, and their powerlessness in the colonial context, African criminals may even have attempted to rationalise their actions in this way. Nevertheless, it is important not to romanticise the Dar es Salaam criminal. As elsewhere in Africa, it was the poor who were most vulnerable and who were the commonest victims of property crime.[39] As such, those who chose to prey upon their fellow Africans were no doubt feared and detested by the majority, and if caught were vulnerable to a popular form of justice that could be swift and harsh.[40] Neither was 'social banditry' a feature.[41] Crime in Dar es Salaam was much more mundane. Although the quotidian criminality of thefts from European employers or from Indian shops appears to have been widely tolerated, and might be characterised as resistance, its basic motivation was more likely simple economic need, unaccompanied by any form of political consciousness.[42]

[38] The quote is from *Condition of the Working Class*, cited in Crumney, *Banditry*, p. 3. See also E.J. Hobsbawm, *Primitive Rebels: Studies in archaic forms of social movement in the 19th and 20 centuries* (Manchester, 1959).

[39] M.B. Clinard & D.J. Abbott, *Crime in Developing Countries* (New York, 1973), p. 36; Van Onselen, *New Babylon*, p. 397 *et passim*; McCracken, 'Coercion and control', p. 135; Iliffe, *African Poor*, pp. 177 & 189; Kynoch, 'Ninevites'; Glaser, *Bo-Tsotsi*, p. 138 *et passim*.

[40] As occurred in 1957, when Maganga Mnameta — caught stealing merely a bundle of clothing from a house in Buguruni — was tied up and beaten to death by a mob. *TS*, 16 November 1957, p. 1. Commenting on the prevalence of such lynchings in contemporary Dar es Salaam, one of Moyer's informants observed that 'people with almost no money for … basic necessities will quickly hand over whatever cash they have when a collection is made for kerosene to douse an accused thief.' The enduring ambivalence of attitudes towards property and theft in Dar es Salaam is demonstrated by the fact that justification for lynchings was provided to Moyer by one-time participants who were 'itinerant thieves themselves'. 'Shadow', p. 225; see also, p. 288.

[41] The one individual who approached 'social bandit' status was Omari bin Masua, whose activities in the early 1930s won the approval of Africans in Dar es Salaam. However, his criminal career was probably motivated more by the mundanely material than by any desire to redress colonial wrongs. For social banditry, see E.J. Hobsbawm, *Bandits*, 2nd edn (Harmondsworth, 1985); and for Africa, Allen Isaacman, 'Social banditry in Zimbabwe (Rhodesia) and Mozambique, 1894–1907', *JSAS* IV:1 (1977); and Crumney, *Banditry*.

[42] Van Onselen comes to similar conclusions about criminals on the Rand (*New Babylon*, p. 397); as does Laurent Fourchard, writing on Ibadan ('Urban poverty, urban crime and crime control: The Lagos and Ibadan cases, 1929–1945', paper given at the conference on African Urban Spaces, University of Texas, Austin, March 2003).

Crime and colonial knowledge

Crime in Dar es Salaam appears to have grown substantially during British colonial rule. Both the statistical record and impressionistic evidence support this view. It is necessary to stress caution about available sources, however.[43] Any rise in crime rates to be detected in surviving police, court or prison records may be as much a reflection of increased efficiency in policing, the decision to enforce previously neglected laws, or a change in sentencing policy, as it is of rising criminality.[44] In the case of Dar es Salaam, low crime figures in the inter-war period are probably connected to the negligible police presence in the town. Similarly, the rapid escalation of crime rates after WWII was almost certainly related to the enhanced police capacity to detect misdemeanours and enforce the law.[45] Post-war crime rates may have also reflected the greater likelihood for crimes to be reported as a result of increasing public confidence in the apprehension and prosecution of offenders.[46] Both before and after WWII, however, it is likely that a large number of offences remained unreported.[47] Africans in colonial Dar es Salaam were probably hesitant to report crimes to a policing body whom many regarded as more an occupying force than a neutral keeper of the peace.[48] The 'dark figure'[49] casts a considerable, though unquantifiable, shadow over the recorded crime statistics in colonial Tanganyika.

A further problem with official crime records is that in Dar es Salaam the law was imposed differentially. Offences that the police decided to prosecute varied over time. The production and consumption of *tembo* (palm wine), for example, was legally proscribed throughout the inter-war period. The official

[43] For a useful discussion of interpreting crime-related data, see Emsley, *Crime*, pp. 1–55.

[44] For discussion of such factors in operation in colonial Kenya, see Anderson, 'Policing', and Willis, 'Thieves'.

[45] In early post-colonial Uganda the police observed 'that the immediate consequence of the erection of a new police station [wa]s a substantial increase in reported crime'. R.E.S. Tanner, 'Some problems of East African crime statistics', in *Three Studies of East African Criminology* (Uppsala, 1970), p. 9.

[46] In addition, the growth of the urban European and Indian population in the late 1940s and 1950s meant the two communities that were particularly sensitised to the perceived threat posed by African criminality, and that were also more prone to reporting incidents to the police, were substantially larger. I owe this observation to Justin Willis.

[47] In 1940, the headmaster of the Government Primary School in Dar es Salaam observed that while it was 'probable that not a single day or night passes without at least one burglary in the African quarter of the town… Most… are never even reported to the Police, because the victims know quite well that in present circumstances nothing can be done in the vast majority of cases.' R.J. Harvey to Director of Education, 6 March 1940, TNA/61/207/ Vol. II.

[48] By the 1950s, the police in Dar es Salaam were colloquially known as '*ndugu wa mchana*' (brothers by day) because they were believed to be enemies at night, when it was thought they went around arresting people anonymously. Sadleir, *Tanzania*, p. 218.

[49] As historians of crime in the Western world have coined 'the number of offences committed of which there is no record'. Emsley, *Crime*, p. 24.

response to such activity, however, was uneven, varying between tolerance and sporadic attempts at eradication.[50] Such unevenness in the application of the law was most marked in the case of the sex trade. While prostitution was declared illegal by the colonial administration, the laws that prohibited it were not systematically implemented against Dar es Salaam's growing community of prostitutes. At one point, in the late 1920s, an attempt was actually made by the Township Authority to license brothels and to provide for the medical inspection of prostitutes. It was opposed by central government.[51] However, prostitution, in spite of the clauses that outlawed such activity in both the Township Rules and the penal code, was broadly tolerated throughout the period of the British mandate. That prostitutes in Dar es Salaam did not receive the treatment meted out to comparable offenders against the law, such as beggars or street traders, is perhaps surprising. Officials disapproved of it on a number of grounds: the areas in which it was practised were often a haven for the town's more unruly elements;[52] the steady flow[53] of customers to the red light districts hindered the control of these areas; it offered the opportunity to amass wealth beyond the supervision of the state; and finally there was the straightforward moral objection to the sale of sex to earn a living. Nevertheless, prostitution was mostly tolerated by colonial officials. This policy was partly based on expediency; in a town full of single men the contribution of these women to urban stability did not go unrecognised. 'The biological urge', observed the Municipal Secretary in 1944, 'is not lightly repressed without grave danger.'[54]

Equally significant, was the fact that the urban administration was never in a position to eliminate prostitution, even if it desired to do so. When, after the outbreak of an epidemic of venereal diseases during WWII, an attempt was made to curtail the trade 'all attempts to stop it proved futile.'[55] Dar es Salaam's prostitutes appear not to have been specifically targeted in colonial campaigns against urban undesirables. As a result, the sale of sex is one criminal activity the incidence of which is poorly reflected in police and judicial records. For other illegal activities too, the uneven application of the law complicates the interpretation of such records.

Other, more impressionistic sources, including newspapers and official correspondence, are also unreliable. Heightened public perceptions of particular crimes, or of crime waves, can in the end almost prove self-fulfilling.[56] Moreover, human anxiety often leads to exaggerated fears about

---

50 When he was DO in Tanga, E.C. Baker observed 'the abuse of this regulation [against *tembo*] bore certain resemblance to conditions in the USA during the prohibition period.' Tanga DAR, 1936, p. 8.

51 EO, TA (at Health Office) to CS, 28 April 1927; DMS to EO, TA 12 May 1927, TNA/ 10340.

52 See e.g. *TH*, 23 February 1935, p. 6.

53 In Kisutu, according to the *Herald* (23 February 1935, p. 6), prostitutes were 'allowed to carry on their profession day and night'.

54 MS to CS, 16 December 1944, TNA/20887/Vol. II.

55 Westcott, 'Impact', p. 291.

56 See Emsley, *Crime*, p. 26.

the prevalence of criminality, especially violence-related crimes.[57] This in part helps to explain the impression of rampant lawlessness in Uhindini given by Dar es Salaam's Indian-owned newspapers. Claims that a 'native raj' operated in Zone II should be treated with some scepticism.[58] Similarly, the settler press reflected distorted perceptions of the prevalence of crime on the part of the European community, whose anxieties were magnified by a consciousness of being heavily outnumbered. Official observations on the incidence of crime in Dar es Salaam are also probably more unreliable than opinions offered on other aspects of town life: the degree of lawlessness partly depending upon the eye of the beholder. The same may be said of oral sources. By contrast to the tenor of overwrought colonial editorials or the commentary of pressurised officials, informants interviewed about colonial Dar es Salaam, from all races and backgrounds (but particularly African informants), tended to recollect a town in which crime was almost absent. Such a view does not chime with the picture that emerges from surviving records — even allowing for the most exaggerated fears on the part of contemporary observers.[59] As we shall see, crime occurred in myriad forms in the town and its increasing incidence over the colonial period is striking. Nevertheless, it is important to stress that colonial Dar es Salaam was, both in terms relative to other African towns at this time — such as Nairobi, Johannesburg or Ibadan[60] — as well as in historical perspective, a remarkably peaceful place.

The causes of crime

The increase in crime that has occurred in Western societies since the eighteenth century has been associated with the breakdown of communal

---

[57] For the 'black peril' in South Africa, see Van Onselen, *New Babylon*, pp. 257–68.

[58] *TH*, 6 April 1935, p. 4.

[59] This tendency to idealise the situation can perhaps best be accounted for by the post-colonial experience — for those who have remained in the town — of substantially increased lawlessness in Dar es Salaam, mixed with a degree of wistful nostalgia. Pearson (*Hooligan*) notes the cyclical, generational nature of anxieties about lawlessness. The past in popular memory is perennially a quieter, safer place. He highlights the recurring theme of the more orderly societies of a generation (twenty years) earlier that are continually invoked in moral panics over 'crime waves' in nineteenth- and twentieth-century England. It is also present in colonial Tanzania. For example, the district official, G.W. Hatchell, who, when based in Tanga in 1945, confidently asserted that 'there can be no doubt that the average town child is less well brought up and has less respect for his elders than was the case twenty years ago.' Note on Education and Training of Africans, 8 September 1945, TNA/450/404.

[60] For Nairobi in the 1940s, see Throup, *Mau Mau*, chapter 8; and for the 1950s, David M. Anderson, *Histories of the Hanged: Britain's dirty war in Kenya and the end of Empire* (London, 2004), chapter 5; for Johannesburg, see Glaser, *Bo-Tsotsi*; for Ibadan, see Simon Heap, 'Jaguda boys: Pickpocketing in Ibadan, 1930–60', *Urban History* 24 (1997), 3, pp. 24–43, and Fourchard, 'Urban poverty'.

social structures in the face of both industrialisation and urbanisation.[61] Scholars of crime in sub-Saharan Africa and other developing countries have turned to related arguments to explain the apparent escalation in crime rates there since the colonial period.[62] Economic 'development' led to the proliferation of commodities and the creation of new patterns of consumption, new needs and desires.[63] Urban growth, meanwhile, provided an environment in which the opportunities and temptations for theft multiplied considerably at the same time as an impoverished urban class emerged in the midst of relative plenty. Both these phenomena were highlighted by Paterson in his 1939 report on prisons in Eastern Africa:

> A very rapid increase in the demand on life during the last thirty years has led inevitably to a[n] ... increase in theft ... Crime will further increase as this same demand to have life, and have it more abundantly, lures the more spirited and ambitious youngster from tending his parents' cattle to the Gold paved streets of Nairobi, Kampala or Dar es Salaam. On arriving at the town they find the only occupation open to them is to serve in the most menial capacity for Shs.2/- a month in an Indian shop. They are just as hungry as when their parents fed them at home, but food in the town has to be paid for, and moreover there are many things in the town besides food that they want to buy. So they steal.[64]

From the little research that has been done on patterns of crime in the Third World, it appears that poverty has tended to be a crucial factor in determining the identity of both perpetrator *and* victim. According to Iliffe, in tropical Africa 'most urban crime ... was crime by individuals against property ... and most of the individuals were poor.' Clinard and Abbott found that in 1960s Kampala most crimes involved property offences committed by the poor against the poor.[65] In an environment in which 'even the simplest object, such as a used shirt, a light bulb, or a piece of iron pipe, represents a desirable increment in wealth,' they point out, 'the potential market for stolen goods is much greater than in almost any developed country.'[66]

---

[61] Emsley, *Crime*, pp. 93–4. Pearson points out the persistence of this 'modernisation thesis' as an explanation since the nineteenth century, but is sceptical of its explanatory value (*Hooligan*, p. 164 *et passim*). More recent, radical criminology, notably in the form of labelling theory, sought to account for criminal tendencies in individuals through the societal response to their initial (quite possibly, petty) offences; their identification and treatment as miscreants contributing to a self-image that leads to further miscreancy. See Paul Rock, 'Sociological theories of crime', in Maguire *et al.*, *Handbook*, pp. 70–3. The 'labelling' of large numbers of Africans through the criminalisation of many petty activities may well have fostered criminality in colonial Dar es Salaam. Van Onselen (*New Babylon*, p. 377) notes how the enforcement of the pass laws impacted upon crime on the Witwatersrand, providing recruits for the 'Ninevites' gang.

[62] See Clinard & Abbott, *Crime*; and for Tanzania, James E. Blackwell, 'Race and crime in Tanzania', *Phylon* 32 (1971), pp. 207–14.

[63] *Ibid.*, p. 35.

[64] Paterson, 'Report', p. 2; see also, *TO*, 20 November 1937, p. 7.

[65] Clinard & Abbott, *Crime*, p. 36; Iliffe, *African Poor*, p. 176.

[66] Clinard & Abbott, p. 257. The same was true of Dar es Salaam where, in 1924 for example, property stolen in housebreakings was reported to be 'of infinitesimal value, and very often consists of rags of native clothing'. 1924 Police AR. See Burton 'Wahuni', pp. 90–1, for a discussion of burglars' loot.

The prevalence of petty theft emerging amid an environment of impoverishment echoes the findings of historians of crime in industrialising Western societies. The notion of a 'criminal class', beloved of 'respectable' nineteenth-century commentators on crime, has been undermined by recent historical research. 'Criminality, in the form of thefts committed by men from the poorer sections of the working class,' Emsley tells us, 'was transitory behaviour, possibly fostered by economic hardship, probably encouraged by opportunity.'[67] The same was true of colonial Africa, and was acknowledged as such by officials, in Dar es Salaam at least. While Victorian commentators may have focused on 'evil ancestral influences'[68] to explain the tendency to offend, in Tanganyika environmental factors were the most frequently cited explanation, and the breakdown of customary restraints and unemployment were both highlighted.[69] Although an anonymous official in the Kisarawe district book could describe the 'character of the Wazaramo' as 'peace loving and polite (though inclined to theft)',[70] more likely the descent into criminality was understood to result from increasing urbanisation. The urban arena, with its concentration of population, its disparities of wealth, its lack of rigid structures of control, and most of all its restricted opportunities for remunerative employment, was seen to corrupt the incoming African.

As the largest town in Tanganyika, Dar es Salaam posed a particular threat. Surviving statistics, which show the incidence of crime in the capital to be hugely disproportionate to its share of the territorial population, appear to confirm this perspective. However, statistics are opaque and can prove deceptive. Surviving territorial criminal records cover only those areas in which a police officer was stationed and thus exclude a large part of rural Tanganyika. In fact crime — and hence criminality — may have been much more common in the rural areas than colonial officials thought. Certainly recent research into crime in rural Britain in the eighteenth and nineteenth centuries has led to a reappraisal of assumptions about the coincidence of urban growth and criminality there.[71] That similar assumptions on the part of officials (and non-officials) may have been equally ill-informed, or at least exaggerated, should be borne in mind in the following discussion of causative interpretations of crime in colonial Dar es Salaam.

Explaining crime[72]

'The African community in town must unfortunately be regarded with marked suspicion', wrote Orde-Browne, then Dar es Salaam's District Officer, in 1924.

---

[67] Emsley, *Crime*, p. 175.
[68] Victorian pyschologist Henry Maudsley, quoted in Emsley, *Crime*, p. 75.
[69] This is not to say that the notion of individual responsibility was ignored, simply that criminal behaviour was felt to result from the moral weaknesses of African migrants in a corrupting urban environment.
[70] Kisarawe District Book Vol.1.
[71] E.g., Rudé, *Criminal and Victim*; Emsley, *Crime*, p. 98.
[72] The following section contains a discussion of how contemporary observers accounted for the growth of crime in colonial Dar es Salaam. For an analysis of the situation in Nairobi that highlights markedly similar factors — urbanisation, the diminishing influence of communal sanctions, unemployment and low wages — see Throup, 'Crime, politics and the police', p. 132.

While there was

> naturally a very large element of thoroughly respectable people honestly occupied in a reputable calling, there is also a most undesirable floating population of criminals, or quasi-criminals, who thrive on the exploitation of unsophisticated natives who may pass through the town.[73]

The emergence of such malefactors, according to Orde-Browne, writing in a later report, was bound up with the growth of large urban centres. Having left their rural homes for waged labour, Africans drifted to the towns where

> they find some sort of casual work, but probably fail to get steady employment; intervals of idleness between jobs tend to increase, until the individual drifts gradually into the class of unemployable loafer, from which stage it is fatally easy to join the definitely criminal class.[74]

As we have seen, African morals were viewed by colonial officials as prone to corrosion through contact with the urban environment. The descent into criminality was the logical conclusion to this process. Fryer, Dar es Salaam's DO in 1931, observed in the town 'the type of development which produces from the waifs and strays and street urchins of London, the type of being that earns his living by his wits, who is a good judge at summing up his fellow man and has no respect for a law he can break with impunity.'[75] For Eric Reid, author of a book on Tanganyika in the 1930s, '[p]ilfering, lying and crime distinguish[ed]' the urbanised native.[76] Crime was commonly associated with the process of detribalisation. A 1952 *Tanganyika Standard* editorial considered it 'quite obvious that the majority of crimes such as theft and burglary are committed by Africans many of whom travel long distances drawn by the glamour of the big town'. 'In the "new community of strangers"', the author observed, 'these people lose the social responsibility that close village life imposed on them.'[77] Throughout the colonial period the tendency to criminality remained, as far as most observers were concerned, a vice predominantly acquired by Africans on their move to the towns.

Within Dar es Salaam itself the shortage of employment was singled out as the key contributor to African criminality. In the first district report, APO West blamed the high levels of crime that had been prevalent in the early years of British rule on the presence of a large number of jobless Africans.[78] The following year, DO Brett voiced his concern about the return of some of these individuals:

[73] 1924 DAR, p. 6.
[74] Orde-Browne, 'Labour', para. 114. The Destitute Persons Ordinance of 1923 was in part enacted to counter this phenomenon. 'It is common', the memorandum accompanying the bill observed, 'for natives from the interior to come to the coast attracted by stories of high wages. Such natives often become destitute and are then tempted to become criminals.' Explanatory Memorandum, PRO/CO/691/57.
[75] 1931 DAR, p. 7.
[76] Eric Reid, *Tanganyika Without Prejudice* (London, 1934), p. 226.
[77] *TS*, 9 August 1952, p. 4.
[78] 1919–20 DAR, p. 9. See also, 1921 DAR, p. 8.

A number of these people are unable to obtain suitable employment, others have no desire to work; these are potential thieves if they have noone who is willing to support them, since food is not available in Dar es Salaam as it may be at their homes. A successful theft of clothing or other articles which are disposed of outside the township procures the wherewithal for their maintenance for several days.

The editor of the *Dar es Salaam Times* concurred, ascribing 'an orgy of housebreaking and theft on the part of native criminals' in the same year to 'an absence of employment for natives who turn their energies along the line of least effect'.[79] In 1930, with the onset of economic depression, the Commissioner of Police made the same connection. Instances of crime 'were to be expected when the fact is taken into account that at the moment the town is overcrowded with alien unemployed natives who have been thrown out of work'.[80] '[T]he question of unemployment among the native community', observed the Indian editor of the *Tanganyika Opinion* in 1937, was '[i]nextricably tangled with the question of tackling the criminally-minded native … the unemployed is as dangerous to the society as the criminally-minded unless he is shown sympathy and is enabled to eke out an honest livelihood'.[81] Lack of work was also identified as an important causative factor by post-war observers. In 1946, according to Dar es Salaam's Resident Magistrate, out of 365 cases of theft coming before him over a five-month period at least sixty 'were perpetrated as a result of genuine hunger conditions'.[82] An outbreak of burglaries in 1952 was attributed 'to the end of the boom or the beginning of the slump'.[83] 'It is most noticeable', wrote the Commissioner of Police later in the decade, 'that the amount of crime varies with unemployment (which varies seasonally).'[84]

Lack of work was held to have a particularly bad effect upon young Africans. In his 1931 report, Baker commented on the large number of detribalised youths, 'pick[ing] up a living as best they can' who frequently resorted to crime to get by.[85] Pike also singled out joblessness among this section of the community. Between the ages of 14 and 18 children who had originally come to the town as servants seldom found permanent employment. '[T]he four most impressionable years of these boys lives' were, according to Pike, 'spent in the company of loafers, petty thieves and card sharpers'.[86] An African writing to *Kwetu* in 1942 also bemoaned the pernicious effects of joblessness among the young. He regarded 'the number of unemployed youths as shocking'. Their semi-educated status gave them ambitions for urban employment that were not matched by opportunities:

[79] *DT*, 28 May 1921, pp. 2–3.
[80] CP to CS, 12 August 1931, TNA/20219.
[81] *TO*, 20 November 1937, p. 7.
[82] The magistrate was satisfied that they 'had all made their maximum effort to obtain work'. Quoted in Shivji, *Law, State & Working Class*, p. 131.
[83] Min. dated 26 August 1952, TNA/21963/Vol. 1.
[84] Police AR, 1959, p. 45.
[85] Baker, 'Social conditions', p. 94.
[86] Pike, 'Report', p. 9.

What can these youths be expected to do? ...they are people in need and as such in desperation they will turn to what will appear to them to be the easiest means of satisfying their wants, *namely theft, pick pocketing, robbery, bank holding* [sic], *etc* [emphasis in original].[87]

Another correspondent to *Kwetu* pointed out that it was not only unemployment, but also the low level of African wages that resulted in the escalation of crime. Rajabu bin Alfani complained that a monthly wage of Shs. 25/- was hopelessly insufficient when daily food expenses alone could be Shs. 1/50, and that this was leading to the increasing incidence of theft.[88] Officials voiced similar concerns. Paterson observed in 1939 that '[e]mployment at wages too low to allow a sufficiency of food tempts the simple and the hungry to steal.'[89] Seven years later, a conference of district officials in Eastern Province was told that 'a partial review of cases of theft and burglary had indicated that a considerable number of such offences had been found to have been committed by Africans at uneconomic rates of pay.'[90]

Commonly expressed fears about crime in Dar es Salaam were rooted in the wider discourse on African urbanisation. While 'the town' was a focal point for anxiety over social change occurring under colonialism, within the urban centres the problem of crime formed a lightning rod for concerns arising from the social and cultural processes unfolding therein. In particular, they reflected anxiety over the occupation of space. A rapidly expanding urban African population, comprised mainly of poorly educated rural migrants, threatened European, Indian and respectable African predominance in the urban arena. As such, it was the migrant *wahuni* who were stigmatised by the moral entrepreneurs of colonial Dar es Salaam.[91] This partly served as an explanation for the growing incidence of social phenomena labelled 'criminal'. In addition, *wahuni* represented a focus for popular fears arising from such phenomena, and simultaneously a convenient target action against which would help assuage these fears.

[87] *Kwetu*, 26 March 1942, p. 7.
[88] *Ibid.*, p. 4 (original in Swahili).
[89] Paterson, 'Tanganyika', p. 1.
[90] Mins of DCs conference, EP, 2 September 1946, TNA/61/502/Pt.1. See also, Uzaramo DAR, 1946, p. 8, TNA/61/504/1/46.
[91] In nineteenth- and twentieth-century Britain, Pearson likewise noted the tendency to scapegoat recent migrant communities as perpetrators of disorder. *Hooligan*, p. 236.

Seven

The Dar es Salaam Underworld

Like other urban centres throughout the world, Dar es Salaam was the location of distinctive forms of criminality. The concentration of wealth and population provided an environment in which such quintessentially urban crimes as burglary, street robbery or pickpocketing could occur. Criminal opportunities offered by the town attracted individuals keen to exploit these conditions. A small, but active, hard core of 'professional' criminals emerged in Dar es Salaam in the course of the colonial period, though opportunist felony driven by need appears to have been more common. At the same time, a distribution network for stolen property arose, which in providing a market for contraband goods seems to have encouraged crime. Alongside improved communications, and a corresponding proliferation of regional socio-cultural and economic links that evolved in the town, this resulted in a kind of illicit 'enlargement of scale'.[1]

The growth of crime[2]

The installation of the British administration had an inauspicious beginning. The final years of WWI and the immediate post-war years saw a wave of lawlessness sweeping the country in which the capital was also caught up. '[D]ue to the demobilised native follower and soldier', the District Officer reported in 1920, 'crime was a very serious matter in the town and district

[1] See Andrew Burton, '*Jamii ya Wahalifu*'. The growth of crime in a colonial urban centre: Dar es Salaam, Tanganyika, 1919–1961', f/c; and for the 'enlargement of scale' in Tanganyikan Society, Iliffe, *Modern History*.

[2] The following discussion gives an account of criminal activity (and the public response) based on surviving colonial records. It shares the weaknesses of those records, which, without knowledge of how they were produced, are difficult to interpret. Nevertheless, as the main source of information about crime — however unreliable — statistics have been quoted in an attempt to convey an impression of the situation in Dar es Salaam. They should be treated as indicators of trends instead of a reliable guide to the extent of crime at any one time or in any one place.

during the last nine months of 1919.'[3] The repatriation of 'undesirables' and prosecution of offenders helped stabilise the situation. However, it was not until 1921 that the Commissioner of Police could report that 'crime within the territory for the first time since the war was brought within normal limits'.[4] Crime rates soon began to escalate once again, in Dar es Salaam especially. By 1931, 38 percent of all criminal cases in Tanganyika were reported in the capital — 1,723 cases out of a total of 2,217.[5] These included 443 cases of theft. 'Few nights pass without some form of minor appropriation of property taking place in the native quarter', observed Baker in his report that year.[6] In the course of the following decade reported cases of theft jumped dramatically, reaching 1,317 in 1939. Over the same period, the number of Africans convicted in Dar es Salaam rose from 1,041 to 1,596. A UMCA missionary bemoaned 'the prevalence of petty larceny in every quarter of the town', much of it going 'undetected and unpunished'.[7]

In the early years of WWII there was an actual reduction in crime, attributed to the absence from town of a large number of men away on service and the repatriation of 'undesirable sojourners'.[8] By the end of the war, though, crime rates were escalating once again. While few statistics for Dar es Salaam itself are extant, surviving records for the territory as a whole indicate a sharp rise in criminality (or at least a sharp rise in *detected* criminality). In 1939 there had been convictions in 1,618 cases of crime against property in Tanganyika. By 1946 the number of convictions for property offences had jumped by over 300 percent to 5,206.[9] In Dar es Salaam itself, the District Commissioner observed in his annual report, 'burglary and petty thieving, bag-snatching and the like showed a considerable increase.'[10] Almost 2,000 thefts were reported in the town in the course of the year, as compared to 1,115 in 1938.[11] 'Commission of crime', the Dar es Salaam Superintendent of Police informed the Municipal Secretary,

> is only too prevalent at present in the native quarter: far too many thefts and burglaries occur monthly in this area mostly by night, although the individual cases may not be very serious the cumulative effect is most disturbing to the African residents.[12]

[3] 1919–20 DAR, TNA/1733:1. Similarly, it was reported in the 1919 Lindi DAR that for demobilised *askaris* 'the period of transition from military work to their pre-war occupations as tillers of the land was a fruitful time for crime' (quoted in Ranger, *Dance*, p. 67). The increased incidence of crime in the aftermath of war, when large numbers of young men return home, appears to have been a relatively common historical phenomenon. See Emsley, *Crime*, pp. 33–4.
[4] 1921 Police AR, p. 28.
[5] CP to CS, 11 July 1932, TNA/18950/Vol. 1; and Police AR, 1931; n.b. police statistics tend to reflect the crime rate in the urban areas — Native Authorities policed rural communities, so most rural crime does not appear in them.
[6] Baker, 'Memorandum', p. 93.
[7] *Central Africa* (1940), p. 161; see also, Pike, 'Report'.
[8] See Police ARs, 1941 (p. 10) and 1942 (p. 19).
[9] 1939 Police AR; 1946 Judicial AR.
[10] Uzaramo DAR, 1946, p. 8, TNA/61/504/1/46.
[11] Answers to D.K. Patel's questions in the Legco, December 1946, TNA/20219/Vol. II.
[12] SP to MS, 4 February 1946, TNA/540/27/20.

He reported that

> a spate of rumours of assaults and robberies [had] been so strong that native women were refusing to go out alone after dark and men took to carrying knives and sticks to protect themselves against attack.

Crime rates continued to rise through the late 1940s. By 1950, convictions in property cases had increased over the territory as a whole by an annual average of around 750. In the first three months of that year 787 property-related offences had been dealt with by the police in Dar es Salaam division alone. 'Incidents after incidents happen', complained the editor of the *Tanganyika Opinion* in February. How, he asked with characteristic overstatement, 'can people tolerate any more such daily harassments when their mere stepping out of home at night is watched by hooligans and night raiders?'[13]

Over the final decade of colonial rule crime continued to rise. 'Offences against property', noted the Commissioner of Police in his 1949 report, 'are steadily on the increase in all areas which are being opened up or developed.'[14] The development of Dar es Salaam considerably outpaced most of the remainder of Tanganyika, and this was reflected in the statistics. In 1949 the number of penal code cases dealt with by the Dar es Salaam police was 3,864. Three years later this figure was almost matched by the number of cases dealt with in the first half of the year alone, at 3,092. In July 1952 the Municipal Council felt compelled to discuss 'the alarming increase in crime', its members urging 'all those in authority to take vigorous steps to meet it'.[15] Any action taken appeared to have little effect. One year later, in the last quarter of 1953, 124 cases of housebreaking were, on average, reported each month. In the same period 32 thefts from vehicles and 124 bicycle thefts were also reported, making a quarterly total of 528 of these offences. In the first quarter of 1954 this figure rose slightly to 536. The Superintendent of Police reported that 'vigorous action ha[d] been taken to clear the town of would-be thieves.' Once again such action had little immediate impact. In the next quarter the total increased to 695. Nonetheless *wahuni* or 'spiv' raids aimed at removing the unemployed and underemployed from the town did eventually appear to keep crime temporarily in check. Between January 1953 and December 1956 the total number of cases under the penal code dealt with by the municipal police actually declined. However, the Commissioner of Police warned that the raids were 'not the final answer to crime prevention and detection, as the criminal classes will soon learn ways and means of avoiding being caught up in the[m]'.[16] He was right to express caution. The following year the number of convictions once again began to rise. By 1960 the territorial total stood at 10,382. In Dar es Salaam, the

---

[13] Crime analysis, 1 January–31 March 1950, TNA/41124; *TO*, 14 February 1950 (TNA/20219/Vol. III).

[14] 1949 Police AR, p. 10.

[15] CP to CS, 14 August 1952; TC to CS, 14 July 1952, TNA/21963/ Vol. II.

[16] QPRs, Dsm Dist., 1 January–31 March 1954; 1 October–31 December 1955, TNA/90/1011/Vol. 1.

primary location of reported crime throughout the colonial period, crime escalated over the course of the 1950s at a rate that exceeded the rise in Tanganyika as a whole.[17] In the town's Native Courts — presided over by the *Wakili* and *Liwali* — the number of criminal cases dealt with annually more than doubled between 1950 and 1960 from 1,997 to 4,596. A comparable increase was recorded in the Resident Magistrate's court (see Tables 7.1 and 7.2).

Table 7.1 *Criminal cases in Dar es Salaam's local courts 1950–60*

	1950	1951	1952	1953	1954	1955	1956	1957	1958	1959	1960
Kariakoo	n/a	n/a	535	804	701	n/a	n/a	n/a	n/a	n/a	n/a
Ilala	n/a	n/a	535	581	599	n/a	n/a	n/a	n/a	n/a	n/a
Kisutu	n/a	n/a	716	1105	765	n/a	n/a	n/a	n/a	n/a	n/a
Liwali	n/a	n/a	273	313	282	n/a	n/a	n/a	n/a	n/a	n/a
Total	1,997	2,336	2,059	2,803	2,347	n/a	2,967	3,379	3,990	3,998	4,596

Sources: Dsm DAR, 1951, TNA 61/504/1/1951; TNA microfilm, Dsm Extra-Provincial Dist. Book Vol. V.I; & PARs 1956–9

Table 7.2 *Criminal cases in Resident Magistrate's Court, Dar es Salaam, 1951–1961*

1951	1952	1953	1954	1955	1956	1957	1958	1959	1960	1961
2,532	2,951	2,407	2,795	3,026	2,743	3,068	5,343	5,948	5,516	4,416

Source: Judicial Dept ARs

Judging by colonial records then, the escalation in crime in Tanganyika is striking. In 1922, the first year for which statistics survive, the number of criminal cases dealt with by the police stood at 4,960. In the final year of colonial rule the number of cases in which convictions were obtained was over 50,000. Property offences alone had proliferated at an almost comparable rate. From the introduction of the Tanganyikan Penal Code in 1930 to the end of colonial rule they increased from around 2,000 to over 11,000. The escalation was apparent in by-law offences also. In 1928, 8,005 offences against the 'social economy' of the territory were reported in Tanganyika. In the final year of colonial rule the number of such offences had risen to almost 34,000. The extent to which these spiralling figures represented increasing criminality is moot. Nevertheless, at the very least they signified a substantial growth in crime as defined by colonial legislation.

[17] Had crime rates in the capital and Tanganyika as a whole risen at a comparable rate in 1960 approximately 4,412 property offences would have been reported in the town. (The number of cases of crimes against property dealt with by Dar es Salaam police in 1954 was 4,162 representing 43% of the total territorial convictions; the corresponding figures in 1955 were 3,632 and 42%). In fact this number was exceeded by a substantial amount; property offences reported to the police in Dar es Salaam stood at 6,380 in 1960, 61% of the territorial total.

Property crime in Dar es Salaam[18]

The growth of crime against property was a town-wide phenomenon. However, offences differed by area, and the incidence of crime appears to have varied markedly in the three designated zones. Housebreakings occurred in all parts of the town, but appeared to be particularly common in the African and Indian quarters. Petty criminals, such as pickpockets and con-men, were also commonly found working the streets of these areas. Again, it was the inhabitants of Uswahilini and Uhindini who were most likely to be a victim of violent crime; for they were also the commonest location of street robberies as well as the occasional armed heist. The higher incidence of crime in these areas had its roots in the lack of control over the urban population — the ineffective Native Administration and, more particularly, the insignificant police presence in Zones II and III. In Uhindini, at several times between the wars, reports in the Indian press portrayed order here as verging on collapse. Although this is exaggerated, the area was considerably more lawless than would have been tolerated in the predominantly European quarter of Uzunguni.

Housebreaking was common throughout the town. In 1925 police dealt with 256 cases, and it is likely that at least as many went unreported. They occurred with greatest frequency in the African township. Thanks to reports in Indian newspapers, though, it is in Uhindini where we get the fullest impression of such activity. Burglaries from both houses and commercial premises were reported with regularity in the 1930s. Merchant houses occasionally suffered armed raids, while smaller shopkeepers were routinely targeted by petty criminals operating in the area.[19] An escalation of property offences in the town after WWII was viewed with increasing disquiet. The situation in the capital at the end of the war was not too serious; around 200 burglaries were reported in 1945. It was from this base, however, that the dramatic post-war increase took place. By 1952, over 1,200 break-ins were reported in the capital, a monthly average of about 100. In the final year of colonial rule, the monthly average stood at 208. As between the wars, all of Dar es Salaam's communities continued to be the victim of burglaries after 1945, though houses in the African township remained most vulnerable. 'It has been emphasized to me again and again', observed the Superintendent of Police in 1946, 'that the crying needs of the native area are more police and more lights, and in this opinion I heartily concur.' 'Africans going out in the evenings now lock and bar their windows', reported the *Standard* in 1952, 'a few years ago this was unnecessary.'[20]

If burglaries were probably the largest identifiable category of property offences, a variety of other offences, generally more petty, grouped together

---

[18] For a slightly more detailed discussion of criminal activity in colonial Dar es Salaam, see Burton, '*Jamii*'.

[19] Examples, *TH* 14 July 1931, p. 14; 4 August 1931, p. 12; 7 July 1934, p. 12.

[20] SP to MS, 4 February 1946, TNA/540/27/20; *TS*, 1 March 1952, p. 1.

as thefts under the penal code, were actually more common. Theft from the person, for example, was, in various guises, widespread in the town. It could take the form of pickpocketing, bag-snatching, or more seriously of street robbery accompanied with violence (or the threat of violence). The most complete impression of the incidence of such crimes comes once again from the Indian newspapers in the 1930s. Theft from the person was an everyday occurrence in Uhindini. Jewellery was particularly vulnerable to being snatched, often by loosely organised gangs of thieves who purportedly hung around the Indian quarter. 'Petty cases of pilferage, of snatching bangles from children and necklaces from old ladies', observed the *Herald*, 'are too numerous to mention'. 'The Indian public, especially ladies…', observed another editorial the following year, found it 'unsafe to walk the streets even in the daytime. People see a danger in carrying money with them, cyclists must have their eyes fixed on their machines'. Muggings were another urban hazard. Once again they were frequently reported in the Indian press. 'Instances of this nature occur daily', observed the *Herald*, 'and it is difficult for one to get police aid.' In 1937, Gujarati merchants wrote to the Herald complaining that 'during busy hours a gang of thieves armed with sticks and knives, loaf about the bazaar and carry on their profession without any fear of being apprehended'. 'The recent development', wrote the editor, 'is that robbery takes place in broad daylight and any attempt to chase a thief is answered by him with violence.'[21]

Certain areas in the African township also became particularly feared. Ilala Road was one such place, which, according to a letter in the African newspaper *Kwetu*, had 'been infiltrated by enemies who perpetrate violence'. The *Herald* complained that owing to 'the absence of police supervision native residents were being seriously molested' in this area. After WWII, DC Bone observed the continuing 'dangers of assault and robbery' there.[22] Another place singled out by Bone was Mnazi Mmoja, the open space situated between Zones II and III comprising both recreation grounds and remnant bush. This was perhaps the most notorious haunt of muggers in the British colonial period. Both Africans and Indians, men and women, formed their prey. Kichwele Street, which bisected Mnazi Mmoja connecting Uhindini with Kariakoo, was, according to a correspondent to the *Standard* in 1949, 'infested with thieves who take advantage of the poor lighting'.[23] Mkunguni Street, which ran across the upper end of Mnazi Mmoja — had by the early 1950s acquired a particular notoriety. 'Dozens of robberies have taken place in this vicinity', complained a correspondent to the *Standard*, 'so that the area in question has come to be known as "*Tuwa tugawe*" which means "put it down and let us divide".'[24] The incidence of robberies was not helped by the

[21] *TH*, 7 July 1934, p. 12; 23 March 1935, p. 6; 11 August 1931, p. 9; 13 November 1937, p. 6.
[22] *Kwetu*, 14 January 1939, p. 29. Quoted in Anthony, 'Culture and society', p. 191; *TH*, 30 September 1933, p. 5; DC to SP, Dsm, 4 May 1945, TNA/540/271/1.
[23] Letter from Kichwele resident, *TS*, 9 April 1949, p. 9.
[24] Letter from 'Unprotected', 4 February 1950, TNA/20219/Vol. II. Oral informants also recalled *Tuwa Tugawe* as being a notorious location. See Burton, 'Wahuni', p. 95.

Map 7.1 *Central Dar es Salaam in 1935. Kichwele Street is the lowest street bisecting the Open Space; Mkunguni Street is the third street above it crossing the Open Space. Uhindini is situated immediately to the east of the Open Space.*

Source: Based on copy of map in BIEA library (inserted in *Tanganyika Notes and Records*, 20 (1945)

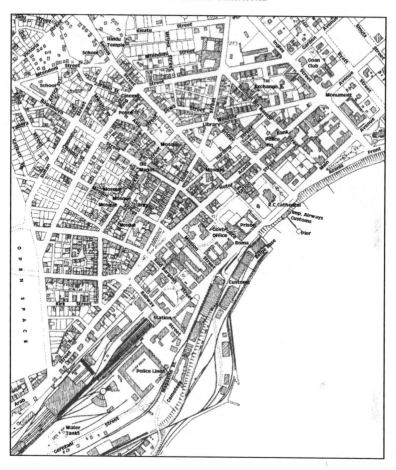

Fig. 7.1 *Eastern Kariakoo/Mnazi Mmoja at Independence. Mkunguni Street is in the upper right hand corner, cutting across Mnazi Mmoja.* Source: Tanzania Information Services

apparent lack of a police presence. 'H.R'. reported in a letter to the *Standard* that:

> I toured the whole area from Arab Street round Msimbazi, Kichwele, New and Livingstone Street, beyond the now notorious Mkunguni Street from 6.15 to past 8pm for a couple of days in succession. But I could not see even a fleeting shadow of an *Askari's* ghost. Later on I looked up things in Zone I and found *Askaris* here, there and everywhere…. I still wonder whom or what they are generally guarding there.[25]

The most plausible answer was, of course, European persons and property. However, while it is probably true that, as in the inter-war period, Uzunguni continued to be better policed than the African or Indian quarters, this did not mean Europeans in Dar es Salaam were not beginning to fall victim to 'muggings' themselves. After WWII, reports in the *Standard* grew more frequent. After two failed attempts of bag-snatching from Europeans in 1946, the paper observed such incidents were on the increase. 'There is in this town', observed Resident Magistrate Platts two years later, 'a considerable number of undesirable Africans who loaf around Acacia Avenue [the main European shopping street] and its adjoining streets for the sole purpose of stealing ladies handbags and anything which is left unprotected.' Later the same year it was reported that in two separate incidents European women

[25] Letter from H.R., *TS*, 16 February 1950. See also *Zuhra*, 18 February 1955, where it is stated 'one cannot meet with policemen apart from in the European residential areas' (Original in Swahili).

had been attacked on Ocean Road, one of them being threatened with a knife.[26]

A criminal economy?

Alongside break-ins and thefts a number of other forms of property crime occurred with increasing frequency over the colonial period. The concentration of population and wealth that existed in Dar es Salaam appears to have led to the emergence of a criminal network exploiting the multiple opportunities for illicit gain. This network consisted of various criminal types engaging in the illegal acquisition, receipt and distribution of property. It centred on the market for stolen goods. Links with areas beyond Dar es Salaam were often vital. Such links were especially apparent in the disposal of stolen property. In 1926, the Commissioner of Police bemoaned the difficulty of dealing with theft cases resulting from 'the proximity of Zanzibar and the facilities which are offered for transporting the proceeds of thefts and burglaries for disposal in that island'.[27] Dar es Salaam's hinterland was also a favoured destination for stolen goods — notably bicycles. A more common means of disposal, however, was through receivers in Dar es Salaam itself.

Receivers were considered to play an important role in the incidence of crime. In the 1927 police report it was observed that they were 'undoubtedly the instigators of a large proportion of the thefts of property'. Three decades later, the *Standard* was attaching 'still more blame to those dregs of human society who go by the name of receivers, without whom the disposal of stolen property would be a difficult and most hazardous process for thieves'.[28] Among Africans, resentment was voiced towards the numerous pawnbrokers that existed in the town, with whom stolen property was frequently deposited. 'These shops', wrote Mary Margaret Mkambe to the *Standard* in 1944, 'are consuming the wealth of the resident African community; encouraging theft, burglary and smuggling.'[29] Between 1928 and 1940 the number of pawn shops increased from eight to fourteen, providing, according to DC Pike, a 'convenient and profitable method of getting rid of stolen goods'.[30] In spite of calls for pawning to be more strictly controlled[31] the number of pawn shops had by the mid 1950s

---

[26] *TS* 23 October 1948, p. 19; 11 December 1948, p. 18.
[27] 1926 Police AR, p. 54.
[28] *TS*, 31 May 1952, p. 24.
[29] Letter to *TS*, 18 November 1944, p. 12; see also, 2 December 1944; 21 September 1946.
[30] Pike, 'Report', p. 16; Amendments by Baker to 'Memorandum', 10 January 1940, TNA/18950/Vol. II; PC Brett to CS, 5 May 1928, TNA/61/286/1 (cited in Brennan, 'Nation').
[31] From both officials (e.g. Pike's report; Baker's amendments; or, somewhat later, QPR, Dsm Dist., 1 July–30 September 1954, TNA/90/1011/Vol. 1) and Africans (e.g. correspondence in *TS*, 18 November 1944; or letter from D. Mtonga, *TS*, 21 September 1946, p. 9).

increased to eighteen.[32] All the shops were Indian-owned.[33] Judging by inter-war police reports it was also Indians, and to a lesser extent Arabs, who usually performed the role of out-and-out receiver in the 1920s and 1930s. And as late as 1954 a magistrate observed that this 'mean, low, despicable' offence was 'one most frequently practised by those who are not natives to this country.'[34] As time went on, though, it appears that more Africans acted as receivers.[35] Assistant Superintendent Young records receiving information from one Mohamed Chande 'better known to the seamier side of Dar es Salaam as Kinyengu [Kinyenga?] a trader in stolen property'. The Shark Market in Kariakoo was well known as a place where such individuals operated, auctioning clothes and other stolen items.

Men such as Kinyengu, along with those scrap dealers not averse to accepting items of dubious origin, helped create a demand for the various types of scrap available to the resourceful urban scavenger. Theft of iron (from the railway and port in particular), observed a Dar es Salaam Magistrate in 1959, was 'a thriving industry from which many people made a dishonest living'.[36] The disappearance of telephone wire and electrical cable was also a problem. According to a 1954 quarterly police report, 'serious thefts of... wire were taking place', while a spate of thefts of stop-cocks and water meters at one time threatened the town's water supply.[37] The Assistant Superintendent of Police recommended that legislation be drawn up for the control of scrap metal dealers in the town. However, by the end of the colonial period theft of cables was beginning to assume its post-independence prevalence.[38] In May 1961, the *Standard* reported that over the previous two months almost eight miles of wire had been stolen by a highly organised gang. The paper considered that 'unscrupulous scrap metal dealers ... [were] as guilty as those who carry out the thefts.'[39] Scrap merchants were also connected with the escalation in bicycle theft that occurred in the colonial period. As cycle ownership grew significantly from the 1940s, the incidence of reported thefts became commonplace. In 1948 thefts totalled 223 — over

[32] Leslie, *Survey*, p. 143. While they continued to provide an outlet for stolen property (knowingly or otherwise), it should be stressed that the shops also performed an important legitimate role in the extension of credit to the impoverished urban populace as documented by Leslie (pp. 142–47); just as they had done in working class communities in eighteenth- and nineteenth-century England (see Emsley, *Crime*, p. 169).

[33] According to Brennan, they were monopolised by Ismaili Khoja Indians until they were banned after independence. Brennan, 'Nation', p. 43.

[34] *TS*, 2 September 1954.

[35] See, for examples, QPR, Dsm Dist., 1 April–30 June 1954, TNA/90/1011/Vol. 1; R.W. Young's Personal Duty Diary, 29 January 1954, RH/Mss.Afr.s.2293; DC Harris to CP, 14 May 1954, TNA/540/3/91.

[36] *TS*, 7 August 1959, p. 3; see also Supt EAR&H Police, Dsm, to OiC Central Police Station (1953?), and following *Tanganazo*, TNA/540/21/8; *TS*, 9 May 1959, p. 1; DAR for 1960, p. 7, RH/Mss.Afr.s. 937.

[37] QPR, Dsm Dist., 1 January–31 March 1954, TNA/90/1011/Vol. 1.

[38] Cables and wires were commonly targeted by criminals after independence. For a series of incidents from 1970, see 'Thieves halt new phone project', *TS* 18 January 1970; 26 February 1970; 5 March 1970; 10 March 1970; and 13 March 1970.

[39] *TS*, 29 May 1961, p. 2.

four a week.[40] By 1953 the number had increased to around one a day; and the following year almost 500 bikes were reported stolen. Stolen bicycles, like cars today, played an important part in the criminal economy. There was a steady demand for parts among Dar es Salaam's mechanics. Meanwhile, disguised bicycles were easily disposed of whole in the capital's hinterland.[41]

The activities of receivers and scrap merchants appeared to be connected to another common form of urban crime, that of theft from the workplace.[42] In 1938, a port official noted that 'stealing from broken packages in the Port was taking place, and that there was liaison between the thieves and certain traders.'[43] However, opportunistic theft was more prevalent. 'Petty theft is common in any dock area in the world', observed Leslie in 1957, 'and this is no exception; pilfering from cargoes and from lorries is too easy to be ignored, and a man who refrained would be considered odd by his fellows.'[44] Whether organised or opportunistic, theft from the workplace was certainly common, perhaps the most widespread form being that of stealing by servants. By 1952, ninety such cases were reported to the police in Dar es Salaam each month. While most cases probably involved just aquisitive employees, professional criminals also forged links with household domestics to gain entry into employers' houses. After a spate of burglaries in Oyster Bay in 1957 in which burglars gained entry with the use of keys, particular suspicion fell upon domestic servants. An earlier editorial in the *Standard* ascribed such offences to a 'black market' in employers' references.[45]

Opportunists and old lags: The Dar es Salaam criminal

Emsley has described how, in nineteenth-century Britain, the notion of a criminal class emerged. Crime was something suffered by all law-abiding members of society and was committed by an alien, maladjusted group. This characterisation absolved respectable members of society from responsibility for the conditions that may have caused individuals to turn to

[40] The *Standard* observed that this was a particularly high figure for a town of Dar es Salaam's size. In Mombasa, a larger town at this time, just 67 were stolen the same year. *TS*, 8 January 1949, p. 3.
[41] QPRs, Dsm Dist., 1 January–31 March 1954; 1 October–31 December 1953; *SN* 22 May 1955, p. 5; 14 August 1955, p. 1. Fourchard ('Urban poverty') notes a similar trade between Lagos and its hinterland (notably Dahomey).
[42] For similar phenomena in Salisbury, Rhodesia, see Phimister, *Zimbabwe*, p. 262.
[43] Manager, Tanganyika Railways to CS, 24 March 1938, TNA/12402/Vol. 1.
[44] Leslie, *Survey*, p. 239; for Tanga, see Kaijage, 'Alternative history'.
[45] *TS*, 5 April 1952. Penvenne (*African Workers*, p. 146) notes the same phenomenon in Lourenço Marques; and links between servants and criminals were also common in Victorian London, Kellow Chesney, *The Victorian Underworld* (Harmondsworth, 1970), p. 192. To combat the problem in Tanganyika a voluntary registration scheme for domestic servants was introduced: see TNA/460/126/2. This file also contains information on a compulsory registration scheme mooted in neighbouring Kenya in 1956, which included a life ban from domestic service for 'former criminals'.

crime. It also served to marginalise the criminal.[46] Colonial Dar es Salaam also had its criminal bogeymen. As with the Victorian class, such a characterisation helped to shift responsibility — in this case away from the colonial organisation of African society — on to the shortcomings of individuals. While structural and environmental causes for criminal behaviour were acknowledged, such as rural–urban drift and the lack of formal employment, it was in the end the *wahuni* who were condemned for their moral weaknesses.

Recent research into crime in nineteenth century Britain has revealed the picture of a criminal class living outside mainstream society to be a spurious one. Rather the conclusion has been reached that in fact 'no clear distinction can be made between a dishonest criminal class and a poor but honest working class.'[47] It appears that the same was true of colonial Dar es Salaam. While the tendency was to stigmatise a section of the population, Leslie, in the only surviving analysis of criminal records in Dar es Salaam from the British period, found that there was little to distinguish offenders from the wider community.[48] The proportion of Muslim offenders was slightly larger than that of the population as a whole, pointing to coastal districts of origin, but the discrepancy was negligible. Single men were more likely to turn to crime (64 percent of offenders as against 39 percent of the general population), although over half of those offenders in the sample considered for probation actually lived with wives, children or other relatives and two-thirds of those sentenced to imprisonment had relatives in Dar es Salaam. In analysing the length of residence of criminals it was found that more recent arrivals provided more than their share, although overall the bulk of offenders were drawn from long-term residents. Neither was it possible to detect distinguishing features from the work record.[49] Neither length of employment nor the receipt of a better wage, Leslie observed, was a 'guarantee that a man will not succumb to the sudden temptation, often for trifling gain'. Indeed, in reviewing the available statistics Leslie surmised that:

> The rather depressing conclusion to be drawn from these figures is that there is comparatively little difference in the circumstances and background of the three classes — the recidivists, the first offenders and the general public. There is a small bias towards crime of those with rather less pay, less work, less family responsibility and less continuity; but it is a small one.[50]

[46] Emsley, *Crime*, pp. 173–5.

[47] *Ibid.*

[48] Leslie, *Survey*, pp. 205–8. In Blantyre, the commercial capital of neighbouring Nyasaland, 'most thieves were part-time amateurs' and crime rates varied 'subject to the rhythms of the agricultural year'. McCracken, 'Coercion and control', p. 134.

[49] From the sample of nine hundred offenders, a quarter had an average of under six months a job, half averaged between six months and three years a job, and a fifth averaged more than three years, 12% had no paid employment at the time of conviction.

[50] *Ibid.* Similarly, LO Bennett in 1952 despaired at the difficulty of finding applicants with no criminal record to register as dockworkers — a 'considerable proportion' of applicants being found to have previous convictions for theft or allied offences. Quarterly Labour Report (ending 30 September 1952), TNA/540/27/7/Vol. III.

Leslie found as much difficulty distinguishing criminals by area of residence as he had by social type. Some parts of the town did develop an unsavoury reputation. From early on Kisutu was considered a location favoured by offenders (as well as Dar es Salaam's principal red light area).[51] Unlike other African residential areas in Zone II, an African community remained in Kisutu into the 1940s and 1950s, and the area continued to be known as a thieves' haven throughout the colonial period, although its notoriety was never as pronounced as it became after independence (before finally being demolished in 1974).[52] Going on convictions reported in the *Tanganyika Standard* in the 1950s, Buguruni was another part of town that had a larger than normal criminal element either living or operating in it. It was characterised by Governor Turnbull in 1959 as 'a favourite haunt for much of the human flotsam that finds its way to Dar es Salaam from up-country'.[53] By the early 1960s it had, according to Ishumi, become known as Alabama 'on account of its long record of urban crime'.[54] Oral informants also remember Buguruni as having acquired a reputation as being 'quite a notorious area' in the late-colonial period (not only as a result of the serious riot that occurred there in 1959). Meanwhile, Leslie recalled it as 'a sort of overgrown village full of all the scallywags'. As a minimally policed 'urban village' on the outskirts of town, it is not surprising if Buguruni was adopted as a place of residence by criminals (as well as a location to pursue their illegal activities).[55] While Kisutu and Buguruni may have acquired reputations as being the haunts of criminals, however, the evidence we have is impressionistic. In his analysis of criminal records Leslie could detect 'no noticeable concentration of [offenders] in any one area of town; the proportion living in each tallied well with the figures for the whole population'. Indeed, an indication of the general prevalence of criminality among Dar es Salaam's population as a whole can perhaps be gleaned from the outcome of a raid conducted in early 1958. '[O]f a total of 331 checked', the Assistant Commissioner of Police reported, 'about one third were breaking the law in some manner in an area selected at random, and without special information regarding its inhabitants.'[56]

While it was difficult to distinguish criminals from the general population, a core of repeat offenders, who appeared to have turned to crime as a

---

[51] See CP to CS, 1 March 1935, TNA/23457; responding to *TH*, 23 February 1935, p. 6.

[52] See Burton, 'Haven', for Kisutu in the 1960s and 1970s.

[53] Turnbull to Lennox-Boyd, 4 July 1959, PRO/CO/822/1795, cited in Brennan, 'Nation', p. 311.

[54] A.G.M. Ishumi, *The urban jobless in East Africa: A study of the unemployed population in the growing urban centres, with special reference to Tanzania* (Uppsala, 1984), p. 84. Ishumi accounts for the appellation by connecting it with civil rights unrest in southern states of the USA — including Alabama.

[55] Other areas identified by oral informants as places where criminals congregated included Mohamed Abeid, Makaburi, Jangwani and Mchikichini (where gambling was common), Mikengeni and above all Tuwa Tugawe (see above).

[56] Though it should be stressed this is probably indicative more of the manner in which colonial legislation criminalised African activities and behaviour than the delinquency of the urban population. Leslie, *Survey*, p. 207; QPR, Dsm Dist., 1 April–30 June 1958, TNA/90/1011/Vol. 1.

Table 7.3 *Recidivism among admissions to Dar es Salaam prison, 1927–38*

	1927	1929*	1930	1932	1933	1935	1936	1937	1938
Recidivists	132	89	178	337	270	255	247	451	391
Total convicted	892	638	722	780	626	832	969	1143	1053
% Recidivists	14.79	13.94	24.65	43.2	43.13	30.64	25.49	39.45	37.13

* Figures for 1928, 1931 and 1934 unavailable
Source: Prisons Dept ARs

Table 7.4 *Recidivism among admissions to Dar es Salaam, Msasani (from 1944) and Ukonga (from 1952) prisons, Dar es Salaam, 1939–60* ➡

	1939	1940	1941	1942	1943	1944	1945	1946
First timers	724	756	808	608	594	800	556	783
Non-recidivists	84	53	130	192	162	178	113	130
Recidivists	296	370	299	164	154	167	197	370
Total admissions	1104	1179	1237	964	910	1145	866	1283
% Recidivists	26.81	31.38	24.17	17.01	16.92	14.58	22.74	28.83

	1947	1948	1949	1950	1951	1952	1953	1954
First timers	871	754	689	1100	1169	1072	1358	1369
Non-recidivists	162	100	136	173	282	362	466	571
Recidivists	385	274	298	384	281	316	358	447
Total admissions	1418	1128	1123	1657	1732	1750	2182	2387
% Recidivists	27.15	24.29	26.53	23.17	16.22	18.05	16.42	18.72

	1955	1956	1957	1958	1959	1960
First timers	1170	855	2302	2344	1656	887
Non-recidivists	453	473	813	784	509	409
Recidivists	445	356	575	670	614	662
Total admissions	2068	1684	3690	3798	2779	1958
% Recidivists	21.51	21.14	15.58	17.64	22.09	33.81

Source: Prisons Dept ARs

profession, was present in Dar es Salaam from relatively early on. The first surviving statistics on recidivism among detainees in Dar es Salaam (from 1927) numbers 132 recidivists out of a total of 892 convicts, a proportion of 14 percent.[57] During the 1930s, the average percentage of recidivists was just under 35 percent. Interestingly, over the following years the number of first-time offenders and those with just one previous conviction increased at a greater rate than the number of recidivists. In the first half of the 1950s

[57] Dar es Salaam (and later Msasani and Ukonga) was the main prison for long-term prisoners from all coastal districts in Eastern Province, including Dar es Salaam itself, though (by 1946) there were others at Bagamoyo, Kingolwira, Kilosa, Mafia, Mahenge, Morogoro and Utete, and there was an additional prison for remand prisoners located at Magazine Street, Dar es Salaam. Recidivism statistics in this paragraph are from the Prisons Dept ARs.

the average percentage of recidivists of all those admitted to Dar es Salaam prisons was down to just 19 percent. Even the actual number of recidivists, considering the rapid growth of both the town itself and crime within it, grew at a remarkably slow rate: the 337 of 1932 actually outnumbering the 316 admitted to Dar es Salaam's prisons twenty years later. Although an increasingly professional criminal class appears to have emerged by the 1950s, the vast majority of crime remained unorganised. In the late 1950s recidivists constituted just 20 percent of admissions to Ukonga prison. This relatively small number would have made up the hard core of Dar es Salaam's underworld, such as it was. While numerically small, it was the activities of this group of hardened offenders that formed the principal source of anxiety for the inhabitants and administrators of Dar es Salaam.

That there were professional criminals in Dar es Salaam was apparent from the earliest years of British rule. On several occasions between the wars, the simultaneous release of a number of ex-convicts was held to be responsible for a mini-wave of housebreaking in the capital. Discharged convicts, complained the Commissioner of Police in 1926,

> come out of gaol one day, and immediately return to crime…. The discharge of a batch of criminals … usually synchronises with a wave of burglary, which continues until the whole gang are back in prison. Orders are passed by the courts… for these habitual criminals to report their addresses to the Police for a given term, on discharge from prison, but this does not prevent them returning to crime and to prison. It merely enables the police to locate them quicker.[58]

The situation was exacerbated by prisoners from the rural part of the district staying in the capital on release.[59] Attempts were made to prevent ex-convicts remaining in Dar es Salaam, although it was not always a straightforward matter. 'Machinery is provided', the Commissioner observed in his 1926 report, 'for repatriating such persons to their homes and such action is invariably taken by the prison authorities, but it is surprising how many of the habitual criminals belong to the towns.'

At least the small numbers involved in serious crime meant that the situation in Dar es Salaam was containable. The recidivism rates appeared to confirm that the control of the relatively few hardened criminals was the key to crime prevention. In the early 1940s, the Superintendent of Police ascribed a reduction in reported crime partly to '[t]he successful conviction before High Court of an appreciable number of old offenders, who are the instigators of crime, which has been a marked achievement during the past year'.[60] By the mid 1950s a system of supervision was in place in which known criminals had to report daily to a local police station (mostly to Msimbazi station), although this regime was insufficiently strict for the Assistant Commissioner who argued for a night-time curfew for all

---

[58] 1926 Police AR, pp. 57/8; see also 1928, p. 18.
[59] AO, Kisarawe to PC, EP, 27 October 1943, TNA/540/3/46.
[60] Supt, Dsm to PC, EP, 15 February 1943, TNA/61/3/XVII.

supervisees.[61] The numbers reporting to police were relatively modest: between 26 and 43 in 1954/5.[62] According to the Assistant Commissioner these constituted 'the hard core of the criminal element'.[63] It is perhaps easier to get a grasp of the activities of this 'hard core' by turning to examples of individual cases.

An impression of the criminal careers of some persistent offenders can be gleaned from official sources and from the Dar es Salaam press. As early as 1922, for example, the *Dar es Salaam Times* reported the conviction — for housebreaking and stealing — of one Musa bin Hassani. In the short period of British rule up till then, he had already acquired three previous convictions.[64] Two years later, Mahomed bin Mursal received a seven-year sentence for housebreaking, theft and assault. Mursal had acquired six previous convictions under British rule.[65] The police report of 1927 recorded the arrest of another persistent offender. Ali bin Sefu, who had an inter-territorial range of activity and five previous convictions for housebreaking, had broken out of prison in Zanzibar and made his way to Dar es Salaam and later Tanga, committing burglaries in both towns before being apprehended by Tanga police sporting a 'loaded revolver'.[66]

The most notorious of inter-war criminals was Omari bin Masua, a Bajuni who made his way to Dar es Salaam from his home district of Mombasa.[67] He was first singled out by the *Tanganyika Herald* — described as an 'old convict' — in November 1932, after his escape from jail and his subsequent recapture with his fellow prisoner, Juma bin Mohammed. Masua had been awaiting trial on charges of resisting arrest and attempting to stab an *askari*, although a subsequent report in the *Herald* noted that he was also 'alleged to have committed a number of burglaries'. Six months later Masua escaped once again and committed at least two fresh burglaries before being rearrested at Kilwa Kisiwani, on the southern Tanganyika coast. Later that year he was tried and convicted on four counts — entry into a King's African Rifles officer's house, two counts of theft, and escape from jail — receiving six months for each charge, which brought the time he had to serve up to ten years. Just 18 months into his incarceration, to the apparent delight of sections of the African population, Masua escaped once again, this time with his fellow prisoner, Hamisi bin Bakari (aka Hamisi bin Kiko — described as a

61 QPR, Dsm Dist, 1 July–30 September 1954, TNA/90/1011/Vol. 1.
62 See QPRs, *ibid.*
63 *Ibid.*, 1 January–31 March 1955. While, at any one time, the number of supervisees was small there was a relatively high degree of reconvictions. In the first quarter of 1955, for example, 11 of the 43 persons being supervised returned to prison.
64 *DT*, 9 September 1922, p. 9.
65 *DT*, 13 September 1924.
66 1927 Police AR, p. 42.
67 Probably via Zanzibar: in evidence to an enquiry investigating a prison riot in Zanzibar in 1928 (in file ZNA/AB61/10), the escape of a juvenile delinquent named Omari bin Msuo in 1927 is reported. Variations in spelling were common at this time — particularly when recorded by European officials — and it seems likely that this delinquent was to grow up into the old lag described in Tanganyika.

Manyema or Zaramo from Dar es Salaam). The police announced they could not 'too strongly impress on all households in Dar es Salaam and the suburbs the importance of taking adequate precautions to secure their property'.[68] The *Herald* observed the town as 'terror-stricken'. Masua was declared 'Public Enemy No. 1' and considerable police resources were devoted to his recapture. The African community of Dar es Salaam was said to be abuzz with rumours about his whereabouts and future movements. Three detachments of police were engaged in the pursuit of the escaped felons, who travelled north through Bagamoyo and Tanga districts. In early March, Masua turned up in Mombasa. Reportedly 'well-known' to the police there, a European and an Arab officer had recognised him walking down a central street in the town and attempted to effect his arrest. Masua responded violently, knifing Sub-Inspector Said in the face, before making good his escape. Three hundred shillings was offered for information leading to his arrest. According to the *Mombasa Times*, however, Masua once again 'vanished into thin air'. He moved further north still, to Kismayu in Somaliland. Here he was apprehended in mid-April by the Italian authorities. Once again Masua got the better of his captors. 'Like love', declared the *Tanganyika Standard* in the wake of his latest escape, 'Omari laughs at locksmiths.' It was not until the following month that Masua's peregrinations of the East African littoral were finally ended, when he was wounded in a shoot-out with Italian police after being caught breaking into a European house in Kismayu.[69]

It is not clear to what extent Masua was, in his sphere of activity, representative of a wider group of criminals operational along the Swahili coast.[70] Both he and Ali bin Sefu obviously travelled widely in pursuit of criminal opportunities. Meanwhile, the 1926 police report complained of 'thieves travel[ling] by *Dhows* and often from ports other than Dar es Salaam'. Experienced criminals on the Swahili coast were clearly willing and able to relocate when a particular town got 'too hot'. Criminals who operated inter-territorially were probably uncommon. However, the activities of Masua and Sefu indicate the presence of a criminal type who was the source of particular anxiety to non-Africans in Dar es Salaam, as is evidenced by the lively correspondence and editorials on the subject of crime in the European and Indian newspapers.

By the second half of the British colonial period the arrest and convictions of offenders with substantial criminal records were being

[68] The police description of Masua gave the following details: 'He is about 26 years old, five feet six inches in height, and very well-built. His features are small for a native [sic] and his complexion is brown. He speaks English, can drive a motor vehicle and ride a motor bicycle. He has a knife wound five and a half inches in length across the left wrist. There is another knife wound across the neck, under the left jaw.' He was thought to be wearing a blue silk *kanzu* (a loose-fitting robe commonly worn on the Swahili coast).

[69] *TH*, 8 November 1932, p. 6; 24 December 1932, p. 9; 5 June 1933, p. 11; 19 August 1933, p. 4; 2 February 1935, p. 3; 9 February 1935, pp. 3 & 10. *TS*, 26 January 1935, p. 19; 23 February 1935, p. 3; 2 March 1935; 20 April 1935; 4 May 1935, p. 20.

[70] For the criminal careers of counterparts of Masua in Nyasaland, see McCracken 'Coercion and control', p. 134.

reported. In November 1942, Hamisi bin Punje (alias Mohammed bin Omari) received a seven-year sentence for breaking into the house of a European police officer. This brought the total number of years to which he had been sentenced between 1918 and 1942 to thirty-three.[71] Issa bin Abdallah (alias Selemani bin Abdallah), convicted of burglary and stealing in 1957, had an equally long criminal career, with a list of previous convictions that ran 'almost continuously' from 1935 to 1956. Similarly Hassani Abdullah, convicted on five charges of 'highway robberies' in 1960, was found to have previous convictions stretching back to the 1940s.[72] Not only were criminals with long records emerging, but also prolific thieves were being apprehended. Two ex-offenders — reporting to the police as supervisees — who were reconvicted in early 1953, had sixteen and fourteen previous convictions each.[73] In August 1960, Juma Saidi, received a 21-year sentence for the grand total of 35 offences in the Oyster Bay area of Dar es Salaam. Six years earlier, the 'notorious thief' Augustino Yusif had been so active that a noticeable reduction in the number of break-ins in the town was attributed to his arrest.[74] Recidivism was not confined to thieves and burglars. The con-man, Abdallah bin Ali, was convicted in 1936 for cheating a man out of Shs. 15/50, for which he served an eight-month term of imprisonment. It was noted he already had five previous convictions of a similar nature. Two decades on, the same individual was convicted of swindling Soga bin Kobezi, a recent arrival from Mwanza, of Shs. 40/-.[75]

A further measure of the degree to which crime became professionalised was the extent of co-operation between criminals. It is noteworthy that organised crime in colonial Dar es Salaam was at an extremely low level, criminals tending to operate singly or in pairs, although this appeared to be changing towards the end of the period when gang activity became more common. Before WWII, serious gang activity made its only appearance in Dar es Salaam in 1931, when an armed gang, comprising of two Indians and two Africans, robbed an Indian merchant house making off with valuable jewellery and Shs. 4,500/- in cash.[76] One reason to which the lack of organised crime was attributed was selective use of the Township Rule that enabled the police and district officials to repatriate undesirables. This was repeatedly singled out in annual police reports. That repatriations were so few at this time gives some indication of the scarcity of serious criminals in the town prior to 1939.

It was not until after WWII that more widespread and serious gang activity in Dar es Salaam was recorded. It was most prominent — in the form of

---

71 The statistical discrepancy can be accounted for by the fact that criminals were often awarded separate sentences for offences committed in the same criminal case that ran concurrently.

72 *TS*, 27 November 1942, p. 8; 29 March 1957; 9 September 1960.

73 QPR, Dsm Dist, 1 October–31 December 1953, TNA/90/1011/Vol. 1.

74 *TS*, 27 August 1960; QPR, Dsm Dist., 1 July–30 September 1954, TNA/90/1011/Vol. 1.

75 Record from 1936 in TNA/20219/Vol. II; Native Court Case record, 11 November 1957, TNA/540/3/38B. For con-men in Dar es Salaam, see Burton, 'Wahuni', pp. 108–12.

76 *TH*, 4 August 1931, p. 12.

petty crime — in the vicinity of Mnazi Mmoja, which by this time had become a rather notorious area thanks to the predatory activities of loosely organised groups of muggers (see above). A greater degree of co-operation in house- and shop-breakings was also beginning to emerge. Three gangs of housebreakers operating in the Oyster Bay area were broken up by the police in 1953. An increase of 170 break-ins in the last quarter of 1954 was attributed to the actions of numerous small gangs. 'Every effort', the Assistant Commissioner of Police reported, 'is being made to exterminate these gangs.' The following quarter he was able to record nine convictions resulting from police infiltration of gangs, although by its very success this method of policing was subsequently ruled out for the foreseeable future.[77] Intensified police activity, however, failed to prevent a trend towards more organised crime, which by the final years of colonial rule reached a peak. In 1960, the Commissioner of Police bemoaned the increase in motorised gangs.[78] From the late 1950s, reports on the activities of armed gangs became increasingly common in the pages of the colonial press.[79] In 1960, in the course of a raid on a *duka* in Ubungo, an Arab was stabbed by a gang of Africans. In the preceding six weeks eleven such attacks had taken place on Arab shops on the outskirts of town. The leader of one of these gangs was sentenced to a total of 67 years in April 1961, having been convicted on thirty-three charges relating to a series of raids in Dar es Salaam, Kisarawe and Morogoro.[80]

The wide sphere of operation of this gang was another indication of the growing sophistication of criminals. Increasingly they switched areas of activity as circumstances allowed. The District Commissioner of Bagamoyo in 1941, for example, blamed a crime-wave on a number of recidivists 'who have made Dar es Salaam or Zanzibar too hot for themselves and who spend a while in Bagamoyo picking up easy money'.[81] Similarly, two years later, the Ruvu and Kikonga sisal estates, situated to the east of the capital, were identified as being used as havens by criminals from Dar es Salaam.[82] Indeed, the Ruvu minor settlement and nearby Ngeta Kikonga were somewhat notorious locations in themselves, singled out by a district official two years earlier as 'one of the worst areas in the district from the point of view of crime'.[83] Ruvu was home to receivers of stolen property and also served as headquarters to one or two gangs led, according to the official, by 'such well known criminals' as Idi Mwinyikondo (alias Idi Benafiri) and his brother Mzee Mwinyikondo (or Benafiri). It is highly likely that these Ruvu gangs were linked to criminal activity occurring in the capital. It is equally likely that they were implicated in crime associated with the central railway line

[77] QPRs, Dsm Dist, 1 July–30 September; 1 October–31 December 1954; 1 January–31 March 1955, TNA/90/1011/Vol. 1.
[78] 1960 Police AR, p. 1.
[79] E.g. *TS*, 24 February 1958, p. 3; 25 February 1959, p. 1.
[80] *TS*, 14 September 1960, p. 1; 7 April 1961, p. 3.
[81] DC, Bagamoyo to PC, EP, 13 May 1941, TNA/61/688/5.
[82] DC, Dsm to SP, Dsm, 28 July 1944, TNA/540/21/8.
[83] Political, Kisarawe to Political, Dsm, 12 March 1942; ADO, Kisarawe to DC, Uzaramo, 3 February 1942, TNA/540/21/8.

which passed through Ruvu. The Provincial Commissioner in 1942 remarked upon the presence of professional pickpockets using Ruvu as a base while they 'worked' the passenger trains.[84] Eight years later, a Dar es Salaam railways official wrote complaining of 'the numerous thefts of consignments from wagons en route from Dar es Salaam to up-country stations'.[85] He reported the activities of an organised gang armed with firearms operating in the district, stealing goods from trains. Thirteen persons were arrested in connection with one incident in January 1950, four of whom were railway employees. In October that year, a further series of burglaries along the railway line culminated in the death of a Khoja railway official.[86]

An overview of the incidence of crime perhaps gives an impression of the problem being more serious than it actually was. Dar es Salaam during the colonial period was mercifully free of serious crime. Nevertheless, while criminal activity may not have been particularly common, for many residents — African, Indian and European alike — it was occurring too frequently for comfort. What is more, crime in the town became both more widespread and more sophisticated as the years passed, a tendency that appears to have accelerated in post-colonial Tanzania, in common with other African countries. However, in assessing rates of criminality it is important to relate surviving criminal statistics alongside those recording the growth of the urban population. The escalation in recorded offences that occurred in Dar es Salaam gives the impression of an urban environment in which crime became increasingly prevalent. It is by no means clear that this was the case. For example, if we take the number of property offences dealt with by Dar es Salaam police, we find that the incidence of crime actually appears to have slightly decreased between 1954 and 1959, with one case for every 25 urban inhabitants in 1954 compared to one for every 29 by the end of the decade. With the capital increasing at the rate it did from the late 1930s, urban crime rates inevitably rose. Commonly expressed anxieties about crime probably reflected this increased incidence rather than a growing tendency to turn to crime. In spite of the commonly stated assertions of European, Indian and African observers linking the two phenomena, criminality in colonial Tanzania was by no means an inevitable by-product of urban growth.[87]

[84] PC, EP to Crime, Dsm, 16 February 1942, TNA/540/21/8.
[85] Regional Assistant, EAR&H to CS, 27 February 1950, TNA/20219/Vol. II.
[86] 1950 PAR. Another instance of the criminal links being forged between Dar es Salaam and its hinterland was the trade in stolen bicycles discussed above.
[87] See also *Jamii*, conclusion.

Eight

Legitimate Lawlessness?

The Informal Economy
in Colonial Dar es Salaam

[A] large number of men (and some women) who break the licensing laws...
or break the by-laws ... constitute a large body of petty offenders, for whom
imprisonment must in the last resort be used. They are not criminals, and
their consciences are untroubled. They are just unwary pawns in the game.[1]

In colonial Africa, it was in the urban areas in particular that the regulatory
impulse of the state was most in evidence. Much criminal activity arose from
the incongruity of colonial legislation and customary and subsistence activities
engaged in by urban Africans. In Dar es Salaam, laws and by-laws that
prohibited activities such as the tapping of palm trees, which without a permit
was disallowed, or a mendicant's right to beg in a society that retained alms-
giving traditions, were widely disregarded.[2] To colonial officials these activities
were held to be disorderly. To Africans engaged in them it was simply a
matter of 'getting by'. Two of these activities, the illegal production, sale and
consumption of alcohol and street trading, form the subject of this chapter.
Alongside begging, their incidence and visibility appeared to increase in the
1940s and 1950s. This partly occurred as a result of important economic
and demographic shifts from around 1940 that transformed the nature of
African urban poverty.[3] Population growth in African towns, Dar es Salaam
included, began to outpace the capacity of urban economies to provide formal
employment (and services): the labour shortage of the pre-WWII era gradually
gave way to widespread joblessness.[4] However, the heightened visibility of
what is now known as the informal sector was also a product of shifts in
colonial governance.[5] British and French administrations in sub-Saharan
Africa were significantly more interventionist after WWII than they had been

---

[1]   Paterson, 'Report', p. 2.
[2]   For begging, see chapter 9.
[3]   Iliffe, *African Poor*, pp. 191–2; Burton, 'Urbanisation', pp. 24–5.
[4]   See Burton, 'Raw youth, school leavers and the emergence of unemployment in late-
colonial urban Tanganyika', (forthcoming).
[5]   In the early 1970s activities such as those discussed in this chapter were identified as the
'informal sector' or 'informal economy'. While the role and definition of the informal sector

between the wars.[6] This had particular significance in the urban arena. While space for the African was now envisaged in colonial towns, heightened efforts were made to control this space. This had its most dramatic manifestation in the purges of urban 'undesirables' (see chapter 12). Of equal significance, though, was the increased attention paid to restricting unlicensed African economic activity. While periodic clampdowns did occur between the wars, greater tolerance was shown towards Africans hawking goods for sale or begging. This tolerance arose from both the lesser incidence of such activity and the scarce resources available for the supervision and enforcement of colonial by-laws.[7] Increasing interventionism from the 1940s, alongside accelerating urbanisation, resulted in a significantly more coercive urban regime.

Alcohol and order in Dar es Salaam

Regulations controlling the production and consumption of alcohol formed a particularly prominent area in which colonial law clashed with African notions of legitimacy.[8] The illicit trade in 'native liquor' was a highly remunerative one, and these restrictive laws were routinely ignored by both producers who brewed and sold alcohol illegally, and by the consumers who preferred these outlets to those licensed and supervised by the state. A variety of regulations controlled the production and consumption of alcohol from the arrival of the British in Dar es Salaam during WWI. Initially, brewing had been allowed for personal use alone and not for sale. However, under this regime 'drunkenness' was considered 'rife among Africans'. In 1921, in an attempt to check consumption, the sale of *pombe*[9] was restricted to licensed premises only, and liquor production prohibited elsewhere.[10] By the end of the year ten premises in the African quarter had received licences to engage

(fn5 cont.) are much disputed, and its application to the colonial era is anachronistic, I use the term for the sake of convenience. The informal sector has come to be most commonly associated with unregulated manufacturing, trading and service activity, and the common usage is employed in this chapter. However, Hart's original concept is actually rather more appropriate for the study as a whole. Hart's formulation included more overtly criminal activity, being akin to what has been termed the 'black economy'; the word 'informal' was employed to highlight not only the lack of regulation but also the contested nature of legislation designed to impose control over the urban arena. Keith Hart, 'Informal income opportunities and urban unemployment in Ghana', *JMAS* 11 (1973).

6   See e.g. D.A. Low and John Lonsdale, 'Introduction: Towards the New Order, 1945–63', in Low and Smith, *History*, pp. 1–63; Cooper, *Decolonization*; and for Dar es Salaam, Burton, 'Townsmen'.

7   Owing to its association with disorderliness legislation prohibiting the unlicensed production, consumption and sale of alcohol was more strictly enforced before 1940. As we shall see, however, important shifts in policy aimed at regulating the trade in alcohol also occurred from around this time. See also, Willis, *Potent Brews*.

8   Notwithstanding the fact that the vast majority of the urban population was Muslim. According to Leslie, in 1956 '[t]he consumption of alcoholic drink by Muslims' was 'almost universal, and so well accepted that it is not considered, except by the few who claim to hold to the strict observance of religion, to need excusing'. Leslie, *Survey*, pp. 210–11.

9   African beer made by fermenting sorghum, bananas, or various other grains and fruits.

10   1921 DAR, p. 22.

in its production and sale. This system proved to be equally undesirable to local officials, who hankered for Government to 'take an active part in the direct control of the liquor traffic in town ... by the establishment of a single compound for the manufacture of beer' along the lines of 'native beer compounds' in South Africa. So, in May 1926, the production, sale and consumption of 'native beer' was forbidden anywhere other than the Kariakoo *pombe* market 'under the immediate supervision of the police'.

Within Dar es Salaam itself, officials congratulated themselves on the more efficient surveillance and control of the trade in alcohol that had done much 'to reduce the drunkenness and disorderliness which once was not uncommon in privately-owned licensed premises'.[11] However, one immediate result was 'that the native residents ... wandered to outside *pombe* markets so as to escape from the exacting supervision to which, under the Native Liquor Ordinance, they were subjected in the *pombe* markets of the townships'. Africans commonly left Dar es Salaam on Saturday night after the termination of *ngoma* in order to continue them outside the town boundary – where the restrictive urban laws relating to alcohol didn't apply – returning on Monday mornings, often 'much the worse for liquor' according to a disapproving Provincial Commissioner. Bars servicing urban residents fringed the township at Kinondoni, Kigogo, Segerea, Mwali, Temeke, Chang'ombe, Buguruni and Keko.[12] While the majority of these bars, being outside the township boundary were technically legal (the exceptions being those bars located in Keko, a popular destination for African imbibers within the boundary), they undermined attempts by officials to order the social life of urban Africans. Accordingly, the Native Liquor Ordinance was extended to cover the surrounding areas in 1940.[13]

Within Dar es Salaam itself prior to 1940 the illegal production and sale of alcohol continued to occur. When East African Breweries took over responsibility for all legally produced 'native beer' in the township in the mid-1930s, it was noted by one secretariat official that '[t]he illicit brewing of probably better beer has continued to flourish.'[14] Indeed, in communicating their decision not to extend the contract to the Township Authority, the brewery indicated that this was not only owing to 'insufficient profit' but also to competition from illicit brewing, 'with the attendant difficulties of suppressing it'.[15] Four years later an editorial by Erica Fiah in *Kwetu* announced that '[a]t present in Dar es Salaam many persons are arrested and fined being found in possession of *Kangara* liquor[16] made by Natives in houses privately'.[17] The Police, Fiah observed, 'were in great difficulties to stop such

11 PC Brett to CS, 21 June 1927, TNA/10491; Police ARs, 1927, pp. 52/3; 1928, p. 21.
12 Chief Insp., CID to SP, Dsm, 25 August 1930, TNA/61/76 (and AgCP, EP to CS, 12 August 1930, TNA/61/76).
13 GN No. 102 of 1940.
14 Min., 5 December 1935, TNA/18893/Vol. II. See Mbilinyi, 'Unforgettable business', for an account of the EAB takeover.
15 Dsm TA mins, 21 November 1935, from notes taken by Martha Honey.
16 *Kangara* is a type of honey beer.
17 *Kwetu*, 27 June 39, p. 3.

contraband'. The tapping of *tembo* (palm wine), both for personal use as well as sale, also appears to have been widespread, although no records of prosecutions survive.[18] Restrictions on the consumption and sale of *tembo* were widely resented. The 'prohibition of tapping cocoa-nut [sic] trees', complained the President of the African Association to the District Officer in 1934, 'is one of the enormous scourges in the history of the Tanganyika Coast.'[19] Official awareness of the customary consumption of *tembo* in coastal societies may in fact have led to a relative tolerance being adopted towards its unlicensed tapping and consumption in Dar es Salaam.[20] Still, it is clear that Africans in Dar es Salaam by no means felt at liberty to freely indulge their taste for palm wine.[21] Indeed, while the illicit *tembo* trade had by 1937 been allowed to grow to such an extent that it was seriously affecting business at the Kariakoo *pombe* market, the following year saw a crackdown by the police and the Native Administration aimed at checking the consumption of *tembo* in the town and its environs.[22]

Restrictions governing African consumption of alcohol proved unsustainable. In May 1940, the tapping of *tembo* under licence was authorised, and by the 1950s a handful of *tembo* bars were dotted about the African residential areas in Dar es Salaam. Similarly, from 1947 regulations governing African consumption of 'European' beers and liquor were slowly removed.[23] Such innovations were in part designed to facilitate administrative control over the trade in alcohol. It was recognised, for example, that inter-war prohibitions relating to *tembo* had, if anything, simply resulted in its unregulated production, consumption and sale. With the introduction of licences for the tapping of palms, and for its sale in African bars, it was hoped that the urban administration would not only boost its revenue, but also play a greater supervisory role. Government intervention was apparent in the small number of licences awarded to African retailers of alcohol and the simple fact that should an individual desire to tap his palms he required a licence issued from the District Office in order to do so legally. As a consequence, the illegal production and consumption of alcohol remained widespread. In Mtoni, the year after licensed palm tapping had been authorised, 46 illegal tappers were found 'in one small area'.[24] The following year the AO at Kiserawe noted:

[18] A territorial ban on *tembo* was introduced in 1923, partly because it was perceived as being too strong for 'upcountry Africans'. See Willis, *Potent Brews*, p. 103.

[19] Pres., AA, to DO, Dsm, 6 December 1934, TNA/12356.

[20] While serving as District Officer for Tanga, E.C. Baker had come to the conclusion that 'prohibition or no, *tembo* will be drunk by young and old alike no matter how severely offenders are punished', and *tembo* was actually decriminalised there from 1935. PC, Tanga to CS, 28 September 1935, TNA/12356/Vol. 1; Willis, *Potent Brews*, p. 103. See also, Tanga DARs 1934 (p. 6); 1935 (pp. 9–10); 1936 (p. 8).

[21] See for eg. editorial in *Kwetu*, 15 July 1939, p. 3.

[22] AgPC, EP to CS, 24 June 1938, TNA/12356/Vol. II. It is likely that illicit spirits were also being manufactured and sold in Dar es Salaam between the wars, although there is little indication of its extent.

[23] See Willis, *Potent Brews*.

[24] PC, EP to CS, 16 July 1941; TNA/12356/Vol. 1.

Illegal tapping of palm wine with its attendant evils of illegal selling of liquor is ... very prevalent in the neighbourhood of Dar es Salaam. Drunkenness and hooliganism were as a result, on the increase especially among the youths of the suburban areas who patronise illegal *tembo* clubs to a very large extent.[25]

Illegal bars were patronised by more respectable urban residents also, partly thanks to the poor condition of those licensed by the Government. 'There is nothing more horrible in this lovely town of Dar es Salaam than the African bars which have been constructed by the government for us', wrote one 'Non-Abstainer' in a letter to the *Tanganyika Standard*.[26] However, drinking in unlicensed bars exposed you to arrest. In 1946 another African correspondent to the *Standard* complained about the criminalisation of such practices:

> When Natives drink from private places where conditions are sweet and sound, but after enjoying for few minutes, there comes the Police – 'Kamata Hawa',[27] both the consumer and the beer maker or keeper appears before the Resident Magistrate who offers them a heavy fine as penalty for drinking in a bar in their own Native Land.[28]

In spite of the possibility of arrest, in the 1940s and 1950s *pombe, kangara* and *tembo* were commonly sold unlicensed from peoples' homes in the African areas of Dar es Salaam.[29] In 1957, the *Wakili* of Kinondoni complained that the town was 'full of crime ... because people are selling *tembo* in their houses without a licence'.[30] In addition, illicit breweries and stills operated on the outskirts of town; in the unplanned African 'villages' police patrols or municipal inspections were infrequent and control was left to the *Majumbe* or *Wandewa* (Native Administration officials),[31] who tended to be more sympathetic towards, or even have a vested interest in, the trade in alcohol.[32] *Pombe* was consumed at unlicensed bars at the place of production as it was difficult to transport. *Moshi* (the commonest spirit produced) and *tembo*, on the other hand, frequently found their way into town and were consumed there by both Africans and (to a lesser extent) by Asians. Raids on the stills and breweries were carried out every two to three months depending on

[25] PC, EP to CS, 16 July 1941; AO i/c Kisarawe to DC, Uzaramo, 8 September 1942, TNA/61/118/1.
[26] *TS*, 24 August 1946, p. 13. European-constructed bars were unpopular elsewhere in Africa. In Northern Rhodesia, according to Gray, 'to Africans the beer-hall was a striking example of the way in which segregation, or the belief that the towns were by right part of the European's preserve, resulted in a rigid refusal to recognize the needs of urban Africans, intruded into the intimacies of their lives, and destroyed their happiness.' Gray, *Two Nations*, pp. 220/1. For Nairobi and Mombasa, see Willis, *Potent Brews*, p. 139.
[27] 'Seize these people'.
[28] Letter from E.J.C. Second Non-Abstainer, *TS*, 24 August 1946.
[29] Interviews Nos. 2 & 5.
[30] *Wakili* Kinondoni to DC, Dsm, 17 June 1957, TNA/540/3/91A (Original in Swahili).
[31] Personal communication from D.J.G. Fraser (Superintendent in the Tanganyika Police, 1952–62), 7 March 1999; Leslie, *Survey*, p. 250.
[32] Baker, in 1941, noted that minor *Wandewa* from the peri-urban fringe were 'loth to enforce the permit system, probably because they themselves derive considerable revenue from the illegal sale of *tembo*'. PC, EP to CS, 16 July 1941, TNA/12356/Vol. II.

information received by the police from the Native Administration.[33] In addition to the consumption of illegally manufactured alcohol there was also, according to Leslie, 'a fair sale of legal liquor but in unlicensed premises'. 'European' beer and spirits were sold at inflated prices to cover the potential cost of the bar-owner's arrest, although if surprised the seller was 'always ready with the excuse that he was only throwing a party for his friends'.[34]

In his social survey, Leslie noted that in comparison to other East African towns regulations controlling the production and consumption of alcohol were not strict in Dar es Salaam. Nevertheless, he remarked, 'the restrictions have bred contraventions, as they must do in any society where they are not backed by public opinion, and the prevalence of such petty contraventions all contributes to the "spiv" mentality.'[35] The liquor laws in Dar es Salaam were ostensibly formulated (and applied) for the preservation of public order. Instead, they promoted disobedience and illegality. Such logic appeared to have little impact on the municipal authorities and the police, who continued to target illegal bars and their customers up to 1961, displaying a Sisyphean determination to impose an alien order.

Street trading and its control

Unlicensed street traders were another group vulnerable to arrest in the name of colonial order. The principal objection voiced by officials was that of the risk to public health. This did not apply to those petty traders of goods other than foodstuffs, however, nor was it the whole story with regard to food-sellers. When, in 1921, DO Brett counselled for the relaxation of the prohibition on hawking that was introduced during WWI, so that 'fit and proper persons' might be granted the licence to trade as they had in German times, he was informed by his seniors that hawking should not be encouraged. A secretariat official, before going on to articulate concerns about sanitation, observed that '[t]he more hawkers wander about European houses the more the chances of theft and probability of annoyance to European ladies'.[36] From the beginning of the British colonial period, official opposition to itinerant trading had as much to do with public order as public health. This is likewise reflected in the apparently gendered nature of official attitudes towards petty trade: little concern was voiced toward the many women engaged in the sale and production of foodstuffs, notably between the wars when they probably constituted a majority of those engaged in informal economic activity.[37] Once again, it was the mobility of male African traders that was the source of such disquiet.

---

33 Fraser communication; Leslie, *Survey*, p. 251.
34 *Ibid.*
35 *Ibid.*
36 Undated sec. min. (1921?) in TNA/2618.
37 See above, pp. 66–8.

Legitimate Lawlessness?: The Informal Economy

In the inter-war period, while unlicensed trading occurred in the town, it was not widespread enough to cause much concern.[38] A sudden increase in hawking from the early 1930s – probably stemming from the reduction in formal employment caused by the Depression – resulted in vociferous complaints from Indian traders about unfair competition, along with a more muted official response raising the health risk and the loss of revenue from licences.[39] However, the numbers involved were small enough for street trading to have been regularised by the end of 1934; 'the bulk of unlicensed traders' were 'swept … into the markets' and 'certain of the aged and infirm hawkers' issued with permits.[40] It was after 1940, when the growth of the town's population outpaced the capacity of the urban economy to provide formal employment, that street trading became more commonly adopted as a means of generating an urban income. Setting oneself up was relatively straightforward. The capital required tended to be minimal, and while returns were usually similarly modest they at least provided a subsistence.[41] A wide range of products were sold by street traders in the 1940s. They included charcoal, firewood, earthenware pots (*vyungu*) and raffia mats (*ukindu*). Fresh fish was hawked around the town by local fishermen; so too was fresh fruit. The most common items offered for sale, though, were prepared foodstuffs: *vitumbua* and *maandazi* (types of fried pastries), *samaki wakukangaa* (cooked fish) and *togwa* (a non-alcoholic millet drink).[42] Meanwhile, itinerant coffee and tea vendors roamed the streets for custom.

Municipal and district officials considered unlicensed street trading as either a public health threat and/or an activity that undermined the licensed and controlled trade conducted (predominantly) in the official markets such as those at Kariakoo and Ilala. On the Township Authority, unofficial Indian members also supported the restriction of informal African trade. They

[38] In the mid 1920s, authorised street trading occurred in the town (though numbers were presumably restricted). Licences were issued by the DO to hawkers of fresh fruits and provisions. After years of complaints, about both the lack of sanitary controls and the loss of market revenues, the Director of Medical and Sanitary Services was in 1929 eventually successful in getting responsibility for issuing licences shifted to the Township Authority, which had its own Medical Officer. See correspondence in TNA/450/249.

[39] E.g. *TH*, 22 September 1934, p. 9, for Indian grievances; and correspondence in TNA/22243 for the official discussion of the problem.

[40] 1934 Report on Township Affairs by MS [hereafter: MS, 'Township affairs'], TNA/625; 1934 Medical AR.

[41] More established traders could actually prosper through informal trade. In his social survey, Leslie noted that 'many [women] have managed to save quite large amounts, enough in some cases to build a house with, from the sale of small quantities of firewood, fish or beans, a few cents at a time.' Leslie, *Survey*, p. 117.

[42] See DC Bone to MS, 5 November 1945, for some of the items traded in the 1940s. I have restricted my discussion to African itinerant traders. Indians played an important part in street trading, providing goods for sale to African (and Arab — see Leslie's notes on the Shihiris in the Dsm District Book) vendors, and — in the inter-war period, at least — hawking goods themselves. Arab Hadhrami (locally known as Shihiri) traders were also common, associated particularly with the sale of second-hand clothing, although existing sources shed little light on official attitudes towards their presence. Baker, 'Memorandum', p. 36; DC Harris to TC, 9 November 1953, TNA/540/3/75A.

appeared to be more successful in serving the interests of retailers among their community than those supposed to be representing the African population.[43] Neither the nominated African member nor the *Liwali* were inclined to support the hawkers' cause. After the war, as more people took to informal trade, the Authority decided to restrict the number of licences issued to itinerant traders, aiming at 'a long term policy to eliminate street hawking altogether'. 'The Police', it was reported the following month, 'were taking the necessary steps to round up the unlicensed squatters selling foodstuffs in the streets'. This policy was retained into the 1950s. 'Police prosecute those [hawkers] they don't like as fast as possible', a district official pointed out in 1953, 'but many still persist'.[44] Some explanation for this persistence may be gleaned from the grievances voiced by three itinerant traders about restrictions on the sale of foodstuffs in the same year. 'We are not trading because we want to', they lamented, 'our problem is there is no work for residents of Dar es Salaam... we are dependent on this business to pay our rent and tax'.[45] Despite the shortage of work, however, the number of trading licences was highly restricted as the Municipal Council (which had succeeded the Township Authority in 1949) maintained its long-held policy 'to keep street trading to an absolute minimum'. There was no relaxation of the restrictions on hawking, and in 1955 a special police squad was set up to apprehend, among other undesirables, unlicensed hawkers. In the first quarter of the year, 111 were prosecuted for trading without a licence and fined a total Shs. 2,402 as a result of police raids.[46]

It is remarkable so few were arrested. Judging by Leslie's 1956 survey, unlicensed trading was widespread in the town by the mid-1950s. It included adult men selling fruit between bouts of formal employment, housewives selling cooked beans or fried fish, and children hawking *kashata* (a peanut sweet) or *dafu* (drinking coconuts). 'Small traders there were in plenty', observes Leslie,

> pedlars of hot coffee, tea-stall holders, sellers of fruit in season, of roast meat, fish, coconuts, firewood, charcoal, onions, or palm-wine, water-carriers, pedlars of milk, old bottles, flattened kerosene cans for roofing, old clothes, and peanuts.

Buguruni was alive with economic activity when Leslie visited the area, most, if not all, almost certainly unlicensed:

> some women have bought lengths of wood and are chopping them for firewood ... women mostly, but one man too, have fish sizzling in a pan over

43 It should be stressed, however, that Indian interests were not uniform. In many cases, African hawkers were actually acting as agents for Indian traders who therefore had no desire to see hawking suppressed.

44 TA mins, 21 March 1947; 18 April 1947, TNA/540/27/3; hand-written note, 3 September 1953, TNA 540/3/75A.

45 Rajabu Tawaleni, Omari Mfaume and Juma Mwinyimvua to DC, TC, and Council of 40, 26 August 1953, TNA/540/3/75A (Original in Swahili).

46 TC to MAAO, 11 November 1955, TNA/540/3/75A; QPR, Dsm Dist, 1 January–31 March 1955, TNA/90/1011/Vol. 1.

a charcoal brazier ... to be sold either to one of the Arab shops or to the men direct when they come home from work; others again have bought a sack of charcoal and laid it out in heaps for sale.

In Keko Magurumbasi the main street was 'blocked with hawkers selling oranges, vegetables, charcoal, firewood, anything that one can get in Kariakoo market; and throughout the morning... this street is thronged with shoppers'. Hawking and peddling were, according to Leslie, 'the standard expedients of those unable to find paid employment'.[47] Trade was often seasonal. Each July, wrote John Cairns, a DO in the mid-1950s,

> Dar es Salaam is flooded with oranges. The spivs and vagrants and the hundreds of youths who drift in from the neighbouring villages have suddenly become fruit sellers. All over town, and particularly in the African areas, they squat by the roadside and under trees with piles of bright oranges heaped before them.[48]

Few of these petty traders were licensed. Various strategies were adopted to combat the unwanted attentions of the police and the municipal authorities in order that unlicensed traders could continue to ply their business. In some cases, a meeting of the Municipal Council was told in 1957, 'hawkers disappear for a day or two when the Police or Health Officers are on the look out for them, and then come back again.' In other cases those rounded up simply reappeared on the streets after a few days.[49]

Despite the obvious inefficacy of municipal policy, the attempt to control street trading through restricting the number of licences was maintained. Unlicensed hawkers continued to be apprehended and taken to court.[50] In May 1959, a round-up of hawkers from Kisarawe Street led to a boycott of business at the Kariakoo fruit auction organised by the Tanganyika African Traders Union. Farmers boycotted the auction in support of the petty traders who bought their produce for resale on the streets.[51] It appears such action had little impact on council officials, however. Later the same year it was reported that instead of increasing the number of itinerant traders' licences (which at that point stood at no more than 80) the Municipal Council had opted for a reduction. Members of the Kariakoo Ward Council bemoaned the decision, pointing out that 'many genuine town residents, particularly widows with young children and the temporarily unemployed had no choice but to scrape together a living by small trade.'[52]

It was not until the election of Dar es Salaam's first African mayor, Amri Abedi, a Manyema poet and Ahmadi missionary,[53] that there was a reconsideration of the long-held municipal policy of restriction. On coming

---

[47] Leslie, *Survey*, pp. 121, 180, 209, 226, 235, 240, 286.
[48] Cairns, *Bush*, p. 140.
[49] Leslie, *Survey*, p. 250; *TS*, 24 May 1957, p. 17; 19 September 1957, p. 4.
[50] See TNA/540/3/38B and 561/DC3/17.
[51] Council minutes, June 1959, p. 189.
[52] DC Winstanley to TC, 26 November 1959, TNA/540/DC9/3.
[53] Iliffe, *Modern History*, p. 551. The Ahmadiyya are an Islamic sect.

to office in early 1960, Mayor Abedi proposed that 'street tea and food sellers should be given licenses to trade freely and hawkers licenses to move freely.'[54] By this time ever-growing numbers were resorting to informal trade as a means of getting by. A review of policy was conducted by the council sub-committee. With its block of newly elected African councillors, there were for the first time elements on the Municipal Council more sympathetic towards the plight of these unlicensed traders. 'The high rate of unemployment in the Municipality is forcing many people to obtain an honest living through street trading', Councillor Kungulilo told a Municipal Council meeting in May 1960. 'These people cannot understand why their efforts should be frustrated by what they consider to be an excessively rigid application of by-laws made in days when circumstances were very different from those of today.'[55] Nevertheless, Indian councillors, keen to protect the interests of sections among their own community, remained stubbornly opposed to the relaxation of trading restrictions. 'To reverse this policy', complained Councillor Jaffer, 'would appear a retrograde step both from the point of view of public health and general tidiness of the town and the abatement of nuisance to traffic and pedestrians.'[56] The outcome of these exchanges was a compromise in which itinerant fruit and vegetable traders were allowed to operate unlicensed as long as they had acquired written permission to trade from the Town Clerk, while regulations were introduced restricting traders of other goods — who coincidentally must have posed a greater competitive threat to established Indian retailers[57] — to operate from approved sites. One hundred and ninety-two licences were made available to such traders. Meanwhile, the Police were 'requested to take action against any such traders operating on the streets or sidewalks and against any other persons (excluding approved fruit sellers) trading on the streets with no permit'.[58] '[T]he new controls', announced a satisfied Councillor Jaffer, 'should go a long way towards solving the indiscriminate trading which was going on "briskly" in Dar es Salaam.'[59]

Such hopes proved misplaced. Four months after the new regulations were introduced, the Markets, Housing and Fire Committee of the Municipal Council was informed of unauthorised markets in Magomeni and Temeke, along with the emergence of itinerant traders at the junction of Acacia Avenue and Suleiman Street in central Dar es Salaam.[60] In June, the Medical Officer of Health observed that 'over the past few months there has been a marked increase of "pavement restaurants".' 'A large, flourishing one exists every mid-day along Azania Front', he pointed out, 'and most central parts of

54 *TS*, 7 April 1960, p. 3.
55 *TS*, 5 May 1960, p. 3.
56 *TS*, 8 April 1960, p. 4; see also, *TS*, 5 May 1960, p. 3.
57 Competition was not simply inter-racial, but also intra-racial, as the hawkers were often acting as agents of other Indian retailers. See fn. 42 above and — for a contemporary example — fn. 22 in the conclusion.
58 Council mins, Markets, Housing and Fire (MHF) Committee, 15 March 1961.
59 *TS*, 5 January 1961, p. 3.
60 Council mins, MHF Cttee, 12 May 1961.

town now have these places where the by-laws are being flagrantly violated.'[61] The municipal authorities lacked the ability or resources to devise a solution to the problem of unlicensed trading in the town. With around 7,000 or more Africans entering the city annually after 1957 (see Table 10.1), when Leslie had estimated unemployment among men between 16 and 45 to be about 18.6 percent, the chances of exerting municipal control over the burgeoning informal economy were slender.[62] In the absence of a more lasting solution, and faced with the proliferation of pavement restaurants and other unlicensed activities, members of the Public Health Committee in June 1961 resorted to a tried, though hardly proven, response: 'that the Town Clerk be directed to seek Police assistance to clear all unauthorised street traders in the town'.[63]

While property offences may have been uppermost in the fight against crime, the informal economy had no place in the orderly town colonial administrators endeavoured to shape.[64] Although social surveys, such as Baker's and Leslie's, brought to light the existence of a flourishing informal sector providing a livelihood to many impoverished town-dwellers, to urban officals this represented a loss of control. By engaging in informal economic activities Africans evaded state supervision. These activities could provide a source of significant accumulation, discomfiting officials keen to regulate African avenues to prosperity. Most of all, though, the emergence of an informal sector formed a very public reminder that officials exercised limited influence over the social, cultural and economic processes accompanying African urbanisation. Its efflorescence from the late-colonial period was to lead to a very different city from that envisaged by colonial administrators; or, for that matter, by their post-colonial successors.[65]

---

[61] Council mins, MOH's Report to Public Health (PH) Cttee, 15 June 1961.
[62] Leslie, *Survey*, p. 122.
[63] Council mins, PH Cttee, 16 June 1961.
[64] The same was true for other Eastern African colonies. See e.g., Claire Robertson, *Trouble Showed the Way: Women, men and trade in the Nairobi area, 1890–1990* (Bloomington, 1997). For a rare case of pragmatic recognition of the role the informal sector might play, see the 1954 Kenya Government *Report on Destitution*, which, while acknowledging that '[q]uestions of hygiene, traffic problems and other factors induce the desire... to impose severe limitations' on petty trade, nevertheless urged 'that the opportunity of a modest livelihood that these activities afford should be provided wherever possible'. The recommendation was ignored. See Robertson, p. 138.
[65] See Burton, 'Haven'; *idem*, 'Urbanisation', pp. 25–6.

Nine

An Unwelcome Presence

African Mobility & Urban Order

To the non-African in Dar es Salaam, while criminals were a persistent source of inconvenience or even menace, they were hard to distinguish from the bulk of the African population. As we have seen, even the best-informed colonial officials had difficulty separating criminals from ordinary residents. This inability to differentiate often led, among officials and (European and Indian) settlers alike, to the perception of an African 'mass' among whom the general breakdown of tribal discipline and consequent predilection to miscreancy posed a constant threat to the wider urban community. These anxieties found expression in the various by-laws that proscribed African mobility in the European and Indian areas. They were magnified by the increasing numbers of migrants making their way to the town. An emerging community of unemployed or underemployed Africans, over which the powers of supervision or control were negligible, was a major concern. Other groups, too, threatened the fragile colonial order. As we have seen, itinerant traders were viewed with suspicion. Likewise, beggars, who reached Dar es Salaam from far and wide, cluttered streets and accosted pedestrians, providing an unwelcome reminder of the shortcomings of the colonial regime. Meanwhile, unruly African youth, who had either come unaccompanied to the town or who were beyond parental control, were also a persistent nuisance. On occasion the position in the capital did deteriorate to the point of the serious breakdown of order. These periodic outbreaks of violence simply served to justify and to reaffirm anxiety about the African urban presence.

Loiterers, loafers and rickshaw 'boys'

Alongside by-laws in the Township Regulations prohibiting unlicensed trade, drunkenness and prostitution, were others aimed at controlling African mobility within the town. Sections 10 and 11 of the 1920 rules restricted the African presence in a 'prohibited area' from the Open Space east to the seashore, disallowing any 'native' from 'loitering' here after 6pm; and after 11pm no 'native' was to be present without 'a dated certificate signed by a responsible householder, stating the purpose for which such native is in such area' (reissued on a daily basis). Other regulations disallowed 'use of streets' anywhere in the town (by bicycle or on foot) without a light between 9pm and sunrise, failing which an individual could be arrested and was then obliged to satisfy the police or a magistrate of his/her respectability.[1] Hamisi Akida, a Dar es Salaam resident from the late 1930s, recalled the prohibitions against all but those employed by Europeans or Indians. Exceptions were made for Africans returning from cinemas in the town centre, although even then movie-goers had, after a show, to go directly from the theatre to Kariakoo, and those using more circuitous routes or travelling in the wrong direction were liable to be apprehended.[2] Prosecutions against Africans 'abroad at night without a light' — an offence in all parts of the town — were among the most commonly enforced of the Township Rules. Out of 149 reported by-law infractions in 1931, 44 were for this offence, four more than for those found drunk and disorderly, the next most common offence.[3] Two decades later this by-law continued to be enforced with regularity, offenders receiving anything up to one month's imprisonment for being in the wrong place at the wrong time (followed by repatriation).[4] In Kinondoni local court in 1957, it was by far the most commonly enforced township regulation, with 73 individuals prosecuted in the course of the year.[5]

The existence of such restrictions indicates anxiety over the need to control the African population. Africans in the town frequently acted in ways contrary to European expectations and desires. Among other things, they entered prohibited areas at proscribed times, and wandered light-less at night. In addition, daytime 'loitering' in Zones I and II was common, which although not technically illegal was certainly regarded as offensive by many Europeans and Indians. The presence of unoccupied Africans in Uzunguni and Uhindini discomfited occupants of those areas. Many preferred the perceived cultural distance between themselves and 'natives' to be reinforced by a physical distance; certainly outside the workplace or the commercial sphere.

These concerns were periodically expressed in local newspapers. A 1925 editorial in the *Dar es Salaam Times* complained of 'a disgraceful state of affairs, which ... old residents of Dar es Salaam have viewed with increasing alarm':

---

[1]   Township Rules, 1923, 149(4). Similar regulations were in place in towns throughout colonial Africa, although they were not restricted to colonial towns. In mid-nineteenth-century Tunis, those found on the city's streets after sundown without a lantern suffered 'a night's detention unless he [the offender] be a respectable person and known to the police'. William L. Cleveland, 'The Municipal Council of Tunis, 1858–1870: A study in institutional change', *International Journal of Middle East Studies* 9 (1978), pp. 22–61, quoted in Clancy-Smith, 'Contested spaces', p. 199.

[2]   Interview No. 1.

[3]   *Report on the Question of Imprisonment in Tanganyika Territory* (Dsm, 1932), App. C, p. 13.

[4]   See repatriation records from 1955/56 in TNA/540/55/10/1.

[5]   TNA/Acc. 122; see also, Asst. CP, Dsm to CP, 5 February 1957, TNA/90/2009/Vol.1.

The system [sic] of groups of native loafers sprawling across our pavements, in main streets as well as in others, coughing and spitting … and occasionally gambling … would not be tolerated in other countries. Surely our trusteeship of the native does not justify such a degree of pampering …

Psychologically, the tolerance of such a condition increases in intensity the contempt of this type of native for White authority. They come to look upon the pavements for sprawling purposes as theirs by right, and no way is willingly made for passers-by, men or women, European or non-European.[6]

A decade later the same prejudices continued to be voiced. A correspondent wrote to the *Tanganyika Standard* demanding that idlers be cleared from the streets. The editor of the paper wholeheartedly agreed that steps should be taken to combat this 'obvious evil':

There is more in this than just a dislike of untidiness (streets can look 'untidy' with loafers just as they can with scraps of paper and orange peel). It is really necessary to lay stress on the ills — evils — that can accompany the presence of street corner idlers, if they are not checked in time.[7]

'Not only' were such 'idlers' 'an offence to the eye but an offence to themselves and the township as a whole'. Similar concerns were expressed in the Indian press. The editor of the Indian-owned *Herald* complained in 1934 of 'unemployed and unemployable natives roaming about in the heart of the township'; and five years later of 'Natives, having no work … found in crowds of 4 to 15 people sitting or sleeping on footpaths, talking and shouting … [who] will not move on from the places but on the contrary sometimes will abuse'.[8]

Such anxieties were not confined to the unemployed. Casuals frequenting the docks were another target. 'We wonder when boat natives are going to be controlled', wrote one correspondent to the *Times* in 1920. 'They are a danger to the life and property of any European who puts in an appearance on the jetty, with their jostling, pushing and screaming for ones custom'.[9] A later correspondent to the paper elaborated on the situation in 1923:

It is a common occurrence to see passengers luggage, and in the case of non-Europeans even their persons, forming the centre of a violent struggle for possession among the loafers of the town and boat boys. The one or two bewildered *Askaris* on the pontoon are no match for the gang of toughs composing the boat crews, and their futile attempts to control them is a common source of wonder.[10]

Once ashore, according to this way of thinking, hapless European travellers were then at the mercy of unscrupulous 'native' rickshaw pullers. 'One hears from time to time', wrote the District Superintendent of Police in 1926,

---

6   *DT*, 19 September 1925, p. 2.
7   *TS*, 4 May 1935, p. 6.
8   *TH*, 21 July 1934, p. 9; 18 January 1939, p. 8.
9   *DT*, 3 July 1920, p. 6. In colonial Lagos a Harbour Police was established in part to deal with the 'bad characters who pester and annoy sailors, merchant seamen and visitors'. Fourchard, 'Urban poverty'.
10   *DT*, 20 January 1923, p. 9.

Fig. 9.1 *A rickshaw outside Dar es Salaam railway station, c. 1930s*
Source: From the collection of Mahmood A. Karimjee

of instances of the gross overcharging of passengers who come ashore from liners and engage rickshaws to see the sights. They are charged say Shs.10/- for a Shs.4/- ride, they protest, the rickshaw boy becomes vehement and to save a scene they pay the amount demanded.[11]

Africans pursuing this line of business were, above all others, the focus of European concern.[12] Rickshaw pullers had an enhanced right of access to Zones I and II, particularly at night, and although in the central area they were supposed to remain at designated stands, this rule was frequently ignored.[13] Their presence made many uneasy. The vehicles and their operators were considered the vectors of disease. In 1921 the *Dar es Salaam Times* drew attention to a new disease that had been identified by the Minister of Health in Nairobi, spread by lice that were found in the upholstery of rickshaws there. They were, according to the paper, 'present owing to the irregular habit of the ricksha boys, who often sleep in the vehicles'. The following month, the paper reported satisfaction 'that among the proposed new laws for rickshas in Nairobi, ricksha boys lying or sitting in a ricksha shall be found guilty of a punishable offence.'[14] Having noted that '[i]n Dar es Salaam the risk is equally great' the paper recommended 'to the authorities here the adoption of similar measures, and insistence on clean and washable covers to all rickshas, as well as on periodical examinations'.

An additional danger of the close encounter between colonial subjects and masters arising from the rickshaw trade was the threat posed to the mystique

[11] Dist. Supt, to CP, 17 September 1926, TNA/61/206.
[12] Less so Indians, judging by their newspapers.
[13] *TH*, 28 October 1933, p. 10.
[14] *DT*, 7 May 1921, p. 6; 4 June 1921, p. 4.

of European superiority. According to Orde-Browne, the pullers' 'employment at night is apt to show an unedifying side of the European character'. 'Every ricksha', he observed anxiously five years later, 'must have a considerable experience of helplessly drunk passengers.'[15] If we accept the criticisms of the *Dar es Salaam Times*, rickshaw-pullers' experience of Europeans *was* resulting in Africans who refused to know their place. A 1925 editorial on 'the growing insolence of the native' singled out 'Rickshaw Boys' for particular ire:

> One can see these lolling in their own rickshaws, which are hauled up on the footpath, while the owners casually invite passing pedestrians to 'N'joo! N'joo! Rickshaw'; or else they pester one in a most impudent and embarassing manner...
>
> We have seen Rickshaw boys, dressed in their filthy clothes, lounging on their rickshaw, which was drawn up on the footpath running along the sea front, leering in a most bestial manner at passing European ladies.
>
> During the week an *askari* attempted to 'move on' a rickshaw boy who had drawn his 'shaw up on the path. As the boy refused to move it the *askari* pushed it out of the way but the rickshaw boy returned it to its former position. This occurred twice, to the accompaniment of much bad language on the part of the boy and much jeering by a crowd of Swahilis, who enjoy seeing authority in any form defied by one of their number.[16]

The relationship between puller and passenger was frequently a tense one. It is likely, though, that the experience for the African puller tended to be significantly more demeaning than for the occasional European whose pride was wounded. Indeed, for all the 'native insolence' that the *Times* complained of, an angry European had recourse to violence in a way that was unimaginable the other way round.[17] Pulling a rickshaw was, in any case, physically (and, no doubt, psychologically) punishing enough in itself.[18]

While the unsavoury effects of the encounter between Europeans and Africans that occurred as a result of the rickshaw trade were widely deplored, it was the rickshaw pullers' purported criminal tendencies that were the focus of greatest concern. The 'class of native' employed in this occupation, it was observed in 1924, 'is a decidedly undesirable one, and it is unfortunate that public convenience necessitates the employment of so many natives in this work.'[19] Even those who entered the profession as upright and honest were considered soon corrupted. Orde-Browne stressed what an 'unedifying education this life must be for an unsophisticated African'.[20] 'The occupation', he pointed out, 'is a demoralising one':

15 1924 DAR, p. 10; Orde-Browne to CS, 18 January 1929, TNA/11205.
16 *DT*, 9 May 1925, p. 2.
17 In 1919, a 'white man was seen in Third Street knocking a ricksha [sic] boy about in a most disgusting fashion, kicking him in the abdomen, and punching his face until the poor boy could hardly stand'. *DT* 24 December 1919, p. 2.
18 Orde-Browne, in 1929, described the 'disgusting and disgraceful sight' of 'two large and portly passengers being dragged up the little hill past the European hospital by one wretched youth, bent almost double and gasping for breath'. Orde-Browne to CP, 9 February 1929, TNA/61/206.
19 1924 DAR, p. 10.
20 Orde-Browne to PC, EP, 19 January 1929, TNA/61/206.

Profits depend largely upon the success with which the passenger can be deceived, or even, threatened, over the amount of fare due; while the owner from whom the vehicle is hired is not exactly an elevating influence.[21]

The rickshaw-puller, Orde-Browne complained, 'is in almost every case an actual or potential criminal', the occupation being 'an ideal mask for theft'.[22] The Commissioner of Police, whose subordinates were responsible for the supervision of rickshaws, refuted this characterisation of Africans engaged in the trade. 'The character of every applicant for a licence is very closely enquired into', he assured the Chief Secretary, 'and there is not one licensed puller with a criminal record which would rightly debar him.'[23] However, the police's assessment was to change. In 1941, a senior officer bemoaned

the idle and unsavoury character of rickshaw boys ... Many so employed are not natives of Dar es Salaam and very few actually keep to rickshaw work, while those who are old hands are without exception persons with criminal or other records against them. There is the famous 'Mumba' who has over fifty previous convictions against him for 'drunk and disorderly'... Another famous character is Juma bin Hamisi; with over thirty previous convictions... These boys are broadly speaking nothing but 'pimps'; they tout for work on boat days and are a perfect nuisance to the visitor when he comes ashore. When the harbour is idle they have very little work and it is not possible for them to earn an honest living.[24]

As a result of the condition of both the vehicles themselves and the persons operating them, the Superintendent recommended the complete removal of rickshaws from Dar es Salaam. It was, in any case, a dying trade, the rickshaw's place being usurped from the early 1930s by the faster and more comfortable — not to mention humane — taxis.[25] Instead of banning their use, licensing procedure became more strict and they were otherwise left to fade away. The small number of rickshaw operators remaining proved tenacious, refusing to recognise that their time was up. They continued to function as late as 1951,

[21] According to the *DT* of 28 May 1921, reporting a strike by rickshaw pullers: 'The method hitherto has been for the boys to hire the rickshas by the day, anything they earn over and above the bike fee being their own profit'. The ethnicity of the vehicle owners is not reported, but it was almost certainly Indians who controlled the rickshaw trade in Dar es Salaam. The strike had occurred owing to a fall in pullers' earnings. The *Times* was surprised by the high degree of organisation the strikers displayed. 'The deputation of ricksha boys', it reported, 'which met the authorities was based on the best European lines, having eloquent spokesmen, and their points clearly and concisely outlined. We wonder if a Ricksha Carriers Trade Union exists?' Such a characterisation of the rickshaw pullers actually contradicts the disparaging tone to be found in other discussions — including *Times* articles and editorials — of this section of the urban population.

[22] Orde-Browne to CS, 18 January 1929, TNA/11205.

[23] CP to CS, 2 February 1929, TNA/11205.

[24] AgSP to MS, 26 August 1941, TNA/30218; see also MS to CS, 20 November 1941, TNA/61/206.

[25] Baker, 'Memorandum', p. 40.

at which time they were reportedly being utilised by prostitutes in the town.[26] After a number of complaints against them in this year, the municipal authorities finally opted for their removal.[27]

By the time the last rickshaws had ceased operating the heightened racial consciousness, on the part of Europeans, that was a feature of inter-ethnic relations in the period between the wars appears to have dissipated. While the editor and readers of the *Tanganyika Standard*— the settler mouthpiece that had replaced the *Times*— in the 1950s may have fulminated on the presence of idlers in the town, such complaints were no longer informed by the racial anxiety that appears to have informed similar complaints in the 1920s and 1930s. The public articulation of concern over 'native insolence', over Africans leering at European women or failing to accord their social betters the respect they felt was their due, was no longer acceptable. In its stead more commonplace worries were expressed over increasing unemployment in the town, and the associated incidence of crime. As part of the effort to address these concerns, municipal by-laws restricting the nocturnal mobility of Africans within the town continued to be enforced. By the late 1950s, though, even these had to be relaxed. From 1958 the by-law prohibiting individuals from walking light-less at night lapsed into disuse, with no prosecutions whatsoever for this offence arising in the Kinondoni court in the last two years of colonial rule.[28] In the changing political circumstances of the late 1950s, the prosecution of un-illuminated pedestrians became untenable. The strength of TANU was the ultimate indication that the colonial 'native' no longer knew his place.

Indigency and urban order

Beggars were another group of 'undesirables' who persistently refused to recognise their allotted colonial space. While their presence may 'have performed a necessary function where almsgiving was a religious obligation',[29] colonial officials were not inclined to accept such visible reminders of the shortcomings of the regime in the territorial capital.[30] Nevertheless, since

[26] The same appeared to be true in Nairobi, where the Resident Magistrate had in 1946 come to the conclusion that 'rickshaws are used chiefly for illegal purposes, that the pullers are mostly pimps and procurers and that these vehicles assist them in their trade'. *TS*, 30 March 1946, p. 10. Similarly, on the Witwatersrand in the early 1900s, owners of horse-drawn 'cabs' sought links with local prostitutes as their technological obsolescence led to their demise. See Van Onselen, *New Babylon*, p. 200.

[27] CP to CS, 28 February 1951, TNA/41119; and personal correspondence from Joan Thompson, 1 March 1999.

[28] TNA/Acc. 122.

[29] Iliffe, *African Poor*, p. 33.

[30] Legislation aimed at the prevention of mendicity included the Destitute Persons Ordinance of 1923. More explicitly aimed at beggars were the sections of the 1930 Penal Code targeting both 'every person wandering or placing himself in any public place to beg or gather alms, or causing any child to do so'; and 'every person wandering abroad and endeavouring by the exposure of wounds or deformation to obtain or gather alms'. Penal Code (No. 11 of 1930), section 166 (2) and (4).

Dar es Salaam represented the principal concentration of population and wealth in Tanganyika, it is likely that beggars were present in the capital from early on, although the first surviving evidence comes from the 1930s. In 1934, an editorial in the *Tanganyika Herald* drew attention to 'crippled, unemployed and unemployable natives roaming about the heart of the township, some with a bowl, others pickpocketing and a few gambling in broad daylight'. The editor displayed little sympathy for these unfortunates. '[N]eeding serious consideration at this stage of the native evolution', he considered, 'is [the] begging habit. It is necessary to do everything possible to root out this growing evil.' His counterpart at the *Standard* concurred. 'One of the nuisances which come under public notice', a 1935 editorial observed,

> is the growing habit of children to beg on the streets. It is not haphazard; the children clearly have been taught. They make a very cautious approach and inform the passer-by that they are hungry. Others may be seen methodically turning out dustbins.[31]

Early the following year, in response to a request in the Legco for control to be exercised over the increasing number of beggars, the Provincial Commissioner reported that there were 'twenty Natives… who have no means of subsistence and beg for a living'. He complained that 'the religious custom of distributing, indiscriminately, alms to door to door supplicants on Holy days, which prevails among Mahomedan and other communities, tends to encourage a class of professional beggars.' He recommended the organisation of a central fund through which 'deserving cases' could receive alms and begging could be controlled. Nothing was done, and the situation continued to deteriorate. The following year, DO Huggins informed the Commissioner that the town was 'full of mendicants, the lame, the halt, the lazy, the unemployable'. By this time there were 40 habitual mendicants (including 15 women) residing in the town. In addition, there was 'a large number of destitutes who come in periodically to beg'.[32] Of the 40, 12 were blind, the others 'paralysed, deformed and deficient of limbs'. The majority were aged. 'The conditions under which they now live are pitiable', commented Huggins. 'Those who cannot obtain lodging from some charitable organisation sleep in temporary shelters and forage in the garbage and refuse of markets and eating houses.' Periodically they had been charged and convicted. They were unable to support themselves except through begging, however, and repatriation was not possible in most cases as they had no surviving relatives. In the circumstances they were only warned and, according to Huggins, '[t]he Police now direct their efforts to keep these people away from the residential and commercial quarters of the town where in the past they have been accustomed to wander on Sundays and Fridays in search of charity.'[33]

---

[31] *TH*, 17 July 1934, p. 9; *TS*, 25 May 1935, p. 6.
[32] PC, EP to CS, 30 January 1936; Huggins to PC, EP, 8 March 1937 and 15 October 1937, TNA/61/261/Vol. II.
[33] The residential areas referred to were most likely the European and Indian areas.

It was recognised that such a state of affairs could not be allowed to persist, and in the late 1930s, on the instigation of the Township Authority, a paupers' camp was built at Kipawa, eight miles from the town centre. Here, reported Pike in 1939, 'the deformed beggars who were such a pest and an eyesore in Dar es Salaam have been sent'.[34] The camp received scant resources, however. Just three years after its establishment, DC Revington declared it was 'squalid and uncared for and should be entirely rebuilt'.[35] Although seventy men, women and children were housed in the camp, this did not appear to have had a significant influence on the numbers of destitute and disabled persons to be found in the town centre. '[T]he number of natives in Dar es Salaam who by reason of old-age, ill-health or physical incapacity are forced to eke out a precarious livelihood by begging appears to be increasing', the Solicitor General told the Chief Secretary in 1942. 'I am informed that a shop-keeper can reckon on being accosted by thirty to forty such natives who parade the streets, particularly on Fridays and Sundays.' 'It must be recognised by now', he continued, invoking the Atlantic Charter, 'even by the extreme die-hards, that the obligation to remove this social evil rests on the Government.' Only if proper facilities were constructed was it 'legitimate for the police to prosecute such persons for begging'.[36]

However, Kipawa remained neglected, and the response to what was described at the end of WWII as the 'swarm of beggars perambulating from house to house and shop to shop ... to the annoyance of the public',[37] was the tightening of Police control.[38] In July 1946, 24 beggars were rounded up and charged with vagrancy. Three weeks later, the President of the Township Authority, Mr. Bryant, thanked the Police 'for the good job carried out by them recently in rounding them up, and for the Police drives still being carried on to rid the town of this nuisance'.[39] At the same meeting, proposals were belatedly put forward for enlarging and improving Kipawa. Government continued to try to absolve itself of responsibility. An attempt to hand over the camp to the Salvation Army in 1948 was only thwarted by resistance from prominent Muslims, who feared inhabitants would be vulnerable to conversion, and any hopes for its improvement remained dependent on substantial donations such as the Shs. 2,000/- received from the East African Muslim Welfare Society in the same year.[40] Although the Social Welfare Department appear to have assumed responsibility for Kipawa in 1948, it provided a refuge for just 45 paupers, 18 less than in 1942. By 1954 the number had fallen to 24.[41]

---

34 Pike, 'Report', p. 12.
35 DC Revington to PC, EP, 23 January 1942, TNA/30134.
36 Ag Solicitor General to CS, 5 January 1942, TNA/22360.
37 The correspondent identified five categories of beggar in the town: the blind, crippled, diseased, insane and paupers. Dsm Social Service League to TA, 15 June 1945, TNA/30134.
38 TA mins, 19 July 1946, TNA/540/7/3.
39 *TS*, 6 July 1946, p. 17; 27 July 1946, p. 9.
40 See TA mins, 23 April 1948, 18 June 1948 and 16 July 1948 in TNA/540/27/3.
41 First [and only surviving] monthly report by the Social Welfare Officer, 3 October 1948; DC's Min., 2 February 1954, TNA/30134.

Within Dar es Salaam, mendicants continued to represent a nuisance to the respectable citizens of the town. In 1950, the Women's Service League of Tanganyika requested for 'arrangements to be made for Africans to be allowed on the streets on Fridays only which is the recognised begging day'. 'Beggars', the Commissioner of Police informed the Chief Secretary in response to this request, 'are a perennial problem and are dealt with periodically when other more pressing duties permit.' According to one secretariat official, the 'beggar problem' was actually exaggerated thanks to the activities of a handful of particularly conspicuous destitutes who were 'so persistent ... that they give the impression of being more numerous than they are':

> There are three in particular — a fat, elderly man, a youth of about 14 who crawls about on the pavement with great agility ... and an elderly blind woman who is led with a stick by a small boy — whom one sees in Acacia Avenue almost every other day. I believe that if the police could manage to eliminate these few 'regulars' the problem would be solved, at least as far as the European shopping areas are concerned.[42]

The narrow concern with the 'European shopping areas' perhaps gives some indication as to why this official remained more complacent than other observers.[43]

By the mid 1950s, with the problem of urban mendicity becoming increasingly severe, it was discovered that large numbers of beggars were coming from further afield than had previously been thought.[44] 'In the last few months, and probably due to famine', complained the District Commissioner in 1954, 'large numbers of blind beggars of ages ranging from 6 to 60 have been coming into Dar es Salaam from Dodoma'.[45] He wrote to the Traffic Superintendent for 'help or suggestions for preventing what is now a serious public nuisance'. Two years later police surveys purportedly revealed the existence of a 'professional class of beggar' in the capital: 'over half of the beggars in Dar es Salaam' were 'indigents who came from long distances, remained a few weeks and returned home'.[46] A *Standard* editorial in 1957 reported 'a well-organised "racket" behind begging

---

[42] Sec. of the Women's Service League to MLO, 13 January 1950; CP to CS, 13 April 1950; Sec min., 23 April 1950, TNA/30134.

[43] Begging in Uhindini appears, from existing sources, to have been common. On the other hand, it is hard to get any impression of mendicity in Zone III, though it certainly occurred there. The African township may not have been so prosperous, although the chances of operating undisturbed were probably greater than in the more strictly policed commercial area. Masudi Ali, who lived in Kariakoo in the 1950s, remembers one particularly prominent female beggar, Binti Hassani Kulomba, operating there. He also recalls that beggars were periodically rounded up and repatriated by the Social Welfare department, although it was never long before they re-emerged. Interview No. 7.

[44] Whether this discovery was evidence of a new trend or simply the belated recognition of the mendicants' mobility is hard to say.

[45] DC, Dsm to Traffic Supt, Dsm, 10 November 1954, TNA/540/3/1.

[46] Tanganyika Council of Social Service [TCSS], mins of meeting, 24 September 1956, TNA/540/1/78.

in Dar es Salaam'.[47] While offering no evidence to support this, an overblown, but nonetheless revealing portrait of the extent of mendicity in the town was painted:

> Something really drastic must be done to rid the streets of Dar es Salaam of the countless beggars which [sic] molest pedestrians, poke their heads — and at times hands — into cars parked in the main thoroughfares and are an extremely bad advertisement for Tanganyika so far as tourists and passengers from the ships are concerned.
>
> During the four days before Christmas, when the streets and the shops were crowded, the beggars simply flocked into town. There were young ones, well able to do a day's work, leading the deformed and the blind, the latter trying to make their pitiful plight still more apparent to passers-by by being clad in the filthiest of rags. One such group of beggars consisted of a young and dirty woman leading an old and allegedly blind man while another young and better clad woman, with a healthy and well-fed youngster of about three strapped to her side, went from shop to shop, or from passer-by to passer-by, all with their hands out, even the toto [child] calling out for money. But they were only four of what must have been hundreds.

By the late 1950s growing numbers of beggars were making their way to the town. This was partly the product of structural destitution, such as the diminishing capacity (or inclination) for rural communities to take care of the disabled. In 1960, the Superintendent of Tanganyika's main mental hospital, Cyril Smartt, complained:

> There is an increasing denial of social responsibility on the part of the African people themselves for their dependants and there is also a tendency to send vagrants, beggars and other social nuisances to mental hospitals as the line of least resistance.[48]

However, cyclical destitution — resulting from weather failure in particular — was at least as significant.

Whatever the causes, the authorities could not tolerate the presence of such large numbers of indigents appearing on the streets of the capital. Several recommendations were made in response to the situation. First, that 'the Police should undertake the regular round-up of persons found begging in the town'. Second, it was proposed that the former Nunge Leper Settlement on the outskirts of Dar es Salaam should be reopened in order to accommodate 30–40 destitute persons in addition to those already residing at Kipawa. This was done in 1958. Finally, echoing the proposals of the

---

[47]   *TS*, 28 December 1957, p. 2. The charge of beggars being frauds has been a common one, both in colonial and post-colonial Dar es Salaam and in other developing countries. In a study of Cali, Colombia, Bromley observed that such representations provide ideological legitimation for coercive action against mendicants (as they have in colonial and post-colonial Tanzania). In the Cali survey, however, those found to be begging were mostly severely deprived individuals among whom the practice of begging was viewed with great shame. R. Bromley, 'Begging in Cali: Image, reality and policy', *International Social Work* 24 (1981), pp. 22–40.

[48]   Quoted in Iliffe, *African Poor*, p. 212.

Provincial Commissioner two decades earlier, '[i]t was agreed that an attempt should now be made to try to canalise the generosity of Muslims and others whose indiscriminate charity was having the effect of encouraging begging in the towns.'[49] However, little headway was made in the attempt to institutionalise alms-giving. By the end of the colonial period, when growing numbers of indigents were making their way to the capital, the official response was much the same as it had been for the past two decades. The Police, the Municipality and the Native Administration co-operated in the periodic removal of 'the various beggars who were infesting the streets [who] would be summoned to the Local Courts … so that a decision could be made as to whether they should be maintained by the Government in the Nunge Pauper Camp or be repatriated to their home districts, if they do not belong to Dar es Salaam'.[50] This was, as ever, a makeshift solution. It was simply a matter of time before indigents drifted back to the town and the whole process had to be started over. A lasting solution to the forces driving the destitute and the disabled to mendicity was beyond the capacity of the colonial state.

Delinquency in Dar es Salaam

Unruly adolescents formed another group whose presence in town officials deplored. The growing number of crimes committed by young offenders first came to be regarded with special concern by the administration in the early 1930s. Crime figures from 1928 and 1929 had revealed a 'disturbing increase in the incidence of juvenile crime'.[51] The phenomenon was blamed on the growth of vagrancy. In Dar es Salaam the usual response to such a state of affairs was to repatriate young vagrants to their area of origin. Frequently those sent home returned to the capital.[52] In other cases, repatriation proved impracticable. When, in 1931, the District Commissioner looked into the background of several boys who had been brought to him by Dar es Salaam police for repatriation, he found himself in a quandary:

> these boys claimed to have been brought by their parents from other districts when they were very young and that they now have no parents living and do not know of the existence of any relatives. To repatriate these lads did not seem to me to be a practicable solution. To whom are they to go? What are they to do? They are a problem.

It was, wrote the DC, 'not desirable to leave them to grow in Dar es Salaam'. Parent-less juveniles in town were vulnerable to a descent into criminality: 'They thieve to obtain the wherewithal to live, and are tools of habitual

---

[49]   See TCSS, mins, TNA/540/1/78.
[50]   MC, mins, 17 February 1961.
[51]   'Imprisonment', Appendix D.
[52]   See statistics of juvenile offenders for 1934 in PRO/CO/691/144/7.

criminals who teach them the trade and relieve them of the proceeds of the theft.'[53]

Juvenile gangs had in fact already emerged that appeared quite capable of operating independently of adult mentors. In his 1931 report, Baker noted the presence of 'particularly impudent' groups of youths who were known collectively as the *kompania ya sinzia*; *kuwevi sinzia* being Swahili for the method used by thieves who stole while one of their number distracted the victim.[54] An editorial on hooliganism (*uhuni*) in *Kwetu* later in the decade complained of young troublemakers '[n]o longer subject to the influence of their parents'. 'Among them', the editorial observed, 'will be found a fair percentage of tax-dodgers, street ruffians, pickpockets, as well as our best athletes ... Most of the petty thefts are committed by them; they are suborned by weaker men to fight out their differences with other people, and they rob our children.'[55] They also victimised Indian residents of the town; snatching jewellery from women and children, harassing shopkeepers in Zones II and III and mugging lone pedestrians in the early evenings. In 1938, 66 Indian retailers from the New Market area wrote a letter to the *Tanganyika Herald* to complain that over the past three months they had been harassed by 'five or six' gangs by day and night.[56]

The gangs contained up to 60 individuals. According to police records, 48 of their number had had dealings with the police in 1937, of whom 43 had convictions recorded against them that year. Their ages and backgrounds were varied. The Commissioner of Police informed the Chief Secretary that some of the *kompania ya sinzia*

> are orphans while others are boys who have run away from home, children who have been neglected and abandoned, and those over whom parents can exercise no control. Their ages average between 8 and 18 years, and they are comparable to the 'street arabs' to be found in any city in the world. With the exception of six who have homes in Dar es Salaam, the remainder have no regular abode, sleep anywhere they can find shelter and obtain food in any way they can.[57]

The Commissioner of Police described the backgrounds of a handful of gang members. Seven were Zaramo, one was Makonde, one Tivi, one Ngindo, one Doe and one Nyamwezi. The youngest, Juma Nassoro, was a 12-year-old Tivi youth, whose father was working as a tailor in Ruvu (a railway town west of Dar es Salaam) and who had been abandoned by his mother in Dar es Salaam after she went off with another man. He was, according to the Commissioner, 'a precocious child and leader of a small gang' who had been dealt with many times by the police. In contrast, the eldest, Nasib Salim, who was 25 years old, from Bagamoyo and had no living relatives, was

---

53   1931 DAR, p. 20.
54   The definition is from Johnson's *Standard Swahili Dictionary*. See also, Baker, 'Social Conditions', p. 93; and for stealing from shops, *TH*, 11 May 1938.
55   *Kwetu*, 21 February 1939. Quoted in Anthony, 'Culture and Society', pp. 159–60.
56   *TH*, 11 May 1938.
57   CP to CS, 13 May 1938, TNA/21963/Vol. 1.

considered 'of weak intellect'. He had eight previous convictions. The others were aged between 16 and 19 years. Some had parents living in Dar es Salaam or in the rural part of the district, others had relatives there or in neighbouring districts, while others had no living relatives.

Officials had difficulty devising a response to the problem of delinquency. In their 1932 report, members of the committee on imprisonment, troubled by evidence that 'frequently children are deliberately employed by thieves and rogues', had recommended that a reformatory be established to 'reclaim' convicted juveniles and to prevent them entering the schools of crime that many took the prisons to be.[58] An Approved School was eventually opened at Kazima, near Tabora, in 1938, after initial opposition by London on financial grounds.[59] While it had some early success with inmates,[60] these initiatives proved to have little impact on the problem of urban delinquency. In 1942, the Superintendent of Police warned the Provincial Commissioner:

> There still remains ... the problem of unemployable youths, who with some precocious youngsters as hangers-on, band themselves into small groups and pester the bazaar and native residential areas. They are mentally unoccupied and by being semi-sophisticated are ripe for any mischief that presents itself from stone-throwing to shoplifting. They are most difficult to control and by their association with bad influences present both a social as well as a police problem which will have to be faced.[61]

The following year it was estimated there were in Dar es Salaam 'about 2,000 young scamps, living on their wits and without any form of parental or other control'. Baker counselled that all parent-less children in Dar es Salaam be removed and the town should become a restricted area into which children could not enter. However, London opposed the introduction of controls over African mobility.[62]

By the early 1950s delinquency had re-emerged as a 'problem of major importance'.[63] In his 1956 survey of the African areas, Leslie uncovered further evidence of 'freedom from parental discipline', detecting signs in Dar es Salaam of 'the revolt of the adolescent, in age and in culture, against the authority of elders'. He found successors to the *kompania ya sinzia* in 'the groups and the gangs who occasionally defy administrative authority ... waging an unceasing though usually personal and defensive battle of wits with the *Jumbes* and the police'.[64] In 1958, the Assistant Commissioner of Police stressed the 'need for a Remand Home in Dar es Salaam for children and young persons who have fallen foul of the law and who, at present,

---

[58] *Report on the Question of Imprisonment in Tanganyika* (Dsm, 1932).
[59] Memo. in PRO/CO/691/132/6.
[60] Up to 1943, of the 44 boys discharged from the school just four had reoffended. Memo attached as App. III to PC's conference mins, 1943, p. 13, TNA/61/702/3.
[61] SP to PC, EP, 20 February 1942, TNA/61/3/XVI.
[62] PC's conference mins, 1943, p. 13, TNA 61/702/3. Other recommendations made by Baker to deal with urban youth are discussed above, pp. 96–7.
[63] Extracts from QPR (Tanganyika) in TNA/540/22/3.
[64] *Ibid.*, p. 112.

constitute something of an embarassment for all who have to deal with them'.[65] Nevertheless, despite the substantial growth of the town and the consequent increase in the number of youths to be found there, delinquency did not appear to be the problem it was in the 1930s. In 1955, the amount of crime attributable to young offenders was, according to the Assistant Commissioner of Police, 'by no means excessive'.[66] 'A number of African youths do come in from the districts in search of work', the same official noted the following year, 'and these men are somewhat of a problem to the Administration although this view cannot, as yet, be shared by the Police.'[67]

It is hard to pinpoint exactly why the position in Dar es Salaam had improved since the early 1940s, or at least had not deteriorated considering the huge increase in the urban population. The Kazima Approved School, which by the early 1950s dealt with a daily average of around 200 offenders ranging in age from 8 to 18, appears to have made some impact. On their return to Dar es Salaam 'a good deal of trouble' was taken over discharged inmates from the school by district officials.[68] Often they were helped to find employment to prevent their returning to crime. For example, within two weeks of their release in February 1947, Ali bin Hassan and Hamisi bin Hassan had, thanks to the efforts of the District Office, been taken on as carpenters in the PWD; Mohamed bin Selemani and Rashidi bin Swedi had joined the Kings African Rifles; Selemani bin Hamisi and Juma bin Abdallah had become registered labourers; and three others had been given chits to assist them in obtaining employment. Of the discharged inmates only Saleh bin Selemani, who had been given a trial by the PWD, had proved to be 'a bad egg'.[69] 'The criterion of any school is the type of boy turned out', the Commissioner of Prisons noted with satisfaction in 1949. 'I cannot overemphasize how impressed I am with the ex-Approved School boys keenness, good outlook and above all, their spirit of independence and confidence in themselves.'[70] Indeed, Kazima's successes had filtered down to African parents. In 1944 Asmani Juma Muna, a government clerk living in Dar es Salaam, sought to have his son committed to Kazima:

> My son Ramadhani Athmani Juma, who is about 15 years, is leading a very notorious conduct. He has the habit of being away from home ... I have instructed him so many times and even punishments but no sign of changing. Moreover I have taken up the same case with the local *Jumbe* Mohamed Sultani who alternatively took the real advice on this boy but merely he despised of and ran away as a rascal young chap.
> ... For his bad example I am afraid he may scandalize the rest and turn up my happy family to be dark one. There is immigration of the school children of such boys, I heard, to somewhere, I here too would take consul to

65 Snr. Asst CP, Dsm to DC, Dsm, 8 January 1958, TNA/540/22/3.
66 QPR, Dsm Dist, 1 October–31 December 1955, TNA/90/1011/Vol. 1.
67 AsstCP, Dsm to CP, 9 March 1956, TNA/90/1011/Vol. 1.
68 Prison ARs 1950–3; Report of PCs' conference, 1943, PRO/CO/691/184/42397.
69 Supt, Kazima to DC, Dsm, 14 February 1947; and note dated 3 March 1947, TNA/540/22/3.
70 Cmmr for Prisons to CS, 31 August 1949, TNA/28692.

recommend for him.[71]

The following week Muna's son was sent to Tabora. Offloading troublesome sons appears not to have been uncommon among educated Africans in Dar es Salaam.[72] For all its achievements, however, Kazima hadn't the resources or the staff to provide a true solution to the problem of delinquency. In 1943, Commissioner Brown had recommended the need to build 'a second school, on the lines of Kazima, to cope with the congestion now existing there'.[73] It was not until 1958, however, that a new institution was opened at Malindi, near Dar es Salaam. Despite the scale of Malindi — it could accommodate 400 boys — the ability of the prisons department to process young offenders still did not expand to the extent that many had considered necessary, as by then the original school at Kazima was closed.[74]

While Kazima and its successor may have taken some credit for the relative lack of delinquency in Dar es Salaam in the 1950s, there were more likely factors at work in the capital itself. A 1958 feature on 'Workless youth' in the *Sunday News* observed that more informal methods of crime control exercised within the African community meant that much of the delinquency that did occur was not reflected in the official statistics. The child offender caught stealing generally was 'given a smart cuff across the ear and told to be off'.[75] Meanwhile, the introduction of a probation office in 1950, established in part as a means of punishing young offenders without exposing them to prison life, appears to have had some impact on juvenile crime. In 1953, 97 probationers under the age of 21 were placed under the close supervision of officers. By the end of the decade this number had increased to a not insubstantial 221.[76] Probably the most important factor accounting for the relative lack of delinquency, though, was the huge escalation in campaigns against undesirables that occurred in the 1950s (see chapter 12). Even before this escalation, youths in Dar es Salaam who had no parents or relatives living in the town were frequently repatriated to their home areas. For those organising the raids in the 1950s, this section of the population represented one of their main targets.[77] It is likely they formed a large proportion, perhaps even a majority, of those ejected from the town. This in turn may help explain why delinquency did not become more of a problem.

Riot and the breakdown of order

European and Indian concern over the African urban presence was at its peak after the occasional outbreaks of disorder that periodically occurred in

[71]   Asmani Juma Muna to DC, Dsm, 12 January 1944, TNA/540/22/3.
[72]   See correspondence in TNA/540/22/3; and the extract from the *Sunday News*, April 1958, TNA/460/1049.
[73]   Report of PCs' conference, 1943, PRO/CO/691/184/42397.
[74]   TCSS meeting mins, 18 March 1957, TNA/540/1/78.
[75]   13 April 1950, extracted in TNA/460/1049.
[76]   Prison ARs for 1953 and 1959.
[77]   See Burton, 'Urchins', pp. 213–14.

Dar es Salaam. While crime against property and petty by-law offences were easily the commonest forms of crime in the town, riot was by far the most explosive and threatening. The causes of such outbreaks were manifold. Most commonly they could be characterised as racial violence, though disorder was also associated with strikes and, towards the end of the period under consideration, with the rising anti-colonial sentiment that emerged in the town.

The best-documented outbreaks of racial violence are those that occurred in Uhindini in the inter-war period.[78] The first of these appears to have taken place as early as 1918, although no reference to it survives other than in a 1932 *Tanganyika Herald* editorial bemoaning the high level of crime in the area.[79] An impression of what occurred can perhaps be gained from details of later outbreaks of violence between Africans and Indians that received prominent, and doubtless somewhat sensationalised, coverage in the Indian press. In one such case, in 1929, the *Herald* complained of a 'Reign of lawlessness' in which a 'native mob' 150 strong (the police estimate was 100) terrorised the Indian community in Ring Street between 9 and 10pm on a Saturday night in December. A description of events gives an impression of significant tension existing between Indians and Africans in the town. According to the *Herald*, the violence began after a group of three or four drunk 'natives' verbally abused Indian children playing on the street, and were challenged by adults. After a short exchange of blows, the Africans left the scene only to return with reinforcements, challenging 'Indians to come out and fight':

> The mob had come prepared and equipped with stones and sticks. They rushed on every Indian house and every Indian passer-by in the vicinity and took command ... Whistles were blown, but it was not until half an hour that police assistance was available ... The native mob was divided into groups of four or five persons having scattered in many directions so as to meet outside people coming to help Indians. Many Indians were hit with stones and sticks as they approached the spot. One Indian was hit with heavy sticks till he fell down unconscious and his pocket was emptied by a group of natives.[80]

[78] Situated in the physical (Zone II), social and economic middle of colonial Dar es Salaam, wielding neither the power of the colonial ruler nor the moral authority of the true indigene, the Indian community was more vulnerable than either the European or African communities. This vulnerability came to the fore in both violent and/or criminal behaviour targeting Indians and in the heightened sensitivity of the Indian community towards African crime. For sources of African resentment towards Indians, see Brennan 'Nation', pp. 54–7, 174–96, *et passim*.

[79] *TH*, 4 June 1932, p. 8. It comments: 'We do not think the authorities have forgotten the 1918 bazaar loot'. That this breakdown of order was referred to fourteen years after it had taken place – and when similar, though presumably less serious, incidents had occurred in between – indicates that it was fresh in the minds of at least one section of Dar es Salaam's population, and testifies to the severity of what had taken place. Unfortunately, it was not until the 1920s that the first Indian newspapers were established in Dar es Salaam, and the first surviving district report dates back to 1919–20, so we are left with just this oblique reference from 1932.

[80] *TH*, 18 December 1929, in TNA/13986.

The next serious incident in Uhindini, in November 1937, also occurred in Ring Street. The immediate origins of the disturbance lay in a shopkeeper's attempts 'to chase a thief and developed into a riot of a very serious nature as crowds of natives began to swell'.[81] For forty-five minutes chaos reigned around Ring Street. The *Herald* reported that a 'rowdy mob' pelted 'stones and empty bottles' on Indian businesses and raided shops. Indian children were beaten by 'stick-wielding' Africans and several people injured, as the street 'became flooded with truculent natives'.

Although such riots were few and far between, the potential for them was always present in Uhindini.[82] In the inter-war period, Indians seemed to have been constantly anxious about the threat of violence or theft perpetrated by 'gangs of natives'. After a scuffle between Africans and the police had occurred on Kichwele Street in 1939, for example, shopkeepers were reported to be 'fearing rioting as in their opinion such disturbances created by hooligans generally develop into rioting if not suppressed at once'.[83] Police officials at the time tended to discount the potential dangers.[84] That the Indian response was not unduly alarmist, however, is supported by testimony from the Commissioner of Police, who, in the early 1950s — when there was a significantly larger police presence in the town — warned the Chief Secretary that in Dar es Salaam it was indeed easy for a riot to develop in a matter of minutes.[85] The Commissioner was writing in response to a serious fracas between Arabs and Africans that had occurred in Magomeni in April 1952. An argument arose after an African struck a cat belonging to an Arab shopkeeper, found sprawling asleep on foodstuffs exposed for sale. Fighting broke out, resulting in the injury of several Arabs and Africans, two of whom were hospitalised. 'The Arabs and Africans at Magomeni', a secretariat official pointed out, 'have not been on the best of terms for some time.'[86] Bad blood between the two communities resulted in further violence the following month, when a fight between 150 Africans and 'at least seven' Arabs was reported in the *Standard*.[87] In the same year, violence was reported at football matches in which African spectators physically threatened the non-African side. On one occasion, the *Standard* recorded that '[s]everal hundred Africans stormed on to the football ground and set about the Agakhan eleven and their handful of supporters with feet, fists, stones and sticks.'[88]

[81] *TH*, 13 November 1937, p. 7.
[82] Indian communities in smaller upcountry towns in Dar es Salaam district (such as Soga and Ruvu) were also victims of violence (see correspondence in TNA/21062). And further afield. Westcott, for example, mentions disorder that broke out in 1945 in Moshi when 'young Chagga rampaged through the Indian quarter'. 'Impact', p. 179.
[83] *TH*, 18 February 1939, p. 8.
[84] E.g. CP to CS, 11 May 1938, TNA/21963/Vol. 1.
[85] CP to CS, 21 April 1952, TNA/50075.
[86] Min., 22 April 1952, TNA/50075. Brennan identifies heightened resentment towards illegal Shihiri immigrants in the 1950s. Shihiri petty traders were perceived as taking business away from Africans also engaged in trade. 'Nation', p. 308.
[87] The tinder that sparked the fire this time was an Arab shopkeeper purportedly trying to swindle an African out of Sh.1/-. *TS*, 10 May 1952, p. 17.
[88] *TS*, 19 August 1952, p. 19.

Notwithstanding such isolated incidents, few serious outbreaks of racial violence were reported in the period between 1945 and independence. This may simply reflect the different news priorities of the settler press (Indian newspapers from after 1948 are largely unavailable).[89] It may reflect an increased police presence acting as a deterrent against such outbreaks. However, two of the most serious eruptions of violence to have occurred in Dar es Salaam in the 1950s can quite plausibly be attributed to the persistence of racial tensions, although in both cases the incidents were blamed on the fear of *mumiani* — a local superstition involving the abduction of individuals who had their blood removed for use as a medicine.[90] The disturbances took place in Buguruni, an unplanned African residential area to the west of the town centre, at either end of the 1950s. The first occurred on a Tuesday evening in January 1950, when, according to Provincial Commissioner Walden, 'a house occupied by two elderly non-British Europeans was stoned and attempts to set it on fire were made by a mob of several hundred Africans.' 'This mob', he continued,

> gathered at an obviously pre-arranged meeting place and marched to the house in question, which belongs to an Indian who has leased it to these Europeans and is in an area which has been scheduled for African housing. The mob over-turned the motorcar belonging to the occupants of the house, ripped the tyres to pieces, smashed all the glass in the car and tore open the cushions.[91]

It was the opinion of the Police Superintendent that '[b]ut for the arrival of the Police … the mob, having once gained ingress into the house, would undoubtedly have murdered the occupants.' Walden attributed the incident to 'the vexed question of availability of land for Africans to build in the township', owing to the fact that the land in question was earmarked for Africans but little had been done about instituting government policy in this area. The word from the African community, on the other hand, was that fear of *mumiani* had caused the attack, after recent murders in the Keko area had been blamed on an unknown European. Whatever the motives for resorting to violence were, it was clear that Africans in the area were not comfortable with a European presence there. 'It has been said', Walden observed, 'that occupation of this house by any European would not be tolerated, but such opposition would not apply to an Indian or African.'

As it turned out, suspicion appeared to attach itself to whoever occupied this house, regardless of racial origin. A recurrence of *mumiani* fears led to particularly serious disturbances nine years later. Once again, according to African testimony, the violence was linked to the disappearance or murder of several Africans in the town.[92] This time rioting involving plantation *askaris*,

---

[89] Cuttings occasionally survive in TNA files.

[90] For *mumiani* and associated phenomena in Eastern Africa, see Luise White, *Speaking With Vampires: Rumour and history in colonial Africa* (Berkeley, 2000).

[91] PC, EP to MLG, 28 January 1950, TNA/5007; see also, *TS*, 11 February 1950, p. 15.

[92] See James R. Brennan, 'Mumiani and Uhuru: Buguruni on the eve of Tanganyika's independence', paper given at ASAC, 1998, for a full account of the riot.

three police officers and around two hundred Buguruni residents, resulted in the death of one officer, the looting of a house and an Arab shop, and the destruction of a police patrol car. The same Indian-owned house that had been involved in the 1950 incident was also at the centre of the 1959 riot. In the later case, however, *mumiani* activities appear to have been blamed on the Indian owner rather than the African *askari* living in the house at the time, Juma Mkuyu. In both cases the events in Buguruni give some indication of the high degree of suspicion that could exist between different communities in Dar es Salaam, and of the potential for violence that could result from these tensions. The two disturbances involved attacks by Africans against individuals from each of Tanganyika's three main immigrant communities: the original European residents, an Arab shopkeeper, and (indirectly) the Indian who owned the house.

While racial factors appeared to be operating in Buguruni, an additional factor that ought to be taken into consideration in connection with the 1959 disturbances is the nationalist fervour sweeping Dar es Salaam's African communities. Both the *Tanganyika Standard* and the Swahili weekly *Baragumu* reported that chants of '*uhuru*' had accompanied the crowds' attacks against the Arab's shop and the police patrol car.[93] TANU, however, were quick to dissociate themselves from the events in Buguruni, so these events cannot be portrayed as a straightforward example of organised (or explicit) opposition to colonialism. They nevertheless took place at a time when British rule was losing its legitimacy. As early as 1955, Machado Plantan, the editor of the Swahili newspaper *Zuhra*, received 'many reports of… people openly defying the law purporting to recognise TANU as the only authority capable to administer justice in the country'.[94] The disturbances at Buguruni fit in with a pattern of outbreaks of violence in the town that occurred as British authority was undermined by nationalist activism in the late-colonial period. These incidents were often associated with the attempted arrest by police *askaris* of African malefactors. In the late 1950s policemen were frequently impeded by hostile crowds that rapidly materialised at the scene of an arrest.[95] In August 1958, for example, around a hundred Africans attacked two detectives attempting to re-apprehend an escaped prisoner in Sikukuu Street. The following June, in Ilala, a crowd of 50–60 persons obstructed the arrest of one Molidi Sultan thus facilitating his escape. The most serious incident of this kind, though, occurred in Msimbazi in September 1957, when a petty arrest degenerated into a minor riot. A crowd of a hundred attempted to prevent the arrest, physically attacking six constables and a European Superintendent. It was not until after the arrival of the riot squad, who subjected a stone-throwing crowd that had grown to about five hundred to a baton charge and finally smoke grenades, that the situation was brought

---

93   *Ibid.*, p. 8.
94   Said, *Abdulwahid Sykes*, p. 178.
95   For the deterioration in police–public relations that occurred in the 1950s, see Burton, 'Brothers by Day'. Similar trends were observable elsewhere in East Africa. For late-colonial Nairobi, see Robertson, *Trouble*, pp. 143–4.

under control. 'Until the last three or four years', wrote the editor of the *Standard* in response to these events, 'there were no more friendly men or women in the whole of East or Central Africa than the average Tanganyika African. No matter where one went, or what one's race or religion, all greeted each other as friends with the familiar greeting of "Jambo"(!). 'It is', he concluded, 'a different story in Dar es Salaam today.'[96] The growing racial tensions implied by the editor arose in a context of increasing disrespect for colonial authority and a diminishing reluctance on the part of Africans to oppose the often heavy-handed actions of the British and their agents. It is in this context, as Brennan has argued for the 1959 Buguruni riot, that we should place such outbreaks of violence in the late-colonial period.

Both racial tensions and growing disillusionment with Government resulted in major disturbances in Dar es Salaam. However, the two most serious breakdowns of order to have taken place during the British colonial period arose out of the labour disputes of 1947 and 1950. Although the violence that occurred can in both cases be seen as expressions of wider alienation, the primary causes were economic. In setting the context for the 1947 strike, Iliffe observed that '[t]his was probably the worst period in the town's history.'[97] As we have seen, from the late 1930s a spiralling population exerted increasing pressure on an overstretched urban infrastructure. Meanwhile, shortages of both consumer items and, more seriously, housing resulted in a spiralling cost of living that was not met by corresponding wage increases. Such was the backdrop to the dispute. The strike began on Saturday 6 September and escalated over the following days. 'For two days', wrote Norman Pearson a British trade unionist stationed in Dar es Salaam at the time, 'mobs ranged the town with their sticks and stones, and organised trade was grinding to a stop.'[98] By the end of the following week Dar es Salaam 'was dead… [t]he strike was general and pickets were out throughout the town.' Iliffe attributes the violence and intimidation that accompanied the strike not to the workers who began the action but to unemployed Africans who joined in shortly after the dispute began.[99] The fact that events represented more than just a straightforward labour dispute is confirmed by Pearson's first-hand testimony:

> [T]here were a number of unruly, lawless and excitedly impulsive mobs. These mobs were augmented by good-for-nothings who were not strikers, but joined in with the mobs merely for the licence of things and any pickings that may come by…
>   Thus we found gangs of Africans rushing about the town brandishing sticks and stones. They considered that all Africans should join them in this grand saturnalia and show the Wazungu 'what was what'. Most joined only too willingly.[100]

96 *TS*, 9 August 1958; 8 June 1959; 26 September 1957.
97 Iliffe, 'Dockworkers', p. 131.
98 Pearson, 'Safari', p. 218.
99 Iliffe, 'Dockworkers', pp. 131–2.
100 Pearson, 'Safari', pp. 215–17.

On 11 September, despite 45 arrests being made and the presence of three hundred special constables patrolling the town, the dockers, according to Iliffe, 'still dominated the situation'. Two days later 'little commercial activity' and 'no tangible improvement' were reported.[101] Police patrols, though, were said to be 'beginning to have effect' and signs were that the strike was breaking. By Monday 15 September the situation was 'much improved'. After a meeting the previous day, dockers drifted back to work.[102] All other labour was back at work. This included African civil servants, many of whom had participated in the strike, though the president of the African Association later stressed that members of his organisation had played no part in originating or inciting '[t]his hooliganism [*uhuni*]'.[103] According to Pearson 'only the fairly-well educated Africans stood out against the mob hysterias which swept the town and the threats which accompanied it.'[104] What happened to those unemployed Africans who took part in the dispute is not recorded, although a wave of repatriations occurred in the following months. As a result of the strike, the dockworkers and other Africans in the town won pay increases of between 30 and 50 percent. Government, meanwhile, was served notice of the danger of collaboration between the disparate elements that made up the urban African population. The threat posed by a similar configuration in Mombasa the same year led eventually to the reorganisation and differentiation of African urban labour in Kenya.[105] In Dar es Salaam, attempts to de-casualise the labour force in the late 1940s were to lead to a further outbreak of strike-related violence three years later.

The disturbances that took place in the course of the 1950 strike do not appear to have convulsed the whole town in the manner of events in 1947. According to the Governor's Deputy, those responsible were 'an insignificant portion of the dock labourers'. 'The vast majority of Africans living within the municipal area', he wrote, 'appear to dissociate themselves from any sympathy with the dock labourers who are regarded with disfavour as tainted with irresponsibility and hooliganism.'[106] The disturbances, however, were the most violent in the whole of the British colonial period, and judging by the large numbers of people involved it seems likely that disgruntled dockworkers were joined by other disaffected elements among the town population — prime candidates being, of course, those people dismissed by officials as *wahuni*. The origins of the strike lay in the introduction of a new

[101] Iliffe, 'Dockworkers', p. 132; PC, EP to Political, Dsm, 13 September 1947, TNA/540/27/13.

[102] Interestingly, casuals were reported to be 'returning better' than permanent employees. CS to PC, EP, 15 September 1947, TNA/540/27/13.

[103] Iliffe, 'Dockworkers', p. 132; *idem, Modern History*, p. 404. While they may have disapproved of the violence once the strike spiralled out of control, the African Association did have a connection with the dispute through Abdulwahid Sykes (son of Kleist Sykes and the Association's Dar es Salaam secretary), who according to Said liaised with 'the underground labour movement' in 1947. See Said, *Abdulwahid Sykes*, pp. 60-7.

[104] Pearson, 'Safari', p. 219.

[105] Cooper, *Waterfront*.

[106] Governor's Dep. to Creech Jones, 11 February 1950, PRO/CO691/209/42540.

gate for labourers entering the docks. The port authorities claimed this had no connection with the implementation of a registration scheme that was proposed to take place at a future date. Union leaders were convinced by these reassurances. The rank and file, on the other hand, remained deeply suspicious of the motivations behind its introduction.[107] In the period leading up to the strike, dockers' attitudes towards registration had been divided. According to the Deputy Governor, registration had actually been encouraged by union leaders in the late 1940s in order 'to protect old established dockworkers whose position seemed threatened by continued demands for and increasing numbers of casual labourers arising from continued pressure of work at the port during the past two years'.[108] 'These casual labourers', wrote the Deputy Governor,

> largely comprise the less responsible element, desiring to work only perhaps once or twice a week and laying up for the remainder. This element gradually gained control of the Union and was opposed to measures favouring permanent employment and insistence on comparatively regular attendance.[109]

With the advent of the new entry procedure in late January 1950, union members overruled their leaders, who had recommended acceptance.[110] They were forced to declare a strike on 1 February. Support was by no means total (the port labour force was not completely unionised), with at least 330 labourers working in the port on the first day of the strike, and as many as 783 on the second.[111] This, along with the determination of the police to prevent intimidation of those who chose to work, led to the eventual resort to violence. On 2 February, the Secretary of the Stevedores and Dockworkers

---

[107] The entry point was described thus in a *Tanganyika Standard* article in the wake of the strike: 'The outer fence has only one main entrance, through which the workers will pass. Inside this, the men pass through another fence and finally go past the administrative buildings and down a stairway to reach the dock' (*TS*, 20 February 1950). It appears that dockworkers were right to be suspicious. The new system greatly facilitated the control of dock labour, particularly when used in conjunction with the registration of workers and issue of ID cards, which occurred immediately after the disastrous events of February 1950. Similar suspicion towards registration was present in Tanga. Former dockworkers interviewed by Frederick Kaijage ('Alternative history', p. 12) 'felt that it was an encroachment on their freedom of movement and on their right to temporarily withdraw from dock work in search of greener pastures'. According to Kaijage's informants a smaller strike also occurred at Tanga in 1950 in response to registration.

[108] Dep. Gov. to CO, 7 February 1950.

[109] For tensions between Union members and leadership in the late 1940s, see Said, *Abdulwahid Sykes*, pp. 70–7.

[110] Internal report in PRO/CO/691/209/42540. A Tanganyika Police Special Branch Intelligence Summary (for January 1950, extract in PRO/WO/276/133 – cited in Brennan, 'Nation', p. 204) interprets the causes of the strike differently. According to Brennan's précis, 'all parties had, up to [1950], tolerated a corrupt system whereby dockworkers had to pass through an old gate guarded by "a gang of bullies", and only dues-paying members of the Stevedores and Dockworkers Union were allowed in, while others had to pay fees, illegally enriching certain union officials. Resistance to the new scheme, this report claimed, was led by those elements that profited from the corrupt status quo.'

[111] In 1950 there were 1,815 labourers registered at the port.

Union wrote a letter to the Chief Secretary, articulating the frustration of the strikers' inability to prevent fellow dockers going to work and predicting 'that surely there will be some great troubles among whole Africans of Dar es Salaam as they are fighting for their colour'. A second letter, presented the following day (presumably written earlier), adopted a significantly more threatening tone:

> I am directed by all Union Members to inform you that as far as the matter effect [sic] that, the Policemen of Dar es Salaam, and their Police Officers interferes with the Dock Labourers Strike and try to fight the Labourers of the Dockworkers Union, therefore, there will be a heavy fight this morning or afternoon between the Policemen and the Union Members, however, this will be for all Africans in Dar es Salaam.[112]

This was indeed what came to pass. Early on the morning of 3 February pickets at the harbour entrance were being moved on or arrested by the police.[113] Those arrested were found to be carrying concealed weapons including knives, axes, iron bars, bottles and clubs. The arrests appeared to aggravate strikers congregating at the harbour:

> At about 7am in the vicinity of the port a party of men attacked Assistant Superintendent Stewart with a blow from behind. In the melee which followed a number of policemen and rioters received injuries. Eight arrests were made and loiterers were then cleared from the dock entrance. Information was received that those dispersed had retired to collect re-inforcements and arm themselves with weapons with which to fight the police, attack their barracks and release arrested persons. The situation in the dock area appeared calm and patrols were sent to detect any concentration of rioters elsewhere.

Reports of such a concentration came in at 8.25am. A patrol car was despatched and, according to an internal report, was stoned 'by a disorderly crowd estimated at some 2,000 men' — the estimate of the *Tanganyika Standard* was a more plausible 400–600 — at Mkunguni Street and Pemba Street where they bisected Mnazi Mmoja.[114] Assistant Superintendent Stewart drove on to Msimbazi station for reinforcements. Returning to Mnazi Mmoja, a force of 30 constables armed with long batons and shields, and three officers armed with service revolvers and ammunition 'was soon surrounded by a large hostile mob which continued to swell... armed with clubs, knives, pangas and rocks':

> The party was stoned at a range of some thirty yards and several constables were injured... Stewart warned the crowd that if it did not desist he would have to shoot. They continued to attack and the two Assistant Superintendents and the Sub-Inspector fired without effect, and the mob proceeded to further violence... Assistant Superintendent McLoughlin and Sub-Inspector Bannerjee...

---

[112] Sec., SDU to CS, 2 February 1950 and 3 February 1950, PRO/CO/691/209/42450.

[113] The following account is drawn from an anonymous internal report in PRO/CO/691/209/42540.

[114] *TS*, 4 February 1950. The paper actually gives a non-existent street — Nmumgumi — along with Pemba Street; this must be Mkunguni Street, which was the street north of Pemba Street, and, perhaps significantly, also the haunt of a number of delinquent gangs.

were cut off and brutally hacked, receiving ghastly wounds from head to foot. At this point the crowd, apparently satisfied with the damage done, dispersed... Stewart recovered the wounded officers and brought them back to barracks... [I]t is not possible to say precisely how many rounds were fired.[115]

The position was deemed serious enough for detachments of the King's African Rifles to be placed on standby at the Central Police Station in case of further disorder. A platoon from a British navy boat, the HMS *Loch Quoich*, then moored in Dar es Salaam harbour, had briefly come ashore — 'armed with rifles and fixed bayonets' — to guard the docks in case the strikers were to break through. After the rioting at Mnazi Mmoja had been suppressed, however, no more violence occurred and the strike was soon broken. The day following the disturbances, the Captain of HMS *Loch Quoich* wired London that the mob appeared still to be in existence but had withdrawn from town.[116] In his despatch the next day London was informed that the mob had finally been dispersed 'in face of a large show of force'. By this time the strike had collapsed and the port was working normally. One hundred and forty-five men were charged with offences connected with the strike and the ensuing violence, including eight 'alleged union leaders' prosecuted for conspiracy. In May, Abdelrehman Musa — not one of the leaders — was found guilty of the attempted murder of Asst Supt McLoughlin and sentenced to ten years. The events of 3 February led to the dissolution of the dockers' union by a High Court order later in the year. Meanwhile, advantage was taken by the Port Authorities and the Labour Department to introduce the new registration scheme.[117]

The riot had a deep impact on all sections of Dar es Salaam's population, official and non-official, African, Indian and European alike. The police stepped up efforts to recruit special constables, and, starting the month after the riots, engaged in intensive campaigns aimed at the repatriation of undesirables from the town. It also led to the introduction of tear gas to the police armoury. Meanwhile, a meeting of officials convened by the Member for Law and Order in late February arrived at the conclusion 'that recent experience in Dar es Salaam particularly in regard to the disturbance at the beginning of the month showed that changes in the administration of African affairs in the Municipal area were essential'.[118] The strike-related violence had a more general impact also, leading to heightened awareness among all communities of crime and policing in the town. After the riot, letters' pages in Dar es Salaam's newspapers became filled with missives from anxious correspondents complaining of a breakdown of discipline and/or the lack of security.[119] Memories of the violence lingered. In conducting a survey of

---

[115] Two rioters died and five others were admitted to hospital with bullet wounds. McLoughlin, Bannerjee and Stewart were wounded alongside 18 African constables (five seriously).
[116] *TS*, 4 February 1950; despatches from HMS *Loch Quoich*, PRO/CO/691/209/42540.
[117] Iliffe, 'Dockworkers', pp. 137/8; *TS*, 20/22 February 1950.
[118] *TS*, 14 March 1950; CP to CS, 13 April 1950, TNA/30134; correspondence in PRO/CO/691/209/42450; Meeting mins, 22 February 1950, TNA/50070.
[119] See clippings in TNA/20219/Vol. II.

the town the following year, two South African sociologists observed that '[a]mong problems relating to the maintenance of law and order in Dar es Salaam, the topic most frequently mentioned to us has been the riots of February 1950.' 'It is commonly said', they continued, 'that the riot took the community completely by surprise.'[120]

Riot was by no means an uncommon event in Dar es Salaam during the British colonial period. It could take the form of anything from a minor skirmish with the police to serious communal violence or organised and widespread strike-related intimidation. The causes of the violence were equally diverse, each disturbance resulting from a combination of factors that might include racial tensions, economic grievances, political disillusionment or even straightforward criminal intent.[121] In all the disturbances to occur, however, there was one constant. In every case, those elements of the urban population categorised by officials as undesirable were directly involved, if not always as the instigators. The unemployed and underemployed not only formed a potential (or actual) criminal element, but were also responsible for the most dramatic breakdowns of urban order.[122] As such, the control of this section of the population became a primary goal of the colonial administration. Laws restricting the urban presence of Africans had formed part of the earliest legislation passed by the British in Tanganyika. However, it was the events of 1947 and 1950, in particular, that led to the increasingly concerted application of these laws in the late-colonial period.

While heavily outnumbered by both Africans and Indians, Europeans in colonial Dar es Salaam were politically, economically, socially and culturally in the ascendant and believed they had determining rights over the occupation of urban space: in particular, over the proper place of the African and how those qualified for urban residence were to behave once in the town. However, sheer weight of numbers overwhelmed European cultural predominance, leading to an unpredictable though vibrant town in which the economic and social struggles of Africans were played out in the streets on a daily basis.[123] It was a far cry from the tidy municipality envisaged by European settlers and officials. Attempts to limit African mobility, and expressions of *angst* over 'boat natives' or beggars, formed

[120] Sofers' Report, p. 63, TNA/18950/Vol. III.

[121] Incidents in Uhindini were often initiated by thieves in order to provide cover for their activities.

[122] The position was much the same elsewhere in East Africa. On the Copperbelt, for example, the violent outcome of the 1935 disturbances was attributed to African workers sharing urban space with 'unemployed or unemployable natives who [we]re not under any effective control'. *Report of Commission Appointed to Enquire into the Disturbance in the Copperbelt, Northern Rhodesia* (Lusaka, 1935), quoted in Cooper, *Decolonization*, p. 59. Similarly, twenty years on, investigation into some disorder in the mid 1950s near one of the mines revealed that 'practically all the rioters were persons who had no business to be in the area'. Prain, 'Stabilization', p. 308.

[123] Moyer ('Shadow', p. 184) makes a similar point about contemporary Dar es Salaam, observing how people engaged in informal economic activities subvert the modernist ideals of the post-colonial state and the 'respectable' classes.

a reaction to a demographic, social and cultural process over which in the final analysis Europeans exercised limited influence. Indian residents of the town also viewed this process with great foreboding. The heart of the Indian community was concentrated in the densely populated bazaar, where the identification of communal space was probably significantly stronger than that among Europeans in the suburbs sprawling to the north of the town. The physical space occupied by Indians matched their social and economic position in colonial society: perched between the rulers and the ruled. Lacking political power, interacting more often with and living closer to the African population, they formed the readiest target for African resentment, yet exercised even less influence over African behaviour than Europeans. Their vulnerability found vent in the anxious newspaper commentary and correspondence on the African presence in what they viewed as an under-policed Uhindini.

Part III

Urbanisation & Colonial Order

c.1947–61

Nearly everywhere natives are on the move.

P.M. Henry, 'The African Townee', *New Commonwealth*, 4 March 1954, p. 221

*It was the old case of 'Bright lights and empty pockets' or
'How're you gonna keep 'em down on the farm.'*

E.G. Rowe (Provincial Commissioner, Eastern Province, 1954),
RH/Mss.Afr.s. 1698, p. 38

Ten

Development, Diversification
& Growth

Dar es Salaam in the Post-war Period

After 1945, Dar es Salaam underwent rapid change. According to one observer, the 'lazy little town which remained almost static in its development … between the two World Wars' was by the late 1940s 'rapidly approaching the dimensions one expects of a territorial capital'.[1] In the following decade, it was transformed further — into the nucleus of what would, before the end of the millennium, become East Africa's largest city.[2] This transformation occurred in part because of its spiralling population. However, it also resulted from shifts in colonial attitudes in the post-war period. A new era of developmentalism meant the town no longer suffered the neglect it had prior to 1939. As with the shifts in strategy in the early 1940s, post-war policies emerged in response to both local conditions and the wider imperial context. In Dar es Salaam, living conditions continued to exercise official concern as administrators sought the elusive answer to the problem of African urbanisation. African grievances were growing and beginning to find a political voice. As we have seen, in the immediate post-war years they found their most dramatic expression in the strike-related disorder of 1947 and 1950, and these events had a significant impact on the evolution of urban policy. In their wake, goals that had been articulated by officials earlier in the decade — notably a better-remunerated and more efficient workforce and increased control over the urban population — were implemented more wholeheartedly.

A substantial increase in resources available for urban development had a significant impact on post-war Dar es Salaam.[3] More concerted attempts to

---

[1] Sir Alexander Gibb and Partners, *A Plan for Dar es Salaam, Report* (Dsm, 1949), p. 4.

[2] Rapid population growth in the post-colonial period appears to have resulted in Dar es Salaam (2,347,000) overtaking Nairobi (2,310,000) in the 1990s. (*Cities in a Globalizing World* (Oxford, 2000), p. 300). It is likely that these figures underestimate the true size of both cities.

[3] Moffett and Hill observe that '[i]n 1946 the financial position made possible a new approach to the development of the Territory', the urban areas being just one of the beneficiaries. *Tanganyika*, pp. 5, 269 and 846. Though the bulk of the expenditure, as Westcott observes, occurred in the 1950s — the early development plans reflecting 'mainly the political forces acting upon those who drew them up'. 'Impact [1986]', pp. 153–4.

shape and control African urban society were now affordable. The Social Development department became increasingly active in the town. Both the urban police force and the district administration were expanded. The sudden availability of development funds also transformed the town physically. Substantial work on the urban infrastructure occurred thanks to grants awarded under the Colonial Development and Welfare (CD & W) Acts. In the first Ten Year Development and Welfare Plan, £1,129,500, £1,000,000 and £300,000 were allocated to Township Development, Public Building and Works, and African Urban Housing. After the arrival of Sir Edward Twining as Governor in 1949 plans were expanded, and the amounts designated under these headings increased respectively to £3,573,000, £3,480,000 and £1,230,000.[4] Pre-war doubts about Tanganyika's status as a British-administered territory had gone, thereby removing an important disincentive for investment. Other factors encouraged industrial development. Faced with a massive war debt to the USA, British imperial policy stressed the preservation of dollar reserves and import substitution was emphasized. During the war, an East Africa Industries Technical Advisory Committee and a Substitutes Committee were set up in Dar es Salaam to encourage small-scale industry; somewhat later, in 1954, guidelines to encourage industrial investment were set by the Licensing Council of the East African Common Services Organization.[5] A wave of small-scale industrialisation occurred after WWII throughout East Africa, which, although more apparent in neighbouring Kenya and Uganda, also had an impact on the Tanganyikan capital. Conditions in Dar es Salaam favoured the expansion in industrial activity. With import restrictions having limited outlets for expenditure, local capital accumulated during the war years sought areas of investment. By the late 1940s the town was enjoying an unprecedented increase in industrial, commercial and building activity.

The urban population

This heightened activity provided further stimulus to urbanisation, which occured at an ever-accelerating rate. By the time of the first territorial census,

---

[4] Seven million pounds was earmarked for Dar es Salaam harbour between 1948 and 1956, and three deepwater berths were completed in 1956; a further £2,075,000 was allotted to 'Railways and Ports'. Between 1950 and 1955, £2,010,000 was spent improving Dar es Salaam's water supply, and £450,000 on a new sewage scheme covering the town centre. Msimbazi Creek was drained as an anti-malarial measure, parts of the reclaimed land being converted into playing fields. Road construction proceeded apace within the town and on the main arterial routes leading out of it: on the Bagamoyo road and the new Dar es Salaam–Tanga (and Morogoro) highway. New hospitals and clinics were established using CD & W funds, and around £1,600,000 was allocated to Public Buildings in Dar es Salaam. Meanwhile, £100,000 was spent on the provision of a serviced area for the location of industrial activities at Pugu Road. Tanganyika, *A Ten-year Development and Welfare Plan for Tanganyika Territory* (Dsm, 1946); *Revised Development and Welfare Plan for Tanganyika Territory 1950–56* (Dsm, 1950); Iliffe, *Modern History*, pp. 442–3; Kironde, 'Land use structure', pp. 242–4.

[5] Martha Honey, 'Asian industrial activities in Tanganyika', *TNR* **75** (1974), p. 65.

in 1948, Dar es Salaam contained almost 70,000 inhabitants: up from around 40,000 at the start of the war. Each of the three racial groupings was expanding apace. A European community numbering just over one thousand in 1940 had grown to 1,726 by 1948. Buoyed no doubt by the great influx of technical and administrative personnel that occurred after WWII, the European population continued to grow, reaching 3,603 in 1952 and 4,479 in 1957.[6] The growth of the Asian population was even more dramatic. This predominantly South Asian community[7] roughly doubled between 1940 and 1948, from 8,825 to 16,270, and by 1957 was just under thirty thousand. Natural increase was responsible for much of this growth. Meanwhile, although the Tanganyikan administration were keen to restrict immigration for fear of sparking African resentment, South Asian workers — who combined higher skill levels than Africans at cheaper rates than Europeans — continued to be recruited from the subcontinent.[8]

The rapid growth of the African community was a source of considerable concern. Between 1940 and 1948 it had increased by about fifty percent, from 34,750 to 51,231. Rural–urban migration was the principal cause. Although wages remained low and living conditions poor, Africans were attracted by the boom conditions that prevailed up to the mid 1950s. Despite the re-emergence of serious joblessness at this time, migrants continued to stream to the town. Salaries were rising, and although acquiring waged work immediately was unlikely, informal economic activities provided an opportunity to obtain a subsistence while awaiting formal employment, or failing that relatives could be relied upon for support. An increase in school-leavers (Standard VI and above) after WWII, whose education fitted them for work in the 'modern' as opposed to the agricultural sector, was also partly responsible for the influx of immigrants.[9] From 1948 the urban African population grew by over 4,000 annually,[10] and by 1957 over 93,000 Africans were residing in the town (see Table 10.1).[11] The urban population continued to be characterised by a gender imbalance, the female:male sex ratio being approximately 74:100. Nevertheless, at 39,516, a substantial number of female Africans lived in the town. In this respect especially, the town stood in stark contrast to most urban centres in the region.

Dar es Salaam's African population remained ethnically diverse. Zaramo predominance was accentuated in the thirty years between 1928 and 1956, by which time they constituted almost forty percent of a significantly larger urban African population.[12] The proportionate increase of the Zaramo

[6] In 1950, two-thirds of Tanganyika's administrative officers had been appointed since 1944. Iliffe, *Modern History*, p. 443.

[7] The 1948 census included 1,067 Arabs, and presumably also a handful of Chinese.

[8] Brennan, 'Nation', pp. 300–1.

[9] Cttee of Enquiry into problems of African housing mins, 18 December 1953, TNA/225/ DC01/3/23; see also, Burton, 'Raw youth'.

[10] Statistically, it had also gained as many as 10,000 extra inhabitants that year, as a result of the town boundary being extended to incorporate the peri-urban periphery.

[11] Leslie, *Survey*, p. 152.

[12] Leslie, 'Appendices'; Tanganyika, *African Population Census* (Dsm, 1957).

Table 10.1 *Dar es Salaam, population growth, 1948–61*

Year	Approximate increase in Dar es Salaam's population[1]	Approximate total population
1948		69,200 (census)
1949	4,429	73,629
1950	4,712	78,341
1951	5,014	83,355
1952	5,335	88,690
1953	5,676	94,366
1954	6,039	100,405
1955	6,426	106,831
1956	6,837	113,668
1957	7,275	120,943
1958	7,740	128,683
1958		128,742 (census)
1959	8,239/10,042	136,981/138,784
1960	8,767/10,825	145,748/149,609
1961	9,328/11,670	155,076/161,279

[1] These are approximate figures calculated by multiplying the town's population in one year by the average rate of increase over the periods 1948–57 (when the town experienced a 6.4% growth rate *per annum*); and 1957–67 (when it grew at 7.8% p.a.). Two calculations (at 6.4% *and* at 7.8% — the latter being second figures in the table) are made for the years 1958–61, as the rate as reflected in the 1967 census may be distorted by accelerated growth after independence.

resulted partly from the incorporation of peri-urban settlements, as Dar es Salaam expanded physically. However, it was also indicative of trends in rural–urban migration. Ethnic groups from Eastern Province formed a significantly larger proportion of the urban population than they had in 1931 (see Table 10.2).[13] Uzaramo/Kisarawe,[14] Rufiji, Morogoro, Bagamoyo, and to a lesser extent Kilwa, in neighbouring Southern Province, formed the principal districts of origin for urban immigrants in the 1940s and early 1950s.[15] The urban profile of groups from other provinces tended to have

[13] In the 1957 census 55.4%, compared to 44.6% in 1931. Lockwood also notes that after WWII 'coastal migrants predominated in the growth of the city'. *Fertility*, p. 31.

[14] Up to 1938, both Dar es Salaam town and the rural areas surrounding it — including Kisarawe, Soga and Ruvu to the west, Mbezi and Kunduchi to the north, and Vikindu and Kisiju to the south — were part of Dar es Salaam District. The rural areas were then separated to become Temeke District. In 1942, they were combined once again and renamed Uzaramo District, which in 1949 became Kisarawe District. In 1950, Dar es Salaam was separated from Kisarawe to once again form its own district. By the end of the decade the town had reached a sufficient size to be declared an extra-provincial district, separate from the surrounding Eastern Province.

[15] Lockwood observes a significant increase in Rufiji migration to Dar es Salaam after WWII, compared to the earlier twentieth century, when Zanzibar and Mafia were 'equally important destinations' for migrants, and to a lesser extent Kilwa and Lindi. *Fertility*, p. 30.

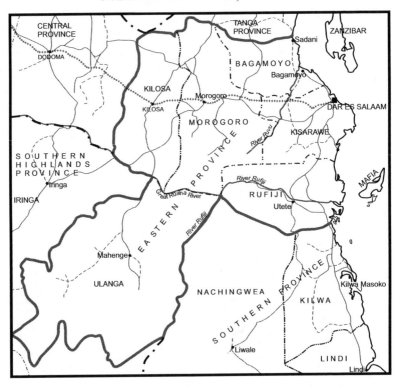

LEGEND

Eastern Province	▬▬▬▬
Provincial Boundary	▬ · ▬ · ▬
District Boundary	▬··▬··▬··
Road	▬▬▬▬
Track	▬ ▬ ▬ ▬
Railway	+++++++++++

Map 10.1 *Eastern Province*
Source: Based on insert in J.P. Moffett, *Handbook of Tanganyika* (Dsm, 1958)

Table 10.2 *Ethnic groups as a proportion of the urban African population (%)*

	1931	1956	1957
Zaramo/Nyagatwa	31.7	39.1	36.4
Rufiji	8.9	9.4	6.8
Luguru	0.4	5.6	6.0
Nyamwezi	3.7	3.2	4.3
Ndengereko	2.8	4.7	3.7
Ngindo	3.6	3.2	3.3
Yao	5.6	2.8	3.1
Nyasa	4.2	1.7	2.7
Ngoni	2.4	1.8	2.5
Pogoro	0.8	1.7	2.5
Makonde	2.2	1.4	2.3
Mwera (Lindi)	2.2	2.3	1.8
Manyema	5.4	1.5	1.8
Matumbi	0.9	2.1	1.7

Sources: Native Census, Dar es Salaam Township, 29 May 1931 in TNA/61/167, Leslie's appendices* and Tanganyika, *African Population Census* (Dsm, 1957)

* Leslie collected information from every ten houses in the township, in the course of which he found the existing register hopelessly outdated — particularly in 'urban village' communities such as Buguruni. (Interview No. 11.) His survey is taken as broadly representative of the urban African population. The discrepancy between his results and the census results, which tend to reflect lower percentages for those groups from Eastern Province (the exception being the Pogoro who originate from the far west of the province), can perhaps be explained by the fact that his survey was conducted in August, the start of the growing season in Dar es Salaam's hinterland. Conversely, this might help account for the boosted percentage of the other groups in the census (except the Mwera, who also hailed from a coastal region). Ethnic groups predominantly resident in Eastern Province (excluding Dar es Salaam) marked in bold; those predominantly resident on the coast south of Eastern Province in italics.

diminished (notably the Manyema and the Yao) or stabilised.[16] Nevertheless, the expanding town was also home to increasing numbers of immigrants from neighbouring territories. Alongside well-established Manyema and 'Sudanese'[17] populations, new groups had emerged by the early 1950s: Rundi communities (from the Belgian Congo) in Temeke and Makaburi; Hiwa (from Portuguese East Africa) in Msasani; Luo (from Kenya) in Kinondoni and Makaburi; and Nyasalanders in Magogoni and the African Government Quarters.[18] By the late 1950s, Kenyan Kamba were also established in the town, engaging in a flourishing trade in woodcarvings.[19]

In other respects, the population showed signs of demographic continuity. The relative proximity of the districts of origin for many urban immigrants no

[16] The main exceptions being the Matumbi — who originated from nearby Kilwa — and the Nyamwezi.
[17] Described as *Wanubi* in the 1931 census.
[18] Quoted by TC Baxter to MLG, 6 April 1950, TNA/28685.
[19] See correspondence in TNA/540/1/5.

doubt played its part in the high level of mobility that the urban populace continued to display. In 1951, when the African community was around 70,000, it was estimated that as many as 15,000 people temporarily joined the urban population in the agricultural off-season between February and June.[20] The flexible livelihood strategy pursued by residents of Rufiji, involving agriculture, fishing and labour migration to the capital, revealed in Bantje's post-colonial study of this drought- and flood-prone area, was no doubt also characteristic of the earlier period.[21] Large numbers of workers continued to pass through Dar es Salaam en route to employment in Zanzibar or on plantations in other parts of Tanganyika.[22] Although mobility among the general population remained high, however, there was evidence of increasing permanence. Almost 26 percent of male Africans surveyed by Leslie in 1956 were born in the town, and over 35 percent of the females. Fifty-seven percent of male respondents, and 52 percent of females, had lived in Dar es Salaam for six or more years.

Youth in post-war Dar es Salaam

One notably consistent aspect of the town's demography was the youthfulness of the population. Leslie found that almost 27 percent of urban Africans were under 16 years of age[23] and an overwhelming 93 percent of the population was 45 or under. Once again this appears to reflect prevailing patterns of migration. By the early 1950s it was clear that government initiatives the previous decade aimed at stemming the flow of young Africans had had little, if any, effect. '[J]uveniles between fourteen and eighteen', complained a secretariat official in 1950, remained 'a very real problem.' The Labour Department report of 1952 recorded 'there may be as many as ten thousand children and juveniles in Dar es Salaam municipal area who have come into town of their own accord and are not under the care of their parents or any recognised guardian.' 'No effective measures', it continued, 'have yet been devised that will send them home and keep them there.' Children of town-dwelling parents also remained a problem. In spite of the good intentions of the previous decade, in 1952 three-quarters of these children received no schooling.[24] Moreover, even those who had received an education often failed to behave in the manner desired by colonial officials. According to G.W. Hatchell, a district official serving in Tanga after WWII, the towns were 'full of ill

[20] Report on a possible sociological survey by R & C Sofer, 21 April 1951, TNA/18950/Vol. III.

[21] H. Bantje, 'The Rufiji agricultural system: Impact of rainfall, floods and settlement', BRALUP Research Paper no. 62 (UDsm, 1979), pp. 12–14.

[22] E.g. MLG to TC, Dsm, 22 May 1950, TNA/12556.

[23] The 1957 census recorded almost identical findings in this regard.

[24] Surridge to Rogers (CO), 4 January 1951, TNA/21616/Vol. III; AR of Labour Dept for 1952, p. 41; 1952 Soc. Devt AR, p. 5. For a brief account of education in the town from the late-nineteenth century to ca.1970, see J.E.F. Mhina, 'Education in and around Dar es Salaam', in Sutton (ed.), *Dar es Salaam*, pp. 175–80.

disciplined and selfish youths of the Std. VIII class whose only thought is their own comfort and convenience'.[25]

Labour officers were greatly alarmed by the presence of large numbers of youth in and around the township, not only for economic reasons.[26] Colonial Office officials were also aware of a problem that needed addressing which while 'not sizeable or serious yet in Tanganyika would come as surely as the tribal organisation was disintegrating'.[27] In his report on Tanganyika in 1951 W.H. Chinn, the Colonial Office Social Welfare adviser, was critical of the 'lack of adequate machinery' to deal with the phenomenon.[28] By contrast, both social welfare officers in Tanganyika itself, and, perhaps most significantly, Governor Twining, were more complacent about the situation, placing their faith in tribal structures for the care and control of young Africans. Twining disdained governmental intervention in Dar es Salaam, arguing this would further undermine tribal cohesion and responsibility. He had the support of the Tanganyikan Commissioner for Social Development, who argued that thanks to '[t]he social security provided by the traditional tribal system ... abandoned children are almost unknown, except occasionally in the larger towns'.[29]

Such an interpretation of the situation betrays signs of either fiscal convenience or wilful ignorance. In his 1956 survey, Leslie found that 29 percent of children between the ages of 6 and 15 had no parents in town.[30] Admittedly most of these 'parent-less' children would — nominally at least — be under the charge of town-dwelling relatives. However, officials felt that these relatives had negligible interest in the 'practice of disciplinary authority' and that children in such a position were particularly exposed to the temptations and vices of town life. Leslie identifies a further 9,000 children (a maximum estimate) of broken marriages who were also potentially more vulnerable than most. While none of these children could be described as 'abandoned', they were the very section of the community whom Colonial Office officials had earlier singled out as needing attention.[31] By the mid 1950s, in an attempt to meet these needs, the Social Development Department had set up boys' clubs in towns throughout Tanganyika aimed at 'character training based on a recreational approach'.[32] The Dar es Salaam club

[25] G.W. Hatchell, education and training of Africans, 8 September 1945, TNA/450/404.
[26] Nor was it just Dar es Salaam that was singled out by them as a cause for concern. So, for example, 'the presence in Arusha township of an increasingly large number of WaChagga youths from the Moshi district who are seemingly without parents and guardians and roam the streets and get into mischief' is recorded in the 1951 Labour Department report (para. 178).
[27] Mins of the Colonial Social Welfare Advisory Cttee — Reports Sub-Cttee — undated 1952, in CO 822/675.
[28] Report on a tour of Tanganyika by W.H. Chinn, 1951, para.18, in PRO/CO/822/675.
[29] Twining to SSCol, 18 March 1952, PRO/CO/822/675; UN Report 1960, para. 414.
[30] The proportion was 34% in Kariakoo, the heart of the African quarter. Leslie, *Survey*, p. 244.
[31] For a contemporary expression of concern see 'Workless Youth — Problem of our future', *Sunday News*, 13 April 1958, extracted in TNA/460/1049.
[32] *SN*, 9 December 1956, p. 4.

reportedly contained 'some of the toughest boys in town' who could let off steam at their twice-weekly meetings through boxing, football, and physical training, or through camping trips to the Kisarawe hills. The situation in Dar es Salaam required more than a bi-weekly schedule of juvenile sports, however. Ironically, a combination of both action and inaction with regard to recommendations made a decade earlier was contributing to the problem. Thanks to the shortage of school places, boys who did not make the grade left school after Standard VI, aged 11, four years before they could legally obtain work. They found themselves 'thrown on the streets ... and for three or four years they are at a loose end with nothing to do but learn the "tricks of the trade"'.[33] Molohan's investigation into detribalisation in 1956 uncovered the same problems regarding urban youth that had characterised the situation in the 1940s: the exploitation of child labour and its impact on adult wages; the difficulties of apprehending and removing unaccompanied children from the town; and the corruption of youth and descent into delinquency. These remained some 'of the greatest problems with which the urban administrator is faced'.[34]

Controlling the town

The rapidly expanding African population posed significant complications for urban governance. The foundation of the township administration was a network of African officials that had been reorganised in 1942 and retained the same basic structure for the remainder of the colonial period.[35] At its head was Hamed Saleh el Busaidi, the *Liwali* of Dar es Salaam between 1937 and 1959. *Liwali* Saleh's duties were primarily judicial, administering Islamic law within the township. However, he also performed a number of other advisory functions, including serving as a representative for the African population on the Municipal Council and its African Affairs sub-committee. Beneath the *Liwali*, the three *Wakili* (increased to four in 1953) performed a similar role. While the bulk of their time was taken up with judicial duties, they also acted as the chairmen of their respective Ward Councils up to the early 1950s and often as arbitrators in the many petty disputes that arose in their wards.[36] However, it was the *Majumbe* or town headmen who in terms of the everyday administration of the urban African population were the most important African agents of government within the town. They had responsibility for a number of sub-divisions within the township, which might incorporate just one street in the more densely populated heart of Zone III or larger areas in the less urbanised outskirts such as Kinondoni or Msasani. At the end of the war, Dar es

---

[33] QPR, Dsm Dist, 1 Oct.–31 December 1954, TNA/90/1011/Vol. 1.
[34] Molohan, *Detribalization*, para. 104.
[35] The next two paragraphs are based on Burton, 'Adjutants'.
[36] For the Ward Councils, see Burton, 'Townsmen'.

Salaam had 24 of these Town Headmen, rising to 28 in the early 1950s. By 1956, though, this number had, in spite of a substantial increase in the urban population, been reduced to just 14. *Majumbe* combined 'the roles of local special constable and petit fonctionaire'.[37] They acted as the '"eyes and ears" of the District Commissioner',[38] passing on instructions and explanations of policy in one direction, and people's complaints and information about events and individuals in the African areas of the town in the other. They were, in addition, expected to ensure that the communities over which they presided remained orderly and well-behaved; they liaised with the police over the prevention of crime and control of undesirables, and with the tax department over the collection of taxes.

The needs of government remained paramount in the selection of the *Majumbe*. However, direct appointment of its agents did not mean the African areas were administered to the satisfaction of district officials. In 1950, the DC complained that the efficiency of the headmen was 'closely associated to the amount of pressure exerted from above'.[39] No doubt *Majumbe* of widely differing abilities were appointed, but it is also the case that the balance of their sympathies — between their loyalty to government and their empathy with the inhabitants of the areas they administered — may have been equally varied with all the implications that this entailed. One of the prime responsibilities of the *Majumbe* was to help organise tax raids in order to apprehend defaulters. It was just as likely, though, that some at least were warning residents about the raids that they had helped organise.[40] In the main, according to Leslie, the *Majumbe*'s 'loyalties lay with their people and not the government', and they failed to provide the degree of control over their respective areas to which district administration officials aspired.

Given the divided loyalties of the *Majumbe*, government influence over the urban African population often depended on the abilities and energy of the DC and his staff. In 1945, the Uzaramo establishment included three European officers, of whom two, the DC and an ADO, had some responsibility for Dar es Salaam and its environs. The DC also acted as the African Affairs Officer for the Township Authority. This set up had functioned reasonably well since its introduction in the early 1940s. It was retained up to 1949. In that year, however, Dar es Salaam became a municipality and the decision was taken to redistribute responsibility for the African population to an employee of the new Municipal Authority. The post of Municipal African Affairs Officer (MAAO) was established, with responsibility for all aspects of African affairs in the town, excepting the supervision of the system of Native Courts. Meanwhile, the DC was moved to Kisarawe, from where he administered the remainder of the district, leaving behind an ADO in the town to liaise with the MAAO and supervise the native judiciary.[41] It was

[37] PC, EP to Sec. for African Affairs, 7 September 1949, TNA/540/27/28.
[38] Molohan, *Detribalization*, para. 65.
[39] 1950 DAR, p. 2, TNA/61/504/1/56.
[40] Leslie interview.
[41] Notes of Meeting on the future native administration of Dsm township, February 1948, TNA/20795/Vol. V.

soon apparent that such a dispensation was flawed. In February 1950, the dramatic breakdown of order that accompanied the dockworkers' strike shocked and surprised officials, who concluded it was partly a product of a vacuum of authority that had existed in the township since the removal of the DC. At a meeting convened by the Member for Local government in the wake of the violence, the decision was made that changes in the administration of African affairs in Dar es Salaam were, once again, essential.[42] Above all, the incident 'demonstrated the need for a representative of Central government in the town to be responsible for law and order'.[43] Accordingly, in July 1950 Dar es Salaam was excised from Kisarawe and declared a separate district. Its DC assumed complete responsibility for African affairs in the township from the MAAO, who retained control of the more technical concerns only in the African areas, such as the construction of housing and infrastructure and the licensing and inspection of businesses.[44] The DC was also appointed an ex-officio member of the Municipal Council.

Problems remained in spite of this reorganisation. The rapid expansion of Dar es Salaam resulted in an African population that was, thanks to its size and its growing sophistication, becoming increasingly unwieldy from an administrative point of view. Mindful of such developments, in 1954 the Dar es Salaam District Commissioner, C.C. Harris, concluded that '[t]he urgent necessity for improvement and intensification of African Administration in large towns is clear.'[45] In part, the problem was the lack of statutory powers invested in the administration. While the African population tended to assume that the *Liwali* and his Town Headmen had executive authority similar to that of Native Authorities in the rural areas, according to Harris these powers had 'no legal basis whatever'.[46] The administration of the town, he observed, was based on 'consent — or bluff'. In rural areas, E.G. Rowe — the Provincial Commissioner at this time — commented in hindsight, 'the behaviour of the African population could be regulated through subsidiary legislation under the Native Authority Ordinance.' No such device was available to urban officials. '[T]he District Commissioner's influence over the African population rested on persuasion only'.[47]

The administrative position in Dar es Salaam in the 1950s was further complicated by the shortage of specialist staff in the District Office. In 1957 there were 43,000 more Africans living in the town than in 1948. The District Office staff responsible for this much increased population had only been augmented by the introduction of a DC in 1950. 'Dar es Salaam is being administered "on the cheap" as far as Senior Service Officers are concerned', Harris complained.[48] Molohan came to similar conclusions. The district

[42] Recommendations of meeting, 22 February 1950, TNA/50070.
[43] Molohan, *Detribalization*, para. 59.
[44] See Division of duties of DC and MAAO, 28 May 1950, TNA/39159.
[45] Memo by DC, Dsm, 14 December 1953, TNA/225/DC/3602.
[46] *Ibid.*
[47] Rowe interview, p. 39, RH/Mss.Afr.s. 1698; see also, DC, Dsm to DC, Mwanza, 24 February 1956, TNA/540/3/75/A.
[48] DC, Dsm to PC, EP, 12 May 1954, TNA/540/3/75/A.

administration in Dar es Salaam, he warned, 'is not so strong now as is desirable, and the present system is not adequately geared to cope with the rapid expansion of the high density areas'. The District Office staff, which consisted of a DC, one DO and one African ADO, together with a Revenue Officer, Office Superintendent and a Secretary, was 'a meagre establishment for a district containing over 90,000 [African] people'. This compared unfavourably with the situation in Kenyan towns. Nairobi, for example, with an African population of 140,000, had a supervisory staff consisting of 'a District Commissioner, two Administrative Assistants and four District Officers, apart from the Officer i/c Extra Provincial District and his own staff'. Meanwhile, the DC in Mombasa, with 90,000 Africans in his district, had 'three District Officers to assist him, in addition to the equivalent of a Woman Administrative Officer, and other staff'. The numbers of Africans employed in Dar es Salaam's Native Administration were similarly modest. The Tanganyikan capital had just one *Liwali*, one deputy *Liwali*, four *Wakili* and 14 headmen, compared to the nine chiefs, 27 headmen and 70 tribal police on the DC's establishment in Nairobi.[49]

Rapid urbanisation inevitably also had important repercussions for Dar es Salaam's police force. 'The economic and social conditions of the people are undergoing rapid changes', observed the Commissioner of Police in 1957, 'and there is a strong urge for Africans to leave their tribal areas for the towns.' 'This', he added, 'naturally leads to new problems for the Police.'[50] Partly to tackle these 'new problems', the Tanganyika Police was substantially reorganised after 1945. The post-war period witnessed the true emergence of a modern force in Tanganyika: one which was not only better equipped and organised, but also numerically stronger.[51] In part this resulted from the successful drive to attract more educated recruits in the late 1940s. With a growing proportion of literate officers it was possible to adopt more widely the use of certain basic policing techniques, such as the keeping of police notebooks and the routine collection of statements, which hitherto had been somewhat neglected. Meanwhile, the dramatic increase in detected crime after the war had an impact on central government, and increasing resources were made available to the police in an attempt to combat this trend (though the consequent improvement in detection rates was partly responsible for it).[52] While these may not have matched the amounts that senior officers felt were necessary, the injection of such funds nevertheless resulted in an unprecedented expansion in the scale, frequency and sophistication of policing. The number of police stations in the town, which in 1952 consisted of just one 'with any claim to such title'[53] — the Central Police Station — had by the end of the following year been expanded to six: at Chang'ombe, Kilwa Road, Oyster Bay, Msimbazi and Temeke. Moreover, by the mid 1950s, there were also police posts at Ilala, Kawe and

[49] Molohan, *Detribalization*, paras 38, 52, 65.
[50] 1957 PAR.
[51] The foregoing is based on Burton, 'Brothers'.
[52] See Table 9.3.
[53] CP to CS, 14 August 1952, TNA/21963/Vol. II.

Fig. 10.1 *Police motorcycle squad in 1950s Dar es Salaam*
Source: Courtesy of Joan Thompson — whose husband was in the Tanganyika Police

Magomeni. Motorised patrols were introduced in 1952, along with a wireless comunications system that connected the patrols to each other and to the various stations. This enhanced the police's ability to cover a town that extended over an ever-growing physical area. Undercover operations and later dog patrols targeted Dar es Salaam criminals in the 1950s; and riot control procedures were established after the violent outcome of the 1950 strike. Meanwhile, a Special Branch was active in the town (and elsewhere) engaging in political surveillance. In addition, a squad of volunteer civilian 'special constables' numbering several hundred augmented the police proper.

In spite of the growing size and sophistication of the force, however, Dar es Salaam remained a substantially under-policed town throughout the colonial period, in which an imposed colonial order was never as pervasive or robust as police and administrative officers, or for that matter European and Asian, and to a lesser degree African, residents, hoped. One major problem was the need to operate over an ever-increasing area. Substantial new residential communities, housing Africans, Asians and Europeans, emerged in the late 1940s and 1950s and the capital's physical expansion prevented the police from providing adequate protection or control of its expanding population (in itself a further complicating factor). Certain parts of town — including, in 1950, Magomeni, Keko, Makaburi and parts of Ilala — were even considered off-limits to patrolling policemen. The force was allocated greater resources in the final years of colonial rule than at any time previously. However, it was never enough. In 1958, the Commissioner of Police observed '[t]he greatest difficulty faced was that of finance.'[54] With growing demands placed upon them as a result of not only a rapidly escalating crime rate but also African nationalist agitation, senior officers became increasingly frustrated at the inadequate amounts placed at their disposal.

Housing in Dar es Salaam

Rapid urbanisation also placed considerable strain on Dar es Salaam's housing infrastructure. Extensive construction that occurred in response to the accommodation shortage — in the African and Indian communities in particular — resulted in the physical transformation of the town. The compact capital of the inter-war period, which (apart from the outlying embryonic suburb of Oyster Bay) was hemmed in by the Msimbazi Creek to the north, and extended only as far as Ilala to the west and Keko to the south, grew into a town of sprawling suburbs, stretching from Msasani to Tandika. Inter-war zoning gave way to urban planning organised around types of residential (and non-residential) areas, which although not envisaged as being as racially exclusive as the former Zones I–III, nevertheless mostly resulted in segregated communities. So-called low density residential areas, covering large swathes of the northern and southern reaches of the town, were in the words of the 1949 Masterplan 'generally assumed as for European housing'.[55] It was in the late 1940s and early 1950s that Dar es Salaam's exclusive Oyster Bay area was extensively developed.[56] Comfortable housing in spacious surroundings was constructed here by government for European officials, and by private companies such as Brooke Bond (East Africa) and Cable and Wireless for their managerial staff. Parts of Kinondoni and Regent Estate were also designated as low density areas for European residence, as were the older residential areas at Sea View and around the botanical gardens. Smaller 'European' suburbs also emerged to the south of the town at Kurasini and Mtoni, occupied mainly by employees of the port and associated industries.

Medium density residential areas were allocated for Dar es Salaam's Indian population. These complemented the bazaar — designated as a 'commercial area' — which remained the principal place of residence for the bulk of this community. Indeed, overcrowding in the bazaar forced government's hand in opening up other parts of the town for Indian residence. Upanga,

---

[54] 1958 PAR.

[55] Gibb, 'Plan', p. 29. Unless indicated the remainder of this paragraph is based on the Masterplan, the AR of the Surveys and Town Planning Department for 1952, and Kironde, 'Land use structure', chapter 5.

[56] See Kironde, 'Land use structure', pp. 281–5.

Fig.10.2 *Housing, Oyster Bay, c. 1960*
Source: Tanzania Information Services

immediately to the north of the bazaar, was designated as the main area for medium density housing.[57] According to the 1949 Masterplan, plot sizes in Upanga were scheduled to vary from one-sixth of an acre in those areas adjoining Kariakoo to half an acre on the side approaching the low density area of Sea View. To the north of the town, Regent Estate North (though no development appears to have occurred here) and part of Kinondoni were planned as medium density areas. To the south, a section of Chang'ombe was earmarked as medium density, where Asian government housing was constructed and the Ismaili community built a small estate in the early 1950s.

After WWII 'high density' African residential areas emerged throughout the town in the former Zone I as well as what used to be Zone III. However, housing for the African population remained one of the most serious problems facing the Tanganyikan administration throughout the late-colonial period. The situation was particularly serious in the immediate post-war years. With building materials in short supply during the war, little construction had occurred at a time when the urban population was growing faster than ever. As a consequence

---

[57] Though it was some time before development in Upanga actually began — a combination of spiralling urban land prices (in Upanga above all) and African claims to ownership of land held up development there. See Kironde, 'Land use structure', pp. 273–9; and Brennan, 'Nation', chapter 4.

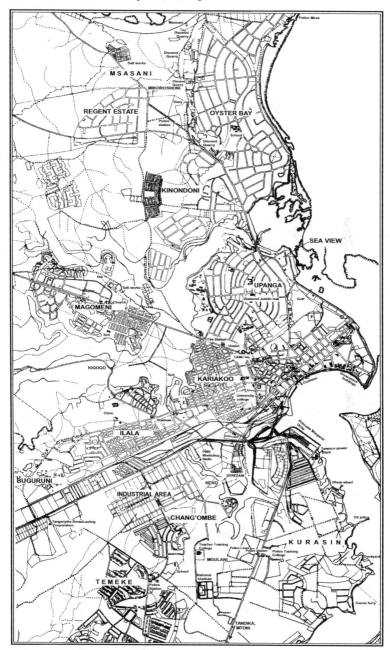

Map 10.2 *Dar es Salaam at Independence*

Source: Based on *City of Dar es Salaam Guide Map* (Dsm, 1962) — copy in BIEA map collection

rents doubled between 1943 and 1947.[58] Overcrowding in Kariakoo and the other main African residential areas worsened. In a survey undertaken by the Medical Officer of Health in 1947 of 674 houses in the African township, 69 percent contained rooms that broke municipal by-laws relating to overcrowding. Serious fires that occurred in Ilala in August and September 1945, destroying a number of houses there, exacerbated the accommodation shortage.[59] In addition, Asian occupation of the more desirable parts of Kariakoo, to the west of Msimbazi Street — in 1944, 111 'Indians' were reported to be renting houses in Zone III, three years later, in 1947, there were 340 'Asian' families living in Kariakoo alone[60] — contributed to escalating rents, magnifying African discontent.[61] As we have seen, this discontent found dramatic expression in the general strike of 1947, the principal object of the strikers' grievances being rising prices and in particular the high cost of housing.

With officials aware of the desperate need for more African accommodation, shifting attitudes towards government provision of housing had been in evidence before the strike, although the spiralling urban population continued to overwhelm official efforts to address the massive housing shortage.[62] A scheme had been initiated in 1946 to construct a 'better class residential suburb for artisans and clerks' on a site near the Msimbazi Mission, north of Ilala, in which — to prevent more overcrowding — subletting was prohibited.[63] Midway through 1947, seventeen 2- and 3-roomed houses were available for occupancy at Shs. 12/- and Shs. 20/50, and a further 60 were planned. By the end of the year 24 more houses had been completed, but with building costs having escalated the rents charged were raised to Shs. 18/- and Shs. 35/-. In spite of the increase, 550 applications were made for the 24 plots. It was clear that progress at such a sluggish pace would have little if any impact on the accommodation crisis. The strike further concentrated officials' minds. A plan to build 1,000 houses in temporary materials, originally raised in August 1947, was swiftly endorsed in the wake of the strike, although a shortage of affordable land and materials meant that just 79 houses were eventually erected.[64] Even the few that were built proved a major disappointment: costs entailed in their construction meant that a 50 percent increase in rents was required in 1949 if the scheme was to remain economic, making the rents, according to the MAAO, 'extortionate'.[65] Meanwhile, the poor quality of construction added to costs thanks to the

[58] Iliffe, 'Dockworkers', p. 131; Gibb, 'Plan', p. 58.

[59] Note on African housing, 1948 (n.d.), Dsm District Book; Uzaramo AR for 1945, p. 12.

[60] Director of Intelligence Unit Bureau to PC, EP, October 1944, quoted in Kironde, 'Land use structure'; Note on African Housing 1948.

[61] Recommendations of Native Affairs Sub-Committee, *TS*, 1 May 1945; Letter from SAVAGE, 12 May 1945.

[62] For urban housing policy, see J.F.R. Hill and J.P. Moffett, *Tanganyika: A review of its resources and their development* (Dsm, 1955), pp. 833–9; and for shifting attitudes in the 1940s, Kironde, 'Land use structure', pp. 248–52.

[63] The quote is from an earlier memorandum in which the extension of Zone III was originally proposed by Molohan and Pike, 27 July 1943 (in TNA/24387), quoted in Kironde, 'Land use structure', p. 263.

[64] PC, EP to CS, 25 August 1947, TNA/36707.

[65] MAAO to TC, 28 December 1949, TNA/36707.

Table 10.3 *Residential location by ethnic group, 1952*

Area	Euro	Indian	Goan	Arab	Somali	Coloured	Other non-African	African	All races
1	1,158	207	5	7		3	10	1,926	3,316
2	4	21		50				1,980	2,055
3	41	10		4				182	237
4	829	282	19			7	17	294	1,448
5	65	492	109	1		16	61	1,135	1,879
6	316	11,589	835	85	5	23	103	707	13,663
7	10	384		15			11	757	1,177
8	39	1					2	362	404
9	480	31		34		3	5	1,141	1,694
10	444	428	71	24		8	68	3,668	4,711
11	1	414	69	3			17	18	522
12	1	11		37				3,098	3,147
13	10	5,073	345	897	4	54	137	22,901	29,421
14	7	385	101	248	1	7	43	16,941	17,733
15	1	6		79		5	5	4,747	4,843
16				7				2,504	2,511
17	51	37	3	45		12	10	3,789	3,947
18				29				4,912	4,941
19	146	11	38	5		1	22	1,268	1,491
Total	**3,603**	**19,382**	**1,595**	**1,570**	**10**	**139**	**511**	**72,330**	**99,140**

1. Oyster Bay
2. Msasani
3. Msasani (Regent Estate)
4. Gymkhana-European Hospital-Sea View
5. & 7. Upanga
6. Central Commercial Area
8. Magogoni
9. Kurasini
10. Gerezani
11. Chang'ombe Estate
12. Chang'ombe Village-Keko Juu
13. Kariakoo
14. Ilala-Buguruni (part)
15. Magomeni-Kigogo
16. Kinondoni
17. Buguruni (part)-Makaburi-Msimbazi Mission
18. Temeke Village
19. Temeke

Source: Census of 13 February 1952, East African Statistical Dept (in Dsm Council Mins, September 1952)

ongoing need of repairs. '[T]hrough the need to deal urgently with a pressing social problem', observed one official in 1949, 'we embarked on a "dud" scheme.'[66]

The dilemma of providing urban workers affordable accommodation remained a perennial one. To complicate matters, by the late 1940s Africans were demanding what they considered their entitlements. 'Housing is the

[66] Min. dated 5 January 1950, TNA/36707.

main problem', wrote 'H.R'. in a letter to the *Standard*:

government has failed in its duty towards most of its employees in this regard. The commercial employers have criminally neglected this aspect of their duty towards most of their employees. All new bungalows in Kingsway and Oyster Bay are for the Big Bosses and nothing is done for the members of the small fry who are required to make do somehow with whatever they get.[67]

Officials too had by this time acknowledged certain responsibilities on the part of government. 'In an age of political and social advancement', wrote the Commissioner for Development in 1951, 'the indigenous African has a right to expect that schemes will be implemented for the betterment of housing conditions.' If government did not accept this obligation it must expect 'some degree of political and industrial unrest of the nature of that evident in… 1947'.[68] With the financial resources available, however, if sub-economic schemes were pursued then this would severely restrict the amount of housing constructed, thereby failing to address the problem of overcrowding, which by 1950 was considered so extreme that it was 'affecting the health of the community'.[69]

In the event, officials chose to continue building 'economic' public housing or 'quarters',[70] while at the same time allocating surveyed plots to individual Africans, whom they hoped would allay the accommodation shortage through constructing their own homes. Between 1949 and 1954 a further 334 houses were constructed in Ilala.[71] Although expensive, the central location and relative luxury of these more upmarket bungalows, made them popular among better-paid Africans, and by the mid 1950s there was a three year waiting list for this accommodation.[72] Meanwhile, new 'high density' suburbs emerged to the south and west of the town at Temeke and Magomeni. Each contained a mixture of government-built quarters and plots for self-development in either semi-permanent or permanent materials. Temeke suburb was originally planned as a residential area for workers employed in the nearby industrial zone along Pugu Road. Work was begun there in 1950 and 256 1-, 2- and 3-roomed semi-detached houses had been constructed in the area by 1954, renting at Shs. 26/-, Shs. 35/- and Shs. 52/- per month.[73] Meanwhile, 2,640 plots were demarcated for allocation for development by individual Africans. Initially, housing in Temeke was unpopular owing to its distance from town. However, by the mid 1950s better transport links, improved facilities and the rising cost of housing in Kariakoo and Ilala resulted in a waiting list developing for

[67] *TS*, 15 May 1948, p. 10.
[68] Undated memo on African housing (by the Commissioner for Development) at f. 36, TNA/225/DC3602.
[69] MOH in *TS*, 15 April 1950, p. 10.
[70] See Leslie, *Survey*, p. 156.
[71] Mins of PC's conference, July 1954, TNA/225/DC01/3/23.
[72] Leslie, *Survey*, p. 151.
[73] Mins of PCs' conference, July 1954, TNA/225/DC01/3/23; Kironde, 'Land use structure', p. 267; Leslie, *Survey*, p. 173.

government quarters there.[74] In the 1957 census the planned area of Temeke was found to have an African population of over 14,000.[75] Magomeni, an area to the west of the Msimbazi Creek that was opened up for development after the construction of the Dar es Salaam–Tanga road, was another area which, despite having limited initial popularity, had by the end of the decade become a substantial suburb.[76] It was planned as the main overspill area for the densely populated Kariakoo and Ilala, and considerable resources were allocated to its development. By 1954, 644 government quarters had been constructed there. Lessons learnt at Temeke resulted in a reduction in construction costs — partly because the housing built in Magomeni was mostly terraced — and rents were therefore lower (at Shs. 12/-, Shs. 20/- and Shs. 29/- for 1-, 2- and 3-roomed units). In addition to these houses, 3,800 plots were demarcated for allocation to Africans — of which 1,772 had been allocated by late 1958.[77] Magomeni (together with the small 'urban village' of Kigogo) was found to have an African population of almost 14,000 in the 1957 census. The other substantial new suburb where planned development occurred was in Kinondoni, although here only plots for African development, and no quarters, were provided. Situated close to the 'low density' suburbs, part of Kinondoni was designated for African housing in order to provide a convenient residential location for domestic servants employed by Europeans.[78] A total of 3,200 plots were designated for African housing there, and by 1957 the area had a population of over four thousand inhabitants.

In contrast to other towns in British East and Central Africa, there was a large landlord class in Dar es Salaam — numbering, according to Leslie, over 8,000 Africans in 1956.[79] In response to the post-war housing crisis, regulations governing building standards and overcrowding rules were relaxed for housing constructed of non-permanent materials built for and by Africans.[80] The high rents obtainable that resulted from the accommodation shortage provided a great incentive for house construction, and substantial developments of Swahili houses, built from poles, mud, wattle and thatch, emerged in areas throughout Dar es Salaam in the course of the 1950s. In his 1956 survey, Leslie found that 57 percent of all housing in the town was of the Swahili type, and that as much as 72 percent of the population lived in this type of accommodation.[81] It was largely as a result of these initiatives

---

[74] 1956 Provincial AR, p. 21.

[75] For a breakdown of the Dar es Salaam census, see Leslie, Appendix 11.

[76] Municipal Treasurer complained that 237 houses in Magomeni remained empty in January 1955. Letter to Cmmr for Development, 7 January 1955, TNA/540/29/17.

[77] Town Planner, Dsm to Cmmr for Development, 8 December 1953, TNA/225/DC01/3/23; Leslie, *Survey*, p. 173; Hill and Moffett, *Tanganyika*, p. 836; Kironde, 'Land use', p. 270.

[78] This was first mooted in the late 1930s; Scott to CS, 17 June 1938, TNA/26179/Vol. III. See also, Kironde, 'Land use', pp. 272–3.

[79] Leslie, *Survey*, pp. 151 and 153.

[80] *Ibid.*, pp. 154–5.

[81] Leslie, Appendices.

that government felt able to report, in 1958, that the Dar es Salaam housing shortage had been solved mostly by 'the people themselves'.[82] There was no room for complacency, however. Although overcrowding had been reduced, with the urban African population growing at upwards of 6,000 a year the supply of housing remained critical up to (and beyond) independence. Kariakoo had a population of around 29,000 in 1957, giving a density of 116 persons per acre — far in excess of the 'designed' population of 20,000 or 76 persons per acre.[83] The District Commissioner warned of the health hazards associated with 'certain parts' of Dar es Salaam where people were living six or seven to the room.[84] Although government had, from the late 1940s, taken greater responsibility for the provision of housing to urban Africans, the amount of public housing built was negligible. Quarters formed just ten percent of the housing stock at the time of Leslie's survey and accommodated a mere six percent of the urban African population. Waiting lists were large. In 1960, there were over 2,500 applicants for government housing.[85] Moreover, although — for the space and amenities provided — quarters represented excellent value, the rents remained beyond many Africans. 'We are not touching the fringe of the problem', observed one anxious official in 1953:

> There is little need for me to stress the political aspect of our failure to house the African... and unless some real measures are taken I am completely convinced that we shall meet with troubles in this Territory.
>
> ... I really don't see a solution to the problem as unless we are going to reduce rentals considerably we shall not be able to house the number and types of population that we should do.[86]

A solution was partly sought in the provision of surveyed plots. However, this policy also had serious deficiencies. Although large numbers of plots were made available for African development, in the rush to expand housing supply most of the high density areas were provided with only the barest minimum of services, often lacking such basic infrastructure as proper roads and drainage.[87] The policy caused strain between different branches of government, and in 1960 the Municipal Council imposed restrictions on new development on all housing estates until 'the vexed problem of essential services' was resolved.[88] The policy of cost-cutting in relation to services had in any case failed to result in sufficient housing to meet the requirements of

---

[82] *Report on Tanganyika for the Year 1958* (London, 1959), p. 155; Kironde, 'Land use structure', p. 299.
[83] Town Planner to TC, 20 February 1953, TNA/540/27/5; Leslie, Appendices. While Leslie was unconcerned by a township-wide density that averaged out for Africans at about two persons per room, this mean figure no doubt concealed important variations — both between different areas and different house types (quarters presumably housing fewer persons per room). Leslie, *Survey*, pp. 170–3.
[84] *TS*, 9 March 1957, p. 3.
[85] 1960 Labour AR, p. 16.
[86] Min by M.D.W., January 1950, TNA/225/DC01/3/16.
[87] 1957 EP, AR, p. 19; Kironde, 'Land use structure', pp. 294–5.
[88] 1960 Dsm DAR, p. 2, RH/Mss.Afr.s. 937.

Fig. 10.3 *Aerial photo of Dar es Salaam, c.1960. Note the different types of housing: Planned high rise in the town centre (Uhindini); unplanned African in Kisutu (barely visible to the bottom left of Uhindini); planned Indian in Upanga (to the bottom left); and planned African Swahili housing in Kariakoo (to the bottom right).*

Source: Tanzania Information Services

Dar es Salaam's rapidly expanding population. Demand for plots continually outstripped supply. There were 2,000 applicants waiting for plots in Magomeni alone in 1958.[89] While the housing shortage was certainly ameliorated by the provision of surveyed plots (and to a lesser extent the construction of public housing), as it turned out crisis was only averted thanks to the growth of a number of unplanned African settlements that emerged in the town in the late 1940s and 1950s. Expanding shanties such as those at Buguruni, Kigogo, Chang'ombe/Toroli, Keko and Mikoroshoni housed approximately 17 percent of the African population according to Leslie's survey — in 1957 this would have amounted to almost 16,000 persons. These mushrooming shanty settlements formed a conspicuous contradiction to the urban order that the late-colonial administration was aiming to impose. However, in the circumstances they were mostly tolerated, and were to form an enduring legacy of colonial rule.[90]

---

[89] Kironde, 'Land use structure', p. 299.
[90] Durdant-Hollomby to Mhuto, 25 September 1961, RH/Mss.Afr.s. 937; Marshall Macklin Monoghan, *Dar es Salaam Masterplan* (Toronto, 1979), p. 58.

Industry and labour in post-war Dar es Salaam

The substantial growth in population that occurred after WWII was in part a response to the proliferation of income-earning opportunities that emerged in Dar es Salaam in the 1940s and 1950s. Political and economic conditions were favourable to a significant expansion in industrial, commercial and building activity. Development funds entering the territorial economy contributed to a post-war building boom through an extensive public works programme. Although not directed at industrial development, they also helped provide a more conducive environment for manufacturing and service industry.[91] So too did a general increase in economic activity that was reflected in a substantial expansion in the tonnage of imports and exports handled at Dar es Salaam port — up from 182,800 tons in 1938 to 431,800 in 1947. This was sustained into the early 1950s, with Tanganyikan exports rising from £8.6 million in 1945 to £48.3 million in 1952, and imports from £6.3 million to £40.9 million.[92] This increased dynamism was reflected in an urban economy that was itself expanding and diversifying from the late 1940s, as unprecedented — though limited[93] — industrial development occurred. In 1948, the Tanganyika Packers factory was commenced at Kawe (Fig. 10.4) as a joint enterprise by the colonial government (with a 51 percent stake) and Liebig's Extract of Meat Limited. It produced tinned beef for the British market, both to allay post-war shortages and to preserve imperial dollar reserves, and was to become the largest single industrial employer in Dar es Salaam. By 1949, over 800 Africans were working there, although full production did not actually begin until 1950. Three years later, the factory was handling 50,000 to 60,000 head of cattle per year.[94] The Metal Box Company in 1950 also opened a factory at the Pugu Road industrial area largely to provide raw materials — tin cans — for Tanganyika Packers.[95]

Various other multinationals established subsidiaries in Dar es Salaam in the post-war period, and a host of smaller concerns also emerged.[96] A combination of factors — including surplus capital generated from rising export prices, an expanding and increasingly educated South Asian

[91] The Groundnut Scheme, for example, provided a demand for specialised engineering services located in the capital. Iliffe, *Modern History*, p. 447.

[92] *TS*, 24 January 1948, p. 4; Low and Smith, *History*, App. 4.

[93] Thanks in part to a tariff system that had — up to 1945 — favoured enterprise in neighbouring Kenya, industrial activity was more widespread there in the 1940s, and continued to develop from this base at a faster pace than in Tanganyika after WWII. See E.A. Brett, *Colonialism and Underdevelopment in East Africa: The politics of economic change, 1919–1939* (London, 1973); Andrew Coulsen, *Tanzania: A political economy* (Oxford, 1982), chap. 9; Shivji, *Law*, pp. 110–11.

[94] District Office, Dsm to DC, Kisarawe — data for Blue Book 1949 — in Kisarawe District Book; Shivji, *Law*, p. 112; Hill and Moffett, *Tanganyika*, p. 759.

[95] *Ibid.*; Coulson, *Tanzania*, p. 78. The factory also supplied tins for meat-canning factories in Southern Rhodesia and the Sudan.

[96] See Honey, 'Asian industrial activities', p. 66; *TS*, 11 August 1951; list of companies and firms in Dsm, 1951, TNA/540/16/15; J. Rweyemamu, *Underdevelopment and Industrialization in Tanzania: A study of perverse capitalist development* (Nairobi, 1974), p. 128.

Fig.10.4 *Tanganyika Packers, Kawe*
Source: Tanzania Information Services

population, and the desire to diversify from their well-established role as merchants and middlemen — led to a substantial increase in Indian industrial activity.[97] Most prominent among these Indian industrialists was the Chande family who from the late 1940s set up several plants in Dar es Salaam (and elsewhere), including a flour mill, an oil crushing plant and a soap factory. Indians also established numerous smaller-scale concerns.[98] Moreover, the building boom the town experienced in the late 1940s and 1950s resulted in the proliferation of construction companies — from two before WWII to a dozen in the late 1940s — and of factories servicing the construction industry.[99] Many of the new industrial concerns were located in the Pugu Road industrial area, which, according to the District Commissioner, was by early 1950 'unrecognisable from what it was a year ago'.[100]

The working population of Dar es Salaam underwent a considerable expansion from the estimated 14,000 employed in the town in 1931. Some of the biggest employers in the district were still located on the outskirts of the town. A total of sixteen sisal estates employed over 6,000 workers in 1949.[101] Twenty quarries, notably those located in the Kunduchi, Ngeta, Mbagala and Mjimwema areas, as well as out towards Pugu, provided employment for around 1,000 in the same year, excavating material for the

[97] *Ibid.*

[98] See e.g. the survey of existing users of Kisarawe Street go-downs in May 1951 in TNA/ 540/16/15 — which included oil mills, soda manufacturers, soap makers and carpentry/ joinery businesses, 80% Indian-owned.

[99] *TS*, 15 January 1949, p. 13; 1949 Kisarawe DAR, TNA/540/1/4/B.

[100] Two years later, visitors to the site who had last seen it in 1950 were once again said to be 'unable to recognise the factory site' owing to 'its large number of new buildings'. 1949 Kisarawe DAR, TNA/540/1/4/B; 1951 Dsm DAR, TNA/61/504/1/1951.

[101] The closest being located at Msasani, Mkoche, Mbezi, Kunduchi and Ununio to the north of the town, and Mbagala to the south. Data for Blue Book 1949, Kisarawe District Book; map of the Bagamoyo–Dsm Coastal Strip, adapted in Map 4.1 above.

booming construction industry.[102] In the town itself, 24,445 male workers were employed.[103] In addition, there were almost five thousand domestic servants.[104] By 1952, the number of employed Africans (excluding domestics) had increased to almost 31,000: 19,000 working for private industry and 12,000 for public services. The main private employers included Tanganyika Packers (over 800 workers), Shell (300) and Metal Box (218);[105] over two thousand dockworkers were registered at the port as casuals or permanent employees. Meanwhile, numerous smaller companies had a substantial combined workforce.[106] The main public sector employers were the PWD (2,436 African workers in 1952), East African Railways and Harbours (1,459) and the Municipality (1,382).

As with other aspects of the social economy of the territory greater governmental intervention in relation to labour was apparent in the post-war period. An employment exchange was set up in Dar es Salaam in July 1945 (and later in other towns throughout Tanganyika), initially to place demobilised *askaris* in work. At the end of the year 821 out of 1,016 Africans registered at the exchange had found jobs.[107] By 1948 it mainly served as a recruiting office for the Overseas Food Corporation (for the Groundnut Scheme) and allied companies.[108] In February 1946, a training centre was also established, at Mgulani, on the Kilwa Road; initially intended to provide ex-servicemen with technical skills, it was later earmarked for 'young educated Africans'. Former *askaris* received an allowance of Shs. 1/25 and civilians -/ 75cts per day while undergoing training for six to nine months as driver-mechanics, tailors, carpenters, masons, painter-signwriters, shoemakers, blacksmiths, tinsmiths, plumbers and — at the request of the Women's Service League — 'trained' domestic servants. Graduates went on to obtain employment both in Dar es Salaam and in their districts of origin. Almost 2,300 trainees passed out of the centre before it was moved to Ifunda in

[102] *Ibid.*; 1950 Kisarawe DAR, TNA/61/504/1.

[103] Including 15,467 labourers, 2,187 shop and office 'boys', 1,201 masons and bricklayers, 764 clerks and 674 drivers.

[104] Labour Census 1949, TNA/225/DC3602.

[105] 'Enquiry into the wage rates of African industrial workers in Dar es Salaam, November–December 1952', N.H. Bull, LO, PRO/CO/822/660; data for Blue Book 1949, Kisarawe District Book; notes on a visit to Dsm by E.W. Barltrop, August/September 1952, PRO/CO/822/660; Coulson, *Political Economy*, p. 78; Quarterly Labour Report (ending 30 September 1952), TNA/540/27/7/Vol. III.

[106] E.g. 33 woodworks engaged 1,415 employees in 1952; 20 garages employed almost 600 Africans; 439 workers were employed in over 150 tailoring businesses; 20 mills of various types engaged 398 workers; and 349 employees worked at the town's nine sheet metal works. Bull, 'Enquiry'.

[107] Correspondence in TNA/33196. I am grateful to Nicholas Westcott for providing me with a copy of his notes on this file.

[108] An African-owned employment bureau was established by the Sykes brothers in November 1950 'to supply good domestic servants to households in the town' (the domestics section in the Government employment exchange was closed as early as February 1948). In early 1951 it had 170 Africans on its books who were charged a registration fee and 10% of the first month's salary after work was obtained. Uzaramo DAR 1948, TNA/540/1/4/B; *TS*, 7 April 1951, p. 13.

Iringa, combined with an Overseas Food Corporation training centre there, and converted into a 'trade school'.[109] The labour inspectorate, founded in 1939 and in 1945 combined with the Manpower Department (set up separately during the war) to form a new Labour Department, was increasingly active from the early 1940s.[110] Numerous reports on territorial labour, with direct relevance to the situation in Dar es Salaam, were published in the final decade and a half of colonial rule.[111] Moreover, within the capital itself the department played an increasingly active role, producing (or initiating) a series of surveys of labour conditions including regular quarterly and annual reports.[112] In addition to their supervisory role, inspecting places of employment and monitoring work conditions and wage rates, the Labour Officer's time was also taken up with arbitration — by 1956 the Dar es Salaam Labour Officer was hearing some 3,000 'small disputes' per year, as well as negotiating between workers and employers.[113] Increased metropolitan intervention was also a feature of the post-war period, with officials such as the British unionist, Norman Pearson (in 1947–49), and the Colonial Office Labour Advisor, E.W. Barltrop (in 1952), visiting Dar es Salaam to investigate conditions in the town and offer advice to local officials and workers.

As was the case prior to the 1947 general strike, conditions of employment and the cost of living remained a primary concern of both Labour Department *and* district officials. Boom conditions in the late 1940s and early 1950s resulted in a proliferation of employment opportunities in Dar es Salaam. Joblessness, which in the early 1940s was a serious problem, was more or less non-existent and the perennial complaint of urban employers at this time was of an acute labour shortage.[114] However, conditions varied greatly depending on the level of skills Africans brought to their work. The limited numbers of African (and Indian) artisans resulted in 'a real sellers market for the skilled trades'. 'Anyone with any pretensions of ability in masonry or carpentry', observed the District Commissioner in 1948, 'is enjoying a hey-day'. Artisans' rates increased rapidly from just Shs. 2/- per day in 1945, to Shs. 5/- in 1947, and Shs. 8–Shs. 10/- by 1948.[115] By contrast, unskilled labour, which constituted the vast majority of those working or looking for employment, remained a problem. 'The Township', complained DC Bone shortly after WWII, 'is as full as ever of unskilled labourers looking for work and accepting it at almost any wages, no matter how low'. While

---

[109] *TS*, 5 November 1949, p. 12; Hill and Moffett, *Tanganyika*, pp. 293–4.

[110] The original Labour Department, established in 1926, was disbanded after the onset of the Depression in 1931. Hill and Moffett, *Tanganyika*, p. 272.

[111] E.g. K.C. Charron, *The Welfare of the African Labourer in Tanganyika* (1944); *Report of the Committee on Manpower* (1951); Molohan, *Detribalization* (1957).

[112] E.g. *The Pattern of Income, Expenditure and Consumption of African Labourers in Dar es Salaam, August 1950* [hereafter, *Pattern*], East African Statistical Dept (1951); Bull, 'Enquiry'; 'Budget Survey of African Consumers in Dar es Salaam 1956/7', East African Statistical Department, unpublished (interim report in TNA/PA.8/06A); Quarterly labour reports (1949–50), TNA/61/503/1.

[113] Leslie, *Survey*, p. 116.

[114] E.g. *TS*, 15 January 1949, p. 13.

[115] 1948 Uzaramo DAR, TNA/540/1/4/B ; Westcott, 'Impact', p. 222.

the position improved over the next few years, the Labour Officer in 1949 bemoaned that casual labour remained in excess of demand.[116] As a consequence unskilled wage rates stayed low, a situation exacerbated by continuing inflation in the post-war years.[117] Tanganyika Packers, for example, were in 1949 engaging casual labourers at just Shs. 1/25 per day plus monthly rations to the value of Shs. 12/- — a monthly total of Shs. 44/50 if six days per week were worked.[118] The following year, the Statistical Department calculated that a family budget — for a man, wife and child — worked out at about Shs. 70/- per month.[119] Even the government minimum rate of Shs. 1/50 plus rations fell well short of this figure. An East African Statistical Department report conducted in 1950 found the average wage to be just Shs. 53/-, although with additional sources of income — principally money earned by wives — this was boosted to Shs. 67/- per month.[120] The minimum daily rate was increased to Shs. 1/75 and subsequently to Shs. 2/- in February 1951. Nevertheless, on a visit to Dar es Salaam two years later, E.W. Barltrop found the situation alarming. While he estimated the family budget figure had increased to about Shs. 90/-, large numbers of workers earned under this amount, some of them receiving as little as Shs. 45/- for a six-day week (12 hours per day) and no rations.[121] Once again, those receiving the government minimum[122] earned less than was required to raise a family. On Barltrop's recommendation, Labour Officer Bull conducted a survey of the wages and working conditions of industrial employees in Dar es Salaam in November/December 1952. He found that an estimated 5,500 workers in private industry were in receipt of wages below the government minimum rates, and that 19,000 workers in private industry and government employment — a full two-thirds of the workforce — were in receipt of wages below the 'family budget' rate. Only a quarter of the workers surveyed earned over ninety shillings (See Fig. 10.5).

[116] 1945 Uzaramo DAR, p. 9, TNA/61/504/1; Labour report for quarter ending 30 June 1949, TNA/61/503/1.

[117] Inflation was stoked by the limited number of imported goods available for purchase, increases in prices received for Tanganyikan exports, and the substantial increase in skilled artisans' rates of pay.

[118] DC Bradley (Kisarawe) to Exec Engineer i/c PWD, Dsm, 24 February 1949, TNA/540/16/15.

[119] Bull, 'Enquiry'.

[120] *Pattern*, para. 68. 'Wages accounted for only 4/5ths of the average earnings', observed the *Standard*, reporting a follow-up survey in 1951, 'the rest coming from such activities as mat-weaving, sale of firewood and water, brewing beer and making soft drinks'. These activities are often managed by the women and', notes the report, enumerators faced some delicate situations when the wife's income was not precisely known by the husband'. *TS*, 28 April 1951, p. 24.

[121] Barltrop to Twining, 28 September 1952, PRO/CO/822/660.

[122] Shs. 2/15 per day; Shs. 55/90 for a 26-day month.

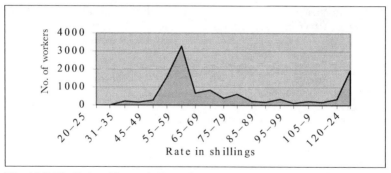

Fig. 10.5 *Distribution of incomes in Dar es Salaam, 1952 (adapted from Bull, 'Enquiry')*

Emerging over-urbanisation

As had been the case ten and twenty years earlier, the colonial administration was once more alerted to the poor conditions of employment suffered by the majority of African workers in the territorial capital. The enduring nature of the problem indicated the need for a radical rethink of policy that would have major consequences for both the organisation of labour and the administration of the township. The problem of urban labour, however, was just one of a number of phenomena that necessitated such a reassessment. Rapid urbanisation was placing ever-greater strain on an urban economy and infrastructure that was not developing at a rate sufficient to keep pace with the growth of population.

Between the end of the war and the early 1950s the Tanganyika economy experienced a healthy rate of growth, principally thanks to rising sisal prices. From around this time, however, there was a decline in foreign trade and it was not until 1959 that 1952 rates were once again reached.[123] Dar es Salaam, in particular, suffered in the ensuing economic downturn. 'It is now apparent that development reached its peak at the end of 1951', observed the Dar es Salaam Labour Officer in 1952, 'and tempo is now slower in almost every branch of industry'. The following year he reported that 'noticeable unemployment' had arisen in the town for the first time in his tenure there. Thanks to the shortage of work there was an increase in applications for *vyeti vya njia* (travel documents) to go to work in Zanzibar harvesting cloves.[124] Many Africans residing in Dar es Salaam were beginning to feel the pinch. 'At the moment', the *Tanganyika Standard* observed, 'the territory is passing through a stage of great prosperity, but in Dar es Salaam there is definite hardship.'[125] '[T]o obtain money for the bare necessities of life', the paper reported, 'the score of "duka ya rahani" [pawn shops] scattered strategically in the African areas of town have a constant stream of clients.' These

---

[123] See Ehrlich, 'The Poor Country'.
[124] Labour Office ARs, Dsm Area, 1952, p. 3; and 1953, p. 2, TNA/61/503/Vol. III.
[125] *TS*, 8 March 1952, p. 19.

'insignificant little shops' with their 'piles of clothes and stoves' were 'a red danger signal which the leaders of all communities might do well to bear in mind'. The following year, a report by the British Legion observed that the average worker

> enjoyed good meals for the first few days of the month and thereafter is faced with the alternatives of:
> a) Semi-starvation for the remainder of the month, or
> b) Frequent visits to the pawnbroker, or
> c) Petty theft and pilfering, or
> d) Various forms of spivvery, or (b), (c) and (d).[126]

These low-paid workers also suffered from poor housing and services. In spite of efforts to address the accommodation crisis since the late 1940s, there remained, according to the District Commissioner, 'an acute shortage of houses' in 1953.[127] The shanty towns emerging as a result of this situation were 'a menace to health and a breeding ground of discontent'.[128] Even in the planned African areas urban influx was resulting in the modest infrastructure and amenities becoming increasingly overburdened. 'Overcrowding', observed the Medical Officer of Health, 'in presence of the deficient piped water supply and food shortage has reached a stage dangerous to the health of the public and especially disadvantageous to the normal development of children.' He viewed the 'number of Africans arriving in Dar es Salaam' as 'beyond comprehension'.[129] Rapid town expansion, he told the Public Health Committee later the same year, was 'causing relative breakdown in several health services':

> In my opinion the town is dangerously overcrowded and is expanding too fast ... for the safety of the public health. This state is being aggravated by inadequate public utility services, such as hard roads to new areas, water supplies and drainage of surface sewage water.[130]

Refuse collection in the African areas was in a 'deplorable condition', and cheap food retailers springing up throughout the town raised concerns about public hygiene.[131] 'Measures are required urgently', he concluded, 'to restrict migration into town until food, water and housing conditions approach normal'. Three years later, the Director of Town Planning, L. Sylvester White, came to similar conclusions. Rapid urbanisation was simply unsustainable, placing an ever-escalating financial burden on Dar es Salaam's wealthier residents:

[126] Report by British Legion on Cost of Living in Dar es Salaam, 4 February 1953, TNA/540/16/15; see also *TS*, 28 April 1951, p. 24.
[127] DC, Dsm to MLG, 27 February 1953, TNA/540/27/19. Leechman, Secretariat, Dsm to Rogers, CO, 18 November 1953, similarly observes '[t]he acute housing position in Dsm brought to notice by workers associations, still remains.' PRO/CO822/660.
[128] PAR for 1949, p. 38.
[129] Quoted by TC Baxter to MLG, 6 April 1950, TNA/28685.
[130] MOH to Public Health Cttee, 18 October 1950, TNA/540/27/7.
[131] *Ibid.*; and MOH to Public Health Cttee, 17 August 1950, TNA/540/27/7.

There is a growing flow of people from the country to the town, and these people, when they arrive, contribute little to the economic or industrial structure of the towns. Enormous new neighbourhoods have to be provided, which tend to spread the towns over ever-increasing areas, all of which must be supplied with some form of public services. The continual expansion of public services has to be paid for, and the tax revenue from the African is insufficient for this. Thus towns are becoming increasingly expensive to run and maintain, with no concomitant increase in revenue from those causing the increased expense. A relatively small body of heavy taxpayers is carrying around its neck an ever increasing number of people who do not (and can not) pay their way, and the whole economic structure of our larger towns is … becoming unsound.[132]

As in other colonial East African cities, it was in fact Europeans who enjoyed privileged access to urban amenities, benefiting from an inequitable racial distribution of development expenditure.[133] Nevertheless, Sylvester White hit upon a central aspect of the urban problem. Rapid urbanisation resulted in Dar es Salaam consuming ever-growing amounts of the colonial state's resources, in both its attempts to administer and control the urban population and to provide this population with adequate infrastructure and amenities. Neither the pay nor the productivity of the African workforce was sufficient for it to make a meaningful contribution to these rising costs. By the mid 1950s it was clear this position could not be sustained indefinitely; for political as well as administrative reasons. A significant shift in colonial policy was required for a solution to the problem of African urbanisation.

---

[132] Minute by D.T.P., 7 March 1953, TNA/225/DC3602.

[133] Kironde, 'Land use structure', pp. 244–5 *et passim*. Similarly, Mary Parker, in her 1947 report on municipal governance in neighbouring Kenya, demonstrated that Europeans — in spite of constant complaints about the fiscal burden of African and Asian communities — were 'in fact ridiculously under-taxed *vis à vis* the value of their properties, their income levels and the services they enjoyed'. Achola, 'Colonial policy', p. 125.

Eleven

Remaking Urban Society

Stabilisation & Citizenship
in Late-colonial Dar es Salaam

The need for a revised urban policy had been recognised by some Tanganyikan officials as far back as the early 1940s. Pike and Molohan, for example, when stationed at the Dar es Salaam District Office during WWII, had advocated that a greater colonial investment in the African was required: both through giving him (the problem was viewed in gendered terms) an enhanced role in municipal governance and by improving wages and conditions of employment. The result of such initiatives, it was hoped, would be a more responsible and productive African now enjoying urban citizenship. A combination of inertia, and a lack of sufficient resources and political will, meant that, while there was some movement in this direction in the late 1940s and early 1950s, it was half-hearted at best. Municipal bodies were established that were supposed to promote African participation in urban governance — the Ward Councils. However, a reluctance to devolve any real responsibility to the councils rendered them useless as vehicles for African political ambitions or as tools for colonial social engineering.[1] Similarly, improvements in African working conditions were negligible. Although a minimum wage had been introduced for government labour, it continually lagged behind a spiralling cost of living (until 1954, at least, when living costs actually began to diminish); meanwhile no universal minimum wage was imposed upon private employers in the town. Recommendations made after WWII by Orde-Browne, the former Tanganyikan official, now labour adviser at the Colonial Office, for the stabilisation of labour and for greater responsibility to be taken by government for workers' welfare, were rebuffed.[2] By the early 1950s, the picture emerging from the numerous reports on conditions in Dar es Salaam indicated the problem of urban labour was as serious as it had ever been. The situation demanded a response. Parallel shifts in thinking on urban issues elsewhere in East and Central Africa, and

---

[1]   See Burton, 'Townsmen'.
[2]   G. StJ. Orde-Browne, *Labour Conditions in East Africa* (London, 1946). See Westcott, 'Impact', pp. 222–3.

in Whitehall, in the late 1940s and early 1950s provided a context that was conducive to a reappraisal of policy.

Colonial knowledge and African urbanisation

Official ignorance of what was actually going on in the African areas of the town was recognised as a prime obstacle to the formation of any realistic new policy. A preliminary survey of Dar es Salaam was commissioned in 1951. It was conducted by two South African sociologists who had just completed research on the town of Jinja, in neighbouring Uganda.[3] In their estimation a comprehensive survey of Dar es Salaam was essential as a foundation for any new approach to dealing with the African urban population. When details of the proposed full-scale survey reached the Standing Finance Committee (SFC), however, members of the committee blanched at the envisaged costs and the Sofers returned to Jinja. Officials responsible for the urban African population reacted to this setback with dismay. The Member for Social Services berated the committee's short-sightedness:

> The rapid 'urbanisation' of our African population is one of the most solid, urgent and vital facts of the time, and it is giving rise to a great number of important problems ... It is not possible to walk or drive from here to Ilala Football Ground or to the Hide Sheds on the Pugu Road without seeing evidence of the fact.[4]

Entrenched attitudes towards the place of the African in town were difficult to dislodge. However, as the decade progressed the situation in Dar es Salaam became serious enough for the SFC to revise their decision, and in 1956 a detailed social survey of the town was carried out.[5] Indeed, such was the interest in Tanganyika's urban areas in general that two further surveys were conducted of towns within the territory around the same time: one of Africans living in the northern town of Arusha, and another that looked at the situation

---

[3]   R. and C. Sofer. Their report on Jinja was published as *Jinja Transformed*, East African Studies no. 5, EAISR (Kampala, 1955).

[4]   Minute by MSS, 25 September 1951, TNA/18950/Vol. III.

[5]   Nevertheless, Government remained reluctant to incur the expense of recruiting professional sociologists. Instead, J.A.K. Leslie, an administrative officer between posts, was enlisted to conduct and write the survey. Leslie's colonial career up till that point had been entirely conventional. Arriving in Tanganyika from Yemen in 1946, in his first two years he worked as an ADO in Dar es Salaam, after which the bulk of his time was spent on two tours as the DC in Kasulu District, Western Province. However, his social survey was anything but conventional, being quite distinct from the numerous surveys of other African cities conducted by professional social scientists around the same time. Thanks to his lack of sociological training, after spending 'six months wandering around Dar es Salaam, up and down the streets finding out what I needed to find out', Leslie produced a most idiosyncratic and personal urban survey; rich in human detail and revealing of both what was going in the African town and of official attitudes towards these phenomena. Quote from Leslie interview.

of detribalised workers in both the plantation areas of Tanga region, as well as in Tanga town itself.[6] In addition, a government-appointed committee — whose report was submitted in 1957 and eventually published in 1959 — examined the phenomenon of detribalisation in the territory as a whole, with special reference to the urban areas, and to Dar es Salaam in particular.[7] In conjunction with the material on East African towns produced by the (slightly earlier) East Africa Royal Commission (EARC) report, this burst of activity in the mid 1950s was unprecedented.[8]

The same fundamental problems continued to vex colonial administrators in Dar es Salaam as had done in the previous decade. Of greatest concern was the uninterrupted tide of rural–urban migrants. 'One of the biggest problems which faces us', complained the Provincial Commissioner of Eastern Province in 1953, 'is the question of uncontrolled migration into the big towns, with the presence of a floating, constantly changing, moneyless, propertyless, and often jobless class amounting at present often to thousands.'[9] It was not only the numbers of the urban immigrants that caused concern but their character also. According to the Labour Department report from the same year, it was 'probable that the greater proportion [we]re attracted to the towns by the possibility of making a living by dubious means'.[10] Despite increasing tolerance towards the process of African urbanisation, in the official imagination the urban environment continued to be one in which moral degeneracy abounded. Increasing rural–urban migration meant that growing numbers of Africans were at risk of contamination. According to a 1952 memorandum by the Acting Member for Local Government: 'The evils and dangers which can result if this drift is allowed to continue unchecked are well known'.[11]

These 'evils and dangers' included not only the lure of petty crime but also urban alienation. According to the administration's Senior Sociologist, '[m]odern conditions were forcing Africans into a position where they had no cultural anchor and were therefore liable to become discontented.'[12] The authors of the EARC report concurred:

> In the towns Africans are confronted with a new way of life in which they
> join as isolated individuals, who must provide for their own material, mental
> and emotional needs. ... [T]he facilities for doing so are lacking, which leads
> to the resort to drunkenness and crime by those who, fresh from a life in a

---

6   Social Survey of Arusha Township Africans by C.J.K. Latham (Social Development Officer), 1957, TNA/225/PA8.06B; Dr. P.H. Gulliver, *Alien Africans in Tanga Region* (Dsm, 1956).

7   Molohan, *Detribalization.*

8   Though it reflected a continent-wide trend. For useful summaries of urban surveys in 1940s and early 1950s Africa, see UNESCO, *Social Implications* (London, 1956).

9   1953 PAR, p. 40.

10 Labour Dept AR, 1953, p. 33; see also, Twining to Rogers, 21 November 1952, TNA/21616/Vol. III.

11 Memo. No. 68 for Executive Council, 6 May 1952, TNA/21616/Vol. III.

12 Extract from minutes of Provincial Advisory Council, Tanga, 27/28 September 1955, TNA/225/PA.8/06A.

community which exercises considerable control over the thoughts and actions of its members, are almost entirely lacking in those resources of mind and character which would give them the capacity to develop interests at their leisure.[13]

There was precious little evidence of the 'civic consciousness' that officials in the 1940s had hoped could be nurtured in the urban African population. In their preliminary survey the Sofers had reported 'an ignorance among citizens which may be widespread concerning their rights, obligations and responsibilities'.[14] E.G. Rowe, Commissioner for Eastern Province in 1954, recalled 'it was very difficult to get any civic sense, even in the crudest interpretation of that term, going among this shifting population.'[15]

A number of initiatives were adopted in an effort to slow African urbanisation. Repatriation campaigns against 'undesirables' were the most significant (see chapter 12). Most unusual was the propaganda film *Mohogomchungu* (translated by the *Tanganyika Standard* as 'The country bumpkin'[16]), which sought to persuade rural folk of the evils and dangers of town life. The film was about 'a country-boy who ... feels the age-old urge to visit the big city — in this case Dar es Salaam':

> the bumpkin ... has a most trying time in the big city, where his rusticity is ill-suited to the streamlined urban mode of life.
>
> After being sent sprawling by a car, fleeced of his money by cardsharps, robbed of his clothes, mixed up in a dripping wet fire-fighting incident, struck on the head by the irate husband of an African girl he admires, and generally subjected to a very tough passage — the bumpkin is well content to return to working the *shamba* with his parents.[17]

Ironically, the most this film can be said to have done was to promote the career of its star, the future unionist and nationalist, Rashidi Kawawa, who, as an employee of the Social Development Department, had landed the leading role.[18] There is no evidence of *Mohogomchungu* having any influence whatsoever on the growing number of migrants making their way to the capital.[19] Even if it had, this would only have had a mitigating influence on

---

[13] Quoted in: Social Development to MLG, 28 November 1955, TNA/17396.

[14] Sofers' Report, p. 1.

[15] Interview, p. 38, RH/Mss.Afr.s. 1698. This supposed absence of 'civic sense' is belied by the diverse African institutions that existed in the town. See Burton, 'Townsmen'.

[16] A more accurate translation is 'Bitter Harvest'.

[17] *TS*, 21 June 1952, p. 8.

[18] According to J. Vinter, who served in the Tanganyika service in the post-war period, Kawawa became the first Tanganyikan film star: 'his films were immensely popular long before he became PM, whenever one of Rashidi's films appeared in Tabora marketplace, roars of applause. So he had ... the same sort of pull which a radio personality, or TV personality, in England now, who goes into politics, he immediately has an enormous advantage.' Interview, RH/Mss.Afr.s. 1999.

[19] *Mohogomchungu* was not the first cinematic attempt in Tanganyika to persuade Africans of the undesirability of town life. Some films made as part of the 1930s 'Bantu Kinema Experiment' (notably *Gumu*) conveyed the same message. Meanwhile, *Chalo Amerudi* ('Chalo has returned'), made around the same time as *Mohogomchungu*, depicts an office worker who 'is shown leading a

the problems facing Dar es Salaam. These required a much more dramatic solution than a simple restriction of internal migration — by propaganda or other means. By the mid 1950s a more substantial answer had begun to emerge.

The East African Royal Commission and urban development

While certain officials had long counselled that a rise in African wages coupled with the control of immigration into the towns was the best approach to dealing with the problems of the urban areas, it was not until the early 1950s that such views got a public airing. In 1951, a committee on manpower in Tanganyika recommended a territorial policy of labour stabilisation.[20] In the towns this would have the benefit of not only promoting greater productivity, through the reduction in casual labour, but it would also, according to the 1951 Labour Department report, promote the civic consciousness, which up till that point had been noticeable by its absence. 'Problems inherent in urban areas today', declared the report, 'are the regular employment of African unskilled labour and the evolution of a social order by which some form of moral discipline will be imposed on detribalised urban Africans'.[21] A policy of stabilisation would address both these difficulties in one fell swoop. However, in the early 1950s all that was done to promote labour stabilisation was the extension of the maximum permissible contract for workers accompanied by their wives and families from two to three years.[22] The initiative passed to neighbouring Kenya, where, in 1954, the publication of the influential 'Carpenter Report' introduced a systematic new approach to the question of urban labour. It recommended the replacement of Kenya's irregular and poorly paid migrant workforce with a smaller, permanent urban African population, receiving higher wages that would enable them to establish and maintain their families in the towns.[23]

The following year, the same approach was adopted by the East African Royal Commission. Set up principally in response to Kenyan Governor, Philip Mitchell's concerns over land shortage and population growth, the EARC

(fn 19 contd) profligate life in town; when he returns to his village … and discovers he has been cuckolded, he beats off his wife's lover and decides to stay in the village'. Rosaleen Smyth, 'The feature film in Tanzania', *AA* 88 (1989), pp. 389–96. For a discussion of the 'Bantu Kinema Experiment', see Ivaska, 'Negotiating culture', chapter 2; for a discussion of censorship and the cinema in colonial and post-colonial Tanzania, see Brennan, 'Democratizing cinema'. Brennan notes that mobile film units for rural areas were actually set up in Tanganyika partly to reduce the appeal of urban cinema shows, which it was feared might 'develop into yet one more magnet to attract rural Africans into towns'. The quote is from Baker, then acting as Social Welfare Officer, to CS, 28 January 1946.

20   *TS*, 23 June 1951, p. 8.
21   Labour Dept AR, 1951.
22   *TS*, 30 August 1952, p. 12.
23   See chapter 1. For Kenya, see Cooper, *Waterfront*; and *idem*, *Decolonization*, for a discussion of late-colonial labour policy in British and French Africa.

eventually took the form of a regional commision with a wide remit that included the instruction to examine 'conditions of employment' and 'the social problems which arise from the growth ... of urban and industrial populations'.[24] The Commission's final recommendations, which advocated a significant extension of market relations in African society, went too far for many more paternalistic officials.[25] However, with regard to urban policy, its proposals were broadly in line with those put forward by officials with first-hand experience of urban administration.

'The part played by Africans in the towns', the Commissioners' observed in their report,

> is now more important. ... They are still, however, regarded socially and financially as liabilities... The problem is to make it possible for them to become an element in town life which shares responsibility with other communities for the development of the towns and which also contributes to urban revenues.[26]

However, both the poor conditions of town life and the high turnover of temporary labour were creating an environment in which it was difficult to forge such a community of responsible Africans. Indeed, according to the Commission, the communities emerging in East African towns were shifting and impermanent ones among whom 'crime, immorality and drunkenness' were rife. These communities contained individuals who were freed 'not only from the influences that customarily control (their) behaviour but also from the responsibilities of family life'. Individuals, that is, with no stake in the urban order. 'The maintenance of order', complained the authors,

> depends in the last resort on the active support of public opinion, which hardly exists where the majority of the population consists of rootless and irresponsible individuals, who have neither family responsibilities nor property to give them an interest in supporting the authorities.

'The first step in the formation of a healthy urban society', the authors advised, 'is the growth of a settled urban population whose loyalties are directed towards the town rather than to their areas of origin.'[27]

One way to achieve this was through greater African participation in municipal government — including giving some executive and financial authority to Africans. This would encourage 'a sense of responsibility among [urban residents] and would result in a full contribution from them towards the services which they enjoy'. In addition, various recommendations were put forward to improve housing conditions, improvements which, it was hoped, would also promote long-term urban residence. Home ownership was to be encouraged 'wherever possible'. Priority of access to educational

---

[24] *EARC Report*, p. xi.
[25] For background on the EARC, see Hugh MacMillan, 'The East Africa Royal Commission 1953–1955', in Low and Smith, *East Africa* (1996), pp. 544–57; and, with special reference to Kenya, Cooper, *Decolonization*, pp. 358–60.
[26] *EARC Report*, p. 201.
[27] *Ibid.*, pp. 214; 209; 237.

facilities for the children of town-dwelling Africans was also mooted, as was the extension of provident fund schemes and the introduction of old age pensions for long-term urban workers to replace the social security implicit in the organisation of rural communities. The principal plank of stabilisation policy, though, was an increase in wage rates.

Better pay would enable the African worker to move his family to the town, would lead to an improvement in his conditions of existence there, and would diminish the importance of maintaining links with his rural home. The permanent urban employee would be a more efficient worker, he would be easier to administer, and in addition would be better equipped to contribute towards municipal revenue. It was recognised that economic expansion was essential in order for wages to rise towards a level that would support family life in the towns, and that consequently the process of stabilisation would be a slow one. Nevertheless, the authors observed the 'paramount need to create a settled African labour force' and recommended that '[e]very effort must … be made to create conditions which are favourable to it.'[28]

It was anticipated that one of the likely side effects of this policy of stabilisation was an increase in the number of urban immigrants. Although the authors of the report had noted that considerable concern over urban drift already existed among officials in East Africa, they concluded that control over movement to the towns was undesirable. In the first place, it was disagreeable on economic grounds 'because it restricts mobility and therefore inhibits the development of the exchange economy'.[29] The extension of market relations, at the core of EARC recommendations, would encourage increasing specialisation of labour, which in the view of the Commission was necessary in order to raise standards of living in both rural and urban areas. Second, it was simply impracticable. 'Systems of control', the authors observed, 'although rigorously enforced have broken down even in territories where the population is sparser and the towns more isolated than in East Africa.' They advised that while steps should be taken to improve conditions in the rural areas, and so limit the attraction of an urban life, '(t)he continued growth of the population of the towns at a rate which is unpredictable must be accepted.'

Tanganyikan initiatives

The immediate response of officials in Dar es Salaam was ambivalent. While the benefits of a policy of stabilisation were broadly accepted, the practicalities of achieving it in the territory were questioned. Tanganyikan administrators were particularly concerned about the consequences of stabilisation for those Africans who had severed links with their home areas only to find themselves without an income at the end of their working life, or as a result of

[28] *Ibid.*, pp. 249; 158; 214.
[29] *Ibid.*, p. 240.

unemployment.[30] Although officials could see the benefits of stabilisation, the administration could not afford to establish some form of adequate social security to replace that which resulted from Africans' continued links with their country kin; neither were they in a position to persuade employers to do so. Of equal concern to Tanganyikan officials was the apparently *laissez-faire* attitude adopted by the Commission towards rural–urban migration. For those responsible for the administration of Dar es Salaam, there was no way that the unfettered movement that the Commission recommended could be countenanced. Indeed, the years following the publication of the report saw more concerted — if, as the EARC predicted, not entirely successful — attempts to control the flow to the towns, and by the mid 1950s more Africans were being repatriated from Dar es Salaam than at any previous time.[31] However, the Tanganyikan government was sympathetic to the broader recommendations of the EARC. The spectre of detribalisation had been superseded in the official mind by the recognition of the need to foster a new urban identity among town-dwelling Africans, and Tanganyikan officials were very much in step with EARC proposals that greater civic responsibility should be fostered through extending the scope for African participation in town life.

Just one year after the publication of the EARC report, the government was instigating its own investigation into 'the development and growth of new communities in urban and peri-urban areas'. The emergence of such communities was now seen as both inevitable and, from the point of view of enhanced economic efficiency and the productivity of labour, as advisable. *Detribalization*, the report that resulted from these investigations, was authored by M.J.B. Molohan, a Labour Officer in Dar es Salaam during WWII and later Labour Commissioner for Tanganyika in the early 1950s. It took its place alongside the Kenyan 'Carpenter Report' and the EARC chapter on urban development as another influential contribution towards the revision of colonial urban policy. Molohan addressed himself 'entirely to the problem of finding the most effective means whereby these [urbanised and/or detribalised] persons can be assisted to settling down peacefully and contentedly in their new environments and becoming good citizens'. He reduced the problem to two main parts: 'the establishment of an efficient system of administration in which the people concerned share and secondly the provision of greatly increased social and cultural amenities for these new communities'.[32]

---

[30] 'Preliminary observations by the Tanganyika Government on EARC report, PRO/CO/ 822/1113.

[31] According to MacMillan, EARC recommendations on urban development were 'primarily inspired by its Uganda secretary'. Uganda was more wholeheartedly committed to a policy of urbanisation and industralisation. This, alongside the more generally *laissez-faire* outlook of the Commission's principal members (though MacMillan qualifies this widely held interpretation), might help explain recommendations that to Tanganyikan officials appeared reckless.

[32] Molohan, *Detribalization*, para. 7.

Addressing the problems of urban administration first, he observed that Dar es Salaam had always been too loosely governed and recommended that the African population 'required a higher degree of closer administration'.[33] The District Office should be moved from the area known by Africans as Uzunguni ('place of the Europeans') to the African quarter, and in addition two sub-district offices should also be constructed in the high density areas. Not only would this decentralisation bring government 'nearer to the people' but it would also facilitate (and intensify) the direct administration of the African areas.[34] The peri-urban areas around the town should be incorporated into a single district along with the town, in order to subject the increasingly urbanised communities that existed there to direct control by the District Office. A substantial increase in the establishment of Dar es Salaam district was counselled, with, among others, four administrative officers and a Woman AO added to the staff. Similar recommendations were made with regard to the African executive staff. The system of *Wakili* and *Majumbe* required strengthening 'both as regards the quality of the staff employed … and by an increase in its number'. In addition, the introduction of 'a stratum of sub-headmen (*wazee wa mji*)' was favoured 'below the level of the headmen to be responsible each for his own particular little area and to get to know all its inhabitants'.[35]

Molohan also counselled for a reinvigoration of urban local government. There was, according to the report, 'a very great need to make the inhabitants of the [African] areas take a greater interest in the administration of their own units and the management of their own affairs and so become civic conscious'. The introduction of local elections for Ward Councils,[36] along with the Councils' acquisition of executive and financial responsibilities, would, it was suggested, stimulate civic consciousness. This would be augmented by making each of Dar es Salaam's five wards 'a self-contained unit with its own council, court and *hakimu* [magistrate], dispensary or clinic, schools, shops, market, pombe market, assembly hall, cinema, recreation and playing fields, post office, public telephone, bus service, etc'. 'By providing such facilities', Molohan concluded, 'the inhabitants will begin to feel that they are part of a single community with a common interest.' The wards would also become 'the natural base[s] for the maintenance of law and order'; each would have its own police station, and the formation of 'special constabulary' units 'should be encouraged in order to impress upon the inhabitants their duty and responsibility for aiding the enforcement of the law'.[37]

Recommendations aimed at what many officials felt was the most pressing problem, rural–urban drift, were also contained in the report. While Molohan acknowledged the impracticality of establishing some form of pass system

---

[33] *Ibid.*, p. 2.
[34] Similar actions in Nairobi and Mombasa had, Molohan observed, had beneficial effects there. *Ibid.*, paras 36–8.
[35] *Ibid*, paras 32–5; 53; 65.
[36] Up to June 1957 unofficial representatives on the Ward Councils were selected at open meetings by residents of each sub-ward. See Burton, 'Townsmen' for more on the Ward Councils.
[37] Molohan, *Detribalization.*, paras 70; 80.

to control internal migration, he nevertheless recommended — contrary to the EARC report — measures aimed at reducing this drift. Above all, he deemed it 'essential to strengthen the administrative powers for getting rid of drones and spivs'. The problem was identified as being intimately connected to the question of labour, and Molohan made a number of proposals that modestly advanced what he acknowledged as the 'accepted policy of encouraging the stabilisation of the working population'. The regulation of casual employment was recommended, which, in the absence of 'any effective scheme to control entry into and residence in the town', was felt might be of value as 'employers would be forced progressively to rely on a more permanent labour force'. Action also needed to be taken against the employment of children in the town, which was common, chiefly taking place in domestic service. Although child labour had been acknowledged as having a depressive effect on wages since the late 1930s, administrators had yet to come up with adequate controls over the phenomenon. Molohan counselled the strengthening of the Employment Ordinance along with an increase in the inspectorate staff of the labour department. Finally, employers were encouraged to play a greater role in meeting the social needs of their employees, including providing housing and other amenities and by establishing provident fund schemes for as many of their employees as possible. With regard to government housing policy, Molohan felt that greater emphasis should be placed on African construction and ownership of houses on serviced plots. 'If we are to encourage the formation of a stable and contented urban middle class African populace', he observed, 'house ownership must be encouraged in every way.'[38]

The position of women in the town also came under more active consideration. As the 1950s progressed, welfare work among African townswomen had been identified as playing an important part in the wider design of stabilisation and the growth of citizenship.[39] Increasingly, the uneducated partners of urban workers were viewed as exerting a regressive influence on both their husbands and children. 'There can be no real advance of raising of the standard of life among Africans', observed a *Standard* editorial in 1952, 'until African women become educated and show some desire for better living conditions, for more personal belongings, and a pride in themselves, their clothes and their homes.'[40] In *Detribalization*, Molohan advised 'that more encouragement should be given, and training facilities made available, for women to obtain paid employment'. Although opportunities in industry were 'not as yet very great', he found it 'ludicrous that domestic service in Tanganyika should be the perquisite of the male', recommending that plans for a training course for women in domestic service should be acted upon.[41] Increased female participation in the workforce would

---

[38] *Ibid.*, paras 95; 102; 106; 112; 156.
[39] This and the following paragraph is based on Burton, 'Townsmen'.
[40] *TS*, 1 March 1952.
[41] Molohan, *Detribalization*, para. 103. However, male predominance in domestic service continued up to and after independence, see Bujra, *Serving Class*.

not only free male labour from unproductive employment, but it would also facilitate the process of stabilisation among lower-paid African urban workers. As the report pointed out '[a]t current wage rates a man and his wife who are prepared to do a proper day's work should be able jointly to earn a handsome wage and in congenial surroundings.'

However, it was anticipated that most women would be coming to the towns for the first time to live with their husbands as wives and not as workers. This category of immigrant was seen as being particularly vulnerable and ill-prepared for an urban existence. 'She is', states the report, 'bemused by the town way of life and often in need of advice and assistance'. Molohan believed the inculcation of urban domesticity among this category of women would have beneficial effects for the wellbeing of themselves, their husbands and their children. Accordingly, he recommended that 'increased facilities for both the formal and informal education of women are necessary throughout the territory and particularly in the towns … [O]nly in this way will the general standard of living be improved'.[42] Although with the implementation of a policy of stabilisation women acquired a place in the colonial urban vision, it was strictly an ancillary position: independent African townswomen remained marginalised. Revealingly, although the proportion of unmarried adult female migrants was rising during the 1950s — from 13 percent before 1952 to 36 percent in 1956 — no explicit consideration in the formation of policy was given to this section of the population.[43] While African townswomen had to a certain extent lost their 'invisibility' thanks to the post-war development agenda and the encouragement of African family residence in the towns, the 'proper' place for the African woman remained either beside their husbands or, failing that, in their rural areas of origin.

Administrative reform in late-colonial Dar es Salaam

Both central government and the provincial administration were by now conscious of the consequences of inaction, and many of Molohan's recommendations were implemented in the closing years of colonial rule. In the late 1950s the district establishment was expanded, with the District Office itself being moved to Ilala in 1958 and administrative officers posted to the Wards, having their offices attached to local courts.[44] There was also a substantial reorganisation of the African administration. By 1960, the number of *Wakili* was doubled from four to eight and an additional two headmen

42 Molohan, *Detribalization*, paras 103; 148–9. The policies towards women in the towns outlined in *Detribalization* were subsequently endorsed by participants at the Ndola Conference and adopted as recommended policy for the British colonies throughout the region. See 'Ndola Report', p. 28.

43 These statistics have been derived from the 1971 Tanzanian Urban Mobility, Employment and Income Survey by Nwanganga Shields, 'Women in the Urban Labour Markets of Africa: The case of Tanzania', *World Bank Staff Papers*, 380 (April 1980), cited in Susan Geiger, *TANU Women*, pp. 38–9.

44 1959 PAR, p. 23.

installed.[45] In the same year, the peri-urban *Wakili*-ates of Kunduchi, Kigamboni and Mbagalla were transferred to the municipality and placed under the direct control of the Dar es Salaam District Office. Moreover, so-called vigilance committees were established in the town during the late 1950s, with District Office, police, and African official (*Majumbe*) and unofficial (Ward Council) representation, in order '[t]o encourage and foster cooperation between the people and the Police in the maintenance of Law and Order'.[46] For the first time since 1919 substantial resources were devoted to Dar es Salaam's African administration. Government, belatedly aware of the importance of the urban African population, recognised the pressing need for more sophisticated methods aimed at its guidance and control.

There were also significant shifts in labour policy. A budget survey of Africans in Dar es Salaam conducted in 1956/7, around the same time Molohan was writing his report, found the position largely unchanged from the early 1950s.[47] The workforce remained characterised by its poverty, its impermanence, its unreliability and its lack of productivity. Leslie observed a vicious circle of inefficiency: 'So long as there is an abundance of low-quality labour at low rates of pay, the labourer has no incentive to improve output, nor the employer to improve the quality of his staff.'[48] Molohan's report signalled an important move towards better pay and stabilisation.

The benefits of regularisation of the workforce had long been recommended. However, the only group among whom it had occurred prior to 1957 was the dockworkers. As we have seen, port employers had actually attempted some form of de-casualisation before 1950. The calamitous events associated with the strike in February that year strengthened the employers' hand and in its wake registration of casual labour occurred. As port traffic increased, the registered pool of labourers actually grew over the next few years — from 1,815 men in 1950 to 3,164 men in 1953. Thereafter, increased mechanisation, alongside a more efficient use of labour, resulted in a dramatic reduction in the numbers employed at the port: the registered casual pool falling to 2,220 in December 1954, 1,792 in January 1958 and 1,306 just seven months later (still 300 too many according to the annual labour report). At the same time, productivity increased: average tonnage handled per man was almost 45 percent higher in the first quarter of 1954 than that handled during the same period two years earlier.[49] Further legal controls over dock labour were introduced in 1955, regularising recruitment of dockers, wage rates and conditions of employment.[50] In tandem with these controls over their work, dockers were, according to Iliffe, 'becoming a more prosperous, better treated, and less militant group'. From late 1955, wage increases at

[45] Political, Dsm to Direstabs, Dsm, 13 August 1959, TNA/226/PM.110/67/037.
[46] See Dep. PC, Dsm to DC, Dsm (?), 3 November 1958, TNA/225/UW.80.131/Vol. 1.
[47] Budget survey of African consumers in Dar es Salaam 1956/7, TNA/225/PA.8/06A.
[48] Leslie, *Survey*, p. 6.
[49] Iliffe, 'Dockworkers', pp. 140–1; Shivji, *Law*, p. 177.
[50] The Dockworkers (Regulation of Employment) Ordinance, GN No. 20 of 1953 (implemented in 1955) and Dar es Salaam Dockworkers (Regulation of Employment) Order, GN No. 222 of 1955. See Shivji, *Law*, p. 177.

last began to outpace inflation: for the first time since 1939 dockworkers' incomes were on an upward trend. By 1956 they received three times the wage of an unskilled labourer. In 1959, the pool of casuals was dispensed with and all dockworkers were employed on permanent terms — the number engaged being further reduced to 1,200 men.[51]

By the time Molohan submitted his report to government, evidence of a changing policy towards urban labour as a whole was becoming more apparent. In April 1957, the Wages Regulation (Area of Dar es Salaam Municipality) Order for the first time set down a legal minimum wage applicable to all urban employers, public *and* private.[52] Wages were raised from the prevailing daily rate of Shs. 2–2/50 to the statutory rate of Shs. 3/ 36, giving a monthly wage of just under Shs. 90/-.[53] Leslie concluded from the results of a June 1957 re-survey of individuals covered in his original research (conducted the previous year) that the introduction of the minimum wage was 'fairly effective in raising to the minimum level the wages of those hitherto below it'.[54] About a fifth of the urban workforce were said to have benefited from the order, and by 1958 66 percent of all African adult male wage-earners received over Shs. 100/- per month. In the following year, this had increased to 68 percent, and wages offered by most major employers in the town started at between Shs. 115 and 130/-.[55] This represented a substantial improvement on the position in the early 1950s.[56]

Despite the introduction of the minimum wage, however, many workers remained underpaid — in some cases by mutual consent with their employers in order to obtain work at a time when urban unemployment was rife.[57] According to the *Report of the Territorial Minimum Wages Board* (the 'Chesworth Report'), appointed in August 1961, the wages order was 'ignored by large numbers of employers, particularly in the fields of retail distribution, smaller hotels, and bars, casual work, and domestic servants employed by certain classes [sic] of the community'.[58] In addition, more economical use of labour in the wake of its implementation only served to exacerbate the unemployment problem.[59] However, increased efficiency was an important aim of stabilisation, and if this entailed a reduction in the workforce — as was the case with the dockworkers — then that price had to be paid. '[O]ne of the most valuable results of the minimum wage', observed Leslie,

[51] Iliffe, 'Dockworkers', pp. 140–4; Leslie, *Survey*, p. 105.

[52] GN No. 80 of 1957.

[53] Mins of Labour Department Conference, Dodoma, 5–7 June 1957, PRO/CO/822/1632; see also Shivji, *Law*, p. 135.

[54] Leslie, *Survey*, p. 127.

[55] Chesworth Report, p. 11; 1959 Labour AR, p. 49.

[56] In December 1952, when the cost of living index stood at 110, it had been estimated that two-thirds of the workforce earned under Shs. 90/-; in December 1959, when the index had only increased to 116, more than two-thirds of employees were earning over Shs. 100/-. See the Retail Price Index in Labour ARs.

[57] Leslie, *Survey*, p. 126; 1959 Labour AR, p. 49.

[58] Chesworth Report (Dsm, 1962), p. 11.

[59] Mins of Labour Department Conference, Dodoma, 5–7 June 1957, p. 4, PRO/CO/822/ 1625; 1959 Labour AR, p. 49; Chesworth Report, p. 32. See Burton, 'Raw youth'.

was that it drove a number of unnecessary men out of employment — a harsh human fact but economically speaking a tonic to both worker and employer, forcing the latter to prune staffs, consider schedules, tighten up supervision and begin to make a real effort to get value for money; where this happened the moral effect on remaining workers of having enough to do was equally advantageous.[60]

By the late 1950s, there were signs that the African workforce was indeed 'stabilising'. A 'gradual accretion of settled workers' encouraged the transition from a casual, migrant labour force to one that was better paid and more permanent.[61] This trend was consolidated by housing policy initiatives, which also served to promote stabilisation. One involved the reinvigoration of the African Urban Housing Loan Scheme, established in the mid 1950s to assist more affluent Africans in constructing their own homes. This had met with little initial success. However, after the required deposit was reduced and building specifications relaxed, demand grew. The favoured type of house built was of the six-room Swahili type (though in permanent materials), which provided the owner with the opportunity to earn an income from renting out rooms not used by his own family. Towards the end of the decade, however, preference was given to those constructing family 'homes with individuality and privacy'. 'Home ownership', as opposed to 'house ownership' based on the 'economies of a boarding house', was encouraged.[62]

Respectable African urbanism

One of the principal objectives of late-colonial policy was to nurture an African community in Dar es Salaam that was sympathetic to the orderly urban vision of European administrators and planners. Stabilisation was a key part of this project. The family man accompanied by his wife and children, in long-term, remunerative employment, and occupying — ideally owning — a comfortable urban home, was the model adopted in opposition to the seemingly ever-increasing preponderance of shiftless, underemployed, young single migrants who bedevilled the official imagination.[63] Success in this regard was in part a product of earlier processes of differentiation that were evident long before the adoption of the new urban policy. As we have seen,

---

[60] Leslie, *Survey*, p. 134.
[61] Iliffe, *Modern History*, p. 541; 'Chesworth Report', p. 7. A 1958 survey found that in one (unspecified) urban area as many as 25% of the population 'no longer had roots in their villages' (Mins of 13th Conference of East African Labour Commissioners, Nairobi, 17–19 November 1958 PRO/CO/822/1630). Nevertheless, at the end of the colonial period the 'Chesworth Report' noted the persistence of poverty and indebtedness among urban workers, and the continuing inadequacy of most wages to cover the costs of an urban family.
[62] OiC Afriloans to Development Secretary, 19 March 1959, TNA/225/DC01/3/3; Leslie, *Survey*, p. 156.
[63] *Wahuni*, observed DC Harris, 'had the least to lose in terms of property and valuable employment'. *Donkey's Gratitude*, p. 343.

an emerging elite was present, who in the 1930s already voiced similar concerns to those expressed by officials over 'indiscriminate' urbanisation.[64] The social distance between this elite and the urban poor was great. According to Norman Pearson, who visited Tanganyika as a trade unions adviser in the late 1940s, 'educated Africans tend to hold themselves aloof from the common people in the towns.' 'It has been said', he continued, 'that there is a greater gulf between the well-educated and the uneducated African, than there is between the latter and some Europeans.'[65] 'The educated class, generally clerks', confirmed a 1952 social welfare report, 'were social snobs' who 'were not prepared to mix' with the 'largely illiterate' manual workers.[66] The presence of unpropertied *wahuni* was viewed as a threat by such respectable Africans, while their unruly behaviour was an affront to elite sensibility. 'We, under the British government today', wrote Lawi Kardi in 1957, bemoaning urban lawlessness, 'are in fear of every kind.' To counter the growth of the *wahuni*, Justino Mponda, a UMCA-educated African member of the Legco, in the same year encouraged the administration to introduce 'African productivity schemes':

[In] the hope that the time wasted by the number of Africans roaming about the trading centres and big towns would be spent in increasing production and those who were not employed would return to their respective districts and join in the shamba development.[67]

Anxiety over the presence of the *wahuni* paralleled concerns among the more 'traditional' elite. 'It is high time', hereditary chief Msabila Lugusha informed the Legco in 1953, 'that the large number of idlers in the town are reduced to the lowest number possible.'[68]

Late-colonial reforms sought to entrench 'respectability' among the beneficiaries of stabilisation, not only through a revised labour policy but also through local government and Social Development Department initiatives. With the introduction of urban Ward Councils officials aimed at nurturing responsible African townsmen, planting a civic identity among the formerly 'detribalised'. Social development officers, meanwhile, were responsible for preparing 'plans which will both stimulate the growth of new social groups and will also teach the skills necessary to successful and happy living in the towns'.[69] However, these initiatives did not always produce the desired result.[70] The higher wages, which formed an integral part of a revised labour policy, for example, instead of encouraging a more respectable, settled

[64] See above, pp. 73–6.
[65] Pearson, 'Trade Unionist', p. 225.
[66] Colonial Social Welfare Advisory Committee, Reports Sub-Cttee mins, 4 November 1952, PRO/CO/822/675.
[67] *TS*, 18 June 1957, p. 4; 20 September 1957, p. 4. For Mponda, see Liebenow, *Colonial Rule*, pp. 180–1.
[68] *TS*, 5 December 1953, p. 12; see also Mins of Second Convention of Representative Chiefs of Tanganyika, 6–8 January 1958, TNA/225/80070.
[69] Commissioner for Social Development to MLG, Statement of Policy of the Soc. Devt Dept, 28 November 1955, TNA/17396.
[70] For the failings of local government and social development, see Burton, 'Townsmen'.

lifestyle, could actually lead to the promotion of an unrespectable modernity, that both officials and elite Africans viewed with disdain.[71] Leslie was disappointed to find among dockworkers, the one section of the blue-collar workforce to have received significant salary hikes at the time of his survey, that although they had 'escaped poverty … they have not put the additional money into attaining … a permanently better standard of life'. Instead they indulged in conspicuous consumption. It was 'well known to all that a docker never lacks for a girl or a drink'. According to Leslie, they were likely adherents of what he termed 'the cult of the cowboy', a working-class fashion involving the acquisition of such expensive accoutrements as the wide-brimmed hat, tasselled shirt, tight jeans and suede boots. With this *de rigueur* apparel went slang derived from Western films and an anti-establishment philosophy. Instead of becoming paragons of proletarian respectability, dockworkers — more than half of whom were, according to Leslie, Zaramo or Rufiji — were in some cases providing negative role models for the many uneducated migrants in the town, who aspired to their lifestyle without having the wherewithal to pay for it.[72]

Nevertheless, partly as a result of shifts in policy, a class of urban Africans emerged in the town, who, thanks to property, occupation or position, had a vested interest in the maintenance of 'order', and who after independence were to ensure there was significant continuity in urban policy.[73] Molohan observed the existence of 'the nucleus of an African middle class which enjoys a relatively comfortable standard of living and regards itself as a different and superior stratum of African society', consisting of clerks and small-scale entrepreneurs and traders.[74] Above all, it was those who had a school certificate standard education or above — 0.1 percent of the urban population — to whom the future belonged. 'Those who can look forward to an improving status, pay and standard of living', observed Leslie, 'are mainly the educated, for whom prospects are indeed rosy, with the chance of very rapid promotion as Africanization gathers speed.'[75] Alongside these enhanced career prospects, they were given preferential treatment when it came to housing. Plotholders in Block W, Magomeni — an area planned at a lower density than other African areas and with higher building standards, set aside for the emerging elite by government — were notable beneficiaries of the African Urban Housing Loans Scheme.[76] Wealthier Africans also obtained favoured access to government quarters, in which better living conditions and amenities were available at a lower rent than those prevailing in private

---

[71] Moyer ('Shadow', p. 91) reaches similar conclusions about the impact of developmentalism in contemporary Dar es Salaam: 'If development does indeed bring about modernization and modernity', she writes, 'then it brings about a modernity that looks quite different from the Western Euro-American modernities that many of those engaged in the development process expect.'

[72] Leslie, *Survey*, pp. 105; 112; 131; Leslie interview.

[73] See Burton, 'Haven'.

[74] Molohan, *Detribalization*, para.128.

[75] *Ibid.*, p. 130.

[76] Kironde, 'Land use', p. 319.

accommodation. According to Leslie, occupants 'had to be better off than the mass of the population', preference being given to those with a wage not under Shs. 150/-. Just 15 percent of respondents in his survey received such a wage, and occupants of quarters were overwhelmingly drawn from the 'clerical and [skilled] artisan class'.[77]

By the mid 1950s, a sense of ownership of the town, not dissimilar to European attitudes before WWII, had emerged among this privileged urban class. An African clerk who came to DO Cairns' aid after his car broke down in Magomeni, for example, had a clear sense of his place in Dar es Salaam. Some Africans who were by the roadside and had refused to assist Cairns, were dismissed by this clerk in

> horn-rimmed glasses ... black shoes, white cotton socks, white drill shorts and stiff white shirt: 'These are savages, sir. Bush men. Very dangerous.' He leaned closer and spoke confidentially. 'We must be very careful of such people in *our* town'.[78]

The Ndola Conference

In 1958, a major conference on 'Urban Problems in East and Central Africa' was held in Ndola, on the Northern Rhodesian Copperbelt. Attended by administrative and social services officials from throughout the region, conference discussion and the final report served to reconfirm policies of stabilisation as advocated by Molohan, Carpenter and others (notably a family wage and home ownership).[79] Nevertheless, the conclusions eventually arrived at by conference participants were in the event modest and cautious; a reflection perhaps, of the widely differing circumstances found in each of the participating territories. It was observed that the 'division of labour', a process that was held to be accelerating in the region, should be encouraged. This was important both for reasons of industrial efficiency and from the point of view of establishing a more affluent — and 'progressive' — agricultural sector in which increasingly cash crops were produced on land held under individual tenure. An 'essential part of this process [was] the stabilisation of some Africans as town-dwellers'.[80] On the other hand, it was considered wise that not all African workers' links with their rural homes should be severed. The colonial state could not afford to provide for old

---

[77] Leslie, *Survey*, pp. 173–4; and Appendices. Leslie also observed a cultural preference for quarters that 'in particular appealed to the man who wanted to live with his own family, and to have some of the modern amenities ... they have not appealed to the traditional Coastal man who is not so interested in privacy as in company who prefers to live with others of his kind in the traditional areas and housing of Dar es Salaam'. *Ibid.*, p. 151.

[78] *Bush and Boma*, p. 139. Emphasis added.

[79] According to an undated (*c.*1956) Proposal for a Professional Conference on Urban Problems in East and Central Africa in PRO/CO/955/40, it was 'assumed that policy in all territories is now directed towards the growth of a permanent African population in the towns'.

[80] 'Ndola Report', p. 5, TNA/225/UW80.131/Vol. 1.

people or those made redundant in the event of recession. Better to maintain a proportion of migrant labour and for some of the Africans who spent their working lives in towns to be encouraged to retire to the countryside. Nevertheless, stabilisation was identified as the key to the new urban policy. The need to restrict urban citizenship to a limited class of formally employed Africans was highlighted in the final section of the conference report — on the 'control over movements of Africans to, within, and out of urban areas'. At the outset, the consequences of a policy of urban stabilisation for such movement was identified:

> Possibility of gainful employment and the amenities of towns are liable to act as a magnet to rural populations, and in particular to the young men from the villages. There is, therefore, a tendency for more people to drift to the towns than the towns can readily absorb; and the surplus is apt to become a danger to law and order and/or a social security problem.

It was recognised that the long-term solution was an improvement of economic conditions in the rural areas. In the meantime, administrators would have to make do with the piecemeal — and largely ineffective — measures already in place in the various territories. With regard to removing those unwanted immigrants who had reached the towns it was concluded that:

> Where there is a lack of balance between urban and rural economies or where there is no system of social security operative in the towns, we consider that there should be provision for sending back to their last place of permanent residence unemployed or underemployed persons who are not permanently urbanised and who cannot reasonably be expected to secure employment in the immediate future.[81]

As was also the case with both the EARC report and Molohan's *Detribalization*, there was no acknowledgment of the role that informal economic activities could play in providing a livelihood to the growing number of town-dwellers. These represented a loss of control over the urban arena, and not the reassertion of government influence over the course of urban development officials were attempting to achieve.

The recommendations made by conference participants were broadly in line with the existing policy of the Tanganyikan government and were endorsed in a despatch by R.H. Gower, the Governor's Deputy.[82] Indeed, Gower indicated the Tanganyikan government's prior implementation of many of the proposals made by officials at Ndola. He could thus boast of the high proportion of African-owned houses in Dar es Salaam and of the 'comprehensive wage' received by the majority of urban workers. The unanimity displayed between the authors of the report and Tanganyikan

[81] *Ibid.*, pp. 63 and 69.
[82] R.H. Gower to SSCol, 22 June 1959, PRO/CO/955/83. The one area with which issue was taken was the wisdom of establishing a state-administered social security scheme. Tanganyikan officials displayed a distinct reluctance to assume the burden of social insurance.

officials was hardly surprising. By 1958, most of the arguments raised at Ndola had been well rehearsed and a consensus had emerged among those responsible for the administration of urban areas throughout British East and Central Africa. The Ndola Conference simply served to strengthen this consensus, while at the same time giving an opportunity to discuss the ways and means of achieving the fundamental objectives of late-colonial policy.

In the course of British colonial rule perceptions of the urban arena had been transformed. Viewed as a moral sink in the inter-war years, by the 1950s the towns were acknowledged as an ideal location in which to mould a new non-tribal (not 'detribalised') African, who had internalised Western attitudes to work, and whose tribal values had been replaced by civic ones. However, the state of the colonial economy restricted the number of Africans who would form the new urban communities. Urbanisation among the remainder of the African population continued to promote anxiety. Existing outside the planned residential estates and employment in the formal sector, this African *residuum* was as much as ever a cause for concern. At the same time as the African urban presence was gradually accepted, a stricter definition of what constituted a 'legitimate' town-dweller was inserted in successive versions of the Townships (Removal of Undesirable Natives/Persons) Ordinance. In 1944, in order to have a right to urban residence you had to have paid poll tax in a town the previous year. A decade later this was amended to having lived in a town for eighteen months out of the past three years. In 1958, qualification was extended to four out of the past five years. The colonial urban vision was always an exclusive one. What a policy of stabilisation required was

> people with regular employment who can settle down to a stable life and by being good citizens can make their contribution to the high reputation that the capital of Tanganyika should enjoy.[83]

While the 1950s was a time when the respectable Africans' place in the colonial urban vision was at last confirmed, it was also a time when more concerted action was simultaneously taking place against the growing numbers of Africans who did not fit this vision. In their forty years in Tanganyika the British had helped create a society in which the lure of the towns grew ever stronger. They had also been engaged in a constant struggle against the consequences of this attraction. With no dramatic transformation of the underdeveloped Tanganyikan economy on the horizon, the principal weapon in this struggle remained attempts to control the mobility of the African population.

[83] Gov. Twining's speech at the opening of Ilala Boma, 20 May 1958, TNA/540/27/11/A.

Twelve

Purging the Town

The Removal of Undesirables
1941–61

The rapid growth of Dar es Salaam's African population in the last two decades of colonial rule placed a district administration, lacking the financial resources, the manpower, and even — having as it did but limited knowledge about the movements, motivations and activities of African urban residents — the imagination to deal with this phenomenon, under increasing pressure to retain control over the urban arena. Informal economic activity and the construction of unauthorised housing became increasingly common. The municipal and district administrations exercised minimal influence over such initiatives, and while these activities provided needy individuals with an income and home, they remained technically illegal, and were generally perceived as illegitimate by urban officials. Their emergence signalled a loss of colonial control; as did the post-war rise in crime. In apportioning blame for these urban ills, officials were inclined to point to African immigration as the principal factor. Tackling the 'surplus' urban African population was an essential element in any attempt to reassert control. Although urban administrators had always disparaged the presence of jobless Africans in the town, only rarely between the wars was action taken against individuals on these grounds alone. From the early 1940s, such action came to be seen as entirely justified and occurred with growing regularity. A system of raids emerged whose objectives included the apprehension of tax defaulters, but which over time increasingly targeted the unemployed and underemployed.

Influx control initiatives

The issue of influx control slipped off the agenda immediately after WWII. This can be attributed both to the decline in unemployment that occurred in the late 1940s and to the difficulty in coming up with a system of controlling African mobility that would satisfy both urban administrators and officials in the Secretariat and at the Colonial Office, who were sensitive to potential criticism from UN overseers. However, in the early 1950s serious unemployment re-emerged, which this time would not go away. The many thousands of Africans making their way to Dar es Salaam overwhelmed an urban formal economy failing to create employment at a sufficient rate. Urban employment had expanded from around 31,000 in work in late 1952 to 37,000 in late 1956.[1] With the population growing at an annual rate of around 6,000 to 8,000 (see Table 10.1), this was woefully insufficient. In 1954, the *Tanganyika Standard* reported the presence of around 20,000 unemployed Africans in and around town.[2] An overstretched urban infrastructure, alongside increasing unemployment and underemployment, formed the backdrop for a renewed outbreak of official anxiety about urban growth, in the course of which arguments about the desirability, practicality and morality of influx control all surfaced once again.

In the post-war period, in the absence of the more comprehensive legislation that many officials desired, district staff in Dar es Salaam continued to rely upon Cap. 104 (the Townships (Removal of Undesirable Natives) Ordinance) and the Employment of Women and Young Persons Ordinance to deal with the surplus population. In order to stem the flow of juveniles to the town, 'continual and active steps' were taken to ensure that sections 3(a) and 4 of the latter — which prohibited the employment of children except under certain conditions — were observed.[3] The principal weapon against unwanted immigrants, though, remained Cap. 104. As more and more Africans found their way to the capital, repatriation through the use of this ordinance became an increasingly common phenomenon. Despite its importance to urban administrators, however, it was not immune from criticism. '[A]ny severe application of this law', acknowledged the acting Chief Secretary in 1946, 'or any extension of the control of movement of persons, would be an invasion of the liberty of the subject.'[4] Moreover, officials in Whitehall remained distinctly uneasy. The Kenya Government, in May 1946, had attempted to have an ordinance along similar lines endorsed by the Colonial Office. It was reported later that Creech Jones, the Colonial Secretary,

> objected to 'its discriminatory nature, which is reflected both in its title and provisions'. In addition he considered that the provisions imposed drastic conditions on the rights of the individual which could not be justified ... and he doubted whether there were adequate safeguards to ensure its proper administration.[5]

[1] Report on developments in the sphere of industrial relations in Dsm, Aug–Dec 1956, Department of Labour to CO (Secret), 24 January 1957, PRO/CO/822/1625.
[2] *TS*, 28 December 1954. This figure was disputed by the Labour Department, but it was probably a fair reflection of underemployment at least. As Leslie observed in 1957, unemployment was 'not at all a clear-cut term', there being 'a very large number of irregular jobs ... last[ing] anything from a few minutes to a day' alongside 'temporary jobs' lasting a month or so. Leslie, *Survey*, p. 121.
[3] Mins of DCs' conference, EP, 2 September 1946, TNA/61/502/pt. 1.
[4] Legco questions, 25 July 1946, TNA/20887/Vol. II.
[5] Quoted in Memo. no. 68, 6 May 1952, TNA/21616/Vol. III.

He went on to state his desire that early steps be taken to repeal the equivalent ordinance in Tanganyika. The Tanganyika Government was instructed to consult with Kenya over the terms of a new ordinance to replace Cap. 104.[6] In response to these criticisms the application of the ordinance, in January 1947, was restricted to six major townships: Dar es Salaam, Morogoro, Tanga, Korogwe, Moshi and Arusha. However, this remained the extent of the action taken by officials, who, appearing to stall for time, failed to respond to further Colonial Office correspondence on the issue after a revised ordinance was passed in Kenya in September 1949.[7]

If these were indeed delaying tactics, then the motivation behind them is readily apparent. Far from going away, concern over rural–urban migration re-emerged with particular force after the violent outcome of the 1950 strike. Heightened public awareness of urban lawlessness led to growing demands to tackle the 'surplus' urban population. 'No law-abiding citizen', wrote the editor of the *Tanganyika Standard* in March 1950,

> will oppose any step taken to eliminate all doubtful characters from our midst … [T]he faster these undesirables of no fixed abode or occupation are sent out of town and back to their own villages, the sooner will it be possible for their housing accommodation to be made available to really deserving cases at present living in overcrowded quarters.[8]

A correspondent to the newspaper advocated the introduction of a pass system, a policy endorsed later in the year by the Dar es Salaam Chamber of Commerce who 'wanted to see a system of registration as comprehensive as possible — like the *kipande* system in Kenya, which recorded past employment and wages'.[9] The *Standard* thought the Chamber's proposals deserved 'full support'. Registration would

> enable the authorities to check up immediately on all and sundry; it would eliminate the presence in the towns of parasites living on their fellows and would make the task of those concerned far easier in running to earth any illegal immigrants in our midst.[10]

To the dismay of the *Standard*, however, no such system was introduced. After a series of robberies three years later, the paper's editor returned to the subject:

> From such lawlessness it can be assumed that there must be hundreds, probably thousands, of people wandering the streets of the town without regular employment which would do away with the necessity to resort to crime for a livelihood, and it is a known fact that most of these are Africans without any means of support whatsoever, who pass the night on the lookout for easy money, unless asleep in the corner of some hovel or other.

[6]   E.L. Scott to P. Rogers (CO), 30 November 1950, PRO/CO/691/208/42431. *Ibid.*
[7]   Letters in February and April 1950 from the CO were ignored. PRO/CO/691/208/42431.
[8]   *TS*, 18 March 1950, p. 21.
[9]   Letter from 'Old Resident', *TS*, 9 February 1950; 1 July 1950.
[10] *TS*, 1 April 1950, p. 20.

These homeless, jobless, ne'er-do-wells have no intention of doing an honest day's work, and what is worse, they never will work so long as they can remain in town with little fear of being found out.[11]

While settler opinion lined up behind some form of registration of Africans, Africans themselves were resolutely opposed to such measures. 'It must be clear to all concerned', wrote Kenneth Msomali in a letter to the *Standard*,

> that the Africans do not want to have that silly system of *kipande* that inconvenienced so much our African brothers in Kenya. Time and again Africans used to be stopped by the Kenya police who would ask them to produce their *kipande*.
> … It is premature at present to introduce any system of identification upon the African. Do you think your *kipande* or ID card will have any meaning to a Mgogo or Mporoto? The answer is: No, thank you. The African wants nothing of a passport for his identification.[12]

In April 1950, when the municipal Public Health Committee recommended that the attention of central Government be drawn to the need to control migration to the town so that overcrowding could be alleviated, an African councillor, Ali Meli, argued against the proposals on the ground that this was 'a political measure rather than one of health'. Unsurprisingly, his amendment was defeated.[13]

Despite African disquiet over population control measures and Colonial Office anxiety about Cap. 104, the Tanganyikan administration was unwilling to concede ground on the issue. In his eventual reply to correspondence from London, Surridge, the Chief Secretary, dismissed concerns over the liberty of the colonial subject under prevailing conditions. With the urban infrastructure under strain, he argued, 'methods of control which might not be justifiable in normal times should be allowed.' Cap. 104 was, in any case, regarded by Dar es Salaam officials 'more in the light of a humanitarian measure by which the DC can repatriate quasi-criminals rather than imprison them'.[14] The Colonial Office nevertheless continued to urge milder legislation. Officials in Dar es Salaam retorted that the maintenance of the existing ordinance was the very least that was required in the circumstances.[15]

In May 1952, as a sop to Whitehall, it was suggested that Cap. 104 be scrapped but that repatriations should continue as usual under the Destitute Persons Ordinance, which gave similar powers over unemployed Africans. After discussion by the Executive Council, however, the proposal was rebuffed as the time was 'inappropriate'. '[I]n view of the opposition to the withdrawal of the Ordinance locally', it was observed, 'it would be very difficult to make

---

[11] *TS*, 27 February 1954, p. 4.
[12] *TS*, 6 May 1950, p. 27.
[13] *TS*, 15 April 1950, p. 10.
[14] Surridge to Rogers, 4 January 1951, TNA/21616/Vol. III.
[15] The Attorney General, for instance, held that 'the most effective course would be to have Cap. 104 plus provision for registration'. Min., 31 March 1952, TNA/21616/Vol. III.

any change now.'[16] Indeed, towards the end of the year, Governor Twining requested permission from the Colonial Office to extend the application of Cap. 104 to three more towns: Mwanza, Musoma and Shinyanga. 'I consider', he wrote,

> that in spite of the objections which have been raised to its continued use, the Ordinance should continue in force and I must emphasize that I am supported in this view by responsible public, as well as official, opinion.[17]

In the face of the persistent defence of Cap. 104, the Colonial Office finally conceded that it could remain on the statute book. However, Whitehall insisted the ordinance be amended: first, to remove the 'unfettered discretion of the executive' bestowed by the existing legislation (under which appeal against decisions by a DC was to the Provincial Commissioner), and second, to address its racially discriminatory nature. In July 1953 an amended ordinance was passed.[18] It enabled, in theory, action to be taken against undesirable *persons* not just natives, and appeal was allowed to the District Court (with eventual appeal to the High Court). Meanwhile, the stipulation that in order to prove urban residence an individual should be liable to house tax, or to have paid municipal poll tax for the current and previous year, was also changed: the new stipulations requiring either parents legally residing in the town or the ability to prove residence there for at least eighteen months out of the last two years.

While secretariat officials may have been satisfied with the retention of Cap. 104, urban administrators were soon urging once again the need for further controls. 'Constant, uncontrolled and uncontrollable immigration', complained the DC in 1953, 'is a very serious problem and must if allowed to continue, ultimately threaten the whole working of the Municipality.'[19] He bemoaned the inefficacy of the existing machinery for tackling the surplus population. Those responsible for housing in the city were equally concerned. Earlier in the year the Director of Town Planning had written of a 'basic error … in quietly accepting the phenomenal increase of African population in towns'. 'Some means', he concluded, 'will have to be found of limiting this continual immigration from country areas, if only to put a firm limit on the urban housing problem.' The Labour Commissioner likewise viewed the situation with some anxiety.[20]

A number of proposals were put forward from various quarters to address the situation. In its 1952 annual report, the Town Planning Department announced a regional plan based 'on the thesis of providing a ring of satellite settlements around Dar es Salaam, situated on the main radial roads focusing upon the town'. One of its principal objects was 'to provide attractive halting places for the current drift of population to the town' (as well as to produce

---

[16] Note for PCs' conference, July 1952, TNA/21616/Vol. III.
[17] Twining to Rogers, 21 November 1952, TNA/21616/Vol. III.
[18] Townships (Removal of Undesirable Persons) Ordinance, No. 15 of 1953.
[19] DAR for 1953, pp. 7–8.
[20] Min., 23 February 1953, TNA/225/DC/3602; 1953 Labour Dept. AR, p. 33.

food for the urban population).[21] The Labour Commissioner considered that compulsory registration at an Employment Exchange of all incomers to Dar es Salaam was a solution.[22] After a visit to Elisabethville, DC Harris advocated the introduction of identity cards such as those used in the Belgian Congo.[23] The issue was a perennial on the agenda of the Provincial Commissioners' conferences in the mid 1950s. Each time different recommendations were made, yet none were acted upon. In July 1954, Provincial Commissioners urged to restrict businesses using casual migrant labour in Dar es Salaam to employing just three or four casuals (unless the Labour Department permitted more), as was the case in Mombasa. In January the following year it was decided 'that a system of voluntary registration could with advantage be introduced in Dar es Salaam, and that this, while providing a most useful measure of control, would be acceptable generally to the African population'. Five months later, at their June conference, Provincial Commissioners discussed no fewer than fourteen measures aimed at solving the problem of African immigration into towns (a problem 'of long standing but one which is progressively becoming of greater urgency'). These included action to be taken in Dar es Salaam itself: such as the introduction of an African Authority in the township with the powers and responsibilities of a Native Authority; the registration of new arrivals; and compulsory education to the age of 15.[24] Several rural initiatives were promoted for discussion by the Commissioner for Eastern Province, who stressed that in Dar es Salaam it was 'apparent that unilateral action can do no more than maintain an already unsatisfactory status quo, at considerable expense'.[25] Compulsory registration, improvement of the machinery for removal of undesirables, and the application of a *cheti cha njia* (pass) system in the rural areas were all rejected once again. Policy recommendations emanating from central Government and/or Whitehall, were dismissed as impractical. The Commissioners questioned the wisdom of introducing a family wage in order to encourage stabilisation, noting that one of the consequences would be to 'militate against the control of immigration by attracting rural workers'. Meanwhile, propaganda to emphasise the expense and difficulties of urban life to rural-dwellers was ruled out, on the grounds that it could lead to a shortage of labour or to a demand for higher wages by urban workers. Measures to control African mobility were, throughout the 1940s and 1950s, repeatedly repudiated

21 1952 Town Planning AR, p. 12. The plans were at a 'preliminary stage' and appear not to have been implemented.
22 Labour Dept AR for 1953, p. 33.
23 Harris' scheme was vetoed on the grounds that 'it would probably be said to be an infringement of the liberty of the subject and liable to arouse political opposition.' Harris, *Donkey's Gratitude*, p. 320.
24 PCs' Conference mins, July 1954, Item 39(B); Jan. 1955, p. 31; June 1955, pp. 25–7 and App. D.
25 Only one of the fourteen proposals received the whole-hearted endorsement of the conference – the uncontroversial suggestion that a social survey of the immigrant and floating population be carried out in order to ascertain its seasonal fluctuations and motivations for the move to the town, which Leslie conducted in 1956.

on the basis of being impractical and/or politically unacceptable. However, with the urban administration under increasing strain from the flow of migrants, officials continued to lobby central Government for influx control measures that it was compelled to refuse.

In his 1957 report, Molohan, who had previously been a strong advocate of such measures, appeared to understand this predicament. He completely ruled out the introduction of a pass system to Tanganyika, principally on the basis of its cost and likely (in)effectiveness. However, the drift of population to the town was acknowledged as a pressing problem, and he put forward a number of other proposals to address the phenomenon, most of which were, for a change, acted upon.[26] To facilitate the operation of Cap. 104, power to repatriate individuals was extended to the *Liwali* and *Wakili*. Another amendment made proof of urban residence more demanding; the length of time necessary to have dwelt in the town was extended to four out of the previous five years.[27] As a further measure to discourage migration, an attempt was made to shift the cost of repatriation from Government (up till then costs had been covered by the provincial budget) on to the Native Authorities in the district to which undesirables were removed. Meanwhile, a voluntary registration scheme was initiated in Dar es Salaam, Arusha and Moshi, which it was hoped would 'strengthen the status of the respectable'.[28] While Molohan's recommendations predominantly covered urban initiatives, he nevertheless observed that 'systematic development' of the rural areas may result in 'the attractions of town life' diminishing and a reduction of rural–urban migration. He was in fact bullish about the impact improving rural conditions had already made:

> Since the end of WWII and more particularly during the last five years ... it is possible to detect a new trend in Tanganyika. While the urban areas continue to prove a magnet and attract the younger African ... there are signs that with the progressive economic development of the tribal areas and the introduction of more intensified and modern systems of agriculture, Africans are beginning to realise that with the greatly increased prices of agricultural products there are now as many, if not more, lucrative means of livelihood to be found on their own doorsteps than there were in the past and that it is as, if not more, profitable, and certainly less irksome, to work for oneself than for another for an equal and perhaps greater gain. The consequence has been a falling off in the number of men proceeding from certain tribal areas to the areas of employment, and I think it is unlikely that this tendency will decrease.[29]

[26] The 'Ndola Report' documents action taken upon Molohan's recommendations.

[27] The Townships (Removal of Undesirable Persons) (Amendment) Bill, 1958. For the Legco discussion, see Legco mins, 19 February 1958, pp. 65–7.

[28] CS to Gorell-Barnes, 27 March 1957. No records remain detailing the success or failure of this scheme, although with TANU so effectively organising opposition to the colonial government it is unlikely that there was much demand for the new identification cards. Molohan also recommended that a system of reporting the presence of new arrivals on a ward basis should be implemented in the town, and that the rules regulating casual labour in Mombasa should be examined with a view to duplicating them in Dar es Salaam. These proposals, like countless others over the years, do not appear to have been acted upon.

[29] Molohan, *Detribalization*, paras 4 and 94.

247

It was an overoptimistic appraisal. While a more dynamic rural economy was emerging in areas such as Chaggaland and Buhaya, and other areas were the focus of colonial development initiatives (for example, cotton production in Sukumaland or the Ubena Wattle Scheme), the rural parts of Eastern Province — from which the bulk of Dar es Salaam's population was drawn — were mostly underdeveloped and vulnerable to drought. In 1959, Eastern Province had the second smallest number of African agricultural marketing co-operatives in Tanganyika after Tanga Province (whose agriculture was dominated by the plantation sector) — just 27 compared to the 324 in Lake Province.[30] Conditions in the villages of Kisarawe, Rufiji and Bagamoyo districts did little to diminish the allure of the capital among their younger inhabitants. Moreover, the introduction of a minimum wage in Dar es Salaam in 1957 was followed in 1958 by a poor harvest in Eastern Province, both of which made the urban option considerably more attractive. At this time the decision was made to use propaganda once again in the rural areas in order to discourage movement to the capital. Upcountry, labour officers stressed the restricted opportunities for employment, while weekly radio broadcasts from Dar es Salaam transmitted the same cautionary message.[31] These efforts had little, if any, impact. The situation was complicated by the inappropriate schooling many officials felt rural children received, which triggered dissatisfaction with rural life and work among African youth. 'Districts sending their young folks to schools', a meeting of the Eastern Province Advisory Council observed in 1958, 'were "rewarded" by losing them to the towns.' 'Rural communities', the Council concluded, 'must be made more attractive.'[32] While lip service was paid towards the need to improve conditions in the rural areas, however, both the political will and the financial resources to take any action in this regard were noticeable by their absence. Instead, ongoing campaigns against undesirables, that had their origins in tax raids in the 1940s, remained the principal means of controlling the urban population.

Repatriation campaigns in the 1940s

Campaigns against tax-evaders were a perennial feature of life in Dar es Salaam in the last two decades of colonial rule; their frequency increased as the scale of evasion became ever more apparent.[33] While the apprehension of defaulters may have helped enhance colonial revenues, the 'chief significance' of the raids, as noted by DC Bone in 1945, was 'political and disciplinary'.[34] Payment of tax signified a form of submission to colonial authority and increasingly, as colonial discourse on African participation gathered pace, it constituted a civic responsibility. However, the 'political and disciplinary' function of the raids

[30] Coulsen, *Tanzania*, p. 68.
[31] Labour ARs, 1957, p. 43; 1958, pp. 5/19.
[32] *TS*, 26 June 1958, p. 5.
[33] For tax raids in the 1940s and 1950s, see Burton, 'Defaulter'.
[34] Uzaramo DAR, 1945, p. 5, TNA/61/504/1.

was by no means confined to fiscal issues. Indeed, over the final decades of colonial rule it was 'undesirables' rather than defaulters who became their primary target. Action against undesirables occurred as local officials from the early 1940s made increasingly arbitrary use of legislation that, it was claimed, existed for the benefit of the African (as well as the wider urban) community as a whole.

There is a good deal of irony in the timing of Justice McRoberts' ruling, in March 1941, that Township Rule 136(2) was an unjustifiable interference with the liberty of the colonial subject.[35] Up to this time the machinery for repatriation had generally been restricted to African criminals. In the years 1938, 1939 and 1940 only 32, 15 and 35 'undesirable sojourners with several criminal convictions' respectively were forcibly removed from the town using this legislation.[36] Exceptional use of it against unemployed Africans in the inter-war period occurred only at times of emergency such as the years following WWI, or in the early 1930s, when large-scale redundancies led to mass unemployment. It was actually after McRoberts' ruling that unemployed and underemployed Africans were singled out as a routine target of official action. Such measures were necessary in the eyes of urban administrators anxious about the re-emergence of joblessness. Writing immediately after the ruling, Baker argued that it was

> vital that unemployment and ill-doing must be checked so far as is possible in urban areas and, with this end in view, it is imperative that those who can find no work or are habitual criminals must be repatriated for their own good as well as that of the community.[37]

Such a view clearly carried weight. Within a month of Rule 136(2) being declared *ultra vires* new repatriation legislation had been introduced.[38]

These new regulations were soon put into operation. Records survive of the repatriation of 14 youths from Dar es Salaam in early September 1941.[39] In reporting the expulsion of a further six 'undesirable natives' two weeks later, DC Revington remarked upon the 'likelihood of many more being repatriated in the next few months as it is considered that any native who ... is unemployed is an undesirable'.[40] McRoberts' judgment clearly had no impact on the actions of urban officials. In 1942, the Commissioner for Prisons reported an 'abnormal number of Remand Juveniles' (83) received at Dar es Salaam. This followed a round-up of undesirables who had ignored earlier warnings to return to their rural homes.[41] Some indication of the impact of these repatriation campaigns on the African consciousness can be gauged by the reaction to the arrest of 15 African 'vagabonds' in May 1944.

[35] See chapter 5.
[36] PC Baker to CS, 12 March 1941, TNA/61/688/5.
[37] *Ibid.*
[38] See above, p. 106.
[39] See record dated 11 September 1941, TNA/61/688/5.
[40] DC Revington to PC, 24 September 1941, TNA/61/688/5.
[41] Cmmr for Prisons to CS, 4 November 1943, TNA/21122.

In the wake of this action, Baker reported whisperings in the township that 'Africans were being taken from their houses at night, loaded into lorries and taken to an unknown destination.'[42] It was rumoured that police had recently arrested 400 men in a single night. Such a figure is not entirely implausible. Three years later, in the last nine months of 1947, a total of 904 removal orders — which usually constituted a fraction of those picked up by the police in the first place — were made under Cap. 104.[43]

From the limited data to have survived, it appears that a high level of action was sustained throughout the war years as officials attempted to retain a grip on the town. A correspondent to the *Tanganyika Standard* in 1950 recalled:

> During the war Government decided that owing to the influx of Africans from up-country and the food situation in the town all Africans without work not domiciled in Dar es Salaam would be rounded up and sent back to their respective villages.[44]

By the end of the decade there is evidence of an even greater increase. The 904 Africans repatriated between March and December of 1947 indicate official determination to reassert control over the town after the strike in September that year. Following this, intermittent action continued to be taken. A year after the 1947 strike, the Superintendent of Police reassured members of the Township Authority that 'the problem of unemployed Africans was borne constantly in mind' by police officers in the town and periodic round-ups of undesirables were carried out as and when it was felt necessary.[45] Timothy Mayhew, whose first posting on arrival in Tanganyika in the late 1940s was as a DO in the Dar es Salaam office, recalled weekly raids in which a section of 'high density housing' was cordoned off before daybreak and '[t]hose with no fixed abode in the town were given government railway warrants to the stations nearest their homes and put on the train.'[46]

Repatriation campaigns in the 1950s

The trend towards the more frequent and indiscriminate use of repatriation legislation accelerated. By the mid 1950s Cap. 104 had become the principal means of controlling the rapidly expanding urban African population, and as many as 2,000 individuals were removed from the town annually. *Wahuni*

---

42 Baker to DC, Uzaramo, 29 May 1944, TNA/540/3/58. See White, *Vampires*, for a discussion of similar rumours in colonial East and Central Africa.

43 Uzaramo DAR for 1947, p. 16, TNA/540/1/4/B.

44 *TS*, 9 February 1950.

45 SP, reported at a Dsm TA meeting, 23 January 1948, TNA/540/27/3. A total of 385 removal orders under Cap. 104 were made in Eastern Province that year, the vast majority of which would have been from Dar es Salaam. The only other town in Eastern Province where Cap. 104 applied was Morogoro, from where in 1951 just one repatriation was made. EP response to Memo from MLG, 12 May 1952, TNA/21616/Vol. III.

46 Mayhew, 'Reminiscences', p. 18.

Table 12.1 *Repatriation of undesirable persons, Dar es Salaam, 1938–58*

1938	32
1939	15
1940	35
1947	904 (March–December)
1949	385 (Eastern Province)
1950	425 (-do-)
1951	234 (-do-)
1953	500
1954	1,094
	1,230*
1955	551 (January–September)
	1,027*
1956	638*
1957	2,335*
1958	2,034

*Includes prisoners immediately repatriated on release from Ukonga.

Sources: 1938–40 from PC Baker to CS, 12 March 1941, TNA 61/688/5; 1947 from Uzaramo DAR for 1947, p. 16, TNA 540/1/4/B; 1949–51 from info in TNA 21616, Vol. III; 1953 from PC, EP to MLG, 22 April 1954, TNA/28685; 1954, 1955 & 1958 from Qrtly Police Reports in TNA 90/1011, Vol. 1 (these may actually underrepresent the numbers repatriated — see footnote 54 & 56); 1954–7 figures from 1957 PAR.

(or 'spiv') raids, as they came to be known by the Police, also played a major role in restricting informal sector activities, apprehending tax defaulters, and more generally in the fight against crime. The first evidence of a more concerted campaign against undesirables is, predictably, connected with the strike in February 1950. By the end of the month a police 'drive' was on against 'spivs and drones, known undesirables, and others of dubious value to the town'. Three weeks later a 'very mixed bag' was reported to have been apprehended.[47] It was announced that the drive would continue, and 'to avoid inconvenience' employers were asked to supply their employees with a letter to establish them as 'respectable citizens'. Over the course of the year 425 removal orders were made in Eastern Province.[48] Intermittent raids continued to be staged. The following June, a morning sweep of Dar es Salaam and its outskirts was reported to have resulted in the arrest of 40 Africans 'who could not give a reasonable explanation of what they were doing at the time'.[49] The total number of removal orders served in Eastern Province in 1951 was 234.[50]

[47] TS, 18 March 1950, pp. 19,21.
[48] EP response to Memo. from MLG, 12 May 1952, TNA/21616/Vol. III.
[49] 'Some of the Africans who were picked up', it was reported, 'were sleeping on the beach and in the cemetery in Upanga Road'. TS, 2 June 1951, p. 17.
[50] EP response to Memo. from MLG, 12 May 1952, TNA/21616/Vol. III.

Towards the end of 1952 the scale of the repatriation campaigns escalated dramatically. On 7 November, in the largest operation of the kind conducted up to then, 676 African 'spivs' and tax-evaders were apprehended in raids on Wireless Village and other areas of the town.[51] After this, *wahuni* raids became a recurring feature of African urban life. A police report for the third quarter of 1953 records that 'a number' were carried out between July and September.[52] In the next quarter, six raids along with 'normal routine checks of undesirables ... by beat-duty constables' were reported to have resulted in the removal of 68 persons 'who were found to have nothing better to do than to hang about the centre of Dar es Salaam looking for what they could pick up'. In total, some 500 repatriations were executed in the course of the year.[53] By 1954 the campaigns were in full swing. In the first six months 31 raids netted 395 repatriatees.[54] Towards the end of June they were suspended, in part because the District Office had used up all its repatriation funds. However, further resources were soon pledged for this purpose, and while in the next quarter fewer raids were conducted, more than three times the number of people were screened: 2,307, of whom 400 were served with removal orders.[55] In the last quarter raids occurred almost every other day, and by the end of the year 1,094 Africans had been repatriated as 'undesirables'.[56] The following year, according to the Assistant Superintendent of Police, 'the rounding-up of "spivs" ... continued unabated, with gratifying results.' As many as 7,009 individuals — 10 percent of the urban African population — were screened, leading to 1,024 repatriations. In 1956, action under the ordinance eased slightly, with a significantly smaller total of 638 being repatriated — an indication, perhaps, that after a year of vigorous action against the surplus population 'undesirables' were getting thinner on the ground.

Any respite was brief. With over 5,000 migrants arriving in the town annually, it was unlikely that any scarcity would last for long. In his report for 1957, the Provincial Commissioner observed that '[u]nemployment and law and order problems demanded an increase in the attention paid to repatriation and expulsion of undesirables'.[57] In January that year the leader of the Tanganyika African National Union, Julius Nyerere, made a speech criticising

---

[51] *TS*, 8 November 1952, p. 8.

[52] Except where otherwise indicated figures in this section for 1953–8 are from Quarterly Police Reports for Dar es Salaam, in TNA/90/1011/Vol. 1.

[53] PC, EP to MLG, 22 April 1954, TNA/28685.

[54] It appears these raids were only one way in which undesirables were identified. The numbers of repatriatees for January–March and for January–*May* 1954 given by provincial administration officials were 200 and 423 respectively, in excess of the police figures of 127 (January–March) and 395 (January–*June*). PC, EP to MLG, 22 April 1954; DC Harris to MLG, TNA/28685.

[55] CS to CP, 16 July 1954, TNA/34184; PAR for 1954, p. 12.

[56] The provincial annual report recorded an even higher total of 1,230 removal orders from Dar es Salaam in 1954. The discrepancy can perhaps be accounted for by the immediate repatriation of Ukonga detainees on their release from prison. PAR for 1954, p. 12. A later report (1 April–30 June 1955) records the repatriation of 29 released prisoners separately from those apprehended in raids.

[57] 1957 PAR, p. 30.

European and Indian racial prejudice. Governor Twining interpreted his motive as an attempt at attracting support among Dar es Salaam's *'wahuni* element', and responded by increasing police action against 'hooliganism'.[58] The scale and frequency of the raids were intensified yet further, becoming, by 1958 at least, a daily occurrence. In both 1957 and 1958 over 2,000 people were repatriated from Dar es Salaam, 842 in one quarter alone. Comprehensive records for 1959 have not survived, although early in the year the screening of over 1,000 men during a raid at Keko Juu was reported in the *Tanganyika Standard*.[59] The largest operation to take place in the colonial period also occurred around this time. After rioting had resulted in the death of an African policeman at Buguruni, 2,817 Africans were screened in a clampdown designed to catch the killer/s.[60] The violence in Buguruni was associated with rumours about the disappearance of Africans in which *mumiani* superstitions were connected to the colonial administration. Brennan has rightly observed that in the context of the late 1950s 'the idea that government officials were responsible for the disappearance of Africans from urban areas is not at all far-fetched.'[61] Indeed, when over two percent of the African population of the town were being forcibly removed by the administration annually,[62] attributing the disappearance of individual Africans to Government action probably made powerful sense to those missing friends or relatives.

This was especially true when, as the decade progressed, increasingly arbitrary use was made of the repatriation legislation. More than ever before, by the mid 1950s to be unemployed in Dar es Salaam was in itself enough to be categorised as 'undesirable', and hence subject to repatriation. Reviewing action taken in the course of 1954, a police spokesmen told the *Tanganyika Standard* that:

> [C]hecks carried out during the year after 9 a.m. when presumably all law-abiding Africans were at work, tended to indicate that there were too many undesirables and Africans of the casual labourer class for whom there was no work ... They were the people who were being repatriated.[63]

DC Harris concurred, singling out 'drifters' unqualified to do anything but labouring work as legitimate targets for removal, as 'the completion or near-completion of several post-war capital works meant that that there was no employment for them.'[64] Looking back in his memoirs, the same official describes his role in the intensification of action under Cap. 104:

> [I]t seemed to me that a certain 'showing of the flag' might be useful ... I therefore increased the already regular attempts to keep out of town those

---

[58]   Copy of min. by H.E. the Governor, 16 March 1957, Lushoto, PRO/CO/822/1361/29, cited in Brennan, 'Nation', p. 305.
[59]   *TS*, 5 March 1959, p. 1; see also, 27 February 1959, p. 1.
[60]   *TS*, 19 March 1959, p. 5.
[61]   Brennan, 'Mumiani', pp. 1,12.
[62]   Based on annual totals for 1957/58.
[63]   *TS*, 28 December 1954.
[64]   *Ibid.* Many of these 'drifters' had presumably been welcome urban residents for as long as their labour was required.

young, unemployed and often tax-defaulting elements.… There existed on the statute book an Ordinance making provision for the expulsion of undesirables … This Ordinance had been used for some time to repatriate persons convicted in the local courts, and, with the cooperation of the police, I saw no reason why its use should not be extended to repatriate those who, whether through their own fault or not, 'toiled not neither did they spin' and could therefore not even make a contribution through their tax to the management of Dar es Salaam.[65]

As we have seen, unemployed Africans had actually been targeted for some time under Cap. 104. However, it was during Harris' tenure as DC that a substantial intensification took place leading to increasingly blameless individuals being defined as undesirable. As a result the tiny office of his assistant, John Cairns, was constantly filled with '*wahuni* awaiting repatriation'. Later on Harris appears to recognise the injustice of repatriations, but concludes that public order imperatives necessitated such action being taken:

Hard and sometimes unsympathetic — unfair even — this culling of the *wahuni* might have seemed. In reality they were often the young pioneers of the African population, leaving home in their dissatisfaction with the futureless subsistence agricultural economy of the rural areas. However, the African residents of Dar es Salaam genuinely felt that law and order, as well as internal security, could only be ensured by controlling the numbers of *wahuni* present in the town to indulge in petty theft and similar offences against property and person.[66]

Harris is unjustified in claiming widespread African support for the repatriation campaigns. A large proportion of Africans in Dar es Salaam were close to those sections of the population vulnerable to repatriation, through kin or social bonds, or simply because they were in danger of becoming jobless themselves. The vast majority of African townsmen were poor, as Leslie points out, and they resented those 'in authority, fixing the low wages, opposing the strikes, arresting those who steal, harassing those who do not pay their tax, repatriating those who cannot give a good account of themselves'.[67] Moreover, while there is evidence of elite anxiety about the presence of unoccupied Africans in the town, educated Africans were generally not at this time inclined to view repatriation as a solution to the problems of over-urbanisation.[68] This could be for political reasons. African nationalist leaders could not afford to alienate the urban population by supporting such action, and anyway found Harris' so-called 'rabble' a useful presence at political rallies (at least up to independence). It could be for practical reasons. Lawi Kardi, in a letter to the *Tanganyika Standard* in 1957, acknowledged the need for something to be done to reduce the surplus population (and hence

[65] Harris, *Donkey's Gratitude*, p. 298.
[66] *Ibid.*, p. 341.
[67] Leslie, *Survey*, p. 106.
[68] Though the policy occasionally met with African approval. See, for example, *Zuhra*, 13 August 1954, where a raid in which 2,000 Africans were screened is commended for helping to 'clear the city of crimes and theft' (original in Swahili).

crime). He ruled out repatriation, however, as being ineffective. '[Y]ou say that Police should round them [*wahuni*] up and send them to their villages, such assumption is without foundation for the reason that they all come back within a few days'.[69] Kardi's preferred solution was for the Department of Agriculture to find them employment in the rural areas, as African politicians were in fact to attempt to do after the assumption of responsible government.[70] The Convention of Representative Chiefs, held in January the following year, counselled for similar action:

> The Conference distinguished between children and youths under twenty, who should be subject to repatriation to their homes as at present: criminals who should be dealt with as criminals: and unemployed loafers. To teach these last the habit of discipline, it requested Government to consider the introduction of some form of compulsory labour service.[71]

In carefully breaking down those groups currently subject to repatriation for differentiated treatment, the conference acknowledged the same dangers of indiscriminate application of repatriation legislation as Justice McRoberts had seventeen years earlier. These were dangers that urban officials conveniently ignored.

The discrepancy between Harris' belief to be acting on behalf of 'respectable' urban citizens and Africans' attitudes towards repatriation campaigns — which actually represented a massive intrusion into the everyday life of the African community as a whole[72] — are perhaps best illustrated by the general response to a radio broadcast he made in the wake of some raids.[73] In an ill-judged attempt to inject some humour into the subject, Harris reported that:

> we had been fishing at Msasani early that morning, and went on to say that perhaps some of my listeners had seen the police lorries full of fish being taken to the Ukonga prison to be dried.

The audience response was — as far as Harris was concerned — unexpectedly negative. 'It was not long', he wrote, 'before I learned that some Africans were deeply hurt at being referred to as fish "when they were just humans like everyone else"'.' For Harris, this illustrated 'the extent to which nationalist, anti-government propaganda had so charged the atmosphere with emotions as to impair the customary quick and reliable sense of humour'.[74] While nationalism may well have played a part in the articulation of such grievances,

[69]   *TS*, 18 June 1957, p. 4.
[70]   See Burton, 'Haven'; 'Raw youth'.
[71]   Mins of Convention of Representative Chiefs of Tanganyika, 6–8 January 1958, TNA/ 225/80070.
[72]   No African was spared the humiliation of screening.
[73]   Harris tells us his 'predecessor had very cleverly encouraged the Broadcasting Corporation Sauti ya Dar es Salaam into inviting him to give a short talk occasionally on affairs in the town, and this had become a useful calming and morale-boosting occasion, much appreciated by the householders and more stable, respectable and conservative citizens'. Harris, *Donkey's Gratitude*, p. 298.
[74]   *Ibid.*, p. 299.

perhaps a more plausible interpretation of the African response to defaulters and 'undesirables' being described as fish was simply that it was too close to the bone. When a community is treated inhumanely it is not surprising if it bristles when members of that community are singled out for flippant dehumanisation by persons in authority.

De-spivving Dar

Substantial resources were devoted to campaigns against undesirables in the 1950s. The police occasionally took action unilaterally, as occurred early one Saturday morning in June 1951 when a sweep by 60 plain clothes policemen and four mobile patrols occurred.[75] More commonly, however, representatives from several different bodies participated in increasingly systematic raids. In the first major raid of this type for which details survive, in November 1952, the *Standard* reported the use of '[a] force consisting of 40 police, 40 tax-collectors and 6 vehicles' along with the police bicycle squad.[76] These 'District Teams' included representatives from the Native Administration to check on such details as the employment status and place of residence of persons screened. 'The local *Jumbes* and *Wazee*', it was observed in 1954, 'rendered valuable assistance in assuring that respectable citizens were released from the "net" with minimum delay.'[77] Someone from the District Office was also expected to be present 'to keep an eye on things' — one of the DOs or even the DC himself. Occasionally, officials from Kisarawe and other districts in Eastern Province also participated in the raids, though they were primarily concerned with collecting tax, in contrast to urban officials' desire to simply 'reduce the number of people who were floating around'.[78] Tax collectors were, of course, an integral part of any '*wahuni*' team, checking up on tax receipts for recent years: they were usually Native Administration employees, such as messengers from the district office.[79] Finally, there were the Police themselves, who were responsible for the arrest of potential undesirables, and their eventual removal to prison to await prosecution and repatriation. The Police Motorised Company played an important role.[80] The four patrol vans with radios installed were used to cover the municipality, which by this time stretched to 36 square miles. The task of the other cars, meanwhile, was 'to cordon off an area while the District Team sorted out the "sheep from the goats"'. Alongside the Motorised Company there were up to 50 or 60 African constables under two or three

75 The plain clothes men, it was reported, had concentrated on the town area while the mobile patrols 'swept the outskirts'. Their efforts led to 40 Africans being apprehended. *TS*, 2 June 1951, p. 17.

76 *TS*, 8 November 1952, p. 8.

77 QPR, 1 July–30 September, 1954.

78 Leslie interview.

79 *Ibid.*

80 Being used 'in force' in 10 out of 19 raids carried out between July and September 1954, for example, and 24 out of 31 in the first three months of 1955. See QPRs.

(European) commanding officers. Civilian 'Special Constables' were also sometimes used in the raids. ASP Young mentions the assistance of one — appropriately named — Mr Eager who took part in a morning raid at Chang'ombe in August 1954. A police report the following year notes the use of 'a large number of Special Constables ... as telephone operators, R/ T operators, drivers, control room operators and with executive Police Officers on the ground'. The operation was conducted partly 'to instruct ... Special Constables in rounding up and screening undesirables'. In 1955 these District Teams were augmented by a special police squad composed of 'the more energetic constables, under an intelligent probationary corporal', which 'was given the task of apprehending loiterers, unlicensed hawkers and the "crafty" type of "spiv", who is generally too cunning to be caught in a normal raid'. In their first two weeks operating in central Dar es Salaam they apprehended 74 undesirables, of whom 34 were defaulters, and 36 were repatriated.[81]

The location and timing of *wahuni* raids varied considerably. In June 1951 a sweep of the town was conducted in the early hours of the morning. Seven years later, in 1958, small raids were said to have taken place in the Ring Street area in the evening.[82] More commonly, though, raids would begin in the early daylight hours and continue throughout the morning, 'when', according to Harris, 'employed persons had either gone to work or were going to it'.[83] ASP Young's notebook entries for 10 and 11 February 1954, may be taken as typical in this regard:

10.2.54
1350 hrs around Temeke 'H' setting up tomorrow's raid with Paul Roberts and Weston of Mot[or] Co[mpan]y
11.2.54
0730 hrs to St[atio]n — getting *wahuni* raid under weigh [sic]
0800 Kilwa Rd Division men on way to muster at Chang'ombe
...0825 to PTS to pick up Mot[or] Co[mpan]y with 2 pickups
...0845 drive to raid
0900 Arrive spot on: cordon round rapidly: only one man made break — nabbed: raiders[?] through looking for *wahuni*, stolen prop etc.
1100 Poor haul — only 18, include 2 bad boys, 3 bags cement and 5 yds KD
1130 Mot[or] Co[mpan]y Kilwa Rd Division returned.[84]

Raids occurred throughout the town, in Zones I and II as well as the main African areas. Records survive of action taken in Oyster Bay, Upanga and Uhindini, in addition to the more obvious locations such as Buguruni, Temeke, Msasani, Keko and Kigogo. Even communities on the Kigamboni peninsula, separated from the town by the Kurasini Channel, did not escape the occasional raid.[85]

---

[81] *TS*, 14 August 1954, p. 5; QPRs, Dsm Dist, 1 June–30 September 1954; 1 October–31 December 1955; 1 January–31 March 1955; ASP Young's Personal Duty Diary, 10 February & 5 August 1954, RH/Mss.Afr.s.2293.
[82] *TS*, 2 June 1951, p. 17; QPR, Dsm Dist, 1 April–30 June 1958.
[83] Harris, *Donkey's Gratitude*, p. 298.
[84] ASP Young's Personal Duty Diary, RH/Mss.Afr.s. 2293.
[85] QPR, Dsm Dist, 1 October–31 December 1955.

The police would usually choose to be located at a bridge or some other form of bottleneck in order to facilitate screening.[86] At other times, house-to-house searches were conducted. Harris recalls that he used to accompany the raids 'to provide them with magisterial cover (as a sort of human, walking search warrant if any householder protested at the invasion of his privacy in our search for undesirable lodgers)'.[87] Anyone apprehended in the course of a raid would have their tax receipts checked. Those without proof of having paid tax for the current year or either of the two preceding ones were taken to the tax office (in the *boma*), where they would have the opportunity of having their receipts brought from their homes, or be prosecuted for failure to pay. Ex-offenders and those caught in breach of the law — unlicensed traders, returned repatriatees, beggars etc. — were taken to the police station and charged. The campaigns were highly effective. After an early raid conducted in the 1940s, inconvenienced Europeans complained that 'only those Africans who were exceptionally meticulous or successfully cunning were able to comfort their employers with their customary early morning tea.'[88]

On arrival at the tax office, defaulters were questioned, in order to sift out 'undesirables'. John Cairns describes one such scene in his lightweight — and to the post-colonial reader often supercilious — account of colonial service in Tanganyika. The scene is set with a preliminary invective against the urban 'undesirable':

> In the tax office a defaulter is being questioned by one of the clerks. The defaulter is about thirty. He wears a black and white check shirt, green trousers, torn tweed jacket and bare feet. He is one of the problems of urban Africa, one of the new parasitic class: the spiv who lives by his wits without work. But he does not think of himself like this. The city has given him freedom, which he wants. He lives here without restriction. He can come and go as he pleases, vanish, change his name a dozen times, have different women nightly. Best of all, he can live on others, for in the elaborate family and tribal communities there is always someone to help him. There is always a cousin or uncle or tribal brother who will give a place to sleep or a little food from the family pot. His only responsibility is to pay tax, and that is no responsibility unless he is caught. When this happens, of course it is bad luck. Still, sometimes even this can be bluffed out.
>
> 'You', the clerk asks. 'What is your name?'
> 'Me?'
> 'You'.
> 'Shomari Rajabu.'
> 'Where is your home?'
> 'Here. I am from Dar es Salaam.'
> 'You were born here?'
> 'Born? Not born here, *bwana*.'

[86] Leslie interview.
[87] Harris, *Donkey's Gratitude*, p. 298; see also *TS*, 14 August 1954, p. 5.
[88] *TS*, 10 October 1941, p. 6.

'Ehehh. Where were you born?'
'Up-country, *bwana*. Mwanza.'
'Where is your father?'
'My true father?'
'Yes', the clerk says angrily. 'Your true father.'
'He is not here. He is up-country. Mwanza.'
'And your mother?'
'Mwanza.'
'Hehhh! When did you come to Dar es Salaam?'
'Me, *bwana*?' A look of surprise.
'Yes, you.'
A long silence. This is the time to lie. Still, what sort of lie?
Finally, 'Last year, *bwana*. Year 1954 I came to Dar es Salaam.'
'So you are not from Dar es Salaam?'
'Not really, *bwana*.'
'What work do you do?'
Astonishment. Then injured innocence. Then an inspired triumphant smile.
'I have good work, *bwana*.'
'What is it?'
'In the docks.'
'Yesterday you worked?'
A pause.
'Not yesterday.'
The clerk is sarcastic now. 'The day before?'
'No, *bwana*.'
'Last week?'
A long silence. Finally, 'No. Not last week.'
'But you do work as a docker?'
'Oh yes, *bwana*. *Ndio*. *Ndio*. But not now.'
'Not now?' the clerk asks.
'No, *bwana*. I left that work a long time ago.'
'When was that?'
'You said you didn't come to Dar es Salaam until 1954.'
'Yes.' A silence. The clerk, who is becoming increasingly angry, stares at the man.
'That was the second time. Year 1953 was the first time.'
'I see.' The clerk realizes he is facing what he faces continually; a mixture of lies, deceit, exaggeration and bad memory.
'What work do you do now?'
'I have no work now, *bwana*. Not since year 1953. Nobody will give me work. Nobody will help me.'
The clerk groans, for now it is falling into a pattern. 'You have done no work for two years? Where did you get your food? Your shirt? Your coat?'
No answer. The man stands sullenly, scuffing his bare foot on the floor.
'Have you paid your taxes?'
'I always pay taxes, *bwana*. How could I not pay taxes to the government? Yes, I have paid. Year 1947, year 1948, year 1949.'
'Those are old years', the clerk shouts. 'The government does not care about

them. Now it is 1955. Have you paid for 1955?'
'Not 1955. I am late, *bwana*.'
'And 1954?'
'Not yet. I wanted to pay, but I forgot.'
'You forgot!' the clerk says savagely. 'And 1953?'
'Oh yes, *bwana*. I paid in 1953.'
'Where is your tax ticket?'
The man looks at the clerk blankly, and then inspiration comes, and he says
triumphantly, 'I paid the money, but he didn't give me a ticket.'
'Who?'
'My headman, *bwana*. Yes, I paid him, but he has eaten the money I gave him
in 1953. He was a thief, and that is why I did not pay this year, *bwana*. Why
should a man pay if he is not given a ticket?'
... The clerk says, 'You will have to see the District Officer.'
'But I will pay my tax. I will pay at the end of next month.'
'The *Bwana Shauri* [DO] must hear about this.' The man is brought to me
where I am waiting at the next table. A messenger stands beside him lest he
run away. The man looks around sullenly. The *Bwana Shauri*, he sees, will
have a heart of stone.[89]

The fate of such an individual was almost inevitably repatriation. In August
1952, a reporter from the *Tanganyika Standard* observed '[o]utside the *Boma* in
Dar es Salaam ... a disconsolate row of Africans, roped together within a
few yards of the tax collection office ... await[ing] removal for failure to pay
tax'.[90] Such individuals were sent on remand to either the town's remand
prison or to Ukonga Prison, on the outskirts of Dar es Salaam, pending the
application of a removal order. Over 300 Africans could be remanded in a
single day. However, prison accommodation was limited, and the raids were
sometimes stopped owing to lack of space. 'The Prison's Officers have been
most helpful', commented the Assistant Superintendent of Police at the time
of one such crisis in 1955, 'but one cannot "get a quart into a pint mug".'[91]

Once the removal order had been served — usually within a few days —
the victim was repatriated to his home district. This was not always the end
of the story, however. Occasionally, repatriatees were returned to districts
that were found after arrival not to be their real districts of origin. In 1955,
the DC at Kigoma complained that large numbers of 'undesirable destitutes'
were being despatched to him whose true homes lay elsewhere.[92] Some of
those Africans removed from Dar es Salaam under Cap. 104 were actually
exploiting the eagerness of officials to reduce the urban population in order
to obtain free transport to areas other than their home districts.[93] In order to

[89] Cairns, *Bush*, pp. 122–5.
[90] *TS*, 23 August 1952, p. 5.
[91] QPR, Dsm Dist, 1 January–31 March 1955. Largely to address this problem, work began
     on a new remand prison in the late 1950s. See, CPris to MSS, 30 July 1957. TNA/489/4/
     2/E/Vol. I.
[92] MLG to PC, EP, 23 April 1956, TNA/540/3/1.
[93] In late May 1954, people were encouraged to come to the District Office to volunteer for
     repatriation. They were sent home 'provided they agreed to the issue of an order forbidding

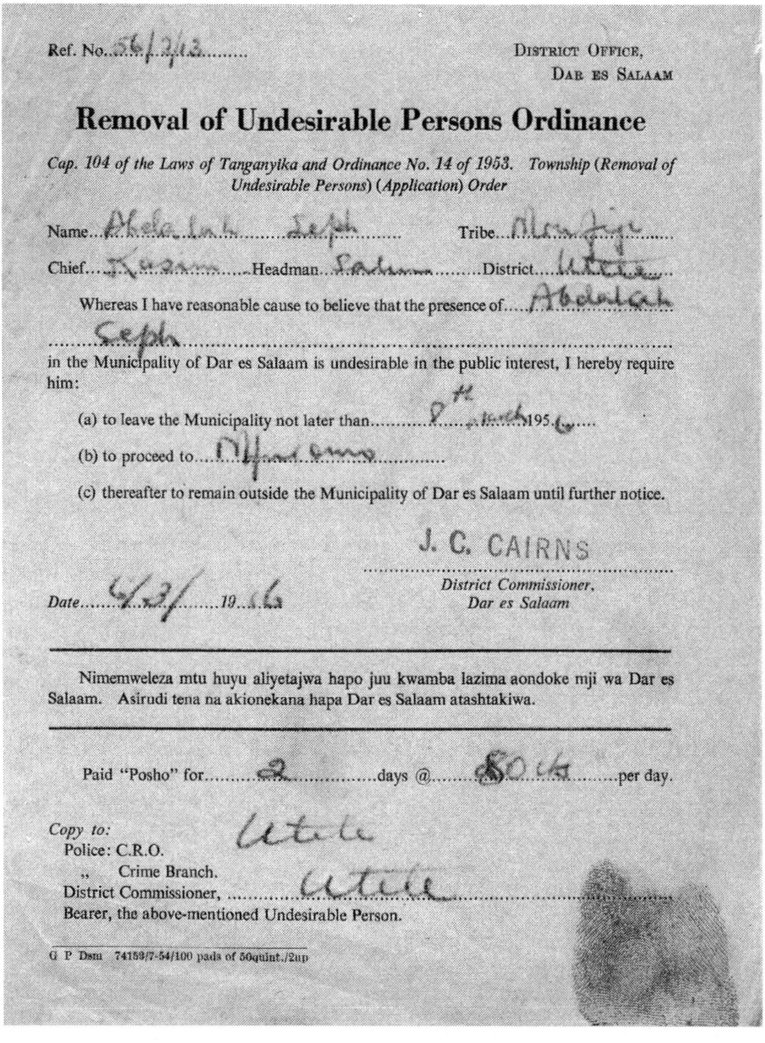

Ref. No. .... DISTRICT OFFICE, DAR ES SALAAM

Removal of Undesirable Persons Ordinance

Cap. 104 of the Laws of Tanganyika and Ordinance No. 14 of 1953. Township (Removal of Undesirable Persons) (Application) Order

Name .... Tribe ....

Chief .... Headman .... District ....

Whereas I have reasonable cause to believe that the presence of Abdalah Seph in the Municipality of Dar es Salaam is undesirable in the public interest, I hereby require him:

(a) to leave the Municipality not later than .... 195....

(b) to proceed to ....

(c) thereafter to remain outside the Municipality of Dar es Salaam until further notice.

J. C. CAIRNS
District Commissioner, Dar es Salaam

Date .... 19....

Nimemweleza mtu huyu aliyetajwa hapo juu kwamba lazima aondoke mji wa Dar es Salaam. Asirudi tena na akionekana hapa Dar es Salaam atashtakiwa.

Paid "Posho" for .... days @ .... per day.

Copy to:
Police: C.R.O.
,, Crime Branch.
District Commissioner, Utete
Bearer, the above-mentioned Undesirable Person.

G P Dsm 74153/7-54/100 pads of 50quint./2up

Fig. 12.1 *A removal order to Utete, 1956 (authorised by John Cairns).* The Swahili reads: 'I have explained to the man referred to above that he must leave the town of Dar es Salaam. He should not return again, and if he is sighted here in Dar es Salaam he will be prosecuted.'

Source: TNA/540/56/56/3

counter this phenomenon the Member for Local Government in 1955 required receiving DCs to be consulted in advance. This was soon found to be impracticable. With scant financial resources and limited prison accommodation at Ukonga, the district administration in Dar es Salaam simply could not afford any delay.[94]

The other, more common, problem associated with repatriatees on arrival in their districts of origin was a disinclination to stay there. Without close rural supervision — usually beyond the capacity of Native Authorities — many took the first opportunity that arose to return to Dar es Salaam. In 1947 the DC complained that while it was 'not known how many [repatriatees] returned to the township ... there have been a number of convictions for failing to comply with Removal Orders'.[95] Mayhew recalled the return of undesirables as a routine fact of life. Those repatriated by train simply 'got off' at the first stop and walked back to Dar es Salaam'.[96] 'Due to the inadequate number of police', the Commissioner of Police observed in 1952, 'it is comparatively easy for these people to re-enter the Municipality and become absorbed into the native population again'.[97] In an attempt to address this phenomenon, an Assistant Probation Officer was sent to Kisarawe district (where the largest number of the repatriatees were sent) in 1954 'to help with the problem of men and youths repatriated to their homes'. '[F]rom present indications', wrote the head of the Commissioner of Prisons at the end of the year, 'it appears that it will prove extremely useful in helping to settle these men in their homes and villages and preventing them from drifting back to town'. By 1958, however, the service was reported to have become overburdened 'owing to the large numbers involved'.[98] In a further attempt to address the problem of returnees, amendments were made to the Police Force Bill in 1958, which allowed the police to retain the fingerprints of undesirables served with removal orders but not convicted of any criminal offence. Without a positive form of identification, the Chief Secretary observed, it was difficult to prove that a returnee was in fact that man who had previously been ordered to leave.[99]

(fn.93 cont.) them to return to Dar es Salaam'. DC Harris to MLG, 15 June 1954, TNA/28685. Over the next two weeks, 15 people came to volunteer for repatriation. However, it seems likely that these individuals were simply taking advantage of free transport home at the end of a spell in the town or – given the difficulties in ensuring repatriatees did not return to the town – with the intention of returning to Dar es Salaam in spite of the order. For '*soi-disants* destitutes' taking advantage of repatriations to visit friends and relatives upcountry, see DC, Morogoro to PC, EP, 6 April 1950, TNA/61/502/50.

94   MLG to PC, EP, 23 April 1956, TNA/540/3/1; Clark to PC, EP, 22 June 1956, TNA/540/3/3/XIV.

95   Uzaramo DAR for 1947, p. 16, TNA/540/1/4/B.

96   Mayhew was an urban DO in 1947. 'Reminiscences', p. 18. See also, Min. by AG, 31 March 1952, TNA/21616/Vol. III.

97   CP to CS, 14 August 1952, TNA/21963/Vol. II.

98   1954 Prisons AR, p. 34; 1958 Social Devt AR, p. 27.

99   Legco Mins, 19 February 1958, p. 447.

Fig.12.2 *Spivs and self-government philosophers*
As depicted in Cairns, *Bush and Boma*, 1959

Some 'undesirables'

Little impression has been gained so far of the identity of repatriatees. While scant information about those subjected to repatriation has survived for the bulk of the colonial period, the contents of a number of files from the mid 1950s does provide us with more substantial background on a limited number of 'undesirables'.[100] Of the 423 persons repatriated in the first five months of 1954, approximately 66 percent were from Eastern Province, 15 percent from Central, Western and Lake Provinces, 14 percent from Southern Province and 4 percent from Tanga, Northern and Southern Highlands Provinces.[101] A random sample from later the same year appears to confirm that the majority of repatriations occurred to districts in Eastern Province. Out of a total of 70 removal orders from August 1954, 39 were to Eastern Province, the majority (18) being to villages in neighbouring Kisarawe district. Among the other repatriatees there were a handful from districts scattered throughout the territory, from Newala in the south to Musoma in the north.

100 TNA Acc. Nos 540/54, 540/55 and 540/56.
101 DC Harris to MLG, 15 June 1954, TNA/28685.

263

Table 12.2 *Districts receiving repatriatees, August 1954*

Bagamoyo (EP)	1	Kilwa	2	Nyasaland	1
Kilosa (EP)	2	Lindi	2	Same	1
Kisarawe (EP)	18	Liwali	1	Singida	2
Morogoro (EP)	12	Mbeya	2	Tabora	6
Utete (EP)	6	Mombasa	1	Tanga	1
Dodoma	1	Musoma	1	Ufipa	2
Kahama	1	Mwanza	1	Uganda	2
Kakanga	1	Newala	3		

Source: Information in TNA 540/54/8/1

Table 12.3 *Tribal breakdown of repatriatees, November 1954*

Zaramo (Kisarawe)*	30	Sukuma	7	Mwera	2
Rufiji (Rufiji)	13	Nyamwezi	5	Ngoni	2
Ndengereko (Kisarawe/Rufiji)	10	Matumbi	4	Kinga	1
Luguru (Morogoro)	6	Gogo	3	Pangwa	1
Nyagatwa (Kisarawe)	4	Yao	3	Rangi	1
Kutu (Morogoro)	2	Hehe	2	Tende	1
Pogoro (Ulanga)	1	Luo	2	Tongwe	1
Ngindo (Ulanga/ + Kilwa/ Nachingwea, SP)	5	Makonde	2	Zigua	1
	71		28		10

* Indicates main district/s of origin in Eastern Province (from J.P. Moffett (ed.), *Handbook of Tanganyika* (Dsm, 1958), pp. 294–7)
Source: Information taken from TNA 540/54/11/1

In addition, six originated from neighbouring territories. A tribal breakdown of removal orders from three months later in November 1954 also indicates a majority of repatriatees from Eastern Province. Over 60 percent were against members of ethnic groups whose main district/s of origin lay within the province. As in August, the majority — Zaramo, Nyagatwa and Ndengereko — were from neighbouring Kisarawe. The main districts of origin for those outside of Eastern Province were once again scattered throughout Tanganyika; the largest were 12 Sukuma/Nyamwezi, which reflects their combined status as the principal ethnic group in Dar es Salaam after those originating in Eastern Province.[102]

The kind of offences forming the basis for applications for removal were varied. Stealing or other property offences were, of course, common. However, the reasons for removal were in many cases petty indeed. One man was repatriated for sleeping under a tree at night; another for walking the streets

---

[102] Sukuma and Nyamwezi are closely related and were often lumped together by colonial officials.

without a light. A removal order was made on the basis that one 'boy' had 'got no job and has been harassing school girls on the way'. Unlicensed petty traders were vulnerable to repatriation. So too were fare-dodgers on the trains. 'Wilful neglect to pay poll tax' was, of course, a repatriating offence, as was affray. Most common of all, however, was the simple fact that the accused was an 'undesirable person'. This could no doubt cover a multitude of sins, but official inability to come up with a specific offence indicates that it is perhaps best translated as joblessness. Unemployment was, above all else, undesirable.[103]

Some of the repatriatees actually took advantage of Cap. 104. As we have seen, it was not unknown for individuals to exploit official keenness to apply the legislation against urban undesirables in order to obtain free transport to districts other than those from which they originated. Commoner still were temporary migrants from the rural areas who, having 'heard of the monthly hundreds who are repatriated, decide to rely on this for [their] return'.[104] One such was Salum bin Juma, who with no money and no relations in Dar es Salaam, made his way from Tabora to see the town.[105] He was repatriated in February 1956. Another group who commonly took advantage of Cap. 104 were Africans who came from the rural areas to seek medical treatment at Dar es Salaam's hospitals, many of whom were repatriated after being treated.[106]

From the isolated examples that turn up in the official record it is possible to begin to sketch a clearer picture of the repatriatees. In a letter about the control of unemployed persons from 1942, for example, DC Pike wrote to Baker of a trio of demobilised soldiers who were prime candidates for removal.[107] Musa bin Saidi had lost a leg while on army service and was discharged at Dar es Salaam on 23 April 1942 with a final payment of Shs. 344/65. Within a month, however, the money had been spent and he found himself destitute. 'He will not go home', complained Pike, 'but wants to stay in Dar es Salaam permanently.' Ibrahim bin Chande provided Pike with a second example of urban profligacy. He was discharged on 1 June 1942 with a substantial Shs. 800/- owing to him. The DC was reluctant to pay the full amount, allowing him to take just Shs. 300/-. To Pike's consternation, within three days Chande had spent the lot, and was back at the District Office demanding the outstanding amount. To paternalistic officials, the exposure of such individuals as Ibrahim bin Chande to the urban environment was bad not only for the person concerned but also for the Native Administration, to whom they represented a potential future burden. The third individual singled out by Pike was Mohamed bin Saidi, a young man who was born and grew up in Mohoro, a village located to the south of the Rufiji delta. He was discharged in mid 1942 after working a year for the E.A.M.L.S. He too

[103] Information taken from removal orders in TNA Acc. Nos 540/54, 540/55 and 540/56.
[104] Leslie, *Survey*, p. 244.
[105] Removal Order, 18 February 1956, TNA/540/3/1.
[106] See TNA/540/3/1 for examples.
[107] DC, Dsm to PC, EP, 4 June 1942, TNA/540/27/13.

was 'determined to stay in Dar es Salaam', expecting Government to supply him with 'some work which he himself considers satisfactory'. 'Government' was inclined to view the matter differently.

While these individuals were likely victims of urban 'cleansing' — Pike wrote to recommend the introduction of a pass system to control such people — there is no evidence they were actually repatriated. To find some examples of actual repatriatees we must go forward a decade. In November 1954, for instance, a removal order was served against one Zacharia Viteris. He was a Tende (Kuria) former prison warder who on his discharge from work — 'sometime ago' — was given a government warrant to return to his home. The lure of the capital proved too strong, however. Returning to Ukonga prison lines he was initially driven away by the authorities there. A few nights later he was found once again wandering around the European officers' quarters at Ukonga. The same night a houseboy at Ukonga had reported having a box stolen. While there was no evidence to connect Zacharia with the theft of the box, it was decided nevertheless that removal was the best option. 'Zacharia has no work in Dar es Salaam', a police officer wrote. 'He has no real place to live in and has not even paid a single poll tax. Please get him repatriated.'[108] A few months later, in March 1955, Maria Salume was found to have made her way to the capital from Bukoba. 'This woman has come again to Dar es Salaam without any reason', complained the DC, somewhat illogically. People had good reasons for travelling to Dar es Salaam (especially from as far away as Bukoba), they were simply not acknowledged as such by pressurised officials. She was expelled under Cap. 104.[109] Judging by the lack of further instances, this constitutes an isolated example of what was a rare phenomenon: the removal of a female 'undesirable'.[110]

A number of probation reports on tax defaulters surviving from early 1956 shed further chinks of light on the world of the repatriatees. The information preserved reflects the priorities (and prejudices) of colonial officials, but for all its weaknesses it at least gives us some insight into those people categorised by officials as 'undesirable'.

Mikidandi Athumani was relatively old to be facing repatriation. He was 45 years old and from the village of Ndundu on the Rufiji River close to the district headquarters at Utete. According to his probation report, he had been in town for just four months, staying rent-free at the house of a 'tribal associate' in Tungi, before his arrest for being in default of taxes. He had just one female relation in the town, a niece. At the time of his arrest, Athumani

---

[108] Chang'ombe Police Station to Central Police Station, 10 November 1954, TNA/540/54/11/11.
[109] DC, Dsm to DC, Bukoba, 16 March 1955, TNA/540/3/1. In Dar es Salaam, as elsewhere in East Africa (see White, *Comforts*), Haya women were prominent in the urban sex trade. It is quite possible that the removal of Maria Salume represents a rare recorded instance of the repatriation of someone engaged in prostitution.
[110] The only other reference to the repatriation of women I have come across is in a 1936 letter from Erica Fiah in which he refers to: 'a few cases of women who were repatriated for a certain crime [prostitution?] to their countries but have privately returned to Dar es Salaam without your knowledge'. TAWCA to MS, 12 April 1936, TNA/22444.

was employed making *makuti* thatch for the roofing of African houses. In previous years he had travelled to the islands of Zanzibar to work on the plantations during the clove harvest. Enquiries were made into his character by the probation service. Hassani Mawazo, in whose home he had been staying at Tungi, confirmed official suspicions: Athumani had many debts outstanding in his home village and was no longer welcome in his house. 'A very doubtful character', the Senior Probation Officer, J.E. Silvertand, concluded: 'To be repatriated'.[111]

Mbegu Salehe came from Msonga in the south of Kisarawe district. When he was apprehended for defaulting in March 1956 he was 22 and unmarried. He moved frequently between Dar es Salaam, where he would work for short periods, and Msonga where he had a *shamba* that he cultivated. When in town he stayed with an uncle who lived in Pemba Street in Kariakoo. In February 1956, Salehe had been in Dar es Salaam just a few days before being picked up for being 'abroad at night without a light', for which he was sentenced to seven days' imprisonment. After his release he was immediately prosecuted for failure to pay tax for 1955. He was in default of taxes for just one year, having paid for both 1953 and 1954. However, neither this nor the fact that he was simply taking advantage of the 'off-season' to leave his *shamba* — as he had done in previous years — in order to obtain some waged labour in the capital[112] was enough to redeem him in the eyes of the probation officer. 'This man', Silvertand decided, 'should be sent back to Kisarawe where he can be supervised by the APO for that district.'[113]

Mrisho Omari was a 19-year-old Kwere from Msoga in south-western Bagamoyo district. He gave as his town address one in Temeke, but most of the fifteen months he had been in Dar es Salaam had been spent serving time inside Ukonga prison, where he had just completed a ten-month sentence. He had also been convicted and imprisoned on two other occasions, although the nature of the offences is not recorded. Prior to his spell at Ukonga, Omari had been employed by an Indian at the rate of Shs. 50/- per month. He had also worked in Dar es Salaam as a labourer on building sites. Unsurprisingly, Silvertand considered him a bad risk. In the Probation Officer's assessment he was 'a very doubtful character who would be very difficult to supervise' and repatriation was considered 'the best thing for him'.[114]

Amiri Zauma, a 20-year-old Makonde from Mikindani, had been living in Magomeni for five months prior to his prosecution in March 1956 for defaulting. Having reached Standard IV, he had completed a full course of primary education. On arrival in Dar es Salaam he first worked as a servant in an Indian household for a couple of months, and then went on to gain employment at the New Africa Hotel, where he was earning Shs. 50/- per month. His only relative in town was an uncle in whose Magomeni house he stayed. In February 1956, Zauma was arrested for loitering and was sentenced

---

[111] Court Report, 29 February 1956, TNA/540/56/1.
[112] As a result of which, he could perhaps have settled his tax arrears.
[113] *Ibid.*, 5 March 1956.
[114] *Ibid.*, 6 March 1956.

to seven days' imprisonment. On his release, after prosecution as a defaulter, he was considered unsuitable for probation and repatriated to Mikindani.[115]

Hamisi Asumani was a 25-year-old Ndengereko from Kitomondo village, close to the coastal town of Kisiju in southern Kisarawe district. Prior to prosecution, he had been in Dar es Salaam for five months. He claimed to have many relatives in the town, one of whom, an uncle, was providing him with free accommodation at his home in Nyamwezi Street, Kariakoo. He also claimed to be working at an Arab restaurant for the monthly wage of Shs. 25/- plus food. In his sixth month in town Asumani was arrested for loitering and given a one-week sentence. He had one previous conviction from the previous year, when he had served two months for an unspecified offence. On his discharge Asumani was immediately rearrested — for tax offences — and the Probation Office looked into his background. The uncle and the employer denied having provided him with either work or accommodation. In fact, the uncle went so far as to give 'a very bad report on his behaviour and character'. It was, wrote Silvertand, 'a good opportunity to get rid of a bad lot'.[116]

Ramadhani Saidi, a 26-year-old Zaramo from Kitunda in Kisarawe district, had been in town for two months when he was apprehended as a tax defaulter. He lived rent-free in a house occupied by his cousin in Kinondoni, and tapped palm wine to earn a living, for which he got on average about Shs. 50/- per month. He had one previous conviction, an assault charge for which he received a six-month sentence. On investigating his background, it was discovered that while he had been living with his cousin in Kinondoni, Saidi had no room there, using instead the passage of the house as his sleeping place. 'The general information obtained was not satisfactory', the Probation Officer concluded, 'and the Cousin is not prepared to take any responsibility. I think this man would benefit from being repatriated to his home.'[117]

As a sample of those people being removed from the town as 'undesirables' it is likely that the above individuals are representative. They are predominantly young and from Eastern Province, although Mikidandi Athumani was over forty, and Amiri Zauma was from Southern Province. In some cases there is evidence of previous (or current) criminal activity, though none could be described as hardened criminals. Others appeared to have fallen foul of colonial by-laws restricting freedom of movement — abroad at night without a light — or been arrested on suspicion for loitering (how justified this suspicion was is of course something we shall never know). Some of the repatriations seem particularly harsh, that of Mbegu Salehe especially so. Colonial officials, though, pressurised as they were by the rapid growth of the African urban population, were — to say the least — not inclined to benevolence, and here too the sample is no doubt representative.

The avenues of investigation pursued by the probation department are revealing. The first thing to establish was the length of residence in the capital.

---

[115] *Ibid.*, 5 March 1956.
[116] *Ibid.*, 26 March 1956.
[117] *Ibid.*, 27 March 1956.

Cap. 104 restricted legitimate urban residence only to those who could prove they had lived in the town for eighteen months out of the last two years (from 1958 four out of the past five years). While most of the people domiciled in town who could not fulfil this requirement were left untouched, this section greatly facilitated the removal of those designated undesirables. The next issue was the marital status of the accused. Each of the six repatriatees above was declared single in the court reports. It is not clear whether this referred only to their position in Dar es Salaam itself. Officials may well have viewed married men — even those with rural wives — as more stable and responsible and hence a lesser risk.[118] It is unlikely that individuals with families in the town would have been repatriated. A third factor in determining the fate of potential repatriatees was the presence of relatives in the capital. To have none at all meant that — without regular employment — you would be highly vulnerable to repatriation. In several of the court reports even the presence of a single relative was not enough to prevent removal. It did not help when relatives were not supportive, as in the case of Hamisi Asumani or Ramadhani Saidi. Why relatives might be inclined to disown the accused is unclear. It may have been a desire to avoid trouble themselves or reluctance to be associated with a malefactor. Alternatively, it could simply have been eagerness to relieve the burden on sparse domestic resources. The inference in some reports is that had the accused been found to have several relatives in the town — who it was assumed would take some responsibility for his behaviour — then he may be allowed to remain. A fourth factor investigated was evidence of a permanent address in Dar es Salaam. Failure to provide one would likely result in eviction from the town. Living with a relative may be enough to avoid this, but not necessarily. In the case of Ramadhani Saidi it appears that his having no room of his own, and sleeping in a passage, was one more factor pointing to removal. In determining repatriation it was also, of course, important for officials to ascertain the employment status of an individual. Lack of a job would almost certainly lead to expulsion. What is more, judging by our sample, even evidence of work was not necessarily enough to prevent removal. Three of the six repatriatees actually had waged employment at the time of prosecution, and another was self-employed. Only two appeared to be jobless, one of whom also claimed to have been employed at the time of his arrest, while the other had only just arrived in town. Finally, the criminal record of the accused was taken into account in any judgment over whether or not to repatriate an individual.

By the late 1950s thousands of migrants were entering Dar es Salaam annually. Admittedly, some did perhaps come to the town unprepared for urban life. In addition, it is likely that a small proportion were attracted by the criminal opportunities that the great concentration of population offered. However, these groups probably represented a minority of urban immigrants. A great deal more were attracted by the opportunity to engage temporarily in waged labour; or by the opportunities the capital provided for income generation in the urban informal sector. For those able only to produce a

---

[118] Harris occasionally translates *wahuni* as 'bachelors'. E.g. *Donkey's Gratitude*, p. 297.

subsistence from their rural *shamba*, a periodic move to the town may have represented the most convenient way of earning the cash that the colonial administration was so assiduous in collecting as tax. Urban officials disregarded such calculations. As Dar es Salaam's African population burgeoned they were increasingly determined to restrict the entry of these rural–urban migrants.

By the end of the colonial period the removal of 'undesirable' Africans was taking place on a massive scale. *Wahuni* raids were conducted daily. Involving mass roadside screening as well as house-to-house searches, these raids represented an extraordinary degree of Government intrusion. Among the African community they were deeply resented and provided a strong basis for mobilising support for TANU. While colonial officials may have acknowledged that the repatriation campaigns were at times unfair, however, they were convinced about the correctness of their actions, perceived as being for the good of the town as a whole. In 1941, Justice McRoberts had warned of the neglect of African civil liberties. His judgment was brushed aside. Almost two decades later these same civil liberties were, if anything, being even more comprehensively ignored. Faced with ever-growing numbers of Africans making their way to Dar es Salaam, the colonial response to African urbanisation grew increasingly coercive. Controlling the human tide, however, was simply beyond the capacity of the colonial state.

Dar es Salaam prior to independence

By the late 1950s a policy of stabilisation, involving the encouragement of more settled African urban communities whose numbers were restricted by the opportunities for formal employment, was in place. In Dar es Salaam, rising wages and increased provision for housing appeared to have resulted in 'a move towards family living'. In a 1959 re-survey, the African community of Magomeni — one of those areas covered by Leslie in 1956 — was, with almost equal numbers of men and women, found to have more of a balance between the sexes than three years earlier. 'This change', according to Leslie, 'which may be an index of "urbanisation", or the adoption of a settled town life and an intention to remain there with one's wife and children, [was] reflected throughout the re-survey.' However, the same factors resulting in greater urban-rootedness were also contributing to an ever-growing flow of immigrants into the town, who, with the 'pruning of staffs' that occurred in the wake of the introduction of a minimum wage, were perhaps less welcome in Dar es Salaam than ever.[119]

As immigration continued unabated, unemployment and its concomitant problems grew. In 1957 (the year in which the minimum wage was introduced), according to the Eastern Province annual report, 'a rise in unemployment figures for Dar es Salaam and a resulting increase in the "spiv" population

[119] Leslie, *Survey*, pp. 123, 281, 290; R.H. Gower to SSCol., 22 June 1959, PRO/CO/955/83.

270

engaged the special attention of the Administration.' In spite of repatriating 'a larger number than usual of workless immigrants' to their 'homes', however, the Provincial Commissioner still reported 'an increased disrespect for the forces of law and order and decreasing assistance from the public in maintaining it'. 'The problem is not new', he complained, 'but it has been intensifying over a considerable period. It arises from a mixed population inexperienced at urban living under modern conditions.'[120] It was not just recent arrivals to the town who were causing the administration a headache. The Provincial Commissioner and the Officer in Charge of the Dar es Salaam police identified a great number of the town's 'spiv' element as being 'persons who have been in the town for a longer period than eighteen months but who have either never been employed or who only take up from time to time temporary or part-time employment'.[121] According to the Chief Secretary:

> many of the spivs and hooligans are a useless type who sleep on shop verandas and other places and who have been in Dar es Salaam for a very much longer period than three years. It is more than probable that these are the worst type and have been living this life of indolence and petty crime for so long that the only cure is to send them back to their tribes where they will come under a certain amount of tribal influence and discipline.[122]

The long urban residency of these undesirables was evidence of the wrong kind of stabilisation. Such was the concern with which the phenomenon was held that a committee was set up '[t]o consider and make recommendations in regard to the problems caused by the presence in Dar es Salaam of large numbers of persons of no fixed abode and no known means of support'.[123] In its initial report, the committee's Working Party drew up a list of 'factors affecting the problem', which, as a litany of colonial concerns, encapsulates perfectly official anxiety about urbanisation. These included:

> [I]dleness and boredom, evidenced by the lessening of the importance of the tribal ties and the waning influence of local heads and leaders.... Thriftlessness.... Unemployment due to labour surplus.... Amorality and irreligion.... Indiscipline in the home.... Lack of respect for law and order.... Difficulty found by the incoming rural African in adapting himself to town conditions and a strictly money economy.... Bright lights and the aura of independent living.[124]

The Working Party put forward recommendations to address the situation, including the draft proposal to construct a so-called 'spiv centre' at which undesirables could be held on remand and repatriations processed.[125] On

120 Eastern PAR for 1957, p. 30.
121 CS to W.A.C. Mathieson, CO, 11 November 1957, in PRO/CO/822/1795. The significance of the 18-month period was that this was the length of time necessary to have resided in an urban area in order to qualify as a 'legitimate' town-dweller under the terms of Cap. 104.
122 *Ibid.*
123 *Ibid.*
124 Confidential Memo., 17 February 1958, PRO/CO/822/1795.
125 CP to Director, Public Works, 4 February 1958, TNA/489/4/2/E/Vol. I.

receiving a copy of the committee's deliberations, however, Whitehall officials were dismissive. 'This is not a particularly impressive report', wrote Chinn, the adviser on Social Welfare, 'and its recommendations are entirely negative.' 'Experience in other territories', he continued,

> proves that it is impossible to deal with the influx of people into the towns merely by using compulsory powers to remove them or to prevent them coming … repressive measures of this kind cannot alone deal with problems which are deep rooted in the social conditions which produce them.

B.E. Rolfe, another Whitehall official, concurred. 'Is it too much to hope', he pondered, 'that we shall hear less about spivs, thugs and hooligans in future and more about human beings?'[126] If these criticisms filtered back to officials in Tanganyika, it was too late. In early 1958, the working party reported that many of their proposals had either been acted upon or were in the process of being taken up. These included the strengthening of powers of repatriation, the extension of the period of residence qualifying an individual to be a 'legitimate' town-dweller, the introduction of a system for voluntary registration, and the expansion of remand facilities to accommodate 'undesirables' awaiting repatriation.[127]

As predicted by Chinn, these initiatives failed to achieve the desired effect. By the end of 1960 it was estimated that out of an adult male population of 41,000, between ten and fifteen thousand were unemployed or underemployed.[128] Now, with a newly appointed 'responsible' government and an African at the helm, Dar es Salaam's surplus population was beginning to be conceived of as more than simply an administrative or social problem. After just two months in office, Chief Minister Nyerere voiced concern about 'the political dangers inherent in the number of unemployed in Dar es Salaam who were easily susceptible to the suggestion that the new Government was doing nothing for them'.[129] 'There was an urgent need', the Minutes continue, 'for an opportunity for the *genuinely* unemployed population to be able to get work.'[130] According to Randall Sadleir, a colonial public relations officer at the time,

> Nyerere did not want to see lawless elements upsetting the apple cart when the country was … proceeding fairly smoothly in the right direction. He

---

[126] Mins, 8 April and 26 March 1958, PRO/CO/822/1795.

[127] Confidential Memo., 17 February 1958, PRO/CO/822/1795.

[128] Memo. on unemployment in Dar es Salaam by the Minister for Health and Labour, January 1961, [Unemployment Memo.], PRO/CO/ 822/2962.

[129] Extract from Minutes of a Meeting of the Council of Ministers, 4 November 1960, in PRO/CO/822/2962. There is some irony in Nyerere singling out the town's surplus population as a political threat. Just three years earlier the Chief Secretary was complaining of the 'spivs and hooligans in the towns, particularly in Dar es Salaam and Tanga, from whose numbers undoubtedly come the majority of the thug element which so obviously supports TANU'. CS to W.A.C. Mathieson, CO, 11 November 1957, in PRO/CO822/ 1795.

[130] Emphasis added.

warned ... that, if anything, TANU's attitude towards law and order would be even tougher than that of the colonial government.[131]

The following year, the TANU Minister for Health and Labour extolled the necessity of 'the formation of a public conscience which actively condemns town idleness'.[132] Like its colonial predecessor, the new Government was anxious to effect the civic education of the urban populace.

[131] Sadleir, *Tanzania*, p. 233; see also Brennan ('Nation', p. 304), who observes that 'preventing disorder became the central concern for both TANU nationalists and the colonial government.'
[132] Unemployment Memo.

Conclusion

Urbanisation, Development & Crime

The colonial legacy

Support for African nationalism in late-colonial Tanganyika was in part mobilised through the articulation of grievances against the petty harassment of individuals struggling to get by in the urban environment. The policy of round-ups and repatriations was at various times condemned by senior TANU figures,[1] and judging by the absence of evidence of *wahuni* raids after 1959 the British responded to such pressures by abandoning the policy in the run-up to independence. Once in office, African politicians initially attempted to respond to rapid urbanisation in a more constructive way than had colonial officials intent on suppression.[2] Schemes to alleviate urban unemployment were initiated in rural areas; there was a modest relaxation of the rules governing petty trading activity; in 1961 a municipal sub-committee was established to look into 'the problem of beggars'.[3] However, faced with the same problems of a rapidly increasing urban population and limited resources with which to deal with the phenomenon, the incoming administration eventually adopted similar 'solutions' to its predecessor. Colonial rule had not only unleashed demographic trends that persisted up to and beyond independence, but it had also established an ideological framework within which the 'problems' of urbanisation were interpreted by officials and an administrative response was improvised.

Continuity in policy was initially particularly marked in the case of labour. In 1962, the Territorial Minimum Wages Board counselled that 'minimum wages should be increased to enable families to live together at a reasonable standard.'[4] In Dar es Salaam, where inflation was once again eating into pay increases, a minimum rate of Shs. 150/- was recommended — with a longer term objective of reaching a Shs. 300/- monthly 'family minimum'

[1] For examples, see Burton, 'Haven', fn. 4.
[2] See Burton, 'Raw youth'.
[3] *TS*, 5 January 1961, p. 3; and *ibid*.
[4] Chesworth Report, p. 34.

within five to six years. Stabilisation and increased productivity remained the key to progress. It was acknowledged that an increase in pay might result in reductions in employment, but the 'desirability of a smaller static labour force with higher minimum wages' was stressed.[5] In the event, in the territory as a whole, employment did indeed decline in the years immediately following independence.[6] A subsequent ILO report highlighted the manner in which the benefits of formal employment were restricted in particular to a narrow group of urban workers (in 'Dar es Salaam and one or two other towns') employed by Government departments and large-scale businesses. If present trends continued, the report predicted, a situation would emerge

in which a very small minority of workers and employees in large monopolistic concerns and in public services enjoy high living standards and social and economic security, but in which there is also a large group of employees in small firms who have low wages and insecure employment, and in which a rapidly increasing peasantry benefits hardly at all from industrial development.[7]

Recommendations were made to curtail wage increases, to attempt to increase employment, and in particular to reduce the rural–urban gap that had widened since independence. The Arusha Declaration reinforced the emphasis on rural development. However, in the decade after 1967 urban wage-earners continued to enjoy a considerably better standard of living than the rural peasant.[8] Moreover, within the towns marked inequality was also evident and according to Collier 'really serious poverty became a problem for the first time' in the early 1970s.[9] Between 1969 and 1975, when Dar es Salaam grew at around 10 percent per annum, urban waged employment increased by just 5.4 percent annually. The urban informal sector and unemployment, on the other hand, expanded at a little short of 20 percent per year. A tide of rural–urban migrants, for whom regular employment (never mind housing, services and amenities) was unavailable, placed increasing strain on the urban administration.

In these circumstances TANU officials, like their British predecessors, were soon anxious to restrict urban citizenship.[10] By the end of the colonial era, as we have seen, rights to urban residence were technically restricted to those who had lived in the town for four out of the past five years. In independent Tanganyika/Tanzania such legal requirements were unsustainable. However,

5   *Ibid.*, p. 32.
6   Employment fell by 14% from 1962 to 1963. Employment in big firms surveyed in 1966 fell by 13% in 1965–6, while wages had increased by 12%. International Labour Office, *Report to the Government of the United Republic of Tanzania on Wages, Incomes and Prices Policy* (Turner Report) (Dsm, 1967), pp. 8, 10.
7   *Ibid.*, p. 12.
8   In 1975, smallholders earned between a third and two-thirds of the average urban waged employee. Coulson, *Tanzania*, p. 198.
9   P. Collier, 'Labour market allocation and income distribution', Annexe III, *Basic Economic Report*, International Bank for Reconstruction and Development (1977), p. 16.
10 See Brennan, 'Sucking with straws'; and Burton, 'Haven'.

the Townships (Removal of Undesirable Persons) Ordinance remained on the statute books[11] and was periodically enforced in an attempt to ensure that urban citizenship was enjoyed by only those who fulfilled certain criteria, notably the acquisition of formal employment.[12] After an apparent hiatus shortly before and after independence, round-ups and repatriations were recommenced by the regional administration.[13] They continued to occur sporadically and with varying intensity through to the mid 1980s. To justify these campaigns, politicians and officials invoked the idle and disorderly nature of the urban poor, alongside the neglect of abundant land in the rural areas and the need to enhance agricultural productivity (a rhetoric that was reinforced after 1967 by the ideological baggage linked with *Ujamaa*). The last campaign of this nature began in late 1983, when an attempt was made to enforce the recently passed Human Resources Deployment Act (popularly known as *Nguvu Kazi* ['hard work']). This innocuously titled act in fact entailed a high degree of coercion aimed at correcting the supposed indolence of large sections of the population (notably those working in the urban informal sector) by forcing them to engage in more 'productive' activities, such as cultivating *shambas* or labouring on plantations. Like previous attempts to 'clean up' the town, *Nguvu Kazi* was a miserable failure. Moreover, the degree of coercion employed led to widespread resentment. In early 1984 enforcement of *Nguvu Kazi* lapsed. Subsequent political shifts in the 1980s and 1990s led to the abandonment of the campaigning style. Meanwhile, the urban informal economy came to be treated with much greater tolerance by politicians and officials. Nevertheless, Tanzanians engaged in lower-level informal sector activities were still periodically targeted, and harassment of unemployed and underemployed urban youth in particular has continued up to the present.

Urbanisation, development and crime

Dar es Salaam forms a good example of the problems associated with rapid urbanisation experienced by many towns and cities in developing countries in the twentieth century. Although by world standards it remains a medium-sized metropolis, from around 1940 it sustained spectacular rates of urban growth matching or exceeding rates of other Third World cities.

[11] As did sections of the penal code targeting 'idle and disorderly persons' and 'rogues and vagabonds' – sections 176 and 177.
[12] See R. Martin, *Personal Freedom and the Law in Tanzania* (Nairobi, 1974), pp. 100–5; Burton, 'Haven'.
[13] In the late 1960s the structure of the raids bore a marked resemblance to those a decade earlier. According to Martin (p. 103): 'the Police ... round people up, and keep them under supervision, but they are interviewed by officers of the Social Welfare [and Probation] Division who make recommendations as to the action that should be taken. If a removal order under Cap. 104 is deemed desirable, the person concerned is sent home under police escort and the local Area Commissioner and TANU leaders are requested to keep him under observation.'

This book has sought to provide a historical context to this phenomenon. The conundrum identified by colonial officials throughout eastern Africa in the early 1950s has grown ever more complex in the decades after independence. Rapid urbanisation was not accompanied by any significant hikes in municipal revenue. As a result, colonial and post-colonial administrations, despite showing a distinct wariness towards urban growth, have been too weak to either prevent over-urbanisation, through rural development schemes or more coercive measures, or to ameliorate it, through the provision of housing and infrastructure or the creation of employment. The loss of control that occurred in urban centres throughout eastern Africa (and further afield), was evident in the burgeoning shanties and an expanding informal sector from the 1950s. These phenomena gave rise to entirely legitimate concerns on the part of urban officials (and others) over such issues as public health, labour practices and living conditions. However, the manner in which officials sought to deal with the problem — in the colonial period and after independence — actually tended to weaken rather than enhance urban order.

At the heart of the problem was the issue of urban citizenship. In the early-colonial period officials had difficulty in even conceiving the truly urban 'native', and restrictions were placed on African residence in towns. A post-WWII shift to a more development-oriented colonial policy saw a significant increase in expenditure on urban infrastructure and amenities. Alongside this came a growing acceptance of the African urban presence. A stabilised urban workforce (albeit one restricted in size) was envisaged, engaged in productive industrial employment, producing manufactured goods for, and consuming the produce of, a reinvigorated rural sector.[14] This scheme hinged around the development and modernisation of African society, which in the urban areas involved the construction of planned housing and of a physical *and* social infrastructure fit for the new African working class. After independence, African officials inherited — and propagated — these late-colonial aims. The legitimacy of the post-colonial state was in large part founded on the notion of development. Modernisation formed a key aspiration for both ordinary citizens and government administrators and politicians.[15] Officials responsible for urban governance envisaged planned towns containing restricted populations that increasingly enjoyed infrastructure and amenities similar to those taken for granted in the urban centres of Europe and North America. This vision had its origins in the late-colonial period, when, concurrently, its viability was undermined by a dramatic acceleration in urban growth rates. Rather than adjusting policy to account for rapid urbanisation, however, the vision of a modern planned town continued to inform the decisions of urban administrators, colonial and post-colonial alike. Faced with the efflorescence of informal networks, in the form of housing, infrastructure, employment and

---

[14] This was advocated most enthusiastically in the *EARC Report*.
[15] Modernity, of course, came in diverse forms, including improved access to services such as electricity and water, as well as increasing industrial production and the consumption of international popular cultural forms.

services, ineffective policies of repression and control were adopted in which rights to urban residence were undermined and/or denied.

In their failure to assert control, officials came to associate the informal networks established by urban-dwellers with a portentous disorder. The urban shanties and the activities adopted by the residents therein posed not only a challenge to governmental authority, but also to public space, public health and public order (shanty communities and informal sector traders were frequently linked with more serious criminal activity by politicians and officials anxious to justify repressive measures).[16] Through the criminalisation of various informal sector activities the state sought to both reimpose authority and to attempt to guide urban development along 'proper' lines. However, rather than strengthening urban order, instead this policy led to a proliferation of crime. Through the enforcement of by-laws proscribing street trading, begging, or even the urban presence of the unemployed, persons who might otherwise have been perfectly law-abiding were consigned to the ranks of the criminal. Valuable time, space and money in police stations, courts and prisons were expended upon petty offenders. More seriously, instead of acting to reassert governmental authority, the sporadic — and ineffective — enforcement of unpopular legislation only served to delegitimise the state and to weaken those institutions responsible for the maintenance of law and order. Faced with a criminal justice system perceived by large sections of the urban population as oppressive, the public co-operation essential to any effort to address crime was withdrawn or offered only partially, thereby undermining the capacity of the police, the courts and local government to tackle the more serious manifestations of urban lawlessness.

Postscript: Dar es Salaam, 2002

In the 1980s and 1990s cash-strapped African governments, subject to strict structural adjustment programmes, scaled down ambitious post-independence schemes aimed at the transformation of African societies. For the victims of what were frequently coercive attempts at fitting local populations to the often ill-conceived, and unpopular, social engineering policies of nationalist politicians (*Ujamaa* in Tanzania being a particularly noteworthy example), this offered respite. In the case of the urban informal sector, greater tolerance was evident — a product of the recognition that the state had few alternatives to informal housing, services and jobs; this was alongside the increasing stress placed on the informal sector by international NGOs and donors as a means to achieve poverty alleviation.[17] Nevertheless, despite evidence of more

---

[16] For an example from neighbouring Zambia, see the ILO *Report on Incomes Prices and Wages in Zambia* (Lusaka, 1969, p. 13) – authored by (presumably) the same Turner who had written the ILO report in Tanzania two years earlier. Cited in MacMillan, 'Historiography'.

[17] For a discussion of the 1980s, see Tripp, *Changing the Rules*; for a recent example of the shift in approach, see 'Informal sector gets new push', *DN*, 1 October 2003.

enlightened policies towards people engaged in informal economic activities, the urban poor remain vulnerable to harassment by agents of local and central Government.[18] Indeed, attitudes towards the occupation and utilisation of urban space that first arose in the colonial period have shown a remarkable resilience.[19] Two examples from contemporary Dar es Salaam serve to underline this point.[20]

In November and December 2002, Dar es Salaam police and municipal *askaris* combined to enforce a provincial initiative to — in the words of a *Daily News* caption — 'rid the Haven of Peace of haphazard trading'.[21] In late November young street hawkers — by this time, colloquially known as *machinga* — were removed from the heart of Kariakoo and forced to trade at the Mchikichi market. Frustrated by the lack of business at Mchikichi, *machinga* drifted back to central Kariakoo. On Saturday 31 November, police armed with *rungus*, teargas and guns engaged in running battles with the *machinga* to prevent them reoccupying the streets.[22] Further action, later the same week, saw the destruction of kiosks and removal of *machinga* from central Dar es Salaam.[23] The Regional Commissioner, Yusuf Makamba, who had initiated the clampdown, instructed Ilala, Kinondoni and Temeke municipalities (which make up the city of Dar es Salaam) to enact legislation providing for

[18]   Young Africans in particular. Andersson and Stavrou (*Youth Delinquency*, p. 48) note that in contemporary Dar es Salaam '[y]outh on the streets ... are often harassed by the police; they are chased, tied up, beaten, searched and taken into police custody' where they often receive further beatings. Young town-dwellers are arrested often merely 'on suspicion' or for vagrancy. For a scholarly discussion, see Moyer, 'Shadow'. For a disturbing account of the police harassment of one Abdallah, a 'street child' in Mwanza, see Rakesh Rajani and Mustaf Kudrati, *Street Children of Nyanza: A situation analysis* (Dsm, 1994), pp. 1–2. The Mwanza raid, which occurred in 1992, targeted — among others — street children because, according to a social welfare officer, 'they were lazy deliquents who would turn into gangsters if left on the streets.'

[19]   To avoid harassment by the police, inhabitants of contemporary Dar es Salaam need to possess official identification cards (*kitambulisho*) demonstrating they are legally permitted to reside in the city. To obtain a card, formal employment and/or residence is required. Young Africans in particular are victimised owing to their lacking *kitambulisho* (Moyer, 'Shadow', pp. 36, 99, 190). The remarkable 'Hali Halisi' (1998) by Tanzanian rapper, Mr.II, provides commentary on such harassment, in which – in a mock court scene – a youth is sentenced to five years' imprisonment for 'loitering'. I am grateful to Alex Perullo for making his transcript of 'Hali Halisi' available to me. See also, Alex Perullo and John Fenn, 'Language ideologies, choices, and practices in Eastern African Hip Hop', in *Global Popular Music: The politics and aesthetics of language choice*, ed. Harry Berger and Michael T. Carroll (Mississippi, 2003), pp. 19–51.

[20]   For an example from Kenya, see the *Daily Nation* of 2 September 2003, which reports a 'police swoop' in Mombasa as a result of which people were charged for 'offences includ[ing] loitering with immoral intent, being drunk and disorderly, roaming purposelessly and being a nuisance to the public'.

[21]   *DN*, 13 December 2002, p. 2.

[22]   See *Nipashe*, 1 December 2002, p. 1. As in the colonial period, many of the *machinga* were acting as agents of owners of shops in Kariakoo's sidestreets. The clampdown on their activities, meanwhile, was heartily supported (if not initiated) by shopowners along Uhuru Street itself.

[23]   *DN*, 13 December, pp. 2 & 4.

Fig. 14.1 *Detail from a* tingatinga *postcard depicting a recent crackdown against* machinga.
Source: Printed by Tingatinga Arts Cooperative Society (2003). (Original painting by Maurus
Malikita. Reproduced with kind permission)

a two-year penal sentence for illegal street trading in place of the current
system of fines.[24]

Eight months earlier, I myself witnessed a related event around the borders
of what, in the colonial period, were known as Zones I and II. A city council
lorry came screeching to a halt at the junction of Ghana Avenue and Ohio
Street. From the back of the lorry jumped a gang of city *askaris* who pounced
on vendors selling *madafu* (drinking coconuts) by the roadside, manhandling
their coconuts, their bikes and the vendors themselves into the back of the
lorry to join fellow vendors who had been apprehended earlier. Their offence
was presumably not to have acquired licences (or alternatively to have failed
to offer municipal officials and/or *askaris* what in local parlance is known as
kitu kidogo ['a little something']).[25] The previous day I had visited the office of
a municipal official who headed a United Nations-sponsored programme
aimed at reducing crime in the city. I asked what were the achievements of
the programme, which by this time had been running for a couple of years.
Alongside initiatives encouraging community policing, the official cited the
removal of petty traders from Maktaba Street in central Dar es Salaam, and
the introduction of a tier of city *askaris* (or 'auxiliary police') responsible for

[24] To avoid 'constant harassment' by city *askaris* Makamba advised that *machinga* relocate to
the city outskirts. *Nipashe*, 12 December 2002, p. 1. The clampdown was predictably ineffective, though the intermittent cycle of repression is never-ending. In early 2004 another
concerted, though similarly unsuccessful, attempt was made to rid the town of street traders and others. (See e.gs., *The Guardian*, 15–17 January 2004). The futility of the exercise
was captured by a later photograph in the *Daily News* of a busy road junction which portrayed '[be]ggars and petty traders ... back in Dar es Salaam in full force and right under
the noses of authorities who only two months ago removed them from the city streets'. *DN*,
14 April 2004, p. 4.

[25] See e.g., 'City askari racket milks the machinga', *Daily Times*, 13 April 2004, p. 1.

the enforcement of municipal by-laws whose 'diligence' I was to witness the following day. On being challenged that such policies not only deprived fellow urbanites of welcome urban services but, more significantly, young townsmen of a source of income (street traders are overwhelmingly male), without which they may be forced to commit more serious criminal acts to get by, the official responded that the kiosks and vendors provided an environment in which crime thrived.

In this study of colonial Dar es Salaam I hope to have demonstrated that, by contrast, crime in the city has in fact proliferated in part as a result of the adoption of inappropriate policies towards the urban poor; policies that have been founded upon a marked antipathy towards urbanisation. In rounding up the *machinga*, and in the quotidian harassment of urban youth, the police and city *askaris* in contemporary Dar es Salaam are simply stoking the problem of urban crime. In these and other cases the Tanzanian state is actually creating criminals. Moreover, the rights of marginalised social groups to occupy and utilise urban space are being infringed. A solution to the problem must begin with an acknowledgment of these rights. In 1922, freedom of movement for all races was written into the League of Nations mandate that was supposed to govern the British administration of Tanganyika. The past eighty years have, regrettably, witnessed the all too frequent abuse of this fundamental right.

Appendix

The Population of Dar es Salaam
1867–2002

	Africans (Male)	Africans (Female)	Africans (Total)	Asians	Europeans	Total
1867						*c*.900
1887						3–5,000
1894			9,000	620	400	10,000
1900			18,000	1,480	360	20,000
1913			19,000	2,500	1,000	22,500
1921			20,000	4,000	600	24,600
1922			20,000 (approx.)			
1923			24,000 (approx.)			
1927			29,000	5,000	774	34,774
1928[1]	12,791	9,139	22,734			
1931[2]	15,299	7,417	22,734	9,000	1,330	33,064
1937	11,550	12,000	23,550	8,800	970	33,320
1940	18,200	16,550	34,750	8,825	1,043	44,618
1948			51,231	16,270	1,726	69,227
1952			77,330	22,547	3,603	103,480
1957	53,847	39,516	93,363	29,986	4,479	128,742
1967						272,515
1978						769,445
1988						1,623,238
2002						2,497,940

The above figures, of varying reliability, are taken from the following sources: 1867–1921 from Table 1 in Sutton, 'Dar es Salaam'; 1922–40, DARs; 1948–2002, census figures. Sutton has the following to say of the figures up to independence: 'The earliest figures are rough estimates not based on counts, and should not… be regarded as at all accurate. It is difficult to say how accurate the counts taken in the German period were.[3] [T]hose of the British period… are believed to fall short of the actual numbers, since the methods of enumeration were not sufficiently thorough to allow for temporary residents, "squatters" and people cultivating on the City's outskirts.' For the censuses up to 1967 he cautions that inclusion of settlements on the outskirts would add significantly to the figures. More recent censuses probably underestimate the population, a majority of whom live in unplanned settlements.

[1] The DAR reports (p. 10): 'Census … of the Township was taken in a single day, and was an enumeration of all the people who had slept in town the previous night … Believed percentage of error very small.'

[2] N.b. figures given in the DAR do not total up correctly. So the number of male and female totals added together give 22,716 not 22,734. In reporting the results of the census DO Fryer gives the total of Africans as 22,732, Fryer to PC, EP, 10 July 1931, TNA/61/167.

[3] Though that of 1913 appears to be relatively reliable, stemming from a census carried out by the *Bezirksamt* (the German equivalent of the District Commissioner). I am grateful to Franck Raimbault for pointing this out.

Bibliography

Archives and Libraries

Colindale Newspaper Library, London
Dar es Salaam Times
Tanganyika Times
Tanganyika Herald
Tanganyika Opinion
Tanganyika Standard
Mambo Leo
Sunday News
Daily News

Kenya National Archive (KNA), Nairobi
Secretariat and regional correspondence and reports

Public Records Office (PRO), Kew, London
Principal accessions consulted:

PRO/CO/691	Tanganyika Original Correspondence
PRO/CO/736	Contains Departmental Annual Reports, Tanganyika
PRO/CO/746	Tanganyika Register of Correspondence
PRO/CO/822	East Africa Original Correspondence
PRO/CO/859	Social Services Original Correspondence
PRO/CO/892	East Africa Royal Commission (1953–55)
PRO/CO/997	Colonial Social Welfare Advisory Committee: Minutes and papers, 1943–52
PRO/CO/1018	Hailey Papers
PRO/WO/276	East Africa Command: Papers

Rhodes House Library, Oxford
Colonial Records Project Papers
Dar es Salaam Extra-Provincial District Book (Microfilm)

Bibliography

SOAS Library (and Special Collection), University of London
Kwetu
Memorandum on Social Conditions in Dar es Salaam (1931) by E.C. Baker
Copy of original social survey of Dar es Salaam (with indices) by J.A.K. Leslie (1957)
Wilfred Whiteley Collection

Tanzania National Archives (TNA), Dar es Salaam
Principal accessions consulted:
Secretariat Files (Early series 1920–27) — File numbers contain four digits
Secretariat Files (1927–1961) — File numbers contain five digits

TNA/54	Dar es Salaam District Annual Reports 1921–37 (these are currently [2004] on the shelves in the TNA reading room)
TNA/57	Kisarawe District
TNA/61	Morogoro Headquarters — Eastern Province
TNA/90	Police Headquarters
TNA/122	Kinondoni Local Court (index only available, which lists offences, dates of cases 1957–61)
TNA/225	Ministry of Local Government and Housing (1946–65)
TNA/226	Ministry of Local Government and Housing (1941–64)
TNA/450	Ministry of Health and Social Welfare
TNA/460	Labour Department
TNA/489	Prisons Headquarters
TNA/561	District Office, Ilala Boma

Dar es Salaam District Books (I–III)
Dar es Salaam Municipal Council Minutes

University of Dar es Salaam Library
Kwetu (copies for 1937–40), *Zuhra* (1955–8) and intermittent copies of various other newspapers in Swahili and English
Provincial Commissioners' Conference Minutes
A. Gibb & Partners, 'A Plan for Dar es Salaam' (the only surviving copy, which has subsequently gone missing)
Legislative Council Minutes
Municipal Council Minutes
History (BA) dissertations
MA and Ph.D. theses

Zanzibar National Archive
Secretariat files

Interviews

No. 1	Hamisi Akida, Arnautoglu Hall, Dar es Salaam, 28 May 1997
No. 2	Mwinyimvua Sultan, Amiri Mngamili and Hassan Mbwana, Buguruni kwa Malapa, Dar es Salaam, 9 July 1997
No. 3	Rajabu Pazi, Yusuf Mkimbizi, Salum Pazi, Saidi Simba and Juma Mtingwa, Manzese, Dar es Salaam, 10 July 1997

Bibliography

No. 4   Mohamed Tugawane, Hamza Mwinyimade, and Seifu Mpimbiluka, Kawe, Dar es Salaam, 11 July 1997
No. 5   Mzee Bogora, Salum Kambi and Hassan Omari, Buguruni kwa Madenge, Dar es Salaam, 28 July 1997
No. 6   Yusuf Mohamed Kifindo, Msasani, Dar es Salaam, 23 July 1997
No. 7   Saidi Amiri Mwinyi, Kisutu, Dar es Salaam, 28 July 1997
No. 8   Masudi Ali and Abdulrahman Mohamed, Kariakoo Maghiribi, Dar es Salaam, 18 August 1997
No. 9   Herbert Kaptua, Stephen Mzinga and Sergeant M. Kilakala, Tanzania Legion, Dar es Salaam, 18 August 1997
No. 10   Randall Sadleir (former official in the Tanganyika Native Administration), London, 5 August 1998
No. 11   John (J.A.K.) Leslie, Berkhamsted, 7 August & 3 September 1998
No. 12   Mabrouk Swedi Mabrouk and Abubakar Saidi Mgomba, Magomeni Kagera, 1 October 2003

Correspondence

Joan Thompson (married to a Tanganyikan Police Officer; living in Dar es Salaam in the 1940s/1950s), letter dated 1 March 1999
D.J.G. Fraser (Supt, Tanganyika Police Force, 1952–62), letter dated 7 March 1999

Unpublished documentary sources (and abbreviations in footnotes)

Baker, Edward Conway (E.C.) 'Memorandum on the Social Conditions of Dar es Salaam', 4 June 1931, copy in SOAS archive (Baker, 'Memorandum')
Mayhew, Timothy. 'Reminiscences of life as a DO 1947–64', RHMss.Afr.s. 2089 (Mayhew, 'Reminiscences')
Molohan, M.J.B. 'Report on Unemployment and Wage Rates in Dar es Salaam', 27 September 1941, TNA/61/443/1 (Molohan, 'Unemployment')
Municipal Secretary. 'Report on Township Affairs', 1934, TNA/61/625 (MS, 'Township Affairs')
Municipal Secretary. 'Memorandum on the administration of Dar es Salaam', 22 February 1937, TNA/61/207/Vol. 1 (MS, 'Administration')
Paterson, Alexander. 'Report on a visit to the Prisons of Kenya, Uganda, Tanganyika, Zanzibar, Aden and Somaliland', 1939, TNA/27062 (Paterson, 'Report')
Pearson, N. 'Trade Unionist on Safari', RH/Mss.Afr.s.394 (Pearson, 'Safari')
Pike, Andrew Hamilton (A.H.) 'Report on Native Affairs in Dar es Salaam Township', 5 June 1939, TNA/18950/Vol. II (Pike, 'Native Affairs')
Pike, A.H. 'Memorandum on the Development of African areas of Dar es Salaam Township', 12 July 1944, TNA/61/643/3 (Pike, 'Development')
Various. Draft copy of 'Urban problems in East and Central Africa — Report of a conference held at Ndola, N. Rhodesia, February 1958', TNA/225/UW80.131/Vol. 1 ('Ndola Report')
Westcott, Nicholas. Notes on interviews with A.H. Pike, 3 November 1978 and 19 March 1979

Unpublished secondary sources

Anthony, David Henry. 'Culture and society in a town in transition: A people's history of Dar es Salaam, 1865–1939', unpub. Ph.D. thesis, University of Wisconsin (1983)

Armstrong, Allen. 'Urban control campaigns in the Third World: The case of Tanzania', Geography Dept, University of Glasgow, Occ. Papers no. 19 (1987)

Bienefeld, Mannfred. 'The self-employed of urban Tanzania', IDS Discussion paper no. 54 (1974), copy in the Institute of Commonwealth Studies library

Brennan, James R. 'Mumiani and Uhuru: Buguruni on the eve of Tanganyika's independence', *African Studies Association Conference paper* (1998)

—— 'Democratizing cinema and censorship in Tanzania, 1920–76', paper given at the first conference on 'Comparative Imperial and Post-colonial Historical Studies', Michigan State University, 14 February 1999, revised draft in author's possession

—— 'Nation, race and urbanization in Dar es Salaam, Tanzania, 1916–1976', Ph.D. thesis, Northwestern University (2002)

Burton, Andrew. 'Wahuni (The Undesirables): African urbanisation, crime and colonial order in Dar es Salaam, 1919–1961', Ph.D. thesis, University of London (2000)

—— 'Raw youth, school-leavers and the emergence of structural unemployment in late-colonial urban Tanganyika' (in preparation)

—— 'Dealing with the defaulter: Native taxation and colonial authority in Tanganyika, 1920s–1950s' (in preparation)

Byerley, Andrew. 'Manufacturing Jinja. Rounds of space production and place making in an African industrial town', Ph.D. thesis, University of Stockholm (f/c)

Chinn, W.H. 'Social problems of rapid urbanisation with particular reference to British Africa', in 'Urbanisation in African Social Change', Proceedings of the Inaugural Seminar, Centre for African Studies, Edinburgh University (1963)

Depelchin, Jacques. 'The beggar problem in Dar es Salaam in the 1930s', History Seminar Paper, UDsm (1978)

Hill, Stephen. '"I am a partial person": the urban experience of rural music', in James R. Brennan, Andrew Burton and Yusufu Lawi. *Dar es Salaam in the Twentieth Century: The history of an emerging East African metropolis* (in preparation)

Ivaska, Andrew M. 'Imagining Dar es Salaam: Culture, morality and urban space in representations of a capital city', paper given at the conference 'Dar es Salaam in the 20th century: Urbanisation and social change in an emerging East African metropolis', UDsm, 1 July 2002

—— 'Negotiating "culture" in a cosmopolitan capital: Urban style and the Tanzanian state in colonial and post-colonial Dar es Salaam', Ph.D. thesis, University of Michigan (2003)

Kaijage, Frederick. 'Alternative history and discourses from below: social history in urban Tanga', Dept of History seminar paper, UDsm, 30 November 2000

Kironde, J.M.L. 'The evolution of the land use structure of Dar es Salaam 1890–1990: A study in the effects of land policy', Ph.D. thesis, University of Nairobi, Dept of Land Development (1994)

—— 'Approaches to dealing with urban poverty in Tanzania: The role of Urban Authorities', paper given at a Regional Workshop on Urban Poverty in Southern and Eastern Africa, March 1995, Nairobi (1995)

Lucas, Stephen (ed.) 'The Magenge of Dar es Salaam', UDsm mimeo, (1976)

Martin, Stephen. 'Music in urban East Africa: A study of the development of urban jazz in Dar es Salaam', Ph.D. thesis, University of Michigan (1980)

Mascarenhas, Adolfo. 'Urban development in Dar es Salaam', MA thesis, UCLA (1966)

Bibliography

Mashisa, W. 'Urbanisation in Dar es Salaam: The case of Manzese', BA history dissertation, UDsm (1978/9)

Moyer, Eileen. 'In the shadow of the Sheraton: Imagining localities in global spaces in Dar es Salaam, Tanzania', Ph.D. thesis, University of Amsterdam (2004)

Mutasingwa, D.R. 'The history of Dar es Salaam — the study of Magomeni', BA history dissertation, UDsm (1978/9)

Mwijarubi, B.E. 'A historical study of class relations in Dar es Salaam: A case study of Buguruni', BA history dissertation, UDsm (1977)

Onstad, Eric. 'A history of Nairobi's petty traders and their organisations, 1899–1975', MA dissertation, University of Nairobi (1990)

Scarnecchia, Timothy. 'Residential segregation and the politics of gender, Salisbury, Rhodesia, 1940–56', Ph.D. thesis, University of Michigan (1993)

Shaidi, Leonard Paulo. 'Explaining crime in Tanzania mainland: An historical socio-economic perspective', Ph.D. thesis, UDsm (1985)

Tsuruta, Tadasu. 'Simba na Yanga: Football and urbanisation in Dar es Salaam, 1920s–1970s', paper given at the conference, 'Dar es Salaam in the 20th century: Urbanisation and social change in an emerging East African metropolis', UDsm, 1 July 2002

Waller, Richard. 'Disciplining youth in colonial Maasailand', paper given at the African Studies Association conference, Boston, 30 October–2 November 2003

Westcott, Nicholas. 'The impact of the Second World War on Tanganyika', unpub Ph.D. thesis, University of Cambridge (1982)

Published sources

Achola, Milcah A. 'Colonial policy and urban health: The case of Nairobi', in Burton (2002)

Admiralty War Staff, Intelligence Division. *A Handbook of German East Africa* (London, 1916)

Akyeampong, Emmanuel. '"Wo pe tam won pe ba" ("You like cloth but you don't want children"): Urbanization, individualism and gender relations in colonial Ghana, c.1900–39', in Anderson and Rathbone (2000), pp. 222–234

Anderson, David M. 'Stock theft and moral economy in colonial Kenya', *Africa* 56 (1986), pp. 399–416

—— 'Policing, prosecution and the law in colonial Kenya, c.1905–39', in Anderson and Killingray (1991)

—— 'Policing the settler state: colonial hegemony in Kenya, 1900–1952', in Dagmar Engels and Shula Marks, *Contesting Colonial Hegemony* (London, 1994)

—— 'Master and servant in colonial Kenya', *JAH* 41 (2000), pp. 459–485

—— 'Corruption at City Hall: African housing and urban development in colonial Nairobi', in Burton (2002)

—— *Histories of the Hanged: Britain's dirty war in Kenya and the end of Empire* (London, 2004)

—— and Vigdis Broch-Due. *The Poor Are Not Us: Poverty and pastoralism in Eastern Africa* (Oxford/Athens/Nairobi/Dar es Salaam/Kampala, 2000)

—— and David Killingray. *Policing the Empire: Government, authority and control, 1830–1940* (Manchester, 1991)

—— *Policing and Decolonization, 1917–1965* (Manchester, 1992)

—— and Richard Rathbone. *Africa's Urban Past* (Oxford/Portsmouth, NH, 2000)

Andersson, Cecilia (with Aki Stavrou). *Youth Delinquency and the Criminal Justice System in*

Bibliography

Dar es Salaam, Tanzania: A snap shot survey, April 2000 (Nairobi (Habitat), 2001)

Armstrong, Allen. 'Colonial planning and neocolonial urban planning: Three generations of master plans for Dar es Salaam, Tanzania', *Utafiti*, 8:1 (1986), pp. 43–66

Barnes, Teresa A. *'We Women Worked So Hard': Gender, urbanization and social reproduction in Harare, Zimbabwe, 1930–56* (Portsmouth, NH/ Oxford/Harare/Cape Town, 1999)

Barnes, W.L.G. 'Urban problems in East and Central Africa: Report of a conference held at Ndola, Northern Rhodesia, February 1958', *Journal of African Administration*, 10 (4)

Becher, Jürgen. *Dar es Salaam, Tanga und Tabora: Stadtentwicklung in Tansani unter deutscher Kolonialherrschaft* (Stuttgart, 1997)

Becker, Charles M. & Andrew R. Morrison. 'The growth of African cities: Theory and estimates' in Mafeje and Radwan (1995)

Beidelman, T.O. *The Matrilineal Peoples of Eastern Tanzania* (London, 1967)

Beinart, William. *Twentieth Century South Africa* (Oxford, 2001)

Bernault, Florence. *Démocraties ambiguës en Afrique centrale. Congo-Brazzaville, Gabon, 1940–1965* (Paris, 1996)

—— (ed.) *Enfermement, prison et châtiments en Afrique. Du 19ème siècle à nos jours* (Paris, 1999)

—— 'The political shaping of a sacred locality in Brazzaville, 1959–97', in Anderson and Rathbone, *Africa's Urban Past* (2000), pp. 283–302

Berry, L. (ed.) *Tanzania in Maps* (London, 1971)

Betts, Raymond F. 'The establishment of the Medina in Dakar, 1914', *Africa* 41 (1971), pp. 143–152

Bienefeld, Mannfred. 'The informal sector and peripheral capitalism', *Bulletin of the Institute of Development Studies* (1975)

Bissell, William Cunningham. 'Conservation and the colonial past: Urban planning, space and power in Zanzibar', in Anderson and Rathbone (2000), pp. 246–261

Blackwell, James E. 'Race and crime in Tanzania', *Phylon* 32 (1971)

Bonner, Philip. 'Family, crime and political consciousness on the East Rand, 1939–55', *JSAS* 14 (1988)

—— 'The Russians on the Reef, 1947–57: Urbanisation, gang warfare and ethnic mobilisation', in Bonner, Peter Delius and Deborah Posel, *Apartheid's Genesis, 1935–62* (Johannesburg, 1993)

—— 'African urbanisation on the Rand between the 1930s and 1960s: Its social character and political consequences', *JSAS* 21:1 (1995), pp. 115–129

Bonsa, Shimelis. 'A history of Kistane migration to 1974', in Burton (2002)

Brennan, James R. '"Sucking with straws": Exploitation and urban citizenship in Tanzanian nationalist thought and rhetoric, 1958–76', in Burton and Jennings, *Emperor's New Clothes* (f/c)

Brett, E.A. *Colonialism and Underdevelopment in East Africa: The politics of economic change, 1919–1939* (London, 1973)

Briggs, Asa. *Victorian Cities* (Harmondsworth, 1968)

Bromley, R. 'Begging in Cali: Image, reality and policy', *International Social Work* 24 (1981), pp. 22–40

Bryceson, Deborah F. 'A century of food supply in Dar es Salaam', in J.I. Guyer (ed.) *Feeding African Cities: Studies in Regional Social History* (Manchester, 1987)

Bujra, Janet. 'Women "entrepreneurs" of early Nairobi', *Canadian Journal of African Studies* 2 (1972); and 'Postcript: Prostitution, class and the state', in Sumner (1982)

—— *Serving Class: Masculinity and the feminisation of domestic service in Tanzania*, London (2000)

Burton, Andrew. 'Urchins, loafers and the cult of the cowboy: Urbanisation and

Bibliography

delinquency in Dar es Salaam, 1919–1961', *JAH* 42 (2001), pp. 199–216
—— (ed.) *The Urban Experience in Eastern Africa, c.1750–2000* (Nairobi, 2002) (also published as a special double volume of *Azania*, XXXVI–XXXVII (2001–2))
—— 'Urbanisation in Eastern Africa: An historical overview, *c.*1750–2000', introduction to *Ibid.* (2002), pp. 1–28
—— 'Adjutants, agents, intermediaries: The Native Administration in Dar es Salaam township, 1919–1961', in *Ibid.* (2002), pp. 98–118
—— 'Brothers by Day: Colonial policing in Dar es Salaam under British rule', *Urban History* (2003: 1), pp. 63–91
—— 'Townsmen in the making: Social engineering and citizenship in Dar es Salaam, 1945–1960', *International Journal of African Historical Studies* (2004)
—— 'The Haven of Peace purged: Tackling the "undesirable" and "unproductive" poor in Dar es Salaam, c.1954–1984', in Burton and Jennings, *Emperor's New Clothes* (f/c)
—— 'Jamii ya Wahalifu. The growth of crime in a colonial urban centre: Dar es Salaam, Tanganyika, 1919–1961', *Crime, History and Societies* 8: 2
Burton, Andrew and Michael Jennings (eds). *The Emperor's New Clothes? Continuity and change in late-colonial and early post-colonial East Africa* (forthcoming)
Buruku, Daisy Sykes. 'The townsman: Kleist Sykes', in Iliffe (1973)
Cairns, J.C. *Bush and Boma* (London, 1959)
Campbell, Chloe. 'Juvenile delinquency in colonial Kenya, 1900–1939', *The Historical Journal* 45: 1 (2002), pp. 129–151
Campbell, John. *Urbanisation, Urban planning and Urban Life in Tanzania: An annotated bibliography*, Occ. Paper No. 4, University of Hull (1987)
—— 'Race, class and community in colonial Dar es Salaam: Tentative steps towards an understanding of urban society', in Colin Creighton and C.K. Omari (eds), *Gender, Family and Work in Tanzania* (Aldershot, 2000)
Cell, John. 'Anglo-Indian medical theory and the origins of segregation in West Africa', *American Historical Review* 91 (1986), pp. 307–335
Chauncey, Jr. George. 'The locus of reproduction: Women's labour in the Zambian Copperbelt, 1927–1953', *JSAS* 7 (1981), pp. 135–164
Chesney, Kellow. *The Victorian Underworld* (Harmondsworth, 1970)
Chevalier, Louis. *Laboring Classes and Dangerous Classes in Paris during the first half of the Nineteenth century* (New York, 1973)
Clancy-Smith, Julia. 'Gender in the city: Women, migration and contested spaces in Tunis, c.1830–81', in Anderson and Rathbone (2000), pp. 189–204
Clayton, Anthony and Donald Savage. *Government and Labour in Kenya, 1919–1939* (London, 1974)
Clinard, M.B. and D.J. Abbott. *Crime in Developing Countries* (New York, 1973)
Clyde, D.F. *History of the Medical Services of Tanganyika* (Dsm, 1962)
Cohen, Stanley. *Folk Devils and Moral Panics: The creation of mods and rockers* (St Albans, 1973)
Connah, Graham. *African Civilizations: Precolonial cities and states in tropical Africa: An archaeological perspective* (Cambridge, 1987)
Cooper, Frederick. 'Urban space, industrial time, and wage labour in Africa', in F. Cooper (ed.), *Struggle for the City* (Beverley Hills, 1983)
—— *On the African Waterfront: Urban disorder and the transformation of work in colonial Mombasa* (New Haven, 1987)
—— *Decolonization and African Society: The labor question in French and British Africa* (Cambridge, 1996)
—— *Africa since 1940: The past of the present* (Cambridge, 2002)

289

Bibliography

Coplan, David B. *In the Township Tonight! South Africa's black city music and theatre* (London/ NY, 1985)

Coquery-Vidrovitch, Catherine. *African Women: A modern history* (Boulder, 1997)

Coulsen, Andrew. *Tanzania: A political economy* (Oxford, 1982)

Crumney, Donald (ed.) *Banditry, Rebellion and Social Protest in Africa* (London/Portsmouth, NH, 1986)

Curtin, Philip. 'Medical knowledge and urban planning in Tropical Africa', *American Historical Review* 90 (1985), pp. 594–613

Davis, Kingsley. 'The Urbanization of the Human Population', *Scientific American*, (1965), reprinted in LeGates and Stout (1996)

Dundas, Charles. *Kilimanjaro and its People: A history of the Wachagga, their laws, customs and legends together with some account of the highest mountain in Africa* (London, 1968, first edn., 1924)

East African Royal Commission. *East African Royal Commission 1953–55 Report* (London, 1955)

Ehrlich, Cyril. 'The poor country: The Tanganyika economy from 1945 to independence', in Low and Smith (1976)

Emsley, Clive. *Crime and Society in England, 1750–1900* (London, 1996)

—— 'The history of crime and crime control institutions', in Maguire, Morgan and Reiner, *Handbook of Criminology* (2002), pp. 203–230

Engels, Friedrich. *The Condition of the Working Class in England*, trans. & ed. by W.O. Henderson and W.H. Chaloner (Stanford, CA, 1958)

Epstein, A.L. *Urbanization and Kinship: The domestic domain on the Copperbelt of Zambia, 1950–1956* (London, 1981)

Ewens, Graeme. *Congo Colossus: The life and legacy of Franco & OK Jazz* (North Walshman, 1994), p. 58.

Feierman, Steven. *Peasant Intellectuals: Anthropology and history in Tanzania* (Madison, WI, 1990)

Fenwick, M. '"Tough guy, eh?": the gangster figure in Drum', *JSAS* 22 (1996)

Ferguson, James. *Expectations of Modernity: Myths and meanings of urban life on the Zambian Copperbelt* (Berkeley, 1999)

Fields, Karen E. *Revival and Rebellion in Colonial Central Africa* (Princeton, 1985)

Fourchard, Laurent. *De la Ville Coloniale à la Cour Africaine. Espaces, pouvoirs et sociétés à Ouagadougou et à Bobo-Dioulasso (Haute-Volta) fin 19ème siècle-1960* (Paris, 2001)

Frederiksen, Bodil Folke. 'African women and their colonisation of Nairobi: Representations and realities', in Burton (2002), pp. 222–34

Freund, William. *The African Worker* (Cambridge, 1988)

Friedman, Lawrence. *Crime and Punishment in American History* (New York, 1993)

Gann, L.H. *A History of Southern Rhodesia: Early days to 1934* (New York, 1969)

Geiger, Susan. *TANU Women: Gender and culture in the making of Tanganyikan nationalism, 1955–1965* (Portsmouth, NH, 1997)

Geschiere, Peter. *The Modernity of Witchcraft: Politics and the occult in postcolonial Africa* (Charlottesville/London, 1997)

Gilbert, Alan and Josef Gugler. *Cities, Poverty and Development: Urbanization in the Third World* (Oxford, 1992)

Giliomee, Hermann and Lawrence Schlemmer. *Up Against the Fences: Poverty, passes and privilege in South Africa* (Cape Town, 1985)

Gillman, Clement. 'Dar es Salaam, 1860 to 1940: A story of growth and change', *Tanganyika Notes and Records* 20 (1945), pp. 1–23

Glaser, Clive. *Bo-Tsotsi: The youth gangs of Soweto, 1935–1976* (Portsmouth, NH/Oxford/

Bibliography

Cape Town, 2000)

Glassman, Jonathon. *Feasts and Riot: Revelry, rebellion and popular consciousness on the Swahili Coast, 1856–1888* (Portsmouth, NH, 1995)

Gluckman, Max. 'Property rights and status in African traditional law', in Gluckman (ed.), *Ideas and Procedures in African Customary Law* (Oxford, 1969)

Goerg, Odile. *Pouvoir Colonial, Municipalités et Espace Urbain: Conakry-Freetown des années 1880–1914* (Paris, 1997)

Gordon, Robert J. 'Vagrancy, law and 'shadow knowledge': Internal pacification, 1915–1939', in P. Hayes *et al* (eds), *Namibia under Colonial Rule: Mobility and containment, 1915–1946* (London, 1998)

Gray, Sir John. 'Dar es Salaam under the Sultans of Zanzibar', *TNR* 33 (1952)

Gray, Richard. *The Two Nations: Aspects of the development of race relations in the Rhodesias and Nyasaland* (London, 1960)

Gulliver, P.H. *Alien Africans in Tanga Region* (Dar es Salaam, 1956)

Hailey, Lord. *An African Survey* (London, 1938)

—— *Native Administration and Political Development in British Tropical Africa* (London, 1940–2)

Hake, Andrew. *African Metropolis: Nairobi's self-help city* (Brighton, 1977)

Hardoy, Jorge and David Satterthwaite. *Squatter Citizen: Life in the urban Third World* (London, 1989)

Harlow, Vincent, E.M. Chilver and Alison Smith. *Oxford History of East Africa, Vol. II* (London, 1965)

Harris, C.C. *Donkey's Gratitude* (Edinburgh, 1992)

Hart, Keith. 'Informal income opportunties and urban employment in Ghana', *JMAS* 11: 1 (1973), pp. 61–89

Hay, Douglas. Peter Linebaugh and E.P. Thompson *et al. Albion's Fatal Tree* (London, 1975)

Heap, Simon. 'Jaguda boys: Pickpocketing in Ibadan, 1930–60', *Urban History* 24 (1997)

Heisler, Helmuth. *Urbanisation and the Government of Migration: The inter-relation of urban and rural life in Zambia* (New York, 1974)

Henry, P.M. 'The African Townee', *New Commonwealth*, 4 March 1954

Hill, J.F.R. and Moffett, J.P. Tanganyika: A review of its resources and their development (Dar es Salaam, 1955)

Hills, Alice. *Policing Africa: Internal security and the limits of liberalization* (Boulder/London, 2000)

Hindson, Doug. *Pass controls and the urban African proletariat in South Africa* (Johannesburg, 1987)

Hobsbawm, E.J. *Primitive Rebels: Studies in archaic forms of social movement in the 19th and 20th centuries* (Manchester, 1959)

—— *Bandits* (Harmondsworth, 1985)

Honey, Martha. 'Asian industrial activities in Tanganyika', *TNR* 75 (1974)

Hyde, David. 'The Nairobi General Strike (1950): From protest to insurgency', in Burton, *Urban Experience* (2002), pp. 235–253

Ibbotson, Percy. 'Urbanization in Southern Rhodesia', *Africa* XVI:2 (1946)

Iliffe, John. 'A history of the Dockworkers of Dar es Salaam', in Sutton (1970)

—— (ed.) *Modern Tanzanians* (Dar es Salaam, 1973)

—— 'Wage labour and urbanisation', in Kaniki, *Tanzania under Colonial Rule* (1979)

—— *A Modern History of Tanganyika* (Cambridge, 1979)

—— *The African Poor* (Cambridge, 1987)

—— *Africans: The history of a continent* (Cambridge, 1995)

Bibliography

ILO. *Report to the Government of the United Republic of Tanzania on Wages, Incomes and Prices Policy* (Turner Report) (Dar es Salaam, 1967)

—— *Employment, Incomes and Equality: A strategy for increasing productive employment in Kenya* (Geneva, 1972)

Ingham, Kenneth. 'Tangayika: The Mandate and Cameron', in Harlow *et al.* (1965)

Isaacman, Allen. 'Social banditry in Zimbabwe (Rhodesia) and Mozambique, 1894–1907', *JSAS* 4:1 (1977)

Ishumi, Abel G.M. *The urban jobless in East Africa: A study of the unemployed in the growing urban centres, with special reference to Tanzania* (Uppsala, 1984)

Ivaska, Andrew M. '"Anti-mini militants meet modern misses": Urban style, gender and the politics of 'national culture' in 1960s Dar es Salaam, Tanzania', *Gender and History* (forthcoming)

Joelson, F.S. *The Tanganyika Territory* (New York, 1921)

Kaniki, M. (ed.) *Tanzania under colonial rule* (London, 1979)

Kenya Colony. *Report of the Committee on African Wages* (Carpenter Report) (Nairobi, 1954)

Kerner, Donna O. '"Hard work" and the informal sector trade in Tanzania', in G. Clark (ed.) *Traders vs the State* (Boulder, 1988)

Killingray, David. 'The maintenance of law and order in British colonial Africa', *AA* 85 (1986), pp. 411–437

King, Anthony D. *Colonial Urban Development: Culture, social power and environment* (London, 1976)

Koponen, Juhani. *Development for Exploitation: German colonial policies in mainland Tanzania, 1884–1914* (Helsinki, 1994)

Kynoch, Gary. 'From the Ninevites to the Hard Living gang: Township gangsters and urban violence in twentieth-century South Africa', *African Studies* 58 (1999)

—— 'Marashea on the mines: Economic, social and criminal networks on the South African gold fields, 1947–99', *JSAS* 26 (2000), pp. 79–103

—— 'Politics and violence in the "Russian Zone": Conflict in Newclare South, 1950–7', *JAH* 41 (2000), pp. 267–290

LaFontaine, J.S. *City Politics: A study of Léopoldville, 1962–63* (Cambridge, 1970)

Larsson, Birgitta. *Conversion to Greater Freedom: Women, Church and social change in North-Western Tanzania under colonial rule* (Uppsala, 1991)

Lees, Andrew. *Cities Perceived: Urban society in European and American thought, 1820–1940* (Manchester, 1985)

LeGates, R.T. and F. Stout, (eds) *The City Reader* (London, 1996)

Legum, Colin (ed.) *Africa Contemporary Record, 1983–84* (New York, 1985)

Leslie, John A.K. *A Survey of Dar es Salaam* (Oxford, 1963)

Lewis, Joanna. *Empire State-Building: War and welfare in Kenya, 1925–52* (Oxford/Nairobi/Athens, GA, 2000)

Liebenow, J. Gus. *Colonial Rule and Political Development in Tanzania: The case of the Makonde* (Evanston, 1971)

Linebaugh, Peter. *The London Hanged: Crime and civil society in the eighteenth century* (Harmondsworth, 1991)

Lockwood, Matthew. *Fertility and Household Labour in Tanzania: Demography, economy, and society in Rufiji District, c.1870–1986* (Oxford, 1998)

Lonsdale, John. 'Town life in colonial Kenya', in Burton (2002)

Low, David A. and Alison Smith. *Oxford History of East Africa, Vol. III* (London, 1976)

Low, David A. and John Lonsdale. 'Introduction: Towards the New Order, 1945–63', in *ibid.* (1976), pp. 1–63

Lugalla, Joe. *Crisis, Urbanization and Urban Poverty in Tanzania* (Lanham, 1995)

Lumley, E.K. *Forgotten Mandate* (London, 1976)

Bibliography

McCracken, John. 'Coercion and control in Nyasaland: Aspects of the history of a colonial police force', *JAH* 27 (1986), pp. 127–147

—— 'Authority and legitimacy in Malawi: Policing and politics in a colonial state', in Anderson and Killingray (1992), pp. 158–186

MacMillan, Hugh. 'The East Africa Royal Commission 1953–1955', in Low and Smith (1976), pp. 544–557

—— 'The historiography of transition on the Zambian Copperbelt — Another view', *JSAS*, 19:4 (1993)

Maguire, Mike, Rod Morgan and Robert Reiner (eds) *The Oxford Handbook of Criminology (Third Edition)* (Oxford, 2002)

Mamdani, Mahmood. *Citizen and Subject: Contemporary Africa and the legacy of late colonialism* (Princeton/Kampala/Cape Town/London, 1996)

Marshall Macklin Monoghan. *Dar es Salaam Masterplan* (Toronto, 1979)

Martin, Phyllis. *Leisure and Society in Colonial Brazzaville* (Cambridge, 1995)

Martin, R. *Personal Freedom and the Law in Tanzania* (Nairobi, 1974)

Maylam, Paul. 'Explaining the Apartheid city: 20 years of South African urban historiography', *JSAS* 21:1 (1995)

Mbilinyi, Marjorie. '"City" and "Countryside" in colonial Tanganyika', *Economic and Political Weekly*, XX (1985)

—— '"This is an unforgettable business": Colonial state intervention in Tanzania', in J.L. Parpart & K.A. Staudt (eds) *Women and the State in Africa* (Boulder, 1989), pp. 111–129

Moffett, J.P. *Handbook of Tanganyika* (Dar es Salaam, 1958)

Mafeje, Archie and Samir Radwan (eds) *Economic and Demographic Change in Africa* (Cambridge, 1995)

Mascarenhas, Ophelia and Marjorie Mbilinyi. *Women in Tanzania: An analytical bibliography* (Uppsala, 1983)

Mhina, J.E.F. 'Education in and around Dar es Salaam', in Sutton (ed.) *Dar es Salaam*, pp. 175–80

Mitchell, J. Clyde. *Cities, Society, and Social Perception: A Central African perspective* (Oxford, 1987)

Molohan, M.J.B. *Detribalization* (Dar es Salaam, 1959)

Moore, R.J.B. "Native wages and standards of living in Northern Rhodesia", *African Studies* 1 (1942)

—— *These African Copper Miners: A study of the industrial revolution in Northern Rhodesia* (London, 1948)

Morris, H.F. and James S. Read. *Indirect Rule and the Search for Justice — Essays in East African Legal History* (London, 1972)

Myers, Garth Andrew. *Verandahs of Power: Colonialism and space in urban Africa* (Syracuse, 2003)

Neuberger, Joan. *Hooliganism: Crime, culture, and power in St. Petersburg, 1900–1914* (Berkeley/Los Angeles/London, 1993)

Nevanlinna, Anja Kervanto. *Interpreting Nairobi: The cultural study of built forms* (Helsinki, 1997)

O'Connor, Anthony. *The African City* (London, 1983)

Orde-Browne, G. St J. *The African Labourer* (Oxford, 1933)

—— *Labour Conditions in East Africa* (London, 1946)

Parker, John. 'The cultural politics of death and burial in early colonial Accra', in Anderson and Rathbone (2000), pp. 205–221

Pearce, R.D. *Turning Point in Africa: British colonial policy, 1938–1948* (London, 1982)

Bibliography

Pearson, Geoffrey. *Hooligan: A history of respectable fears* (London, 1983)

Penvenne, Jeanne Marie. *African Workers and Colonial Racism: Mozambican strategies and struggles in Lourenco Marques, 1822–1962* (Portsmouth, NH/Johannesburg/London, 1995)

Perullo, Alex and John Fenn. 'Language ideologies, choices, and practices in Eastern African Hip Hop', in *Global Popular Music: The politics and aesthetics of language choice*, ed. Harry Berger and Michael T. Carroll (Mississippi, 2003), pp. 19–51.

Phillips, Anne. *The Enigma of Colonialism: British policy in West Africa* (London, 1989)

Phimister, Ian. *An Economic and Social History of Zimbabwe: Capital accumulation and class struggle* (London, 1988)

Platzky, Laurine and Cherryl Walker. *The Surplus People: Forced removals in South Africa* (Johannesburg, 1985)

Pons, Valdo. *Stanleyville: An urban African community under Belgian administration* (Oxford, 1969)

Posel, Deborah. *The Making of Apartheid, 1948–61: Conflict and compromise* (Oxford, 1991)

Prain, R.L. 'The stabilization of labour in the Rhodesian Copper Belt', *AA* 55 (1956), pp. 305–312

Raimbault, Franck. 'Les élites Arabes et Indiennes face à la colonisation. Le cas de Dar-es-Salaam à l'époque de la domination Allemande (1890–1914), *Hypothèses* (2001)

Rakodi, Carole. *Harare: Inheriting a colonial settler city: Change or continuity?* (Chichester, 1998)

Ranger, Terence. *Dance and Society in Eastern Africa: The beni 'ngoma'* (London, 1975)

Reid, Eric. *Tanganyika Without Prejudice* (London, 1934)

Reid, Richard and Henri Médard. 'Merchants, missions and the remaking of the urban environment in Buganda, *c.* 1840–90', in Anderson and Rathbone (2000), pp. 98–108

Rock, Paul. 'Sociological theories of crime', in Maguire, Morgan and Reiner, *Handbook of Criminology* (2002)

Roberts, Andrew. *A History of Zambia* (London, 1976)

Robertson, Claire. *Trouble Showed the Way: Women, men and trade in the Nairobi area, 1890–1990* (Bloomington, 1997)

Rothman, David J. *The Discovery of the Asylum: Social order and disorder in the new Republic* (Boston/Toronto, 1971)

Rudé, George. *Criminal and victim: Crime and society in early 19th century England* (Oxford, 1985)

—— *The Crowd in History* (London, 1995)

Rweyemamu, J. *Underdevelopment and Industrialization in Tanzania: A study of perverse capitalist development* (Nairobi, 1974)

Sabot, R.H. *Economic Development and Urban Migration in Tanzania, 1900–1971* (London, 1978)

Sadleir, Randall. *Tanzania: Journey to Republic* (London, 1999)

Saffery, A. Lynn. *A Report on Some Aspects of African Living Conditions on the Copperbelt of Northern Rhodesia* (Lusaka, 1943)

Said, Mohamed. *The Life and Times of Abdulwahid Sykes (1924–1968): The untold story of the Muslim struggle against British colonialism in Tanganyika* (London, 1998)

Sapire, Hilary. 'Apartheid's "testing ground": Urban "native policy" and African politics in Brakpan, South Africa, 1943–1948', *JAH* 35 (1994), pp. 99–123

Sayers, G.F. *Handbook of Tanganyika* (London, 1930)

Scarnecchia, Timothy. 'Poor women and nationalist politics: Alliances and fissures in the formation of a nationalist political movement in Salisbury, Rhodesia, 1950–56', *JAH* 37 (1996), pp. 283–310

Bibliography

Scott, R.R. 'Public health services in Dar es Salaam in the 'twenties', *East African Medical Journal* 40:7 (1963), pp. 339–353

Seyoum, Seltene. 'Land alienation and the urban growth of Bahir Dar', in Anderson and Rathbone (2000), pp. 235–245

Shivji, Issa G. 'Semi-proletarian labour and the use of penal sanctions in the labour law of colonial Tanganyika (1920–38)', in Sumner, *Crime, Justice and Underdevelopment* (1982)

Smyth, Rosaleen. 'The feature film in Tanzania', *AA* 88 (1989), pp. 389–396

Sofer, R. and C. *Jinja Transformed*, East African Studies no. 5 (EAISR, Kampala, 1955)

Sommers, Marc. *Fear in Bongoland: Burundi refugees in urban Tanzania* (New York/Oxford, 2001)

Southern Rhodesia. *Report of the Committee to Investigate the Economic, Social and Health Conditions of Africans Employed in Urban Areas* (Howman Report) (Salisbury, 1944)

Spear, Thomas. '"A town of strangers" or "A model East African town"? Arusha and the Arusha', in Anderson and Rathbone (2000), pp. 109–125

Stedman-Jones, Gareth. *Outcast London: A study of the relationship between classes in Victorian society* (Harmondsworth, 1976)

Stichter, Sharon. *Migrant Labour in Kenya: Capitalism and African response* (London, 1982)

—— *Migrant Labourers* (Cambridge, 1985)

Stren, Richard. *Urban Inequality and Housing Policy in Tanzania: The problem of squatting in Tanzania*, University of California, Berkeley, Institute of International Studies, Research Series No. 24 (1975)

Sturmer, Martin. *The Media History of Tanzania* (Austrian Development Corporation/Ndanda Mission Press, Ndanda, Tanzania, 1998)

Sumner, Colin. *Crime, Justice and Underdevelopment* (London, 1982)

Sunseri, Thaddeus. *Vilimani: Labour migration and rural change in early colonial Tanzania* (Portsmouth, NH/Oxford/Cape Town, 2002)

Sutton, John (ed.) *Dar es Salaam: City, port and region*: special edition of *Tanzania Notes and Records* 71 (1970)

Swanson, Maynard. 'The sanitation syndrome: Bubonic plague and urban native policy in the Cape Colony, 1900–1909', *JAH* 18 (1977), pp. 387–410

Swantz, Lloyd. *The Medicine Man among the Zaramo of Dar es Salaam* (Uppsala, 1990)

Sweet, C. Louise. 'Inventing crime: British colonial land policy in Tanganyika', in Sumner (1982)

Taasisi ya Uchunguzi wa Kiswahili (University of Dsm). *Kamusi ya Kiswahili–Kiingereza* (Dar es Salaam, 2001)

Tanganyika Government. *A Ten-year Development and Welfare Plan for Tanganyika Territory* (Dsm, 1946)

—— *Revised Development and Welfare Plan for Tanganyika Territory 1950–56* (Dsm, 1950)

—— with Rev. R.M. Gibbons. Appendix C in Tanganyika Territory, *Report on the Question of Imprisonment in Tanganyika* (Dar es Salaam, 1932)

Tanner, R.E.S. 'Some problems of East African crime statistics', in *Three Studies of East African Criminology* (Uppsala, 1970)

Thomas, Lynn M. *Politics of the Womb: Women, reproduction and the state in Kenya* (Berkeley/Los Angeles, 2003)

Thompson, E.P. *Whigs and Hunters: The origin of the Black Act* (Harmondsworth, 1990)

Throup, David. *The Social and Economic Origins of Mau Mau* (London, 1987)

—— 'Crime, politics and the police in colonial Kenya, 1939–63', in Anderson and Killingray (1992), pp. 127–157

Tripp, Aili Marie. *Changing the Rules: The politics of liberalization and the urban informal economy in Tanzania* (Berkeley, 1997)

Tsuruta, Tadasu. 'Popular music, sports, and politics in Dar es Salaam during the British colonial period', *Journal of African and Asian Studies*, 55 (1998), pp. 93–118 (original in Japanese; substantially revised English version in author's possession)

—— 'The development process of dance bands in urban Tanzania–in connection with changes in socioeconomic and political circumstances from the colonial period to the 1980s', *Nilo-Ethiopian Studies* (200), pp. 9–24

UNESCO. *Social Implications of Industrialisation and Urbanisation in Africa South of the Sahara* (Paris, 1956)

United Nations (Habitat). *Global Report on Human Settlements* (Oxford, 1987, 1996 & 2001)

Van Donge, Jan Kees. 'Waluguru traders in Dar es Salaam: An analysis of the social construction of economic life', *AA* 91 (1992), pp. 181–205

Van Onselen, Charles. *Chibaro: African mine labour in Southern Rhodesia, 1900–1933* (London, 1976)

—— *New Babylon New Nineveh: Everyday life on the Witwatersrand* (Jeppestown, 2001) (Originally published as *Studies in the Social and Economic History of the Witwatersrand Vols 1&2* [Harlow, 1982])

Van Velsen, J. 'Urban squatters: Problem or solution', in David Parkin (ed.) *Town and Country in Central and Eastern Africa* (London, 1975), pp. 294-307.

Van Zwanenberg, Roger. *Colonial Capitalism and Labour in Kenya, 1919–1939* (Nairobi/Kampala/Dsm, 1975)

Van Zwanenberg, R.M.A. with Anne King. *An Economic History of Kenya and Uganda, 1800–1970* (London, 1975)

Vaughan, Megan. *Curing Their Ills: Colonial power and African illness* (Cambridge/Oxford, 1991)

von Sicard, Sigvard. *The Lutheran Church on the Coast of Tanzania, 1887–1914* (Uppsala, 1970)

Walshe, A.P. 'Southern Africa', p. 552, in Andrew Roberts (ed.) *Cambridge History of Africa, Volume 7: 1905–1940* (Cambridge, 1986), pp. 544–601

Waweru, Peter. 'Frontier urbanisation: The rise and development of towns in Samburu District, Kenya, 1909–1940', in Burton (2002), pp. 85–97

Westcott, Nicholas. 'Erica Fiah: An East African Radical', *JAH* 22 (1981), pp. 85–101

—— 'The impact of the Second World War on Tanganyika, 1939–49', in David Killingray and Richard Rathbone (eds), *Africa and the Second World War* (New York, 1986), pp. 143–159

White, Luise. *The Comforts of Home: Prostitution in colonial Nairobi* (Chicago, 1990)

—— *Speaking with Vampires: Rumor and history in colonial Africa* (Berkeley/Los Angeles/London, 2000)

Willis, Justin. 'Thieves, drunkards and vagrants: Defining crime in colonial Mombasa, 1902–32', in Anderson and Killingray (1991)

—— *Mombasa, the Swahili, and the Making of the Mijikenda* (Oxford, 1993)

—— *Potent Brews: A social history of alcohol in East Africa* (Oxford/Athens, OH/Nairobi/Kampala/Dar es Salaam, 2002)

—— '"Clean spirit": Distilling, modernity, and the Ugandan state, 1950–1986', in Burton and Jennings, *Emperor's New Clothes* (forthcoming)

Wilson, Godfrey. *An Essay on the Economics of Detribalization in Northern Rhodesia* (Livingstone, 1941)

Wright, F.C. *African consumers in Nyasaland and Tanganyika: An enquiry into the distribution and consumption of commodities among Africans carried out in 1952–53* (London, 1955)

Index